The Chaco Experience

Published with the support of the National Endowment for the Humanities and Colorado College.

The Chaco Experience
Landscape and Ideology at the Center Place

Ruth M. Van Dyke

A School for Advanced Research Resident Scholar Book

Santa Fe, New Mexico

School for Advanced Research Press
Post Office Box 2188
Santa Fe, New Mexico 87504-2188
www.sarpress.sarweb.org

Co-Director and Executive Editor: Catherine Cocks
Manuscript Editor: Kate Whelan
Design and Production: Cynthia Dyer
Proofreader: Sarah Soliz
Indexer: Catherine Fox
Printer: Transcontinental Printing, Canada

Library of Congress Cataloging-in-Publication Data:
Van Dyke, Ruth M.
The Chaco experience : landscape and ideology at the center place /
Ruth M. Van Dyke. —1st ed.
p. cm. — (A School for Advanced Research resident scholar book)
Includes bibliographical references and index.
ISBN 978-1-930618-76-3 (pa : alk. paper)
1. Chaco culture—New Mexico—Chaco Canyon. 2. Chaco architecture—New Mexico—Chaco Canyon. 3. Landscape—Symbolic aspects—New Mexico—Chaco Canyon. 4. Chaco Canyon (N.M.)—Antiquities. I. Title.

E99.C37V35 2007
978.9'82—dc22
2007038748

Copyright © 2007 by the School for Advanced Research. All rights reserved.
Manufactured in Canada.
Library of Congress Catalog Card Number: 2007038748
International Standard Book Number 978-1-930618-76-3
First edition 2008.

Front cover illustration: Fajada Butte © Ruth M. Van Dyke; back cover: Pueblo Pintado © Ruth M. Van Dyke.

Contents

List of Figures and Plates	vi
List of Tables	viii
Preface	ix
1. Orientations	1
2. Locations	11
3. Perceptions and Representations	37
4. Origins	61
5. The Center Place	105
6. Connections	137
7. The Classic Bonito Chacoan World	169
8. The Late Bonito Phase	201
9. Lived Landscapes	237
References	255
Index	305

Figures

2.1	The San Juan Basin	13
2.2	Mired in the mud en route to Chaco	16
2.3	Chacoan veneer styles	20
2.4	Chaco Canyon topography, great house locations, and major road segments	23
3.1	Tewa cosmography	50
3.2	Keres cosmography	51
4.1	Plan of a Late Basketmaker III pitstructure	64
4.2	Plan of Shabik'eshchee Village	65
4.3	Site 423, the Basketmaker III village atop West Mesa	66
4.4	The great pitstructure at Shabik'eshchee Village	68
4.5	Locations of the northern San Juan Pueblo I–period sites discussed in the text	71
4.6	Plan of Site 13, Alkali Ridge	73
4.7	Plan of McPhee Pueblo	74
4.8	Comparison of a late Pueblo I great kiva and an oversized pitstructure from sites in the Dolores River Valley	75
4.9	Early Bonito–phase communities in the San Juan Basin	82
4.10	Plan of Early Bonito–phase Skunk Springs	85
4.11	Plans of five Early Bonito–phase proto-great houses in Chaco Canyon	87
4.12	Bennett Peak and Ford Butte, as seen from atop Newcomb great house	94
4.13	A view of Site 423 from Peñasco Blanco	95
4.14	The author looking out over Kin Bineola, with Hosta Butte on the horizon, June 2003	96
5.1	The major lunar standstill full moonrise at Chimney Rock, December 9, 2006	110
5.2	Plans of Classic Bonito canyon great houses	112
5.3	Banded, Type III Chacoan masonry	120
5.4	Plan of Casa Rinconada	124
5.5	A possible processional route between the Pueblo Bonito mounds and Casa Rinconada	127
5.6	Plan of Pueblo Bonito, showing the East Mound and West Mound	129

5.7	Peñasco Blanco, as approached from the east within Chaco Canyon	129
6.1	Major roads, routes, shrines, and stone circles in Chaco Canyon	138–139
6.2	The Classic Bonito Chacoan world, including major Chacoan roads (chapter 6) and great houses (chapter 7)	146
6.3	Dave Ayers walks along a Chacoan road segment in the western San Juan Basin, September 1991	147
6.4	Entering Chaco Canyon through South Gap	161
6.5	Entering Chaco Canyon along SR 57, through Fajada Gap	162
7.1	(a) Skunk Springs great house, looking east, and (b) plan of the Classic Bonito–phase Skunk Springs great house	170
7.2	Plans of Classic Bonito outlier great houses discussed in the text	172
7.3	Peach Springs great house environs	175
7.4	Andrews great house, with California State University–Fullerton students, June 2000	177
7.5	Andrews great house environs	177
7.6	Cabezon peak, as seen from Guadalupe great house	185
7.7	Mount Taylor, as seen from a shrine in the vicinity of Las Ventanas	188
7.8	Casamero, with the "tecolote" alcoves behind the great house	189
7.9	Whirlwind great house, looking west	189
7.10	(a) Red Willow great house environs, and (b) Red Willow great house, looking west	194
7.11	The road connecting Red Willow great house and Los Rayos great kiva, in the western San Juan Basin	195
8.1	The Late Bonito Chacoan world	203
8.2	Plans of Late Bonito outlier great houses discussed in the text	204
8.3	The Lowry landscape	205
8.4	A comparison of the Aztec and Chacoan landscapes	210
8.5	The Aztec landscape	211
8.6	The Late Bonito canyon landscape—great house locations and alignments	215
8.7	Plans of Late Bonito–phase great houses in Chaco Canyon	216
8.8	Tsin Kletsin, the Late Bonito great house atop South Mesa	221
8.9	The Kin Ya'a tower kiva	228

Plates

1. The Chacoan landscape
2. Fajada Butte at sunrise
3. Kin Nahasbas and Una Vida, as seen from the great kiva site 29SJ1253 in Fajada Gap
4. Pueblo Bonito, center of the Chacoan world
5. Dramatically shaped, highly visible landforms in the Chacoan world
6. A staircase behind Hungo Pavi leads atop Chaco Canyon's north rim
7. Aerial view of Peñasco Blanco
8. Inside the plaza at Pueblo Bonito
9. Cairns overlook the Chaco River and western San Juan Basin at Site 1088 atop West Mesa
10. The badlands in Kutz Canyon, with Angel Peak beyond, near the terminus of the North Road
11. View from a stone circle atop the north rim of Chaco Canyon, looking across Pueblo del Arroyo, through South Gap, to Hosta Butte
12. Peñasco Blanco, on West Mesa, illuminated in the late afternoon light from the end of the Ah-Shi-Sle-Pah Road, atop the north rim of Chaco Canyon
13. Peach Springs great house, looking north
14. Escalon atalaya from below
15. Kin Bineola, from the mesa above, looking northwest
16. Kin Klizhin, with Colorado College students, December 2006
17. Painted Hand, a McElmo-style tower in Hovenweep Canyon, southwest Colorado

Tables

2.1	Time periods for the Ancestral Puebloan occupation of Chaco Canyon	18
4.1	Basketmaker III great pitstructures in northwest New Mexico and northeast Arizona	69
4.2	Proto-great house and great kiva communities in the San Juan Basin, AD 875–925	79
5.1	Estimated height, footprint, room counts, and mass for seven Classic Bonito canyon great houses and one small house	119
5.2	Great kivas in Chaco Canyon	123
6.1	Line-of-sight visibility from Classic Bonito great houses in Chaco Canyon	141
7.1	Classic Bonito outliers discussed in the text	181
8.1	Estimated floor area, height, and room counts for six Late Bonito outlier great houses	208
8.2	Estimated height, footprint, room counts, mass, and visibility for six Late Bonito canyon great houses	214
8.3	Time bridges in the post-Chacoan world	234

Preface

In the summer of 1985, my University of Texas field school class took a weekend trip to Chaco Canyon. At Pueblo Alto, I exulted in the endless sky, the distant snow-capped San Juans, the geometric ruins crumpled darkly against the dunes—and I knew I was hooked. A decade late, in my University of Arizona dissertation, I attempted to use quantifiable architectural attributes to get a handle on the complex relationships between outliers and Chaco. But as I tabulated variables and ran statistical analyses, I continued to think about the landscape. There were intangibles on the Chacoan landscape—intangibles that were difficult to get at archaeologically but that seemed critical to understanding Chaco. I began to read British landscape archaeologists—Barbara Bender, Richard Bradley, Julian Thomas, Christopher Tilley—to think about how some of their ideas might work if applied to Chaco.

Perhaps more ink has already been spilled about Chaco than about any other New World archaeological society. *The Chaco Experience* represents my own attempt at a synthetic contribution to the dialogue. Even as this book goes to press, however, it remains a work in progress. Chaco is too big, too complicated, too cantankerous a subject for anyone to ever completely digest, let alone represent. A noted Chaco scholar once told me that it had been some twenty years since he'd decided he was finished with Chaco, but Chaco still didn't seem to be quite finished with him. I now understand what he meant. Answers lead to new questions, and there is always more to learn.

My intended audience for this book includes Chacoan scholars, students, and the interested public. I have assumed a basic familiarity with Chaco, archaeology, and the Puebloan Southwest, but I have sought to construct a readable book—one not overly burdened with technical jargon and esoterica. Through language and images, I have tried to evoke the wide horizons and sandstone mesas of the San Juan Basin. At times, I found it difficult to part with cherished factoids that are not central to the text. The interested reader will find these and other additional information in the endnotes.

As I worked on *The Chaco Experience*, I benefited from interaction with scores of colleagues, friends, and scholars who gave me insight and support—my heartfelt thanks to all of you. The book began to take shape in 2000–2001, when I was a National Endowment for the Humanities resident scholar at the School for Advanced Research (SAR) in Santa Fe. Thanks to Doug Schwartz, Nancy Owen Lewis, and the SAR staff for the tremendous gift of a year of uninterrupted thinking and writing. Fellow resident scholars during my SAR year—Rebecca Allahyari, Edsel Brown, Kathryn Geurtz, Gary Gossen, Mary Eunice Romero, and Marni Sandweiss—provided insightful discussion and comments on early versions of many of my ideas. Kay Hagan, freelance SAR scholar biographer, provided encouragement at a critical moment. I am especially grateful to James Brooks, fellow SAR scholar, former press director, and now SAR president, for his unflagging belief in this book across years of labor. Catherine Cocks took over SAR Press and helped bring the book to completion—my thanks to Catherine for her support, organizational insights, enthusiasm for the project, and, of course, patience!

The ideas in *The Chaco Experience* have evolved considerably since my SAR year, and this is due in no small part to many conversations and interactions with a wide range of archaeological colleagues. I gained insights into the organization of Chacoan power and society from discussions with Gary Feinman, Jonathan Haas, Tim Kohler, Tim Pauketat, John Ware, and Norm Yoffee. Sue Alcock contributed to my ideas about social memory, Wendy Ashmore encouraged me to think more deeply about landscape, and Randy McGuire helped clarify my understanding of ideology. While working on this book, I was fortunate to participate in several meetings of Chaco scholars, including a Chaco Synthesis session on architecture in October 2000 (organized by Steve Lekson), the Chaco Synthesis Mini-Symposium at SAR in May 2003 (also organized by Steve Lekson), and the Salmon Working Conference in April 2004 (organized by Paul Reed and the Center for Desert Archaeology). At these meetings and elsewhere, I learned much from interactions and conversations with Larry Baker, Gary Brown, Cathy Cameron,

Linda Cordell, Dennis Gilpin, Kelley Hays-Gilpin, Jim Judge, John Kantner, Jim Kendrick, Keith Kintigh, Steve Lekson, Pete McKenna, Joan Mathien, Barbara Mills, Ben Nelson, Bob Powers, Paul Reed, Lynn Sebastian, Anna Sofaer, Wolky Toll, Philip Tuwaletstiwa, Bill Walker, Carla Van West, Gwinn Vivian, John Ware, Dottie Washburn, Laurie Webster, Chip Wills, and Tom Windes. I also gleaned insights from discussions and field trips with Colorado College students, particularly those in my Field Archaeology courses (fall 2003 and fall 2005) and my Archaeologies of Landscape course (fall 2006). Friends and colleagues Jeff Clark, Beth Grindell, Andrea Kayser, Hillary Hamann, Karen Harry, Joshua Jones, Jane McDougall, Louise Senior, and Nicole Ureles, as well as my parents, Paul and Marguerite Van Dyke, lent invaluable encouragement along the way. Sarah Herr, Adam Smith, Wolky Toll, Jeff Ureles, and Phillip and Judy Tuwaletstiwa enthusiastically forged into various draft chapters of the manuscript and provided helpful substantive and organizational feedback. Five especially meritorious individuals—Tim Pauketat, Tom Windes, Gwinn Vivian, and two anonymous reviewers—went through one or more drafts line by line, providing detailed fact-checking and many useful suggestions. The book has been immeasurably strengthened as a result of all these contributions. Of course, the responsibility for any remaining errors in data, interpretations, or judgment rests on my shoulders alone.

The Chaco Experience owes a debt to the work of several other scholars whom I greatly respect and whose ideas have been especially influential. My vision of the Pueblo I period is derived from the work of Rich Wilshusen, who kindly invited me to investigate this issue with him in 2003 and encouraged me to think about the relationships between Chaco and the northern San Juan. Many of my interpretations have been influenced by conversations and other adventures with Tom Windes. Tom's insights into early Chacoan settlement, proto-great houses, shrines, and visibility have been particularly invaluable. Tom also generously shared with me many unpublished data. Also, I owe an intellectual debt to Mike Marshall, John Stein, and their colleagues. My conceptions of Chacoan ritual landscapes and sacred geography were inspired by their visions and draw heavily upon their interpretations. Particularly influential were ideas published in Fowler and Stein (1992), Hayes and Windes (1975), Marshall (1997), Sofaer (1997), Sofaer, Marshall, and Sinclair (1989), and Stein and Lekson (1992). Special thanks to fellow scholars who spent hours traipsing with me across the Chacoan landscape, sharing their ideas, knowledge, and insights. John Stein and Rich Friedman lent me aerial photographs, took me to the Ah-Shi-Sle-Pah Road, and spent a day with me looking for roads and features in South Gap. Bob Powers walked with me across the landscapes of Kin Bineola and

Kin Klizhin. Tom Windes showed me Chaco East, South Fork, Casa del Rio, Padilla Well, and, perhaps most critically, Site 1088. It has been my privilege to work with so many knowledgeable, generous, and supportive colleagues.

For much of the life of this manuscript, I was teaching at Colorado College, where I received financial and logistical support for *The Chaco Experience* through a variety of avenues. My thanks to the Benezet Summer Research Award Committee, the Social Sciences Executive Committee, the Hulbert Center for Southwest Studies at Colorado College, and the Department of Anthropology. My research assistant at Colorado College, Tucker Robinson, conducted line-of-sight analyses in ArcGIS and was an invaluable help during eleventh-hour figure- and fact-checking. The book was born at SAR, but it was completed at the Amerind Foundation. My heartfelt thanks to Amerind director John Ware and his staff for providing an ideal writing environment for completion of the first draft during the summer of 2004 and the second draft during the summer of 2006.

Over the past few years, some of the ideas in *The Chaco Experience* have found their way into other publication venues, including a chapter in *Archaeologies of Memory* (Van Dyke 2003b), an article in *American Antiquity* (Van Dyke 2004b), a chapter in David Noble's *In Search of Chaco* (Van Dyke 2004a), a chapter with Rich Wilshusen in Steve Lekson's SAR Chaco tome (Wilshusen and Van Dyke 2006), a chapter on great kivas in Steve Lekson's Chaco architecture volume (Van Dyke 2007), and a chapter in Paul Reed's Salmon volume (Van Dyke n.d.).

Some of my insights about western outliers were gleaned as I worked for the Division of Conservation Archaeology on the El Paso pipeline project under the direction of Tim Kearns in the early 1990s. I conducted fieldwork in the Andrews outlier community in 1995, 1999, and 2000 with permission from the Archaeological Conservancy and the Bureau of Land Management—thanks to Jim Walker, John Roney, and Gretchen Obenauf of those agencies, and thanks to the National Science Foundation for a dissertation improvement grant that funded early research there. I walked and photographed approaches into Chaco Canyon during 2002 and 2004 with permits from Chaco Culture National Historic Park. Thanks to Dabney Ford, Roger Moore, Russ and Tracy Bodnar, G. B. Cornucopia, Wendy Bustard, and John George for facilitating my research in Chaco and for helping with logistics along the way. I researched various outliers and road segments on the Navajo Nation during 1998 and 2004 with permits from the Navajo Nation Historic Preservation Department. Thanks to Ron Maldonado for these permissions, and thanks to John Stein for help in securing these arrangements. The artistic maps in the book were drafted by

Molly O'Halloran and were developed from base maps that appear in David Grant Noble's *In Search of Chaco* (SAR Press, 2004)—thanks to SAR for permission to use the base figures. Kate Whelan copyedited the manuscript with good grace and meticulous care.

Finally, there are two individuals without whom this book would not exist. The book might never have evolved past multiple, half-finished chapter drafts were it not for the critical insights and unflagging support of Randy McGuire. Randy helped me solve some central organizational problems and served as an excellent proxy audience through more revisions than I can count. Thank you, Randy, for believing in me. And my heartfelt appreciation to Gwinn Vivian, invaluable mentor, colleague, and friend. Gwinn, thank you for all the many ways you continue to encourage, support, and inspire me as I set out on new adventures "in the weeds."

Colorado Springs
February 2007

1 Orientations

> The events of one's life take place, *take place*. How often have I used this expression, and how often have I stopped to think what it means? Events do indeed take place; they have meaning in relation to the things around them.
>
> —N. Scott Momaday, The Names (1976:142)

In a remote canyon in northwest New Mexico, thousand-year-old sandstone walls waver in the sunlight, stretching like ancient vertebrae against a turquoise sky. The stillness is broken only by the occasional crunch of boots on sandstone gravel and distant tourists' fragmentary voices, floating on the breeze like paper streamers. Overhead, a solitary redtail rides an updraft until she disappears. This storied place—Chaco Canyon—carries multiple layers of meaning for Native Americans and archaeologists, writers and tourists, explorers and artists. Here, isolation, arid conditions, and dry-laid construction have conspired to preserve ruins that are monuments to ancient creativity and perseverance. The north wall of Chetro Ketl undulates and bulges, its banded masonry mimicking the Menefee shale and Cretaceous sandstone behind the great house. A line of multiple doorways in Pueblo Bonito telescopes like a corridor through time. The subterranean passageway at Casa Rinconada hints at esoteric ceremonies in the dimly lit great kiva. Light and shadow, stone and sky, come together in the canyon, inspiring those who have lived, worked, and traveled here (plate 1).

Chaco Canyon draws its power not only from the ancient architecture sheltering beneath its walls but also from the ever-changing light and the far-flung vistas of the Colorado Plateau. From high above the canyon floor, the San Juan Basin stretches away in sedimentary waves lapping against mountainous shores. Bands of golden sunlight illuminate distant swaths of

Tertiary and Quaternary sandstone. To the west, the Chuskas sleep the deep blue sleep of the Cretaceous, indented by Narbona Pass with its promises of chert and wood. To the south, flat-topped Hosta Butte peeps coyly above the dark line of the Dutton Plateau. Around a canyon bend, Fajada Butte's isolated knob protrudes like the controls of some giant chronometer (plate 2).

At the heart of this sky-filled landscape lie twelve massive great houses. The Chacoans used a masonry technique called *core-and-veneer* to craft these buildings at an exaggerated scale, with formal symmetry, according to specific designs (Lekson 1986). Over the course of three centuries, they stacked hundreds of very large rooms—many devoid of hearths or other indications of use—in rows up to four stories, or 8 m, high. The rooms surround blocked-in kivas and embrace plazas toward the east or south (plate 3). In great house plazas, Chacoans often built circular, masonry-lined, semi-subterranean great kivas. They constructed great kivas, like great houses, according to formal guidelines for size, layout, and orientation. The Chacoans modified the landscape in other ways as well, building earthen mounds, ramps, staircases, and road segments. Archaeologists use the term *Bonito-style architecture* to refer collectively to all these architectural elements (Gladwin 1945). The overbuilt, monumental, Bonito-style great houses contrast dramatically with the many small, domestic pueblos that form clusters of low mounds along the south side of Chaco Canyon.

The Classic Bonito phase (AD 1020–1100) was Chaco's heyday, and during that time the canyon's influence spread across the surrounding San Juan Basin. Cleared linear alignments, or road segments, extended from the canyon toward the north, northwest, and southwest. Across the Basin's buttes, dunes, and drainages, Ancestral Puebloans built Bonito-style architecture in nearly a hundred *outlier* communities. The collapsed remains of some outlier great houses, such as Red Willow and Whirlwind, form mounded silhouettes against the sky. At others, such as Kin Bineola and Kin Ya'a, multistoried sandstone walls rise tenaciously from the Basin floor. Often, outliers include great kivas, earthworks, and road segments. There is usually a surrounding community of thirty to forty (or more) small, domestic sites (Fowler, Stein, and Anyon 1987; Kantner and Mahoney 2000; Marshall and Sofaer 1988; Marshall et al. 1979; Powers, Gillespie, and Lekson 1983).

Archaeological research has been under way at Chaco Canyon since the days of Wetherill and Pepper in the 1890s. From Hewett and Judd in the first half of the twentieth century, through the Chaco Project in the 1970s and 1980s, most Southwest archaeologists alive today can link themselves to Chaco through less than six degrees of academic separation. Along the way, Chaco has attracted and addicted generations of scholars (Lister and Lister 1981; Mathien 1992; Mills 2002; Vivian 1990:37–78).[1] After more than a century of research, we have gathered an astounding amount of information about Chaco Canyon and about the Ancestral Puebloan farmers who inhabited this place. We know, to the year, when trees were harvested to build great house roofs and floors. We can pick up a potsherd and know, within a 50-year window, when it was made (and sometimes where it was made). We know how the local precipitation changed from year to year, and we can calculate the ways in which this affected corn crop yields. We know that individuals interred in Pueblo Bonito were better nourished than those buried in small house sites. We know that corn, pottery, wood, and lithic materials were carried to Chaco from the Chuska Mountains, 75 km to the west. We know that feasts were held at Pueblo Alto and ritual paraphernalia was cached at Pueblo Bonito and Chetro Ketl.

But we still have more questions than we have answers. Chaco seems an isolated, difficult place in which to live today. It appears strange to us that subsistence farmers should have invested so much of their energy in monuments that have lasted across a millennium. Great houses remain enigmatic structures variously interpreted as apartments, elite residences, storehouses, empty stages for ceremony, and assorted combinations thereof. It seems odd that the largest and best-preserved great houses are in Chaco Canyon, as opposed to the comparably well-watered slopes of the Chuska Mountains or the lush valleys of the Animas and La Plata rivers. The specific nature of the relationships between outliers and Chaco Canyon is not particularly clear.

Although archaeological interpretations for Chaco are sometimes conflicting, scholars agree that planned, massive, Bonito-style structures required a substantial investment of labor and design. Bonito-style architecture "exceed(s) the requirements of any practical functions that a building is intended to perform" (Trigger 1990:119). These large-scale, long-term construction projects suggest the presence of social inequalities and institutionalized leaders, yet the evidence for sociopolitical hierarchy in the canyon is ambiguous. As a result, Chaco has great appeal for scholars of ancient sociopolitical complexity.

Most current explanations for Chaco revolve around the idea of the canyon as a central place for ritual gatherings, with leaders' power legitimated through exclusive access to ritual knowledge (Judge 1989; Kantner 1996; Saitta 1997; Sebastian 1992; Toll 1985; Wills 2000; Yoffee 2001). But how did ritual leaders come to power? Why was their authority perceived as legitimate? Why would people agree to act as subjects—that is, to participate in a situation that was to their social or material disadvantage? Bonito-style architecture looms large in the background of all these questions —were the great houses, great kivas, roads, and earthworks stages for ritual events? The Chacoan landscape, with its formally constructed, carefully situated architectural features, is charged with symbolism (Fritz 1978; Marshall 1997; Stein and Lekson 1992). What can this landscape reveal to us about the nature of Chacoan beliefs and social relationships?

Lived Landscapes

Landscape provides archaeologists with an excellent window through which to construct a comprehensive picture of Chacoan society and polity. This book is built on a vision of landscape as a reflexive dimension of human social interaction. Landscapes both create and reflect ideas we hold about ourselves and our societies, our worldviews and our ideologies. All human experience is spatialized, and some aspects of Chacoan life may have been deliberately and consciously so. For many contemporary Puebloans, there are interrelated, overlapping spatial dimensions to society, ritual, cosmography, and politics. These ideas likely have a deep Ancestral Puebloan history. As Chacoans constructed monumental buildings and positioned structures and features to engage with the natural topography, they communicated aspects of a Chacoan ideology. The Chacoan landscape is laden with meaning, and although we cannot access ancient meanings at a specific level, we can trace the large-scale outlines of a Chacoan worldview.

Landscapes embrace the intersection of the social, the emotional, and the material. Spatial experiences have a powerful aesthetic dimension. The term *place* encompasses the lived experiences and meanings bound up in a particular space. In the Apache ethnography *Wisdom Sits in Places*, Basso (1996) employed the term *sense of place* to describe the ways humans imbue their surroundings with memories, meanings, and aesthetic resonance. Lived, spatial experiences help to affirm and challenge ideas about the world and our place in it. Because worldviews and ideologies are negotiated within a complex web of the social and the material, they are at least partially accessible to archaeologists willing to take an interpretive approach to the past. My interpretively constructed vision of the Chacoan landscape has a twofold purpose. First, I have attempted to understand some of the ideas that resonate through Bonito-style architecture. Second, I have employed these ideas to try to gain a clearer understanding of Chacoan sociopolitical relationships across Chaco's rise, zenith, and decline.

Archaeological Landscapes

Over the past two decades, landscape has emerged as a unifying concept for the archaeological study of place and social reality (for example, Ashmore and Knapp 1999). Many current areas of archaeological interest, including identity, ethnicity, ritual, power, and ideology, intersect at the nexus of landscape. In the American Southwest, the term *landscape* is invoked by archaeologists straddling a wide range of epistemological positions. Some equate landscape with settlement patterns, examining the changing and variable distributions of people and resources across space. Some explore "cultural landscapes," investigating the links—which may involve oral traditions, as well as archaeology—that connect indigenous groups with specific places. Still others view spatial experiences as reflexively constructed over time and landscape as a window through which to investigate less tangible aspects of ancient life, such as meaning and ideology. Although each of these approaches has different theoretical roots, they can be complementary. Material remains, ethnography, and cognitive perceptions can all have a place in well-rounded interpretive analysis.

Settlement pattern studies have enjoyed a long run of popularity in cultural ecology and processual archaeology. Horizontal and vertical measurements describe relationships between people and natural or cultural resources, and landforms provide raw materials or opportunities to engage in various kinds of subsistence behavior. Traditional settlement pattern studies tend to view space as a neutral container for action. Clearly, ancient peoples were concerned with factors such as the presence of competitive neighbors and the availability of arable land or water, but landscapes are more than backdrops or sets of resources waiting to be exploited.[2] Although measurements of physical distances among populations and resources can constitute useful information, reducing landscape to material patterning leaves the meaningful and experiential aspects of place unexplored. People have reactions, perceptions, opinions, and experiences of their constructed and natural spatial surroundings.

During the 1980s and 1990s, geographers, philosophers, and anthropologists began to move beyond "space as container" models, developing a holistic concept of space as a socially produced, relational medium vital to the construction of identity and society (for example, Altman and Low 1992; Lefebvre 1991).[3] Archaeologists seeking ways to move beyond the limitations of settlement pattern studies began to focus on landscape as a way to integrate human perceptions and relationships into the picture (Anschuetz, Wilshusen, and Scheick 2001). In the Southwest and in other postcolonial settings, archaeologists working with indigenous peoples developed the concept of cultural landscapes to weave together oral histories, migrations, and traditional land use (for example, Ferguson and Colwell-Chanthaphonh 2006; Morphy 1993).[4]

But landscapes are not only culturally constructed—they are also inherently ideological. Landscapes comprise the spatial milieu within which bodies and the social and material worlds interact and intersect, as identity and power are negotiated. Highly visible monumental architecture is often employed in the construction of identity or the legitimation of power. The commercial skyscrapers that form the nucleus of the urban landscape may be seen as embodying the dominance of capitalism and capitalists, towering over (yet based in) the wreckage of the inner-city poor (Zukin 1991). Landscapes do not simply evoke meanings—they also constrain and order (Foucault 1977). Spaces are both the site and the stake of social struggle (Harvey 1989, 1996). An investigation into space must extend beyond "the relationship between bodies, forms, and elements" to include "the product of negotiations between an array of competing actors with varying practical capacities to transform relationships" (Smith 2003:72). Archaeologists working on monumental landscapes in Mesoamerica (Ashmore 1989), Roman Greece (Alcock 1993), and Neolithic Britain (Bradley 1998, 2000) have turned their attention to landscape as a way to think about ancient ideologies, worldviews, and power relationships.[5]

Landscapes are more than reflexive representations of social or political relationships. Much of the potency of spatial experiences for enhancing or challenging power relationships comes from the fact that landscapes are also inherently sensual. Place making—the construction of a meaningful landscape—involves sound, smell, taste, touch, sight, and emotion. Tuan's (1974) *Topophilia*, today a classic geography text, was the first book of its kind to deal with the aesthetic and sensual dimensions of landscape. Tuan (1974:27) pointed out that spatial experiences can elicit powerful emotions, particularly when multiple senses are involved. Cathedral interiors provide a familiar example. The exaggerated height and emptiness of the space, the shadowy light shot through with stained glass beams, the suffused odors of incense and candle wax, the blurry echoes of chants or organ music, the coolness of marble underfoot—all combine to create strong aesthetic and emotional responses.

Lefebvre (1991:38–46) proposes a useful organizational scheme for thinking about these interrelated dimensions of landscape. For Lefebvre, space is a tripartite concept that includes the material world, spatial representations, and spatial perceptions. Smith (2003:73–75) has helped translate these ideas into archaeological terms. The material world is, of course, the archaeologically familiar patterning of sites, features, topography, and resources. These physical landscapes are invested with meaning through representations and perceptions. Spatial representations refer to the ways people draw, describe, and imagine landscape, through art, texts, photographs, maps, or cosmographic schemes—this dimension may be accessible to Southwest archaeologists through rock art, pottery motifs, and indigenous oral traditions and histories. Spatial perceptions encompass the sensual, emotional, aesthetic dimensions of landscape, involving such archaeological factors as visibility, memory, and iconic symbolism. Investigations into past perceptions pose no small challenge for archaeologists. One potentially useful method involves phenomenology—experiencing the landscape.

Experiencing the Landscape

Contemporary visitors to Chaco Canyon do not approach the canyon as eleventh-century visitors did. As we drive into Chaco Culture National Historic Park, in the air-conditioned comfort of our automobiles, we are insulated from the sandy dunes underfoot, the gnat-scattering breeze, the sun on skin. We approach the canyon through the Gallo Wash, weaving our way past low cliffs until we round a bend to see Fajada Butte and the sign for the public campground. Those who are a bit more adventurous brave multiple tire punctures to travel rocky Route 57 north from Seven Lakes. Some ancient visitors probably also entered the canyon through the Gallo Wash or Fajada Gap, but many probably arrived from other directions. Major concentrations of outlier communities are situated to the north, the west, and the southwest of Chaco; a few large settlements are located to the east. Ancient visitors likely arrived from all these directions, traveling along the North Road via Pueblo Alto, along the Chaco River from the west, through South Gap from the southwest, along Chacra Mesa from the southeast, or through the canyon from the east. And, by important contrast with our own experiences, Chacoans arrived in the canyon on foot. Time and movement were not compressed along the journey as they are for us today, in our cars and campers.

But once we reach the canyon core and begin to move through constructed spaces such as Pueblo Bonito, some aspects of the contemporary and the ancient Chacoan spatial experience are likely to be similar. All humans know the world through bodily experience, so all humans share body-relational perceptions such as directionality and scale. The builders of monumental architecture intend for their work to be seen and experienced by others. As visitors walk within the canyon today, navigating park service trails through great house ruins, we catch partial glimpses of the Chacoan architects' intentions. We are impressed with Pueblo Bonito's massive, looming walls, exaggerated size, and rigid, repetitive formality. What sensory reactions were great houses originally designed to elicit? What beliefs about the world were they intended to convey? I investigate these questions and others, using a phenomenological approach.

Phenomenological archaeologists such as Tilley (1994) have used the commonalities in all human spatial perception as a starting point for exploring the ways in which ancient peoples might have experienced landscape and architecture. Of course, the contemporary archaeological landscape is but a distorted remnant of the ancient landscape, and interpretations of both are and were culturally situated. We can never replicate the perceptions and reactions of past peoples, and we cannot help but bring our own subjectivities to any experience. Nevertheless, phenomenology provides us with one route of ingress into the ideologically charged, complex social and physical landscapes of the past. Keeping the various caveats and pitfalls of a phenomenological approach in mind, I set out to experience the Chacoan landscape.

Armed with a 35 mm camera, a digital video camera, and a notebook, I made formal and informal data-gathering forays in Chaco Canyon and across the San Juan Basin, visiting great houses, great kivas, shrines, stone circles, small sites, road segments, and high places over a period spanning more than a decade. I walked the last few kilometers of the major road segments and access routes that lead into Chaco Canyon, and I visited more than 50 outlier communities across the San Juan Basin. Along the way, I asked specific questions about spatial perceptions and the ways in which perceptions were directed and enhanced by Bonito-style architecture.

Chacoan travelers, of course, did not carry cameras. I used photography to help create a visual record of these experiences, but the cameras were more than recording devices (Geuens 1994; Himpele 2003). The creation of still and moving images helped focus my attention on the specifics of the surroundings, enabling me to perceive things I otherwise might have missed, such as the way great houses on the north side of Chaco Canyon momentarily throb with golden light when the sun drops below cloud cover on an overcast winter day, or the way a prominent Bonito-style building can appear and disappear from different vantage points within an outlier community.

Maps constitute another important tool of the landscape scholar. I manipulated digital topographic data with ArcGIS and MapTech Terrain Navigator. I used these programs to plot sites on the terrain, compare elevations, measure distances, and look for potential line-of-sight connections among architectural and natural features. I used aerial photographs to help locate Chacoan roads on the ground. However, maps, aerial photographs, GIS databases, and other kinds of large-scale, top-down representations of space do not show us the landscape as Chacoans would have seen it. "Distanced, geometrical, 'outsider's' approaches to space can claim no priority over the social and the experiential" (Thomas 1993:27).

My phenomenological observations coalesce around three perceptual attributes—visibility, movement, and memory—that seem to be of importance on the Chacoan landscape. These observations gain additional support and dimensions when considered together with representations of landscape derived from contemporary and historic Pueblo ethnography (chapter 3). For many modern Pueblo peoples, the social, ritual, and mythic worlds are expressed and represented by physical and imagined landscapes. Memory, movement, and cosmography are three overlapping attributes that emerge from the ethnographic literature.

Interpreting the Landscape

Archaeologists work to understand the past from within a double hermeneutic, developing partial and imperfect interpretations of the meanings constructed by the peoples under investigation, on the basis of material objects that are likely to contain multidimensional, ambiguous, complex, and incomplete connotations. The interpretations offered in this book can represent but one partially understood set of possibilities. But I have attempted to craft my interpretations so that they are faithful to material evidence, ethnographic information, and phenomenological observations.

The Chacoan landscape can be understood as the large-scale spatial representation of a worldview shared by many Ancestral Puebloan inhabitants, builders, and visitors. Chacoan architects actively designed a landscape that elicited a powerful emotional response in visitors. This worldview revolved around interrelated themes that are omnipresent at Chaco, as well as in many other Ancestral Puebloan spaces: sacred geography, balanced dualisms, directionality, visibility, cyclical renewal, social memory, and center place.

When those who shared this worldview moved through the buildings and across the modified landscape of Chaco Canyon, the experience actively reaffirmed their beliefs about the nature of the world and their place in it. Architecture and worldview were transformed into a powerful Chacoan ideology. Leaders' authority was naturalized and legitimated by spatial messages that celebrated Chaco Canyon as the center of the Puebloan cosmographic, social, and ritual world, and visitors transformed themselves into subjects. It seemed inevitable and desirable to travel to Chaco for periodic ritual events and to contribute labor and resources for the ceremonies necessary to continue the Puebloan way of life. And where else should these ceremonies take place but in Chaco Canyon—the cosmographic, social, and ritual center of the eleventh-century Pueblo world?

Notes

1. Early investigations in the canyon include excavations conducted by Richard Wetherill and the Hyde Expedition (1896–1900), Edgar Lee Hewett and the School of American Research

(1920–1921, 1929–1935), Neil Judd and the National Geographic Society (1921–1927), and Hewett and the University of New Mexico (1928–1947). Chaco Canyon became a national monument in 1907, following the passage of the Antiquities Act in 1906, as advocated by Hewett. During the 1950s and 1960s, research continued as part of a stabilization program directed by Gordon Vivian. In the 1970s and 1980s, a joint venture called the Chaco Project was initiated between the University of New Mexico and the National Park Service under the direction of Robert Lister, then James Judge. Coal and natural gas development during the 1970s and 1980s led to regional studies by the Bureau of Land Management and the Public Service Company of New Mexico. One outcome of the Chaco Project was the creation of a Chaco Archive at the University of New Mexico, where copies of all data and publications pertaining to Chaco from the past 150 years are ostensibly housed. However, information and collections from various expeditions are scattered, from Washington DC to the canyon itself. Steve Plog and others are working on the Chaco Digital Initiative, construction of a digital database to facilitate access to information. Over the past several years, Steve Lekson, one of the original participants in the Chaco Project, has spearheaded efforts to create a series of final, synthetic reports on the Chaco Project (for example, Cameron and Toll 2001; Cordell, Judge, and Piper 2001; Kantner 2003b; Lekson 2006; Noble 2004).

2. For examples of absolutist approaches to landscape, see Hodder and Orton (1976), Steward (1955), Washburn (1974), and Willey (1953). For a detailed critique, see Smith (2003:33–54), Tilley (1994:7–11), and Wagstaff (1987).

3. For additional influential examples of geographers who have worked on holistic concepts of space and landscape, see Agnew and Duncan (1989), Cosgrove (1984, 1993), Davis (1992), Duncan and Ley (1993), Harvey (1989, 1996), Jackson (1984), Lowenthal (1985), Schama (1996), Soja (1980, 1988, 1996), and Tuan (1974, 1977). Some influential anthropological landscape investigations of note include Appadurai (1988), Basso (1996), Feld and Basso (1996), Hirsch and O'Hanlon (1995), Ingold (1993), Lawrence and Low (1990), Low and Lawrence-Zúñiga (2003), and Rodman (1992).

4. Other good examples include Carroll, Zedeño, and Stoffle (2004), Ferguson and Anyon (2001), T. King (2003), Taçon (1999), and Zedeño (1997).

5. The ranks of this genre of landscape studies are increasing at an exponential rate. For additional influential examples, see Ashmore (2002), Ashmore and Knapp (1999), Barrett (1991, 1994), Bender (1993), Bowser (2004), R. Bradley (1993), Donley-Reid (1990), Edmonds (1999), Joyce and Gillespie (2000), Leone (1988), Smith (2003), Thomas (1991, 1996), Tilley (1994, 1999), and Ucko and Layton (1998).

2 Locations

> Wisdom sits in places. It's like water that never dries up. You need to drink water to stay alive, don't you? Well, you also need to drink from places.
>
> —Dudley Patterson, in Wisdom Sits in Places, by Keith Basso (1996:127)

The landscape of Chaco Canyon and, indeed, northwest New Mexico carries aesthetic resonance and cultural significance for Native and non-native visitors and inhabitants today. People have been walking this terrain of light and shadow, wind and saltbush, for at least 12,000 years. The hoodoos, rockshelters, badlands, and canyon walls are, of course, much older. Like the Western Apache landscapes encountered by Basso, the Chacoan landscape is imbued with multiple layers of cultural meaning that shift according to the viewer and the purpose of the story. Any construction of meaning requires basic contextual information so that it will make sense. In this chapter, I position my work on the physical and the archaeological landscape, providing background information on the environment, culture history, and sociopolitical issues at stake in Chacoan studies.

Chaco Canyon, as a place, had a number of things going for it that were useful and appealing to settlers and great house builders. Chaco had good soils and reliable water, especially in comparison with the surrounding territory of the San Juan Basin. The canyon contains excellent building material, which may have both attracted and inspired Puebloan masons. But Chaco contained other critical attributes that led to its emergence as a central place in the eleventh-century Puebloan world.

One of these critical attributes was topography. The canyon sits in the geographic center of the San Juan Basin, a logical gathering place for people from peripheral settlements. The canyon also is at the visible center of the

Basin. High atop Chacra Mesa, one can see and be seen by the surrounding world. Ancestral occupations connected the people who gathered here to the more distant past. Early Puebloan horticulturalists lived in two large villages in Chaco during the Basketmaker III period (AD 450–700), centuries before masons laid the first stone at Pueblo Bonito. The canyon was a place potentially charged with ancestral stories and meanings. There is no mystery as to why Pueblo Bonito and the other great houses were built in Chaco Canyon. They could not have been built anywhere else.

Chaco's Physical Landscape

> *The light there is of a certain kind. In the mornings and evenings it is soft and pervasive, and the earth seems to absorb it, to become enlarged with light. About the noons there are edges and angles— and a brightness that is hard and thin like a glaze. There is something strange and powerful in it. When you look out across the land you believe at first that it is all one thing: there appears to be an awful sameness to it. But after a while you see that it is not one thing at all, but many things, all of which are subject to change in a moment. [Momaday 1976:4]*

One hundred million years ago, vast seas covered the undulating gray-green horizons of the Colorado Plateau. Today, the Cretaceous ocean floor has become shales and sandstones settled into horizontal beds, riven by erosion into canyons, mesas, and fantastic spires. On this open expanse, light captures the human imagination. The sun sears this world to midday monochromes and pours distant cliffs with evening liquid gold.

In the San Juan Basin, a topographic depression encompassing much of northwest New Mexico, the sky's prominence is enhanced by recumbent, sedimentary topography. The Basin forms a shallow bowl bounded by the Hogback Monocline and the San Juan Uplift to the north, the Nacimiento Uplift and the Jemez Mountains Caldera to the east, the Zuni Uplift to the south, and the Defiance Uplift and the Chuska Mountains to the west and northwest. It covers an area measuring approximately 160 km north/south and 145 km east/west and ranging in altitude from 1,500 to 2,500 m above sea level (Vivian 1990:26).

The San Juan Basin can be divided into a number of physiographic subregions, based on geology and drainage patterns (figure 2.1) (Gregory 1916; Kelley 1950; Marshall et al. 1979; Vivian 1990:25–31). The Chaco Slope and the Chaco Plateau are two central subregions of the San Juan Basin located to the south and north, respectively. The Chaco Slope is a broad, flat,

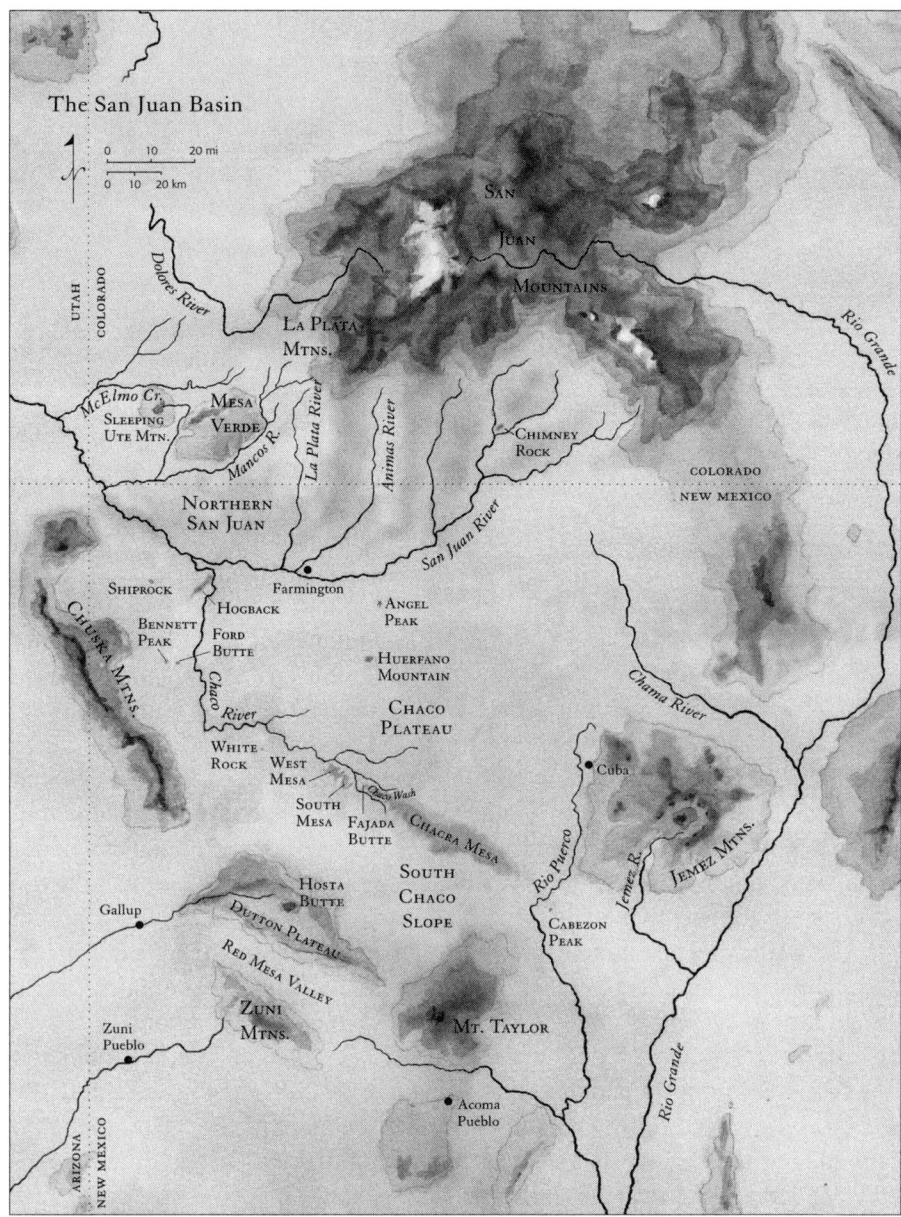

Figure 2.1. The San Juan Basin. Drafted by Molly O'Halloran.

dune-covered expanse characterized by the low relief of small buttes, eroding shale and sandstone ridges, and short valleys. The Chaco Plateau is a similarly open, north-sloping, sage-covered, treeless plain covered in rolling

Locations 13

dunes dissected here and there by badlands, with fewer sandstone exposures. The Chaco Slope and the Chaco Plateau are separated by Chacra Mesa, an uplifted cuesta that runs for 75 km east to west across the center of the Basin. The Chaco Wash cut through the north side of this cuesta to create Chaco Canyon.

> Suddenly the canyon was there: huge cliffs bordering a flat valley bisected by a deep, straight-sided arroyo. As the sun dropped toward the horizon, the rocks' strong red contrasted with the soft tones of valley sand, sage, and grass. Within the arroyo were striking patches of green, the leaves of occasional giant cottonwoods fed by the intermittent waters of Chaco Wash. And dominating the upper section of the scene was that clear turquoise southwestern sky. [Schwartz 1984:ix]

Created by Pleistocene erosion along the north side of Chacra Mesa, Chaco Canyon extends for 30 km, from Pueblo Pintado to the confluence of the Chaco Wash with the Escavada Wash (plate 5; see figure 2.1). The canyon bottom is 0.5 to 1.0 km wide and slopes almost imperceptibly toward the west. Canyon walls range from 90 to 180 m in height, although benches on both sides soften the drop. The north side of the canyon is formed by a massive layer of Cliff House sandstone topped by a dark, thinly bedded sandstone bench, then by a second layer of steeply rising, massive sandstone. The south side of Chaco Canyon is formed by Chacra Mesa, which breaks at Fajada Gap to form Fajada Butte and South Mesa and again at South Gap to form West Mesa. Here, soft, carbonaceous shales of the Menefee formation under harder Cliff House sandstone form long, colluvial talus slopes topped by short terraces and cliffs (Vivian 1990:32). Although less dramatic in appearance when viewed from the canyon floor, Chacra Mesa is higher and steeper than the north side of Chaco Canyon, rising to elevations of 1,800 to 2,300 m above sea level. From the south, Chacra Mesa is a steep escarpment reaching 120 to 150 m above the Basin floor.

This is an important point. The name Chaco *Canyon* suggests depth, so most of us are used to thinking of Chaco as a secluded, protected, sheltered canyon. But the canyon is created from a landform that is also highly visible and vertical. Chacra *Mesa* is a prominent high place on the broad and level expanse of the San Juan Basin floor. Chacra Mesa, Fajada Butte, South Mesa, and West Mesa afford stunning vistas of the San Juan Basin, its encircling mountains and uplifts, and its prominent topographic landmarks. In turn, Chacra Mesa, Fajada Butte, South Mesa, and West Mesa are visible across the surrounding San Juan Basin to the north, west, and south from locations as far as 90 km away.

Additional high places punctuate the horizons of the San Juan Basin, including Huerfano Mountain, Chimney Rock, Cabezon Peak, Mount Taylor, Hosta Butte, and Shiprock (see plate 5). These landmarks figure prominently in the oral traditions of Pueblo and Navajo peoples (for example, Linford 2000; Ortiz 2002; Snead and Preucel 1999). Huerfano Mountain is an isolated, 2,255-m-high sandstone mesa north of Chaco Canyon and east of Bloomfield. The Navajo call this hogan-shaped mesa Dzilth Ná'oodithlii and consider it one of the homes of First Man and First Woman. Chimney Rock and Companion Rock, 400-m-high twin spires on the Piedra River in southwest Colorado, are considered a shrine to the Twin War Gods of Taos Pueblo. Cabezon Peak, a 2,373-m-high volcanic plug, rises above the Middle Rio Puerco Valley 90 km southeast of Chaco. In Navajo stories, this place is the head of a slain giant. From Cabezon's basalt heights, Mount Taylor is clearly visible on the horizon, 66 km to the southwest. Mount Taylor, the 3,445-m-high remnant cone of an ancient volcano, presides in majesty over north-central New Mexico. The Acoma consider Mount Taylor a holy place, and the Navajo view this "turquoise mountain" as the southern boundary of their world. Southeast of Chaco Canyon at a distance of 55 km, Hosta Butte is a flat-topped mesa rising to 2,627 m above the 2,300-m-high Dutton Plateau. For the Navajo, 'Ak'iih Dah Nást'ání (Mountain Sits on Top of Another Mountain) is the sacred home of Mirage Boy and Mirage Girl. Along the eastern flanks of the Chuska Mountains, three jagged volcanic dykes and plugs reach between 200 and 500 m into the sky. The largest and best known of these is Shiprock, with its great fins stretched out like sails or wings. English-speaking settlers thought that Shiprock resembled a clipper ship; the Navajo consider Tsé Bit' a'í to represent a large bird. To the south of 2,188-m-high Shiprock, two companion plugs—Ford Butte (1,876 m) and Bennett Peak (1,972 m)—also rise sharply above the surrounding terrain.

The expanses between these dramatic peaks can appear empty and forbidding to modern travelers, but this a perspective not shared by modern Navajo Basin residents. Many thousands of Navajo live in the San Juan Basin today, in towns such as Shiprock, in small settlements such as White Rock, and in isolated hogans that dot the landscape like small beehives. Far from any major center of modern Anglo population, Chaco Canyon can seem difficult to access, as illustrated by infamous photos of various historic archaeological expeditions mired in the Escavada Wash (figure 2.2). Road conditions have only moderately improved since the days of Judd and Hewitt. The twenty-first-century traveler still must brave extremes of weather and topography in order to make the pilgrimage to Chaco. But Chaco was not an isolated place in AD 1000, nor, for modern Navajo peoples, is it particularly isolated today. Chacoan site densities of twenty to thirty small sites per

Figure 2.2. A National Park Service vehicle mired in the mud en route to Chaco. Photograph by Gordon Vivian. Courtesy of the National Park Service, Chaco Culture National Historical Park, negative no. 77906.

square kilometer give the lie to the notion that the silence and isolation experienced by contemporary visitors characterized the San Juan Basin in 1050 (Hayes 1981).

The weather in Chaco has also contributed to perceptions of the canyon as a bleak and untenable wasteland. Extreme aridity, sudden storms, gale-force winds, temperatures above 100 degrees F in summer and below 0 degrees F in winter, and dramatic diurnal temperature fluctuations in any season inspired A. V. Kidder to infamously opine that Chaco is a land

> little better than a desert; many parts of it, indeed, are absolutely barren wastes of sand and rock which do not even support the usual dry-country flora of the Southwest. It is almost devoid of springs, has no permanent streams, is subject to severe sandstorms, is blistering hot in summer and bitterly cold in winter. It is hard to see how life in the Chaco could have been anything but a continual struggle for bare existence. [Kidder 1962(1924):54]

The climate of the San Juan Basin has not changed substantially over the past two millennia, although there have been many short- and long-term climatic shifts (Dean 1992; Vivian et al. 2006). But rather than the forbidding wasteland conjured by Kidder, Chaco in its heyday might have been something of an ancient farming oasis. Vivian and Mathews

> want to temper the harshness of Kidder's judgment somewhat, for there are portions of the Chaco that are quite green even in dry years. The tributary canyons from the north, particularly the Mockingbird and the Gallo, have a very heavy perennial cover. [Vivian and Mathews 1965:1]

A thousand years in the past, Chaco Canyon may actually have presented an inviting locale for agriculturalists. As it happens, the canyon is the only place in the Basin where deep deposits of alluvium accumulated in a confined area suitable for floodwater irrigation (Vivian and Mathews 1965:4). Recent geomorphic research (Force et al. 2002; Vivian et al. 2006) indicates that an aeolian dune blocked Chaco Canyon at its confluence with the Escavada Wash, creating a recurring dam and possibly even a lake. When the natural dam breached, it may have been replaced with masonry. If Force's interpretations are correct, then Chaco Canyon during its heyday would have been a particularly wet and suitable place for agriculture.[1] Today, despite modern arroyo downcutting, the Chaco Wash flows following summer rains and winter snowmelt. The modern water table is 1–2 m below the surface of the Chaco Wash, and the subsurface stream contains water even during the driest periods.

Regardless of how difficult it may or may not have been to farm in and around Chaco, Ancestral Puebloans did so (and quite successfully) for many centuries. Although detailed understandings of the environment, in and of themselves, cannot tell us why the Chacoans built great houses, periods of escalating construction activity during the eleventh century and the early twelfth century correspond to some of the wettest years ever seen in Chaco (Sebastian 1992; Windes 1993). It does appear likely that surplus resources provided part of the means and motivation for the social and architectural developments in the canyon that have attracted so much archaeological attention.

Chaco's Archaeological Landscape

Chaco Canyon has a lengthy history of occupation, extending from the Paleoindian through the historic periods (Vivian 1990). Thanks to dendrochronology, archaeologists at Chaco have some of the best temporal resolution in the world (for example, Bannister 1965; Bannister, Robinson, and Warren 1970; Hawley 1934, 1938; Robinson, Harrill, and Warren 1974; Windes 2003; Windes and Ford 1992, 1996). Tree-ring dates are available

Table 2.1 Time Periods for the Ancestral Puebloan Occupation of Chaco Canyon

Dates (AD)	Pecos Classification Periods	Chaco Center Phases
450–700	Basketmaker III	—
700–875	Pueblo I	—
875–1020	Early Pueblo II	Early Bonito
1020–1100	Late Pueblo II	Classic Bonito
1100–1140	Early Pueblo III	Late Bonito
1140–1300	Late Pueblo III	—

for structures with standing masonry or where wood has been recovered through excavation. Masonry styles and ceramic types have been cross-dated with tree-ring sequences so that unexcavated sites can still be assigned time spans as tight as 50–100 years on the basis of visible architecture and surface ceramics. Over the past century of archaeological research on Chaco, various temporal schemes have been devised. For the great house era, between AD 850 and 1140, I use the Chaco Center terminology, with phases named in reference to the great house Pueblo Bonito and with dates revised by Windes (1987:244).[2] The Pecos Classification, as slightly modified by more recent research, provides a useful baseline for developments immediately pre- and post-Chaco (table 2.1).

Archaeologists have documented various Paleoindian and Archaic sites in the San Juan Basin, but these time periods are poorly studied and thinly represented in Chaco Canyon. The earliest, clearly relevant roots of Chacoan culture reach back to the Basketmaker III period, when Ancestral Pueblo peoples made gray and black-on-white pottery, raised corn, beans, and squash, and lived in villages of semisubterranean pitstructures. Larger villages sometimes contained an oversized "great pitstructure" that could have served as a community meeting place.[3] Two of the largest Basketmaker III villages in the San Juan Basin—Shabik'eshchee Village and 29SJ423—are located in Chaco Canyon.

During the early Pueblo I period, the Four Corners region attracted settlers from many areas, including the San Juan Basin. By the mid-800s, the Ancestral Pueblo population was concentrated north of the San Juan River in large communities such as Alkali Ridge in southeast Utah and McPhee Village in southwest Colorado.[4] Architecture was changing, too, as people moved out of pitstructures and into surface rooms. These new *pueblos* consisted of linear arcs of connected, masonry-footed surface rooms. Ancestral Puebloans still built pitstructures but began to transform them into *kivas*, used primarily for ritual or other special activities. Some communities contained oversized, circular, underground meeting rooms, or *great kivas*.

By the late 800s, groups of Puebloans began to filter back into the San Juan Basin. The migrants proceeded down the flanks of the Chuska Mountains, across the western San Juan Basin, into Chaco Canyon, and south to the Red Mesa Valley. They returned to ancestral Basketmaker landscapes, and they founded settlements in pristine areas. The new communities consisted of clusters of small domestic pueblos, sometimes centered around a great kiva, sometimes around a *proto-great house*—a prominent domestic pueblo built of simple, stacked sandstone masonry. Ancestral Puebloans built at least six proto-great houses in Chaco Canyon, at Peñasco Blanco, Pueblo Bonito, Kin Nahasbas, Una Vida, Chaco East, and Pueblo Pintado (Windes et al. 2000). Out of this diverse collection of late Pueblo I San Juan Basin communities, Chaco Canyon emerged as a focal point of construction and social activity during the Early Bonito phase.

The great houses, great kivas, and other monumental projects of the Chacoan era were constructed primarily during the Classic Bonito phase. Beds of blocky and tabular Cliff House sandstone exposed in north-side canyon walls provided convenient and durable building materials for great house builders and enabled the development of the core-and-veneer masonry technique. Core-and-veneer is a Chacoan innovation in which the space between two parallel sandstone walls is filled with rubble or stacked masonry. The weight load of the upper stories is transferred from the weaker core to the stronger, outer facing (Lekson 1986:23; Reiter 1933:67). Wall fill, facing, and overall wall widths can vary considerably, depending on the core type, wall morphology, and size of stones used in construction; changing veneer styles are well correlated with tree-ring dates. Chacoans snapped the hard, dark brown, tabular sandstone into long, thin pieces, and they pecked and ground the massive, reddish-brown sandstone into bun-shaped blocks. Over the twentieth century, several scholars developed veneer typologies and cross-dated them with tree-rings (Hawley 1934, 1938; Judd 1927, 1964; Roberts 1938). Judd's Types I–IV together with Vivian and Mathews' (1965) McElmo style constitute the five basic veneer types most commonly referenced today (Lekson 1986:17–21) (figure 2.3). Many Chacoan veneers have a banded appearance that is aesthetically pleasing to the modern eye, but banding probably was not visible after great house construction was complete, because prehispanic masons likely covered great house walls with plaster (Lekson 1986:29, 173).

During the Classic Bonito phase, Chacoan great house builders made formal additions to Peñasco Blanco, Pueblo Bonito, and Una Vida. They also erected four new great houses—Hungo Pavi, Chetro Ketl, Pueblo Alto, and

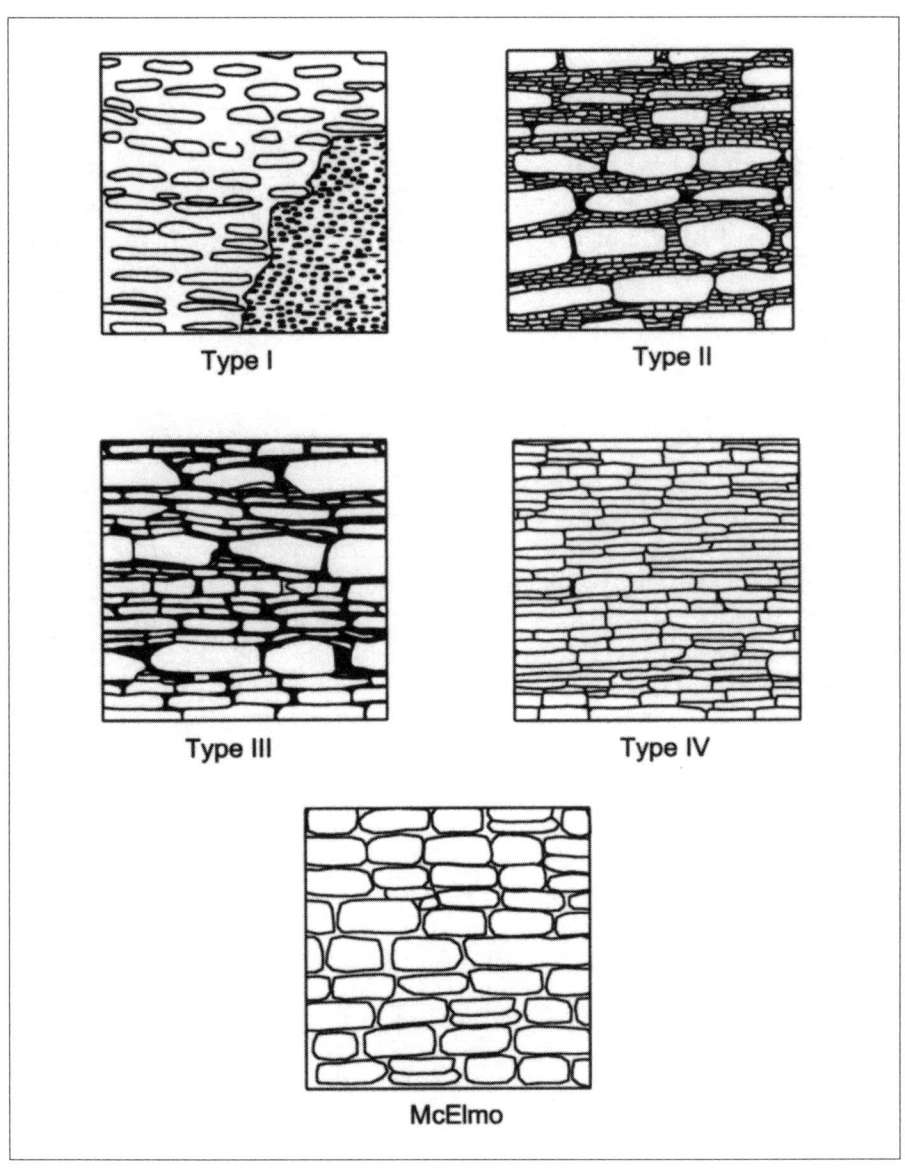

Figure 2.3. Chacoan veneer styles, after Lekson 1986:18, figure 2.4.

Pueblo del Arroyo (Lekson 1986). Chacoans laid out new great houses as a single, linear block of rooms, oriented east-west or northeast-southwest. Perpendicular, symmetrical roomblock wings were added at either end of the linear blocks to create a bracket-shaped, E-shaped, or D-shaped configuration. Roomblocks included kivas enclosed within first- or second-story rectangular rooms. Over the course of the eleventh century, Chacoan builders added higher stories, particularly atop rear rows of rooms, and they added enclosing arcs to plazas (Vivian 1990:270–286). By the mid-1000s, they had added great kivas to the plazas of most great houses and had built four "isolated" great kivas on the south side of Chaco Canyon (Van Dyke 2007; Vivian and Reiter 1960). The south side of the canyon was dotted with hundreds of single-storied, small domestic sites (Hayes, Brugge, and Judge 1981; Kluckhohn and Reiter 1939; McKenna and Truell 1986; Windes 1993).[5] Throughout the Classic Bonito phase, the landscape of Chaco Canyon became increasingly formalized with the construction of shrines, staircases, mounds, ramps, and linear alignments dubbed "roads" (Hayes and Windes 1975; Vivian 1997a, 1997b; Wills 2001).

Conservative estimates for the population of Chaco Canyon during the Classic Bonito phase range between 2,000 and 3,000 people (Lekson 1999:21; Lekson, Windes, and McKenna 2006; Windes 1984).[6] Estimating Chacoan population is difficult primarily because it is not clear how to "count" great houses. Excavated great houses exhibit few hearths or other domestic floor features, but these may have been present in collapsed upper-story floors. Some archaeologists consider kivas to represent domestic spaces; others (notably Lekson 1988a) do not. Windes (2003:32) and others (for example, Bernardini 1999) contend that no more than 100 people lived at Pueblo Bonito at one time and that domestic occupation was most intense during the Early and Late Bonito phases, when domestic trash is most common.

The Late Bonito phase (1100–1140) brought many changes, including the appearance of carbon-painted ceramics and a dramatic shift in architectural construction styles (Judge 1989:246; Lekson 1986:267–269; Toll 1985:483–489). Chacoans continued to build great houses, but the new design consisted of a rectangular block of rooms surrounding a single enclosed kiva. Great kivas were conspicuously absent. At Wijiji, builders experimented with this new, modular building style. Subsequent early 1100s great houses represent McElmo-style architecture and are built of bun-shaped, pecked-and-ground sandstone blocks (Vivian and Mathews 1965). McElmo great houses in Chaco Canyon include New Alto, Casa Chiquita, Tsin Kletsin, and Kin Kletso.

Classic Bonito architectural and political developments in Chaco Canyon cannot be understood outside their larger social context—a world comprising contemporaneous outlier communities stretching across northwest New Mexico and adjacent areas. By the mid-1000s, Bonito-style architecture had spread to nearly 100 Basin communities, where great houses, great kivas, and other Bonito-style elements were built in the midst of small domestic sites. Some outliers were founded in the eleventh century; others were Early Bonito communities that continued as major centers of Classic Bonito occupation.

Scholars have long recognized the existence of outliers (Gladwin 1945; Martin 1936; Morris 1939; Roberts 1932), but until recently these extra-canyon communities and their relationships to Chaco were but poorly explored. In the late 1970s and early 1980s, several major survey projects systematically documented outliers across the San Juan Basin (Fowler, Stein, and Anyon 1987; Marshall and Sofaer 1988; Marshall et al. 1979; Powers, Gillespie, and Lekson 1983). Today, archaeologists have excavated a handful of outlier great houses, and research is ongoing in a number of communities (Cameron 2002; Irwin-Williams and Shelley 1980; Kantner 2003b; Kantner and Mahoney 2000; Pippin 1987), but most outliers remain unexcavated. Outlier great houses and associated Bonito-style features are generally well described, but information for the surrounding communities often tends to be sketchy.[7]

During the 1970s and 1980s, the identification of Chacoan road segments—straight, wide, cleared linear alignments—throughout the San Juan Basin contributed to the recognition that the "Chaco Phenomenon" is regional in scope.[8] At least eight road segments extend into the San Juan Basin from Chaco Canyon (figure 2.4). Through the 1980s, many researchers assumed that these and other road segments were part of a vast network that facilitated travel for economic, ritual, or political purposes. Roney (1992), however, demonstrated that, with the exception of a few very long segments, most roads are short, localized features. Most segments originate near outlier great houses and extend outwards into the landscape for less than a mile before disappearing. Today, most scholars agree that the roads were not constructed primarily to link a Chacoan regional system. Rather, they formalize access to great houses and great kivas, point toward striking topographic features, or serve other ceremonial or symbolic purposes (Marshall 1997; Stein and Lekson 1992; Van Dyke 2003b; Vivian 1997a, 1997b). This does not mean that people did not walk on these roads—only that the practical facilitation of travel was probably not their sole or primary function.

Outliers are linked to Chaco Canyon not only through architectural similarities but also through the movement of materials. The Chacoans imported high quantities of nonlocal materials—including ceramics, lithics, wood, turquoise, and shell—during the Early and the Classic Bonito phases. These materials provide archaeologists with information about the nature and intensity of interaction between Chaco Canyon and outliers in the surrounding subregions of the San Juan Basin.

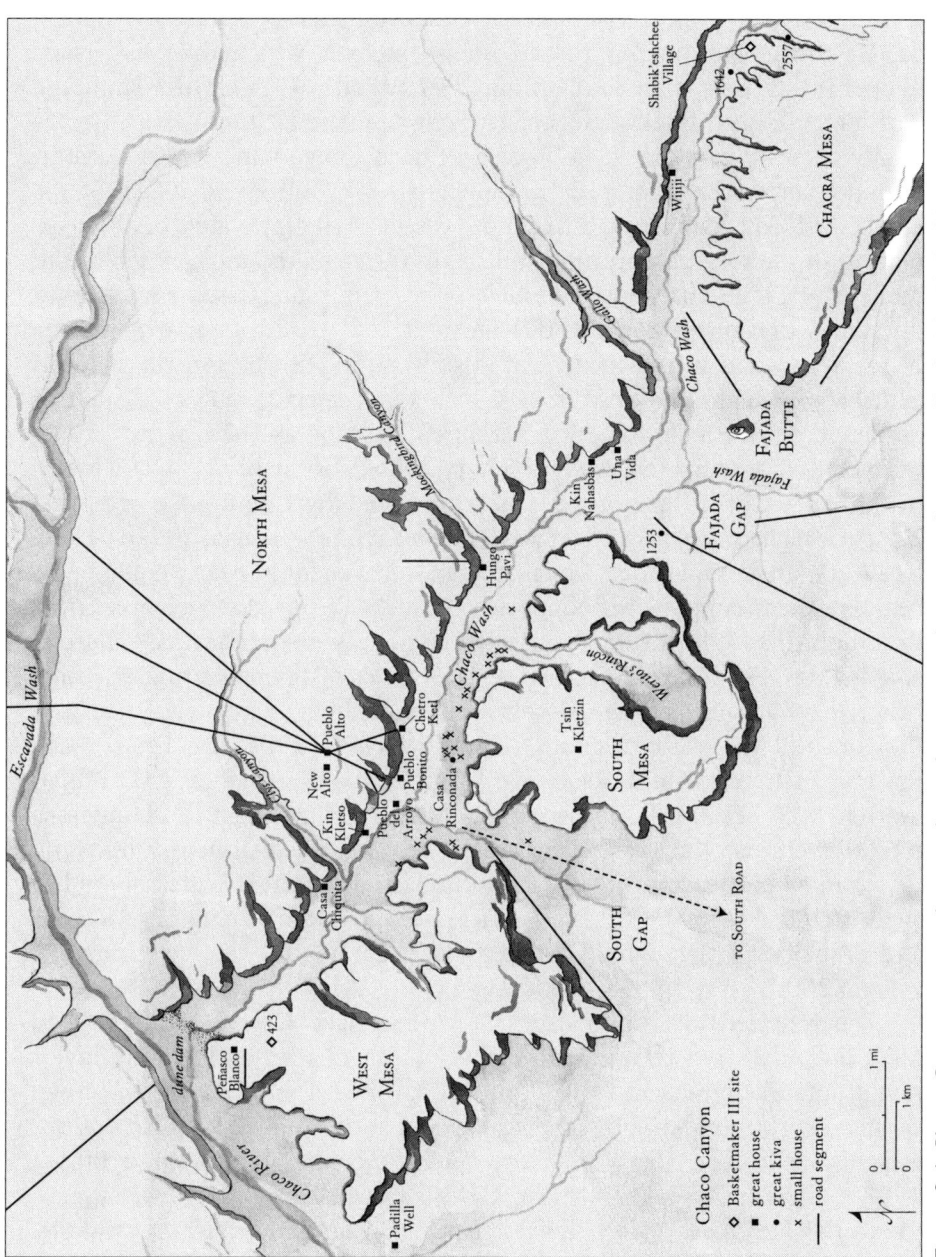

Figure 2.4. Chaco Canyon topography, great house locations, and major road segments. Drafted by Molly O'Halloran.

The Chuskan slopes were an important source for pottery, lithic material, and wood during the Early and Classic Bonito phases. We can easily identify ceramic vessels made on the Chuskan slopes, because the potters used a distinctive, black, crushed rock—trachyte, or sanidine basalt—as temper (Mills, Carpenter, and Grimm 1997; Windes 1977). Throughout the Early and Classic Bonito phases, trachyte-tempered Chuska wares commonly occur in ceramic assemblages in Chaco Canyon and in outlier communities across the western Basin (Shepard 1954; Toll 1985, 2001). By the late 1000s, Chuskan ceramics account for half of all gray wares, or about 30 percent of the total ceramic assemblage, in the trash mound at Pueblo Alto (Toll 1984:115). Chacoans may have prized Chuskan vessels for superior durability, or Chacoans may not have been able to fire their own vessels because firewood would have been in short supply in the canyon. Perhaps Chuskans brought the vessels to Chaco for a specific purpose, such as exchange or use in feasting, or perhaps Chacoans and Chuskans simply enjoyed a close social relationship (Harry 2005; V. King 2003). In any event, the Chuska–Chaco relationship, as represented by ceramics, is strongest along the Chaco Wash corridor west of the canyon (Van Dyke 1997b). Here, local Cibolan and imported Chuskan gray wares occur in nearly equal numbers, but Chuskan pottery frequencies diminish abruptly as one moves onto the South Chaco Slope (Marshall and Sofaer 1988:60–61; Powers, Gillespie, and Lekson 1983:342; Toll 1985:441–442). A distinctive Chuskan lithic material—Narbona Pass chert—also occurs in high frequencies in Chaco Canyon and the western Basin (Cameron 1984, 1997; Jacobson 1984; Powers, Gillespie, and Lekson 1983: Appendix D, table 1; Ward 2004; Warren 1967, 1977). Recent sourcing studies indicate that the Ponderosa pine timbers used in great house roofs were obtained primarily from the Chuskan slopes (Durand et al. 1999; English et al. 2001). Faunal studies show a shift during the Classic Bonito phase from small mammals to deer and antelope, which would have likely been hunted in the mountains (Vivian 2000:5; Vivian et al. 2006:19).

Different relationships existed between Chaco Canyon and the Red Mesa Valley, 80 km to the south. The Dutton Plateau and Mount Taylor might potentially have supplied wood (English et al. 2001). Yellow-brown spotted chert from the Zuni area is abundant at the Red Mesa Valley outliers and in some canyon sites, particularly during the Early Bonito phase (Brandi 1988; Cameron 1984; LeTourneau 1997; Van Dyke 1999a). However, people in the Red Mesa Valley did not participate in Chuskan pottery trade. Chuskan sherds are virtually nonexistent in ceramic assemblages at the Red Mesa Valley sites (Marshall et al. 1979:115–194; Mills 1988; Van Dyke 1997a, 1997b).

Exotic items from more distant regions also made their way into Chaco. Turquoise and shell were fashioned into beads, pendants, and inlays. Turquoise was mined in New Mexico, Colorado, Arizona, and Nevada (Weigand 1994; Weigand and Harbottle 1993). Marine shell came from the Pacific and the Sea of Cortez, and freshwater shell came from California, Texas, and Arkansas (Mathien 2003:129–130). Copper bells and macaws originated in western Mexico or possibly the Mimbres region (Creel and McKusick 1994; Mathien 2003:128–129; Palmer 1994; Palmer et al. 1998). Most of these materials are from two clusters of burial rooms in Pueblo Bonito (Akins 1986, 2003; Judd 1954; Mathien 2003; Neitzel 2003a; Pepper 1909, 1920). Large-scale excavations at Pueblo del Arroyo, Pueblo Alto, and Kin Kletso did not yield similar quantities of exotics.

By the Late Bonito phase (1100–1140), outliers had spread across an area nearly 200 miles in diameter, encompassing northwest New Mexico and neighboring portions of Utah, Colorado, and Arizona. Aztec, located on the Animas River 85 km north of Chaco, was the largest and most prominent of these. As great house construction tapered off in Chaco Canyon, Aztec became the focus of new 1100s building activity.

The late Pueblo III period (1140–1300) was a time of change and gradual migration away from the central San Juan Basin. Great house construction ceased in Chaco Canyon, although occupation continued. People still inhabited some canyon and outlier sites, but settlements had an increasingly domestic flavor. Many Ancestral Puebloans returned to the northern San Juan, where they built large, aggregated pueblos and cliff dwellings. Large pueblos also appeared in the Rio Puerco drainage and in the Zuni area. Architectural references to Chaco at many of these sites suggest that the Chacoan past—both real and imagined—figured prominently into the construction of post-Chacoan Pueblo society. By the fourteenth century, Chaco and the central San Juan Basin lay silent as Ancestral Pueblo peoples moved to the well-watered Rio Grande, to Laguna, Acoma, and Zuni, to the Little Colorado and Hopi, or to southern New Mexico and Arizona.

Perspectives on Chacoan Social and Political Organization

Archaeological interpretations for Chaco are varied and sometimes conflicting, but scholars agree that planned, massive, Bonito-style structures represent a substantial investment of labor and design. Clearly, the construction of Chacoan monumental architecture required the participation of a great many people. Why did these small-scale agriculturalists invest so much time and energy in what Johnson (1989:376) has termed "piling behavior"? Did people participate gladly and willingly, or did others coerce them in some way? What went on in the massive buildings, plazas, and great kivas, and whose interests did these activities serve? What was the basis of power in Chaco? What can Chaco teach us about the negotiation of political authority and social status in nonstate societies? The evidence for sociopolitical hierarchy at Chaco is ambiguous, and therein lies Chaco's appeal for scholars of prehispanic sociopolitical complexity. The configuration of society in the canyon, the organization of labor, the reasoning behind the construction of massive, imposing, nonresidential buildings cannot be neatly explained by analogy with other societies. Chaco must be understood on its own terms.

Chaco is of central interest for scholars investigating the development of sociopolitical power and authority, in part because it does not comfortably fit any ethnographically identified, sociopolitical niche such as "state" or "chiefdom" (Johnson 1989; Saitta 1999; Yoffee 1994, 2001). Over the past century, archaeologists have developed a plethora of models to explain the sociopolitical organization of Chaco Canyon and the outliers that surround it (Mills 2002:77–80; Sebastian 1992:82–97; Vivian 1990:391–419). In the 1970s and 1980s, explanations tended to polarize, with researchers at one extreme positing Chaco as an aggregation of egalitarian, communal farmers and those at the other viewing Chaco as the seat of institutionalized sociopolitical hierarchy.

Gwinn Vivian has been a strong advocate of an egalitarian vision of Chaco in which great houses and small house sites are interpreted as domestic architecture. Following the ideas of Kluckhohn (1939), Vivian (1989, 1990:419–448) argues that great houses and small house sites in Chaco Canyon represent two separate but coexistent cultural traditions, neither of which involved institutionalized, permanent, hierarchical authority. Rather, Vivian sees great house society as organized according to a rotating, sequential hierarchy grounded in principles of dualism, after the contemporary social organization of the Tewa (Johnson 1982; Ortiz 1965, 1969). At small houses, social relationships were organized in terms of lineages.

In the 1980s, Chaco Center archaeologists, including Jim Judge, Bob Powers, John Schelberg, and Wolky Toll, were divided on the egalitarian-versus-hierarchical issue. In the basic Chaco Center scheme, they portrayed the canyon and the outliers as an integrated regional system. Chaco Center scholars considered adaptation to the environment to be the motivating force behind the evolution of this system. The canyon was the center of a redistribution network for subsistence goods—the network protected everyone in the San Juan Basin against unpredictable crop shortfalls due to rainfall fluctuations. In the hierarchical version of this scenario (for example, Judge 1979; Judge et al. 1981; Powers 1984; Schelberg 1984), an institutionalized hierarchy of elites doled out the food at Chaco under a ritual veneer. Leaders gained power through control of food, which led to controlled access to ritual, which legitimated power. In an egalitarian version (Toll 1984, 1985), people periodically came together at Chaco to feast, participate in rituals, and redistribute food, but these activities did not involve hierarchical leaders. Following the latter vision, Renfrew (2001) has recently dubbed Chaco a "Location of High Devotional Expression," where "essentially egalitarian" pilgrims periodically gathered to worship, leaving nonlocal goods in exchange for spiritual experiences.

Many scholars subsequently discarded the redistribution aspect of the Chaco Center model because of a dearth of supporting material evidence (Sebastian 1992:85–91; see Lekson 1999, 2002b:619; and Stuart 2000 for some exceptions), but various permutations of the egalitarian-versus-hierarchical issue continued to vex archaeologists. Sometimes this argument has been cast in terms of the presence or absence of "complexity" (for example, Lekson 1988b). By the late 1990s, Southwest archaeologists were beginning to break free of the gridlock engendered by categorical perspectives on social inequality in Chaco and elsewhere in the Southwest. In a seminal critique, McGuire and Saitta (1996) argue that Puebloan society may be seen as *both* hierarchical and communal and that social change is driven by a dialectical tension between the two. Planned architecture on a monumental scale strongly suggests the presence of some form or forms of social and political authority at Chaco. Rather than asking the categorical question, Was social power present or absent at Chaco? we should be asking, How can we understand the nature and development of social power at Chaco (Nelson 1995)?

Power To and *Power Over*

Power in a Weberian sense refers to the ability of an individual to impose her or his will on others (Weber 1947:152). As Foucault (1977, 1980) demonstrated, power is not merely a property exerted by active agents upon passive subjects. Rather, power can be both enabling and restrictive, involving not only domination but also resistance. Miller and Tilley (1984:5–8) distinguish between *power to* and *power over*. *Power to* enables people to draw upon, create, and control social and material resources. *Power over* involves transformations that must be realized through the actions of others. With *power over*, people get others to do things that are not necessarily in their best interests. At Chaco, *power to* and *power over* are inseparable, coexisting in a dialectical relationship. *Power over*, however, has been the focus of most investigations into Chacoan inequalities.

The most obvious way to establish and maintain *power over* is through coercion, or the threat of physical force. In this vein, Wilcox (1993) proposes a military Chacoan state complete with social, economic, and religious centralization. For Wilcox, canyon great houses were soldiers' barracks, outliers were military installations, great kivas were focal points for tribute collection, and roads were for the efficient movement of Chacoan armies. This scenario rests on little empirical support, however (Van Dyke 1999b:479). Turner and Turner (1999) postulate coercive Toltec cannibals as the founders of Chaco. This idea is not taken seriously by most Chacoan scholars for many reasons, including the fact that there is no compelling evidence for a Toltec presence in Chaco (McGuire 1980; McGuire et al. 1994) and the fact that there is more evidence for violence both before and after the Chacoan period than during it (LeBlanc 1999). The preponderance of evidence for violence and cannibalism is from the Four Corners area, not Chaco, and dates from the 1100s and 1200s, not the Classic Bonito phase (Bustard in press; McGuire and Van Dyke in press).

In the long term, coercion is an expensive and dangerous path to the continuation and maintenance of power, as tyrants inevitably become objects of resistance. Most Chaco scholars have been more attracted to models in which elites wielded authority more by persuasion than by force. In the models of Judge (1989, 1991), Sebastian (1992), and Kantner (1996), "ritual leaders held institutionalized offices, were accorded status, prestige, and authority in deference to their roles as mediators with the supernatural, engaged in alliance building and exchange with other ritual leaders outside Chaco, and controlled the allocation and use of economic resources" (Wills 2000:23–24).

Some scholars have imagined Chacoan elites as controlling agricultural land, subsistence goods, or turquoise and other exotica (Cameron and Toll 2001). In Judge's (1989, 1991) "pilgrimage fair" model, Chaco initially developed as a center for redistribution but then expanded into a pilgrimage site where people met periodically for ceremonies and exchange. Elites gained *power over* through the production and distribution of turquoise and through exclusive access to ritual knowledge. Similarly, the models of Sebastian and Kantner emphasize aggrandizing groups or individuals motivated by a desire for wealth, prestige, or economic control. Sebastian (1992) argues that social inequality emerged at Chaco as a result of differences in land quality and in agricultural strategies. Opportunistic leaders with agricultural surplus doled out the extra food to engender obligations from those less fortunate, directed the construction of great houses as a means to repay the debt, and conducted rituals as a means of legitimation. Bonito-style architecture ultimately became a medium of competition among elites seeking to impress and attract followers. Kantner (1996) closely follows Sebastian's idea of architecture as competition, overtly linking his arguments to game theory and Neo-Darwinian evolution, in which leaders act to maximize their competitive advantages.

There is little question that some individuals at Chaco were accorded special status, at least toward the end of the Classic Bonito phase. Most of the exotic items found in Chaco were recovered from two clusters of rooms in the north and west areas of Pueblo Bonito, where approximately 130 men, women, and children were interred during the late eleventh century (Akins 1986, 2003; Judd 1954; Pepper 1909, 1920:112–163, 216).[9] Burial rooms and adjacent rooms contained great quantities of turquoise, shell, jet, cloth, sandals, cylinder vessels, shell trumpets, ceremonial staffs, macaw skeletons, and clay pipes (Mathien 2003; Neitzel 2003a). Room 33 alone contained 80 percent of the turquoise recovered from Pueblo Bonito, or more than 50,000 pieces. In this room, 16 disarticulated individuals lay above a plank floor. Below the floor were the articulated remains of two middle-aged men, along with a staggering quantity of turquoise and other exotica. One of the men—Burial 14—met a violent end, with chop marks to his left parietal and temporal, as well as on his left femur. In comparison with burial populations from small house sites, the individuals interred in Pueblo Bonito were healthier, had better nutrition, and lived longer (Akins 2003:100; Nelson et al. 1994:89–90; Stodder 1989:179; but see Palkovich 1984:107, 111).

The burials from Pueblo Bonito seem to represent elites, yet there are some ambiguities in this interpretation. Many of the burials were disarticulated, and excavation records from the days of Pepper and Judd shed little light on the reasons. Human remains may have been disturbed by looters or animals, may have been moved by the repeated interment of new burials, or may have been intentionally disarticulated by Chacoans for ritual purposes. The two individuals interred under the floor in Room 33 of Pueblo Bonito are clearly very unusual. They have more exotics with them than all the rest of the exotica from Chaco combined. They may have been very high-ranking persons, or unusual circumstances of death may have contributed to their special treatment, particularly in the case of Burial 14 (Akins 2003:103–104). But two leaders seem too few to represent more than a century's worth of institutionalized sociopolitical authority. Aggrandizing individuals or lineages often erect stelae or similar monuments, but nothing like this exists at Chaco. All we know for certain here is that two small groups of people merited special treatment at burial.

Western scholarship has a difficult time imagining power that is not vested in individuals. In an effort to understand alternative power configurations, Feinman and his colleagues have developed "dual processual theory" (Blanton et al. 1996; Feinman 2000a, 2000b; Feinman, Lightfoot, and Upham 2000). Network strategies fit traditional views of elites vesting authority in economic control and personal aggrandizement. By contrast, corporate strategies locate authority in groups rather than in individuals. Overt displays of material wealth are discouraged, and access to labor and land depends on group membership. Large-scale architecture is for public, communal gatherings, not individual aggrandizement. Although corporate strategies seem to describe Chaco well in some respects (Feinman 2000a; Mills 2002), the explanatory power of this perspective is limited. Dual processual theory encourages researchers to *think* in terms of essential categories and idealized extremes (Heitman and Plog 2005). Labeling Chaco as "corporate" does little to further our understandings of the bases for Chacoan power or the realities of Chacoan social life.

Rather than rush to place Chaco into a corporate box, we should think about the diverse ways in which the evidence both fits and challenges the ideal. Saitta (1999:139–140) suggests that the corporate ideal needs to be "texturized"—within the rather flat concept of "factions" or "groups," traders, ritual specialists, craft specialists, administrators, and others may all be struggling with one another. Wills (2000) points out that ritual specialization does not preclude communal forms of economic and social organization. Yoffee (2001:67) has suggested that "various groups and social identities...coexisted in Chaco" in different contexts and a ritual hierarchy was perhaps in conflict with older, kin-based forms of organization.

Most Chaco scholars agree that ritual played some role in social and political power at Chaco. Archaeologists have found abundant evidence for ritual activities at canyon great houses. In addition to the Bonito-style architecture itself, there are feasting remains and oversized cooking facilities at Pueblo Alto (Windes 1987) and caches of wooden staffs, cylinder vessels, and other unusual paraphernalia at Pueblo Bonito and Chetro Ketl (Neitzel 2003a; Vivian, Dodgen, and Hartmann 1978). Sociopolitical hierarchies within historic and contemporary Pueblo communities find expression in exclusive access to ritual knowledge and control of ceremonies rather than in disparate distributions of material wealth (Brandt 1977, 1980, 1994; Levy 1992; Ortiz 1969; Whiteley 1985, 1986).

But both Wills (2000:23) and Yoffee (2001) critique scenarios that essentially consider ritual to be a veneer for economic relations. Yoffee observes that ritual activities tend to be seen by Western scholars as legitimation for political and economic inequalities. As an alternative, Yoffee invites us to conceive of a *rituality*, in which, rather than ritual providing a veneer of legitimacy for economic differences, economics provide a veneer of legitimacy for ritual power. Somewhat similarly, Saitta (1997, 1999) allows that control of ritual knowledge may have enabled elites to appropriate surplus labor but points out that power can be exercised by a variety of factions with conflicting interests. Beliefs and practices may have constrained the actions of some individuals while enabling others. Change may have been driven less by the activities of individual self-aggrandizers than by struggles between different social groups.

It is easier for us to describe social and political changes than to explain how and why they happen. If exclusive access to ritual authority was the basis for leaders' power in Classic Bonito–phase Chaco, then how did that authority come into being? Why was it accepted? Was it challenged, and if so, how? A nuanced, multidimensional account of the developments at Chaco must ask, What motivated people to participate, and what motivated others to seek power? Both *power to* and *power over* are always present in the dialectical and contingent relationships between these two groups. Charismatic leaders cannot come to power without the consent and participation of followers. As *power over* is negotiated, potential subjects may resist, or they may decide to participate. The concept of ideology helps explain how this process works.

Ideology

In power relationships that enjoy long-term success, people tend to be complicit in their own subjugation, providing tacit consent to social configurations that limit or deny their access to resources or possible fields of action. Consent is preferable to coercion because "once power nakedly reveals its hand, it can become an object of political contestation" (Eagleton 1991:116). Negative sanctions such as force and coercion tend to be costly (Kus 1992). Ideology explains how subjects willingly participate in practices that perpetuate inequalities (Weber 1947:115–121). Multiple definitions of ideology exist (Eagleton 1991:1–31; Geuss 1981:4–44), and two usages are common in archaeology. In the first, ideology refers rather generically to philosophy or worldview. In the second, ideology encompasses the ideas, beliefs, and values specific to a social group that assist in the promotion and legitimation of the interests of the group (Marx and Engels 1939). Both dimensions are relevant at Chaco. I use *worldview* to denote the benign, generic meaning—

Pueblo peoples today, for example, share aspects of cosmology and have many similar values and ideas about the way the world works. I use *ideology* in contexts where social factions drew upon aspects of a shared worldview to promote or legitimate social, political, and ritual inequalities.

Ideologies may be perpetuated through a number of strategies, including the naturalization and universalization of beliefs so that they appear to be self-evident or inevitable, the denigration and exclusion of alternative or contradictory beliefs, and the obfuscation or "mystification" (Miller and Tilley 1984) of social realities and inequalities (Eagleton 1991). However, ideology is more than a tool used to lead subjects into erroneously believing that their interests are coterminous with the interests of the dominant group (Althusser 1969, 1971; Habermas 1976). People are not dupes, and ideology is not a property exclusive to dominant social interests, nor does it always involve dissimulation or distortion. Multiple ideologies exist, overlap, and conflict among different parts of society, just as subjects can simultaneously be members of multiple groups with conflicting interests (McGuire 1992:142; McGuire and Wurst 2003). Some elements of dominant and subordinate groups' ideologies are shared. This explains why subjects consensually support regimes that serve the interests of the dominant. Subjects may resonate strongly with some aspects of these shared ideologies yet may fail to see the aspects of the dominant ideology that support their own exploitation.

The most effective political leaders are those who can win the hearts, or emotional loyalties, of their subjects so that subjects desire and work toward the continuation of the regime. Ideological choices are rational, but they also involve an emotional or aesthetic dimension (Conrad and Demarest 1984: 201). In the mid-eighteenth century, German philosophers developed the concept of the aesthetic in contrast to the overt rationality of Enlightenment thought. Eagleton (1990:13) describes the aesthetic as "the whole of our sensate life together—the business of affections and aversions, of how the world strikes the body on its sensory surfaces, of that which takes root in the gaze and the guts and all that arises from our most banal, biological insertion into the world." The aesthetic is the intersection of bodily experience and emotion and therefore carries great power for the construction of ideology. Emotional and aesthetic dimensions of ideology tend to be archaeologically accessible through artistic representation, through the material remnants of rituals or other emotionally charged events, and through architecture and landscape (Kus 1992). For example, Smith (2000) describes how rulers of the ancient Urartian state used artistic media to elicit emotional allegiances from their subjects. Images portrayed the landscape under Urartian rule as a site of sacred devotion. Subjects conferred legitimacy upon the regime, in part because they resonated with the ideology expressed in the images, which affirmed some of their basic beliefs about the world. In this way, Smith argues, Urartian rulers "rendered the political aesthetic" (Benjamin 1968).

It has long been clear to archaeologists that Chacoan architecture and landscape are heavily laden with symbolism (for example, Fowler and Stein 1992; Fritz 1978; Lekson 1991; Stein and Lekson 1992). Stein and Lekson developed the idea of a Chacoan ritual landscape, arguing that Bonito-style architecture provided settings for ritual activities and symbolized participation in a loosely conceptualized, pan-Puebloan belief system. Building on this idea, I argue that Chaco can be understood, at one level, as the large-scale, recursive, spatial construction of Ancestral Pueblo worldviews. Beliefs and values expressed on the landscape were woven into a Chacoan ideology that enabled the establishment and perpetuation of elite power. During the Chacoan heyday, priestly leaders directed the construction of a landscape that emphasized aspects of a Puebloan worldview that had been in play for five centuries or more. Canyon visitors and ritual participants shared aspects of this worldview. As they moved through the buildings and among the natural spaces in Chaco, their aesthetic experiences reciprocally confirmed their beliefs about the world and simultaneously and seamlessly affirmed the validity of a Chacoan ritual and political order. As Chacoan leaders transformed a shared Puebloan worldview into a Chacoan ideology, visitors and participants transformed themselves into subjects, desiring to contribute their labor and resources toward events at Chaco and to give leaders their emotional allegiance. Through the medium of shared spatial experience, ritual leadership became political authority.

Structuration

But Chacoan leaders' authority did not come to exist in a single, transfiguring, aggrandizing moment (or even a series of such moments). Power relationships are constructed and negotiated gradually, within specific historical contexts. People continuously reproduce and transform the world around them. Political hierarchy does not come to exist through the willful exertion of aggrandizing leaders pitted against followers' naïveté. Social change can be the cumulative result of many decisions, small and large, made over centuries by individuals who could not have foreseen those decisions' ultimate consequences (Pauketat 2000; Saitta 1997, 1999). People can and do have intentionality—in other words, they act, believing that their actions will have a particular outcome—but they are motivated by factors besides self-interest, such as emotional loyalties or religious beliefs.

And, regardless of the motivations for particular decisions, actual outcomes might be quite different from what was intended, because the actors are not omniscient and myriad other individuals are simultaneously acting (Dobres and Robb 2000:4).

Relationships and ideologies are constantly created, negotiated, and transformed. The relationships between decisions, beliefs, practices, and social institutions are such an integral part of daily life that most of the time people are not conscious of them, but each quotidian action is linked to a host of large and small suppositions about the way the world works. These relationships are reflexive, so social realities and perceptions are constantly shifting. Human understandings and actions take place within a social medium that is lived and created simultaneously. Action, cognition, and intentionality occur as a continuous flow. Giddens (1984) developed the concept of *structuration* to capture this interactive intersection of rules, resources, and motives.

To understand how and why Ancestral Puebloans created Chaco, we need to look at the canyon in terms of its deep historical context. The presence of twelve well-preserved, present-day great houses encourages us to collapse time at Chaco, to think of the canyon as temporally flat. Most basic plans of Chaco Canyon illustrate this point, conflating more than three centuries of architectural construction into one two-dimensional map (see figure 2.4). But these great houses do not represent a single moment in time. Some were expanded and remodeled many times between AD 860 and 1200. Some were not built until the early 1100s. Earlier structures were obscured by, or incorporated into, later additions. The architectural features visible today were only contemporaneous at the very end of the Chacoan occupation. The Chacoan landscape we see today is a palimpsest created over the course of centuries. Each particular moment during that span, each construction episode, built on what came before and influenced what came after.

Ideology and landscape are moving targets, shifting over time, as Chacoans incorporated some elements of the past into their present while discarding others. It is primarily the ideas of those who directed construction—the dominant social faction—that we see expressed on the landscape. Chacoan leaders directed the construction of Bonito-style architecture to communicate and extol basic ideas about the way the world works—ideas that legitimated leaders' authority and encouraged visitors to transform themselves into subjects. Undoubtedly, there were dissenting, competing, or alternative social factions with ideologies that overlapped or differed from the dominant ideology to varying degrees. There are moments when these competing ideas are visible on the Chacoan landscape. For the most part, however, it is the dominant ideology of the Classic Bonito phase that is easiest for archaeologists to interpret, as I attempt to do in the chapters that follow.

Notes

1. According to Force and his colleagues, the original dune was in place between AD 660 and 900. The aeolian dam was breached about 900, and a deleterious period of channel cutting continued until approximately 1025. During the eleventh century, channel in-filling occurred, and a masonry dam may have been constructed across the Chaco Wash to replace the breached dune dam. Vivian and others (2006) date this channel filling period between 1025 and 1090. The 1080–1100 decades were characterized by drought and major oscillations in rainfall, but 1100–1130 were some of the wettest years ever seen at Chaco. A second, severe drought took place between 1130 and 1180; after this, occupation of the canyon clearly declined. Subsequently, there were a number of cut-and-fill sequences before modern arroyo downcutting began in the late 1800s. Today, the Chaco Wash is approximately 8 m deep and 30 to 90 m across.

2. All dates used in this text are AD unless otherwise noted. Dates for the Early Bonito phase are modified slightly to reflect recent work on early great house establishment and construction sequences (Lekson, Windes, and McKenna 2006; Wilshusen and Van Dyke 2006; Windes 2003, n.d.a; Windes and Ford 1992, 1996).

3. The great pitstructure is logically the predecessor of the Chacoan great kiva (Reed 2000; Vivian and Reiter 1960). Because construction of the two is separated by three to five centuries, I employ the term *great pitstructure* to refer specifically to these Basketmaker features and to avoid confusion with the formal great kivas of later periods.

4. These relatively new interpretations have been developed primarily by Rich Wilshusen and colleagues (Adler and Wilshusen 1990; Schachner 2001; Wilshusen and Blinman 1992; Wilshusen and Ortman 1999; Wilshusen and Van Dyke 2006; Wilshusen and Wilson 1995; Windes n.d.a), using data collected by the Dolores Archaeological Project (for example, Blinman 1989; Lightfoot 1988, 1994; Orcutt, Blinman, and Kohler 1990; Varien and Lightfoot 1989; Wilshusen 1989).

5. Two clusters of small sites have been investigated in the Fajada Gap and South Gap vicinities. McKenna and Truell (1986) thoroughly review and evaluate all data collected from these sites. Excavated small sites include 29SJ627 and 29SJ629 in Marcia's Rincon (Truell 1986; Windes 1993) and Bc50 and Bc51 near Casa Rinconada (Kluckhohn and Reiter 1939). These structures ranged in size from nine to forty rooms and were generally single storied. Single or compound masonry walls characterize wall construction, although core-and-veneer construction is occasionally present. Like great houses, small houses have formalized kivas, but they may also contain pit rooms of variable design. Domestic trash middens are generally present.

6. See also Adler 1996:104; Dean, Doelle, and Orcutt 1994: figure 4.6; Drager 1976; Hayes 1981; Lekson 1986; Neitzel 1999, 2003b; Pierson 1949; Schelberg 1984.

7. Despite all the general architectural similarities (core-and-veneer masonry, planned, symmetrical layout, enclosed kivas, large rooms) that render outlier great houses easily recognizable as such, these structures exhibit great variability in size and layout (Van Dyke 2003a). For example, outlier great house floor area ranges from 145 sq m (Halfway House) to 15,030 sq m (Aztec

West) (Powers, Gillespie, and Lekson 1983: table 41). Classic Bonito great kivas are often located in close spatial proximity to great houses, either in front or to the southeast, sometimes enclosed within a plaza retaining wall. Although outlier great kiva diameters range between 12 and 22 m, most great kiva diameters fall within the confines of 15 to 17 m (Herr 1994; Van Dyke 2002). Isolated outlier great kivas are often known, but these tend to date from the late Pueblo I period or the Early Bonito phase (Powers, Gillespie, and Lekson 1983:260).

8. Road segments have long been identified across the Chacoan world (for example, Holsinger 1901; Morris 1915). Remote sensing techniques and aerial photography have been used to locate roads both within and extending outward from Chaco Canyon (Ebert and Hitchcock 1980; Lyons and Ebert 1978; Lyons and Hitchcock 1977; Obenauf 1980, 1991; Sever and Wagner 1991). The Bureau of Land Management conducted large-scale road studies across the San Juan Basin and ground-verified many segments and features (Kincaid 1983; Nials, Stein, and Roney 1987; Roney 1992). Vivian (1997a, 1997b) provides the most recent overview of roads research.

9. The north cluster includes Rooms 32, 33, 53, and 56. Here, Pepper excavated 24–28 burials. The remains of approximately 16 disarticulated individuals were found above a plank floor in Room 33. Half were female, half male, and all but two females and one male were middle-aged or older. The west burial cluster includes Rooms 320, 326, 329, and 339. Here, Judd collected 95 burials, 70 percent of which had been badly disturbed or disarticulated. The same kinds of exotic materials were present as in the north cluster, but in dramatically lower percentages, and jet, fossil shell, and clay pipes were absent.

3 Perceptions and Representations

Two spiders crawled toward each other. They crawled on a wall the color of blood. One climbed up the wall, the other down. Each spider left behind it a path of white. Showing through the white path was a thin line of red. The spider inching upward was black, the other spider, except for its black head and legs, was covered with yellow, blue, red, green, and white dots.

When the spiders met, they stopped and spoke to each other. They did not speak in the usual language of spiders, but they spoke in a language of lines and curves, which appeared between them as a white etching. It was a language of permanence and meaning.

—*from "Poovolli's Dream," by Phillip Tuwaletstiwa (2000)*

Tuwaletstiwa's narrative describes the dream of a young Hopi girl visiting Chaco Canyon. Like the language of lines and curves spoken by the dream spiders, the Chacoan landscape may be seen as a language of permanence and meaning. This landscape was perceived and represented by Ancestral Pueblo peoples, and it may be understood by archaeologists today, albeit only partially, from our own culturally constructed perspective. We cannot see the canyon with Chacoan eyes, but we can work toward an understanding of the ideas represented by Chacoan architecture and landscape and how these were integrated into Chacoan ideologies.

If landscapes are a point of intersection for physical, social, and ideological dimensions, then their study must encompass not only the physical environment but also the perceived spaces of the senses and the representational spaces of the imagination (Lefebvre 1991). Spatial perception is sensual, and it is emotional. Phenomenological investigations into the Chacoan landscape provide insights into the experiences and perceptions shared by human bodies in these spaces. Spatial representation involves the presentation of ideas about space through such media as art, literature, maps, models, and the human imagination. An Ansel Adams print, a GIS shapefile, and a narrative describing Tewa cosmography are all examples of spatial representation.

In my interpretations of Chacoan landscape and ideology, I draw together as many lines of evidence as possible to create a coherent picture that fits well with empirical observations. Phenomenology provides me with some tools through which to approach Chacoan spatial perceptions. Phenomenological observations alone, however, run the risk of representing nothing more than the researcher's own perceptions, imposed upon the past. Interpretations are stronger when they can be linked to the meanings and representations inscribed on the landscape by the historic and the living descendants of Chacoan peoples. Accordingly, I view my phenomenological observations through the lens of Pueblo ethnography.

Phenomenology and Landscape

Phenomenology—an approach grounded in existentialist philosophy—has recently gained attention among some British archaeologists as a useful way to apprehend past meanings and social forms (Gosden 1994; Thomas 1996; Tilley 1994). Existentialism developed as one solution to the objective/subjective conundrum in philosophy. We know the world by separating ourselves from it, but at the same time, we can understand ourselves only in relation to the world. There are many strands of existentialism, but the key idea is that we bridge the distance between objective reality and our subjective consciousness through *existence*, or daily experiences and participation in the world. For Immanuel Kant and Edmund Husserl, phenomenology entailed the study of the physical world as it is experienced through the senses. Phenomenologists Martin Heidegger (1962), Maurice Merleau-Ponty (1981 [1962]), and others further elaborated upon these ideas, focusing on the intersections between the body, perception, experience, and place. The human body is the point of dialectical mediation between consciousness and the physical world, subject and object.

Place plays a critical part in our human understanding of existence, because all bodily experiences are spatially situated. This is explored in Heidegger's concept of *Dasein*, or dwelling in the world. Casey (1996) considers place—the intersection of time, space, and self—as the most fundamental form of embedded experience. De Certeau (1984:91–130) explores how people actively construct knowledge of the world by moving through places. Phenomenology has influenced humanistic geography, which focuses on places—locales where people carry out their daily lives, have experiences, and construct understandings of self and society (Buttimer 1993; Casey 1997; Jackson 1984; Tuan 1974, 1977).

Phenomenology involves understandings and descriptions of the world as experienced by cognizant subjects, and it operates from the premise that there are some similarities in human spatial perception. Because the human body is universal in its configuration, it is possible to assume that all humans have generally similar spatial perceptions of such body-relevant experiences as directionality and scale. Spaces are organized by the human body into up and down, front and back, left and right. If we accept these premises, then a phenomenological approach to archaeology can allow us to think about the ways in which past peoples experienced, perceived, and represented landscapes, working from the starting point of contemporary bodies in the same spaces. By moving through ancient landscapes and architecture as past peoples did, phenomenological archaeologists can gain insights into past worldviews.

Of course, phenomenological archaeology is not without shortcomings. Phenomenology encourages reliance on one's own perceptions as a means for learning about the past. Although human bodily configurations are, to some extent, always shared, many aspects of spatial experience and perception are socially constructed (Feld 1996; Geurts 2003). Past landscapes no longer exist—contemporary landscapes can provide researchers with only partial, distorted experiences. Past sensual perceptions were culturally situated and might be quite different from our own. Phenomenological explanations often essentialize description to the detriment of explanation (Smith 2003:67–68). Archaeologists may argue that buildings or landscape elements represent certain ideas, for example, but may fail to give their attention to the social and political processes through which these symbols were negotiated. As I tread the path of phenomenology, I try to keep these cautions in mind.

Visible Landscapes

As Tuan (1974), Feld (1996), and others have argued, the perception of space involves multiple senses. Past sounds, smells, tastes, and textures are difficult for archaeologists to access, although some have made interesting attempts (Hamilakis, Pluciennik, and Tarlow 2002; Houston and Taube 2000). Vision is an easier sense for archaeologists to examine because past landscapes tend to be full of relatively well-preserved visual signifiers. Western culture, like many others, privileges the visual (Thomas 1993). Nonetheless, visibility is likely to have been important to Ancestral Pueblos living on the open, exposed, sky-filled horizons of the arid Southwest (Lekson 2002a; Tuan 1974:79–83).

Exaggerated visibility and its counterpart, invisibility, are bound up with the construction of power in interesting ways (Lefebvre 1991:236). People associate themselves with dramatically visible, ostensibly powerful natural places to tap into their potency in some way. The power might be used for political domination or resistance or to construct social identity. Aboriginal Australians view prominent topographic features as places where different planes of existence intersect (Taçon 1999). The oddly shaped mountain above the Vietnamese temple complex at My Son is said to represent the Hindu deity Garuda (Sharma 1992). At Jemez, cloud beings or spirits are said to reside in mountains (Parsons 1939:172, 173). For the Maya, mountains are the hollow homes of deities, and caves are openings to this supernatural realm (Brady and Ashmore 1999). Shrines, rock art, votive deposits, or ritual structures may mark significant natural landforms (Bradley 2000; O'Donovan 2002). Buildings can be shaped to mimic natural features (Hartung 1981:46). Structures and roads can be aligned to point toward topographic features that carry special meaning.

What evidence exists that Chacoans placed importance on prominent natural features, such as volcanic plugs, buttes, and mountain peaks? As I visited Bonito-style architecture, road segments, and high places in Chaco Canyon, at outliers, and across the San Juan Basin, I addressed this issue through specific observations. Are there shrines, rock art panels, votive deposits, or other ritual structures atop these landforms? Does the positioning of Bonito-style architecture maximize the visibility of these features? Do the shapes of buildings mimic these features? Has architecture been positioned to create alignments or line-of-sight connections with prominent natural features? Do site locations indicate clear choices among alternatives?

People not only associate themselves with naturally occurring, visible and invisible places—they also create their own. Monumental architecture juxtaposes dramatically visible human constructs against the relatively smaller scale of the human body, creating artificial skylines. Jerry Moore (1996) delineated four criteria that characterize high-visibility Andean public buildings: clear forms, contrasting backgrounds, vertical prominence, and solid mass. Visual impact does not always correspond directly to verticality and massive size, however. As the human eye and brain convert the three-dimensional world into two-dimensional images, viewers make errors in judgment, and architects can exploit this possibility to create an illusion of greater size. For example, in Andean buildings, long horizontal planes sometimes create the illusion that intersecting vertical forms are taller (Moore 1996). In the Mayan ceremonial complex of Tikal, on a low hill in the relatively flat plain of the Petén, builders used roof combs to further accentuate the heights of pyramids (Hartung 1981:46).

Bonito-style architecture fits Moore's criteria for maximal visibility. Great houses are easily recognized, highly formal structures. Likely coated in white plaster, they would have burned in the sun in startling clarity against backgrounds of dark shale and sandstone. Many outlier great houses and some canyon great houses are situated in high places atop buttes or mesas. Many—but not all—are two to four stories high. Great houses are quite variable in size, however (Van Dyke 1999b), and many outlier great houses—but not all—tend to be substantially smaller than canyon great houses. Is there a patterned, inverse relationship between great house mass and verticality? Was every great house either massive or placed atop a prominent landform? Are great house mass and verticality mutually exclusive? Is there such a thing as a small, inconspicuous great house in a low place?

I investigated these issues through several means. Other researchers have compiled detailed building plans, estimated wall heights, and numbers of stories for canyon architecture, as well as for many outlier great houses (Fowler, Stein, and Anyon 1987; Lekson 1986; Marshall et al. 1979; Powers, Gillespie, and Lekson 1983: table 41). In a previous study (Van Dyke 1996), I used this information to determine that patterned relationships exist between great house mass, height, and topographic location. I calculated mass as enclosed structural area multiplied by building height. Where outlier community information was available, I examined the differences between great house and surrounding community elevations. These exercises enabled me to demonstrate that great houses are, in fact, quantifiably more massive and more vertical in comparison with small sites.

However, numbers are no substitute for experiencing the landscapes in question. In visits to canyon and outlier great houses, I thought about the ways in which great house builders emphasized these structures' visual drama. Are all great houses, in fact, perceived on the landscape as looming and massive? Are there exceptions? Did builders use elements of the natural landscape to enhance visual impact? What techniques did the builders use—such as doubled walls, walls built over rock faces, and walls built atop boulders—to create great houses that look larger than their actual mass?

These issues are difficult to assess for great houses reduced to rubble mounds, of course—they are easiest to think about at sites where there are standing walls.

If Bonito-style architecture was meant to have visual impact, who was the intended audience? It might seem obvious that residents or visitors in the local community were the targets, but such is not necessarily the case. Certain monuments at the Chimu city of Chan Chan in Peru were highly visible from several kilometers away but were invisible from inside the city, suggesting that the intended viewers were neighbors and travelers, not the residents of Chan Chan (Moore 1996). People build highly visible structures to provide stages for public spectacles, to facilitate long-distance communication, and to convey symbolic messages about power and identity. Communication implies the creation or maintenance of interactive social networks (Carr 1995:195–198). In Renfrew and Cherry's (1986) concept of *symbolic entrainment*, people in one community consciously emulate monumental architecture built by their neighbors, in order to compete for status. Accordingly, at canyon and outlier great houses, I asked, Was the great house sited to maximize its visibility to a surrounding community? Which portions of the community can see and be seen by great houses? Were great houses positioned to be intervisible with one another? Are great houses tied into line-of-sight networks that might include other architectural and natural features as well?

Highly visible structures not only serve to attract viewers' attention—they also provide viewing platforms from which people can look out on the surrounding terrain. Great house builders might wish to gaze upon the landscape from high places for a variety of reasons that imply different kinds of power relationships. I investigated these possibilities by visiting the high places and looking out across the landscape to see what kinds of cultural or natural features could be seen or emphasized from these vantage points. Viewers might wish to see across the landscape to control subjects through surveillance or the threat of surveillance (Foucault 1977). If this was the motive for great houses in high places, then the structures should provide line-of-sight access to the surrounding community, and they should cover potential routes of access up to the great houses. Great houses in high places might enable people to participate reciprocally in a communication network with other communities—if this was the case, then a line-of-sight network should be present, linking communities together.

Viewers in high places might wish, for religious or social reasons, to be able to see prominent, sacred topographic features. Of course, buttes, plugs, mesas, and mountain peaks project into the sky and are therefore visible at great distances from many positions. Does it seem that great houses were deliberately sited to enable views of certain landmarks, rather than positioned in reasonably alternative locations? Great houses in high places might facilitate celestial observations. Do they afford an open view of the horizon? Are there viewports or orientations toward specific solar, lunar, or stellar phenomena?

Landscapes in Motion

Visual perception changes as the viewer moves across the landscape and through buildings. We experience the world and inscribe it with meaning as we move through it (Tilley 1994:27–31). De Certeau (1984:91–130) describes how knowledge of a city is metaphorically and physically created by walking. Routes can be prescribed by social knowledge—there can be "right" and "wrong" ways to enter a building, for example. Roads, pathways, and other access routes can provide indications about the ways in which movement was culturally prescribed in the past.

During Ancestral Pueblo times, visitors to Chaco would have arrived on foot. Topography constrains access to the canyon's interior, with its central core of great houses. Most outliers are located to the north, west, and south of Chaco Canyon. Foot travelers could have entered the canyon easily from the Chaco/Escavada confluence at the west end. Travelers from the south could have arrived through South Gap or Fajada Gap. Visitors approaching from Guadalupe, Pueblo Pintado, and other points to the east could have walked the length of the 300–500-m-wide canyon from its east end. The northern approach, however, is more problematic because two steeply rising terraces of Cliff House sandstone behind Kin Kletso, Pueblo Bonito, Chetro Ketl, and Hungo Pavi prevent easy access. Three tributary drainages—Clys Canyon, Mockingbird Canyon, and Gallo Wash—and a crack behind Kin Kletso provide the only natural access routes into the canyon from the north.

Chacoan builders, however, invested much energy in constructing formalized access into the canyon by means of road segments, ramps, and staircases. In some cases, these features enhanced or facilitated access over natural routes. In other cases, the construction of staircases and ramps created access points across the prohibitive barriers of sandstone escarpments. Jackson's Staircase, which connects the upper two terraces in the tributary drainage behind Chetro Ketl, is but one well-known example. A foot traveler could use the staircase to drop off the uppermost bench of the north mesa and could proceed down to the canyon floor by means of a ramp. Chacoans built at least five other, similar staircases near great houses in the canyon core (plate 6).

At least six major, formal routes lead into Chaco Canyon (Kincaid 1983; Vivian 1997a, 1997b) (refer to plate 11). The North Road arrives at Pueblo

Alto on North Mesa, where it splits into shorter segments (Windes 1987, 1991). From this point, travelers could enter Chaco Canyon via several staircases or trails. The Ah-Shi-Sle-Pah Road approaches Chaco Canyon from the northwest. It reaches the confluence of the Chaco and Escavada washes across from Peñasco Blanco and descends into the canyon by means of Vivian's Staircase. The South Road passes into Chaco through South Gap. A second southern road segment enters through Fajada Gap. The Chacra Face Road traverses the colluvial slopes of the south side of Chacra Mesa before entering the canyon at Fajada Gap. A possible East Road leaves Pueblo Pintado and descends into Chaco Canyon by a series of cut steps; segments of this road are visible near the Chaco East community (Windes 1991; Windes et al. 2000). The Chaco River would have provided a natural access conduit from the west. Although archaeologists have not identified a continuous West Road leading into the canyon, a short, west-trending road segment at Peñasco Blanco, a staircase into the Chaco/Escavada confluence below Peñasco Blanco, and a large shrine complex on the west end of West Mesa all suggest that access from the west was also formalized.

I walked and videotaped the last few miles of each of these formal and informal access routes into Chaco Canyon in order to investigate the following questions: Is walking on road segments easier than walking on adjacent, unmodified terrain? How do the various routes into the canyon differ in terms of spatial experience? Would visitors to Chaco from different areas of the San Juan Basin have had significantly different spatial and visual experiences as they entered the canyon? How does the visibility of topographic landmarks, shrines, buildings, or other features change as one moves along the route? Does the design of the roads maximize the visual impact of the canyon and its architecture?

Road segments and prescribed pathways likely existed within Chaco Canyon as well, but centuries of environmental and cultural impact on the canyon floor have made identifying these virtually impossible (Vivian 1997a, 1997b). Great house layouts nonetheless suggest that there were formal approaches to these buildings. Chacoan great house entry points were generally quite different from modern park service trails. The pueblos are oriented to face a central plaza to the south or southeast, with tiered stories rising higher toward the rear of the building.[1] Formal entry to Classic Bonito great houses was likely from the south or southeast. At Pueblo Bonito, two mounds in front of the great house further constricted access. People approaching the plaza would have had to pass through an opening between the two mounds or circumvent the mounds at either end. I walked toward each great house in Chaco Canyon from the south or southeast to see what it would have been like to enter the building as the Chacoans presumably intended. As I walked, I investigated the ways in which movement contributed to, or detracted from, the visual impact of these structures. Were the buildings situated so that movement accentuated their visual prominence?

Formal routes for movement suggest the possibility that people took part in processions, which often are part of ritual activities. In Moore's (1996) Andean research, he found that monuments fronted by plazas and low mounds were likely used in processions. A series of planes in the form of retaining walls, platforms, or flanking mounds created a sense of depth, making the principal monument seem larger and more distant. "[The] flanking mounds create parallel planes that lead the eye to the principal mound while the large open plaza in the foreground emphasizes the distinctive volume and shape of the mound" (Moore 1996:111). Similar features are present at Pueblo Bonito—do they create perceptions akin to those that Moore observed? Does the design and siting of monumental architecture support the likelihood of processions at Chaco? I extended these investigations to outliers, where road segments sometimes prescribe specific approaches to communities and where roads and ramps at great houses such as Andrews and Red Willow delineate Chacoan routes of access into these structures.

Landscapes of Memory

In addition to visibility and movement, landscapes are experienced through the sensual, emotionally charged dimension of memory. People develop a sense of place through a history of social engagement with the landscape (Altman and Low 1992). We cannot know or recognize a place without keying on the memories and cues that lend it meaning. Social memory involves the construction of a collective notion (not an individual belief) about the way things were in the past (Connerton 1989; Halbwachs 1975 [1925], 1992 [1950]). Like us, past peoples reconfigured and reinterpreted the more distant past, selectively remembering and forgetting people and events to serve the interests of the then present (Alcock 2001, 2002; Bradley 2002; Bradley and Williams 1998; Van Dyke and Alcock 2003).

Memory is often employed to legitimate authority or to support a sense of community identity. Social memory may take the form of general references to a vague but glorious past, or direct links (fictive or otherwise) may be made to specific ancestors or events. Although in archaeological contexts it is easiest to see the top-down machinations of elite groups invoking memory for legitimation, multiple and conflicting versions of events can coexist, as different genders, classes, ethnicities, or other interest groups employ memory in competing ways. The past may be subsumed and dominated, conquered and dismantled.

Buildings, shrines, rock art, and tombs are likely to be symbolically charged in the construction of social memory. There are a number of ways we can recognize the workings of social memory in these places. Past peoples dwelt within landscapes that were reoccupied time and again. When new sites or buildings were constructed on top of old ones, the new builders must have had stories about earlier inhabitants, whether they were seen as enemies, ancestors, mythic figures, or simply vanished ones. Other desirable attributes of the location aside, such an act is never innocent. The juxtaposition of new and old sites or buildings creates a powerful connection with the past. New builders may have been obliterating or subsuming the past, or they may have been accessing it to draw power from it in some way. These observations also pertain to the remodeling of existing sites, whether older portions were left intact, incorporated into the new portions, or razed and replaced. Materials from older sites were sometimes reused or incorporated into new constructions, as in the Greek practice of spoliation, where dismantled pieces of earlier monuments were reused and displayed in later constructions (Papalexandrou 2003).

Masks, figurines, heirloom objects, paintings, and other representational media often possess commemorative functions. Objects may be demolished in the interest of forgetting, as in the destruction of carved *malanggan* images in mortuary contexts (Küchler 1993), or may become heirlooms and valued connections to the past, as in Maya earspools (Joyce 2003). Repetition and secrecy may be involved in the social transmission of knowledge about the past (Mills n.d.; Rowlands 1993; Whitehouse 1992:795–796).

Sometimes places are no longer inhabited by the living but become the residences of mythic or remembered ancestors (Blake 1998; Bradley 2002). Abandoned buildings, tombs, shrines, and natural features might be visited repeatedly over time for ritual reasons. We can recognize these features' relevance to social memory when they are linked across time by the presence of ritual or mortuary deposits dating from multiple time periods or when they are physically connected to later time periods via roads or alignments. New visitors would have seen the signs of previous visitors, and older events, visits, or other occurrences would have been incorporated into the multiple meanings of the place. Assessing the nature of these kinds of meanings is difficult, but we can recognize the significance of acts such as the repeated overlay of new rock art and the repeated deposition of votive offerings.

The past would have been part of the Chacoan experience. In Chaco Canyon and at outliers, I looked for indications that the ancestral past—whether real or imagined—was referenced by Chacoan builders. Evidence on the landscape for the importance of social memory at Chaco might include the juxtaposition of temporally disparate sites, the remodeling and reuse of buildings, the incorporation of older construction elements in Chacoan buildings, votive objects deposited repeatedly over time, and connections and alignments with past sites. Where are these elements present? How do they intersect with observations on visibility or motion? Are references to the past positioned so that they are highly visible, or are they hidden, suggesting that this knowledge was restricted in some way?

Ethnographic Landscapes

A phenomenological approach to landscape can further understandings of visibility, movement, and memory—aspects of lived, spatial experiences in the Chacoan past. One serious problem with any phenomenological interpretation, however, is that spatial perceptions emerge not only out of bodily experiences but also out of situated cultural knowledge. Archaeologists are not Chacoans—we come with our own sets of preconceptions, experiences, and beliefs about the world. Phenomenological interpretations run the risk of expressing nothing more than naïve universalism, or worse, the archaeologist's own culturally situated perceptions. In the Pueblo Southwest, use of the direct historical approach helps to mitigate these problems.

Both archaeologists and contemporary Native peoples view Chaco as a place important to Pueblo ancestors. Archaeological evidence suggests that Ancestral Pueblo peoples moved in many directions when they left Chaco. Some people traveled south to Zuni, Acoma, Laguna, and central and southern New Mexico and Arizona (Lyons 2003; Woodson 1999). Some went west to the Little Colorado River valley and the Hopi mesas. Still others moved north to the Four Corners area, then ultimately to the Rio Grande valley (Lekson and Cameron 1995).

Based on language and geography, anthropologists have grouped contemporary Pueblo peoples into the Western Pueblos (the Hopi of northeast Arizona, whose language is Uto-Aztecan, the Zuni of northwest New Mexico, who speak Penutian, and the Acoma and Laguna of northwest New Mexico, who speak Keres) and the Eastern Pueblos, who encompass 16 pueblos along the Rio Grande River and its tributaries (Eggan 1950). The Eastern Pueblos can be separated into two linguistic groups: 11 Tanoan pueblos (including the language groups of Tiwa, Tewa, and Towa) and 5 Keresan pueblos.

There is little consensus as to which contemporary pueblos might have closer, or more distant, ties to Chaco Canyon, but the presence of similar cosmologies and oral traditions among contemporary or historic Pueblo groups supports the pan-Pueblo origins of many beliefs and stories. Hopi, Zuni, and Eastern Pueblo oral traditions tell of a "White House," where many seminal events took place, particularly relating to the development of

Pueblo ceremonialism (Stirling 1942:83; White 1942:145). Some scholars consider White House to be a metaphor referring to the Four Corners region; others situate White House at Mesa Verde (Ellis 1967). Lekson, however, argues convincingly that White House is Chaco (Lekson 1999:145–150; Lekson and Cameron 1995:194–195). The Hopi specifically describe Chaco as a place where ancestors lived during their migrations (Kuwanwisiwma 2004). The Navajo inhabit Chaco Canyon today and have been there for at least 300 years (Brugge 1980). Although most archaeologists see the Navajo as relative newcomers on the scene, Chaco figures prominently in some Navajo stories and ceremonies, including traditions surrounding several clan origins (Begay 2004). Navajo stories tell about a Great Gambler who lived at Chaco and enslaved the people before he was overthrown (Judd 1954:351–354; McPherson 1992:87–93).

For Pueblo peoples, landscape and architecture carry symbolic meaning and, together with myth and ritual, form an interconnected whole. The social and supernatural are expressed in topographic features, paths of movement, and locations of settlements. It is important to keep in mind that contemporary Pueblo people are not living ancestors—many changes and events have transformed the Pueblo world over the past millennium. Nevertheless, some core ideas derived from recent and historic ethnography are plainly visible at Chaco, and we can learn much about Chacoan ideology by following these threads back into the past. Overlapping ideas drawn from Pueblo worldviews and cosmographies include

- Symbolically laden horizontal and vertical directions converge at a center place.
- Balance is maintained by the dualistic juxtaposition of opposites.
- The past is repeatedly revisited in a pattern of cyclical renewal.
- Individual and mythic life may be experienced as a journey.

It is not my intention here to equate Chaco with any specific, contemporary pueblo or with contemporary Pueblo beliefs in general. But the shared presence of these themes among contemporary Pueblo groups who speak different languages and otherwise have different ritual practices speaks to the antiquity of these belief systems among Pueblo peoples (Dozier 1960). Within the Chacoan world of a millennium ago, there are clear archaeological indicators that similar worldviews were present (Swentzell 1992). And, as among contemporary Pueblo peoples, these beliefs were represented spatially, on the landscape.

Pueblo Cosmography: Sacred Directions, Balanced Dualism, and the Center Place

One of the most basic and pervasive ideas in much Native North American consciousness involves the organization of physical, social, and spiritual worlds into horizontal and vertical dimensions expressed through landscape and architecture.[2] In many contemporary Pueblo cosmologies, nested layers or symmetrical quarters are connected at a center place—the pueblo village. Horizontal divisions correspond to cardinal or intercardinal directions. Vertical divisions include upper and lower worlds. Multiple levels are inscribed on the landscape by highly visible topographic features such as buttes and mountain peaks, and the pueblo itself represents this organization in microcosm. Spatial organization is intertwined with cosmography, social organization, and ritual practice. Spatially expressed social, ritual, and cosmographic systems exist to some degree in all Pueblo societies, but I will briefly discuss examples from Tewa, Keresan, and Zuni peoples.

For the Tewa, who occupy six pueblos along the northern Rio Grande and its tributaries, landscape, social organization, and ritual form an interconnecting cosmographic whole (Ortiz 1969, 1972) (figure 3.1). Tewa society has three hierarchical levels, each of which has counterparts on the physical terrain and in the supernatural world. At the lowest tier, Dry Food People are common folk who do not hold political or ritual positions. In the middle, Towa é form the core of political organization. At the highest tier, Made People direct ritual and are the real power behind the activities of Towa é. The hierarchy is not rigid, however; initiation into higher levels is possible, and most Tewa may potentially become Made People.

This three-tiered division is marked on the physical landscape by natural features and by concentric tetrads of shrines. The innermost level includes the village and nearby farmlands—the sphere of ordinary people and domestic life. Within each village are four dance plazas. Near the edge of each village are four shrines associated with the cardinal directions. The ancestral souls of the common Tewa dwell at these shrines. A second, more distant level includes the hills, mesas, and washes where people hunt and gather. This area is defined by four mesas, each containing a cave to the underworld. Although women and children may visit the second level, it is best if men accompany them. At the third, outermost level, four sacred mountains associated with cardinal directions delimit the Tewa world. Each is associated with a mountaintop earth navel, a lake, a color, and various spirits. People go to these distant, high mountains only to hunt, gather, or make pilgrimages. The supernatural Towa é, who are counterparts to the Tewa political officials, dwell at earth navels located on top of the four

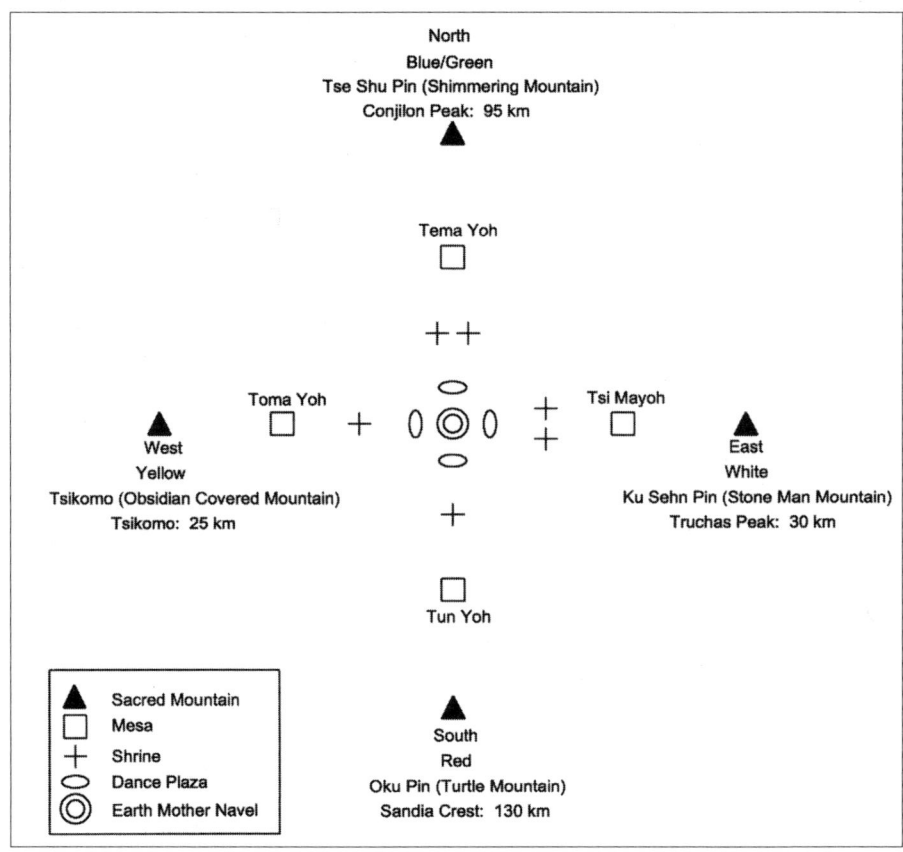

Figure 3.1. Tewa cosmography, following Ortiz 1969:18–21 and based on a drawing in Tilley 1994:64, figure 2.8.

sacred mesas and four sacred mountains. The highest deities recognized by the Tewa dwell within lakes located near the four sacred mountains.

Tewa cosmography is also divided into three vertical levels—an upper world, a lower world, and the middle place, which is the plane of earthly habitation. Sacred mountain peaks, shrines, and earth navels or openings mediate among the vertical levels. The four cardinal and two vertical directions converge or join in the middle place—the center of the village (Harrington 1916:41–45; Ortiz 1972:142). Of course, Tewa physical and social realities do not always conform neatly to these cosmologies. But in ideal conceptions, Tewa meaning and order are imposed on the landscape, and, in turn, the landscape embodies meaning and order that guide Pueblo life.

The Keres, who inhabit Acoma and Laguna, as well as five pueblos along the northern Rio Grande, have a similarly inscribed landscape (White 1960).

Plate 1. The Chacoan landscape: West Mesa and the Chaco Wash near the Escavada confluence, from the north side of Chaco Canyon.

Plate 2. Fajada Butte at sunrise.

Plate 3. Kin Nahasbas and Una Vida, as seen from the great kiva site 29SJ1253 in Fajada Gap.

Plate 4. Pueblo Bonito, center of the Chacoan world. Photo courtesy of Adriel Heisey.

Huerfano Mountain

Shiprock

Hosta Butte

Plate 5. Dramatically shaped, highly visible landforms in the Chacoan world.

Companion Rock and Chimney Rock

Cabezon Peak

Mount Taylor

Plate 6. A staircase behind Hungo Pavi leads atop Chaco Canyon's north rim.

Plate 7. Aerial view of Peñasco Blanco. Photo courtesy of Adriel Heisey.

Plate 8. Inside the plaza at Pueblo Bonito.

Plate 9. Cairns overlook the Chaco River and western San Juan Basin at Site 1088 atop West Mesa.

Plate 10. The badlands in Kutz Canyon, with Angel Peak beyond, near the terminus of the North Road.

Plate 11. The view from this stone circle atop the north rim of Chaco Canyon extends across Pueblo del Arroyo, through South Gap, along the South Road, to Hosta Butte.

Plate 12. Peñasco Blanco, on West Mesa, is illuminated in the late afternoon sunlight from the end of the Ah-Shi-Sle-Pah Road, atop the north rim of Chaco Canyon.

Plate 13. Peach Springs great house, looking north.

Plate 14. Escalon atalaya from below with Joshua Jones, October 1991.

Plate 15. Kin Bineola, from the mesa above, looking northwest.

Plate 16. Kin Klizhin, with Colorado College students, December 2006.

Plate 17. Painted Hand, a McElmo-style tower in Hovenweep Canyon, southwest Colorado.

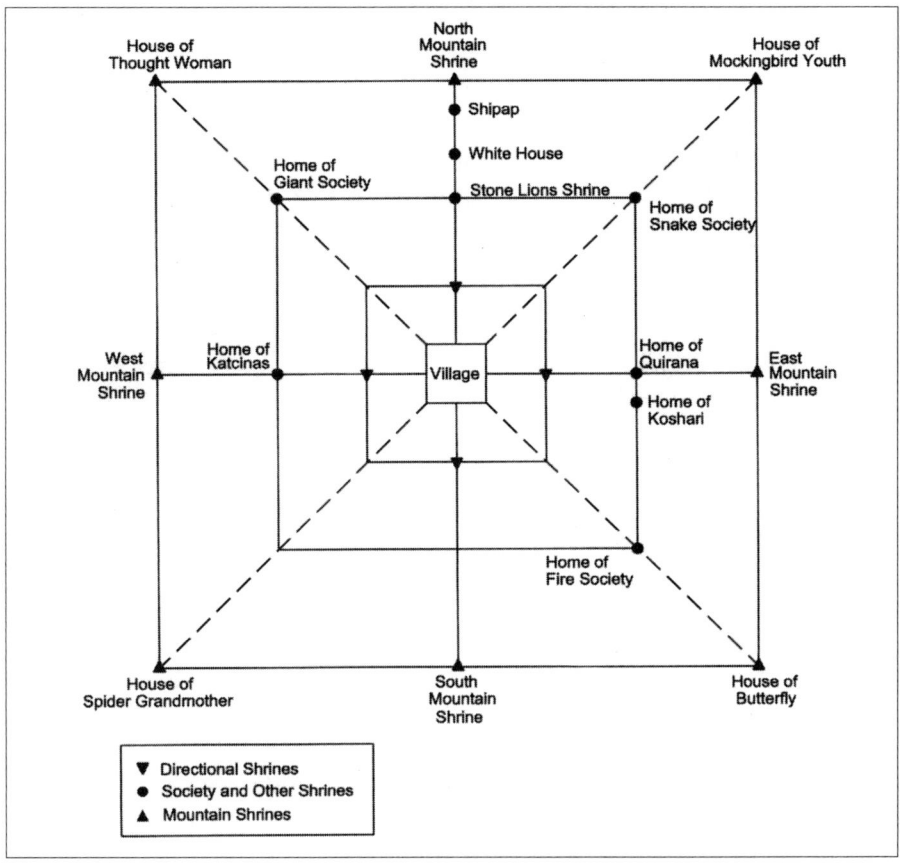

Figure 3.2. Keres cosmography, based on a drawing in Snead and Preucel 1999:177, figure 8.2.

They conceive of the world as a series of nested, interrelated regions focused on the central village. The Keres world is divided in half along gender lines; the west is female, the east, male. The world has four corners—northeast, northwest, southwest, and southeast. Each is home to different supernatural entities; each is associated with different animals and colors. Intercardinal and cardinal directions are important as the world's corners and the halfway points between them. Sacred mountains topped with shrines mark the outermost level of the contemporary world. The next closest region, also marked by shrines, contains homes of supernatural beings. Shrines at the four cardinal directions delineate the symbolic bounds of the village. Finally, plaza shrines are present in the villages themselves. Similar directional affiliations and boundary shrines were present at the ancestral Keresan sites of Los Aguajes and Kotyiti (Snead and Preucel 1999) (figure 3.2).

Perceptions and Representations 51

In Keresan origin stories (White 1960:60), the people lived originally with Iyatiku, their mother-creator, in a white world. In a series of events, they migrated upwards through several successive worlds—red, blue, and yellow—before emerging at the sipapu into this, the current level of existence. The people migrated south from the sipapu to White House, where they lived for a time before continuing southward to their present pueblos. When Keresans die, their souls return to the sipapu and dwell with Iyatiku to the north, in the white world, four layers down (White 1942:177, 1960:89).

The idea of geometric, symmetrical divisions connected at a center is pervasive in the culture and mythology of Zuni. Zuni cosmography involves "a series of concentric circles, all surrounding the ultimate center, 'the heart of the world'" (Young 1988:100). There are six cardinal directions (including up and down), each associated with particular colors, fetishes, and animals (Cushing 1966 [1883]:16–18). The Zuni year is divided into two halves, each containing six months. At the Shalako ceremony, which takes place near the winter solstice, six pairs of rain priests and six pairs of warriors represent the six kivas. With an implied center or connecting point, the ritual number becomes seven. This center corresponds to the middle, the navel, the heart, the Zuni village itself, and the winter solstice (Young 1988:103–104). According to Cushing (1896:139), there were at one time nineteen Zuni clans organized into six groups of three, plus one that represented the central or all-containing clan. Each group of three was associated with one of the six directions. The numbers four and five are also important. There are four independent but interrelated organizational systems: clans, kiva groups, curing societies, and priesthoods (Ladd 1979). Four underworlds are oriented toward the center/nadir, and four overworlds are oriented toward the zenith/center. When the center is included, four becomes five. The five parts of this quatridivision-plus-center are symbolized by the X-shaped body of the water skate. North is associated with the lowest of the worlds below (Stevenson 1904:25) and is the most important direction in ceremonial events and religious leadership (Cushing 1979:188–190). The associations between spaces and elements of the cosmic or mythic landscape are a fundamental part of Zuni consciousness. The village is traditionally "divided, not always clearly to the eye, but very clearly in the estimation of the people themselves," into seven parts corresponding to each of the six directions plus the center (Cushing 1896:367). Each of six sections of the village is "centered" in its sacred space or kiva. The village as a whole represents the seventh part, the center or Middle Place. These orientations and divisions exist in the minds of Zunis whether or not these are physically, architecturally extant. "What is important is the symbolic relationship to those directions, not the actual precision of directional alignments" (Young 1988:105).

Pueblo agriculturalists living on an open horizon follow the movements of the sun and moon with great interest (Parsons 1939:493–497; 554–589). In Tewa pueblos, a sunwatcher is appointed to keep track of the sun's position on the horizon (Harrington 1916:47; Parsons 1939:555). Directions and alignments derive some of their significance from the movements of celestial bodies. Cardinal directions are also solar alignments—on equinoxes, when the sun has traveled halfway between its northern and southern extremes on the horizon, it rises directly to the east and sets directly to the west. North is the "heart of the sky" (Lekson 1999:86), bisecting the daily movements of the sun and representing a fixed point around which the stars revolve. At midday, when the sun is halfway across the sky, any shadow will be cast directly along a north-south meridian. North has particular symbolic significance for Tewa and Keresan speakers as the mythic location of the sipapu, the connection to previous worlds, through which ancestors emerged long ago (Benedict 1931:249; White 1960:85).

For Tewa, Keres, and Zuni, opposing directions—north and south, east and west, up and down—create a center place where they intersect, a transition point around which the directions turn. For some Hopi, the center is a place of transformation, where different realities meet (Tuwaletstiwa, personal communication, December 2004). For Pueblo peoples, the center place is an extremely powerful trope that connects identity with landscape. Many Pueblo groups have origin stories involving migrations to a center place where they believe that they are destined to live (Parsons 1939:215, 230). Zuni migrations culminated in settlement at the middle place, Itiwana (Bunzel 1932; Ferguson and Hart 1985:20–23; Stevenson 1904:73–89). Hopi clans wandered the earth until they arrived at Tuuwanasavi, the earth center (Dongoske et al. 1997:603).

The center place is the point around which the sun, moon, and seasons revolve and the point of balance between opposing dualities. The concept of balanced dualism is deeply embedded in much Pueblo cosmography, social organization, and ritual. A cyclical rotation between two halves characterizes the ritual cycle and, for some Pueblos, the alternating dominance of dual social groups or moieties. Although there are many specific variations on this theme, most Eastern Pueblo social and ritual organization separates the world into two divisions, or moieties, often associated with summer and winter. Dualism and moieties are particularly strongly expressed among the Tewa, Tiwa, and Rio Grande Keresans (Fox 1972; Harrington 1916:61–62; Ortiz 1965, 1969; White 1942:142–144). The western pueblos of Zuni and Hopi lack moieties yet still express links between directions, social divisions, and ritual practices (Cushing 1896, 1966 [1883]; Hieb 1979).

Ortiz (1965:389) describes Tewa dual organization as "a system of antithetical institutions with the associated symbols, ideas, and meanings in terms of which social interaction takes place." The tripartite division of Tewa society outlined above is crosscut by membership in of one of two moieties—Winter and Summer. Moiety affiliation is inherited from one's father, although it can change as a result of marriage or initiation. Each moiety directs activities for half of the year, from equinox to equinox. During the summer, the Summer moiety head is in charge of the pueblo, and activities are centered around agriculture; during the winter, the Winter head is in charge, and nonagricultural activities, especially hunting, are important. In a complex organizational scheme, membership in a number of other societies integrates the three levels of people, as well as the two moieties, so that no single group of people can ever really obtain clear-cut power over others (Ortiz 1969:83–97, 121–137). Asymmetrical relationships present for half the year are balanced when the second group has power during the other half.

Moieties are also present at Keresan pueblos such as Cochiti, Santo Domingo, San Felipe, and Santa Ana (White 1942:142–144). At Santa Ana, people belong to either the Squash or the Turquoise moiety, according to their clan affiliation. At the other Keresan pueblos, as among the Tewa, people normally belong to the moiety of their father. As among the Tewa, moieties alternate in directing ritual activities over the course of the year. In Keresan origin stories, twin warriors—Masewi and Oyoyewi—are represented by today's moiety heads (White 1960:60).

In these Tewa, Keresan, and Zuni examples, important concepts include center place, directionality, and dualism, and the idea that these principles are represented on the landscape and in the natural world. The pervasive presence of these concepts across the Pueblo world, among multiple language groups, supports my interpretation that these ideas, or some version of them, were key components in an antecedent Chacoan worldview.

Social Memory and Cyclical Renewal

Moieties alternate in balanced rotation, the sun, moon, stars, and seasons revolve in an endless cycle, and human souls emerge from and return to the sipapu. The past is touched repeatedly, is revisited and incorporated into the present as a means of keeping the world alive and in balance. Pueblo peoples construct social memory through repetitive patterns that result in layer upon layer of meaning, contained in the same space.

Cyclical renewal is found in the turning of the heavens and the rotation of the seasons. Many Pueblo peoples, including the Hopi, Zuni, Tewa, Jemez, and Zia, follow with interest the peregrinations of the sun and moon

(Harrington 1916:45–48; McCluskey 1977; Parsons 1939:212; Stevenson 1894:29; Tedlock 1983). The winter solstice—when the sun turns back from its southerly course—is an important turning point in the ceremonial cycle (Parsons 1939:554). In solstice ceremonies such as the Zuni Shalako, Pueblo peoples ask the sun to return to the north. Solstice ceremonies usually begin before the actual solstice date, in part to coordinate this solar event with an important moment in the lunar cycle—the full moon (White 1962:227).

Just as the movements of the sun and moon are repeated each year, the past—revisited again and again—is a potent source of meaning and power. Archaeological sites play a part in the construction of social memory for contemporary Pueblo peoples. Some sites are pilgrimage destinations filled with potent spirituality (Ellis and Hammack 1968:32). Some are considered to be places where ancestors dwelled for a time before continuing their journey to the center place (Parsons 1939:214). The Hopi consider archaeological sites to be *ang kuktota*, the "footprints" of ancestors (Dongoske et al. 1997; Ferguson et al. 2000; Kuwanwisiwma and Ferguson 2004). In Zuni origin stories, ancestors left archaeological sites behind on their migrations to Itiwana, the middle place (Ferguson and Hart 1985:22).

Repeatedly touching the past, potentially for the purpose of constructing social memory, is a Pueblo practice that may be traced materially from the contemporary world back into the Basketmaker period. Representational media such as rock art panels, kiva murals, masks, and pottery show signs of superposition or repeated obliteration and redecoration. At Awatovi and Kawaika'a, kiva murals were repeatedly replastered, or paint was washed or scraped away and new layers of designs applied (Hibben 1975:34; Smith 1952:19–21, 1990; Young 1988:192). Some excavated kivas have as many as 100 layers of plaster (Smith 1952:17–19). Chacoan kivas were frequently remodeled and replastered as well—some have as many as 31 layers of plaster (Kluckhohn 1939:8). When Chacoans sealed shell and turquoise ornaments beneath roof pillars or inside great kiva niches, they may have been engaged in memory's counterpart—the formal process of forgetting (Mills n.d.).

At Zuni and Hopi, katsina masks were repainted and refurbished for ceremonial use—old paint is considered sacred and is deposited in a special location (Bunzel 1932:858; Parsons 1939:341; Young 1988:192). Similarly, some whiteware cylinder vessels from Chaco were repeatedly redecorated, either by washing or scraping away the black-on-white designs or by reslipping, repainting, and refiring (Crown and Wills 2003). Crown and Wills (2003:525) believe that these heirloom vessels, with their hidden layers of ancestral designs, express the "dual concepts of rebirth and continuity."

The Chacoan past was a potent symbol referenced by post-Chacoan communities that emerged to the north and south of the Chaco core. Pueblo III people in the Mesa Verde region intentionally used Chaco-era outlier great houses in the area for feasting and burial—but not for habitation. They built Sand Canyon pueblo in an unusual D shape, referencing the form of Pueblo Bonito, and they may have shaped Mesa Verde mugs to resemble the unique form of Chacoan pitchers (Bradley 1996). Pueblo III people in the Cibola region built great kivas that may reference Chaco (Kintigh 1994). In Manuelito Canyon, a post-Chacoan road segment links Atse'e Nitsaa, a great house dating from the 1200s and 1300s, to Kin Hocho'i, a Chacoan great house from the 1100s (Fowler and Stein 1992). At the Pettit site, Saitta (1994) argues, a common memory of the Chacoan past was used to help integrate disparate groups and advance communalism instead of factionalism.

Earlier in time, Ancestral Pueblo peoples referenced the Basketmaker past. Archaeologists working in the La Plata Valley observed that the "superimposition of Pueblo II habitations on Basketmaker structures is so regular in our sample that there can be little question that it was intentional" (Toll and Wilson 2000:33). And the Basketmakers, in turn, linked themselves to the Archaic. Robins and Hayes-Gilpin (2000:237–238) observed that Basketmaker artists superimposed lobed circles over older, Archaic images, perhaps to reference a connection to the past through the sipapu of emergence.

Not only are repetition, renewal, and the construction of social memory very much a part of the contemporary Pueblo world, but they also appear to have a lengthy history extending back into the Pueblo past. This historical continuity strengthens my assumption that memory was likely an integral part of the Chacoan landscape, and it lends added weight to my investigations into the ways Bonito-style architecture might have been designed to reference the past.

Pathways and Pilgrimages

The concept of a journey—whether a migration, a pilgrimage, or simply a metaphor for life—is integral to Pueblo ideas about directionality, center place, dualism, and renewal. The sipapu is the place where the individual's life journey begins and ends, as well as the origin point of mythic Pueblo migrations. The mythic sipapu might be a canyon, a hole (Sofaer, Marshall, and Sinclair 1989:374), or some round and deep place (Lange 1959:416), or it might be located in the mountains (Weslowski 1981:123). A small hole in a kiva floor is also termed the sipapu and represents the place of emergence from earlier worlds into this one, connecting the present world to past mythic events (Smith 1972). After emergence from the sipapu, Pueblo peoples migrated toward the center place. For Keresans, the original sipapu, or place of origin, is in the north, and after emergence, people migrated in a north-south direction (White 1942:177, 1960:89). Zuni ancestors chose from two sets of colored eggs—those who chose one set settled at Zuni, and those who chose the other set traveled to the south (Dutton 1963:112). Roads symbolize the journey from the place of emergence to the center place (Parsons 1939:310, 363). For example, Jemez oral traditions tell about a leader who made four roads for people to travel south from the place of emergence (Parsons 1925:137, 138).

Roads, or spirit paths, are said to be straight (Stevenson 1894:31, 41, 145) and may be represented by a cornmeal or pollen trail (Parsons 1939:360–364). The connection from the center place back to the sipapu is a path traveled not only by Pueblo people as described in origin stories, but also by spirits. At Hopi, the souls of the dead travel to the sipapu in the west (Parsons 1939:216). In Keresan tradition, the dead return to the sipapu along a road to the north (White 1942:177, 1960:89). At Acoma, when someone dies, offerings that represent the person's soul are carried to the north and deposited in a canyon or mesa crevice (White 1973 [1932]:137). Ceramic vessels are broken in rituals relating to the dead (Ortiz 1969:54; Parsons 1939:72, 77). A pot containing a last meal for the deceased can be placed on the road to the north or can be "killed" (by breaking the rim) and then thrown to the north, the direction the soul will travel (White 1942:177). Every year, the souls of the dead return to visit their relatives and to consume food placed on their graves and along the road to the north.

Roads are used for processions (Parsons 1939:360–364). They also represent the human life cycle on both individual and collective levels. Parallel tracks represent social groups traveling in the same direction that diverge, then converge, in origin and migration stories, or they may represent opposite paths for the living and the dead (Tuwaletstiwa, personal communication, December 2004). All Tewa people begin on a single path, but then the path diverges into two parallel paths corresponding to the two moieties. At death, the two paths rejoin into one, just as the moieties eventually rejoined as one pueblo in Tewa oral history (Ortiz 1969:57). Zuni prayers and chants describe four parallel roads on the journey to the middle place (Bunzel 1932:717). Ceremonial races are sometimes run on north-south parallel tracks symbolic of emergence journeys (Dutton and Marmon 1936:12) and sometimes on east-west roads to assist the sun in its journey (Parsons 1939:212, 547).

Pilgrimages are tightly integrated into the Pueblo ritual cycle and are interconnected with directionality, center place, dualism, and memory. Pueblo peoples may undertake religious pilgrimages to sacred locations that are made as part of the ceremonial cycle, sometimes in association with astronomical events such as solstices. Pueblo pilgrimage destinations include a variety of symbolically charged, distinctive landforms such as mountains, canyons, oddly shaped hills, caves, lakes, and springs. Often these sacred places are associated with sipapu openings (Ellis and Hammack 1968:31, 33; Ladd 1983) or access to spiritual realms (Parsons 1939:213), or they may be places visited on the ancestors' migrations. Archaeological sites, rock art, and shrines are also important pilgrimage destinations because they offer material markers of ancestral migrations. For example, Zuni Bow Priests travel to Chaco Canyon (Ferguson and Hart 1985:23).

Pilgrimage routes and destinations are sometimes, but not always, marked by shrines. Shrines take a variety of forms, including stone cairns and rings. At Keresan pueblos and at Jemez, shrines on high places include rings of stones with an opening facing the pueblo (Parsons 1939:308). At Jemez every June, priests visit a shrine on a prominent mountain peak to the north to kick off summer rain ceremonies (Weslowski 1981:117). Ellis and Hammack (1968:32) describe how Keresan pilgrims set out from their pueblo south of Chaco and traveled north, stopping to leave offerings at a shrine on the south side of Chaco Canyon, at Jackson Butte, and finally at a lake or spring in the San Juan Mountains regarded as the sipapu. Zuni ceremonialists periodically undertake a religious pilgrimage to Zuni Salt Lake on a straight road with shrines along the way (Ferguson and Hart 1985:51).

Dance is another way in which movement integrates Pueblo cosmographic principles. Scott Momaday captures this relationship as he describes a dance at Jemez:

> *Through the afternoon the dance went on in the universe. The plaza was thronged with people of every description; they clung there to the adobe walls, looking on; they stood on the housetops, high against the winter sky; and they gave themselves up to the motion and the music of the holy world which was centered there. The dancers came forth in long files of concentrated men and women, first one and then the other of the great Jemez clans, the Turquoise and the Squash, their bodies blue and yellow, taut and tethered to the drums, their feet shaking the hard earth. In them was unspeakable calm and intensity, and these were, I thought and think, unaccountable and unaccountably the same thing. They described every impulse, the whole rhythm of the turning of the earth, the returning of time upon it forever.* [Momaday 1976:134–135]

Very likely, pilgrimages, processions, journeys, and dances—important components of Pueblo cosmography and ritual today—were also integral to the Chacoan experience. My phenomenological investigations focusing on movement across the Chacoan landscape are lent additional weight by these ethnographic observations.

Into the Chacoan World

If the Chacoan landscape was created to be experienced, then a phenomenological approach—walking where the Chacoans walked, perceiving spaces as closely as possible to the ways in which they perceived them—is a viable method through which to learn more about Chacoan ideological uses of space. If contemporary Pueblo peoples, as Chacoan descendants, share some aspects of a Chacoan worldview, then ethnographic information on Pueblo landscape and cosmography provides an invaluable lens through which to investigate the representation of ideas on the Chacoan landscape. In this study, I use a phenomenological approach to investigate the spatial dimensions of visibility, motion, and memory, and I combine these sensual aspects of spatial experience with Pueblo ethnography to create an interpretive understanding of the ways in which Chacoans perceived and represented landscape. Several aspects of spatial experience that were probably important at Chaco emerge from the discussions in this chapter:

> *Sacred geography.* Unusual or highly visible natural places such as mountain peaks and springs might have been the sites of shrines. Lines of sight or roads might have linked sacred places to Chaco.
>
> *Visibility.* Architectural prominence, site positions, and line-of-sight connections might have expressed a Chacoan concern with visibility. Bonito-style architecture was positioned to be highly visible. Some buildings or other features may have been positioned to be in sight of meaningful topographic landmarks.
>
> *Movement.* Roads, ramps, and staircases in Chaco Canyon and near outlier great houses may have enhanced or restricted access and visibility and may have served as routes for ritual processions.
>
> *Memory.* Chacoan architects worked within an ancient and storied landscape. References to the more distant past, ritual renewal, and other dimensions of social memory were incorporated into buildings and landscape features.
>
> *Cosmography.* Cosmographic ideas such as cardinal directions, balanced dualism, and center place were likely represented in Chacoan architecture and landscape and may have been tied into the movements of the sun and moon.

As described in "Poovolli's Dream," the Chacoan landscape is a "language of permanence and meaning." Constellations of buildings, roads, and shrines provide insights into the social and cosmographic world shared by eleventh- and twelfth-century canyon inhabitants and visitors. This landscape, rife with alignments, prominences, and stark juxtapositions, was built to be experienced. Because of the reflexive relationship between space and worldview, as Chacoan peoples moved through the canyon and surrounding areas, they actively reaffirmed their beliefs about the nature of the world and their place in it.

Chacoan leaders traded upon this relationship, formally constructing spatial settings for ritual visitors. As the visitors moved in prescribed ways through the Chacoan landscape, they connected emotionally and aesthetically with shared Ancestral Pueblo ideas expressed by the architecture. Leaders naturalized their authority by constructing line-of-sight connections with sacred landmarks and by making material references to ancestors. Chaco Canyon as a center place was a powerful trope—to Pueblo followers, the canyon seemed the appropriate place for ceremony, and canyon leaders seemed the legitimate caretakers of exclusive ritual knowledge. Leaders and subjects appropriated elements of a shared worldview as they negotiated a Chacoan ideology. Ultimately, visitors from outliers transformed themselves into subjects, contributing their labor and resources toward the success of Chaco as a ceremonial center. This process did not happen instantaneously, of course, but developed and grew more elaborate over the course of three centuries. In the chapters that follow, I explore some of the ways in which Ancestral Pueblo peoples expressed visibility, movement, memory, and cosmography on the landscape. I explain how these perceived and representational elements of an Ancestral Pueblo worldview contributed to a Chacoan ideology, and I deconstruct the negotiation of changing sociopolitical relationships between canyon and outlier dwellers.

Notes

1. There are relatively few openings along the pueblo walls; rather, people likely entered great houses from the direction of the plaza. Initially, most great house plazas were open, but by the late 1000s, builders enclosed plazas with rows of rooms or walls, limiting access to the pueblo interior. Twelfth-century McElmo-style great houses lack plazas altogether. These self-contained structures must have been entered through doorways that led directly into rooms or through the use of ladders.

2. Cardinal directions were important to Mississippian peoples (Emerson 1997), the Maya (Ashmore 1989, 1991), and many other Mesoamerican groups (for example, Aveni 1980; Carlson 1981; Heyden 1981).

4 Origins

I follow their journey in stone

from our third world,

reaching hand over hand,

ascending the reed;

coming into canyons,

reaching higher and higher

like sprouted corn

stretching upward to light.

I feel their words

and hear echoes of past lives.

—*from "They Told Stories," by Ramson Lomatewama (1993:6)*

Pueblo stories tell of great migrations across the landscape, journeys that began at the place of emergence and ended with settlement at a "middle place" or "center place." To understand the spatially complex Chacoan landscapes of the tenth and eleventh centuries, we must first undertake a journey of our own, tracing the origins of Chacoan culture from the Basketmaker III period (450–700) through the Pueblo I period (700–875) and the Early Bonito phase (875–1020). At the beginning of the Early Bonito phase, Chaco Canyon was but one of many locations where Ancestral Puebloans constructed early great houses. By the end of the Early Bonito phase, Chaco was

Chaco, with architecture and social organization on a larger scale than anything previously seen in the Ancestral Pueblo world. Why did Ancestral Puebloan agriculturalists devote their energy to the creation of monumental architecture? Who did the buildings serve? How was Chacoan society organized during the eleventh century? These questions can be answered only by an understanding of the deep social history that led Ancestral Puebloans to this time and place. The preceding five centuries hold the key to understanding how and why social complexity emerged in Chaco Canyon.

The Basketmaker III and Pueblo I periods were times of great social mobility and change as large communities formed and disbanded and people moved hundreds of kilometers back and forth across the landscape. Chaco Canyon was home to two of the largest known Basketmaker III settlements, complete with community architecture. In the Pueblo I period, many of these people migrated north across the San Juan River and aggregated in farming villages larger than any previously seen on the Colorado Plateau. These new villages were hotbeds of social innovation as they brought together peoples from multiple backgrounds and perhaps multiple ethnicities. Two forms of Pueblo I community architecture suggest that there were at least two different ways of organizing ritual and, perhaps, ameliorating social disputes and tensions.

Near the end of the ninth century, Ancestral Puebloans moved back south to the central San Juan Basin, where they founded new farming communities centered around proto-great houses and great kivas. The new communities used familiar Puebloan ideas such as sacred geography, directionality, dualism, and social memory in rituals meant to celebrate social cohesiveness and ensure agricultural success. In the early 900s, like many areas of the Basin, Chaco Canyon was home to several communities that contained one or more proto-great houses. By the early 1000s, however, Chaco Canyon emerged as a central gathering place for periodic rituals that involved much of the surrounding Pueblo world. A shared Ancestral Pueblo ideology made this transformation possible. Between the beginning of the Basketmaker III and the end of the Pueblo I periods, communal ritual became important, and major elements of the Puebloan worldview—sacred geography, cyclical renewal, social memory, balanced dualism—coalesced. By the Early Bonito phase, these ideas were widely held by Ancestral Puebloans living in proto-great house and great kiva–centered communities across the San Juan Basin. They formed elements of an Ancestral Puebloan worldview that Classic Bonito–phase canyon leaders drew upon to enjoin Basin residents to participate in a canyon-based social and ritual order.

Basketmaker III Roots

Aspects of the Ancestral Puebloan worldview expressed at Chaco clearly extend back in time at least as far as the Basketmaker III period (450–700). Archaeologists have long recognized that the origins of Puebloan society can be traced back to the Basketmaker III period (Vivian and Mathews 1965:29). By the late fifth century in the San Juan Basin, early experiments with horticulture and sedentism had led to commitments to agriculture and settled villages. The basic material components of Ancestral Puebloan life—corn, beans, and squash; grayware and whiteware pottery; and patterned architectural configurations—were in place (Reed 2000). Basketmaker architecture in Chaco Canyon indicates that communal ritual and the concepts of sacred geography, cyclical renewal, social memory, and possibly dualism were present or developing during this time as well.

Basketmaker III communities of varying size and configuration are located across the San Juan Basin.[1] In rockshelters or on ridges and bluffs overlooking well-drained valleys, Basketmaker III peoples built homes. They cut pitstructures into the earth, roofing these with mud-covered brush frameworks supported by internal beams or poles. A typical domestic pitstructure was approximately 5 m in diameter and 1.5 m deep, often with an attached antechamber to the south or east (figure 4.1). The Basketmakers used the interiors of these structures in recognizably formal ways. Patterned suites of features included a deflector, a central hearth, roof support posts, and wing walls—the latter sometimes demarcated storage or grinding areas. The Basketmakers sometimes lined pitstructures with sandstone slabs and built arcs of slab-lined surface rooms behind the pitstructure to the west or north. Most settlements consisted of several pitstructures, slab-lined storage cists, and a refuse area. Villages probably represent associated kin groups organized by lineage (Reed 2000; Steward 1937, 1955; Ware 2001). Larger villages contained 30 or more pitstructures and associated features. In addition, some large villages sported paved "walking areas" and a communal meeting space in the form of a "great pitstructure."

Interestingly, both of the two largest centers of Basketmaker III settlement in the San Juan Basin were located atop the south rim of Chaco Canyon, indicating that the canyon was a center of Puebloan settlement as early as the sixth century.[2] Shabik'eshchee Village (29SJ1659) is in the eastern part of Chaco Canyon, high atop a north-trending finger of Chacra Mesa. Roberts (1929) originally excavated parts of Shabik'eshchee, and the Chaco Project revisited the site in the 1980s (Wills and Windes 1989; Windes n.d.a). A second major Basketmaker III village—29SJ423—is on West Mesa at the west end of Chaco Canyon, on a high bench of Cliff House

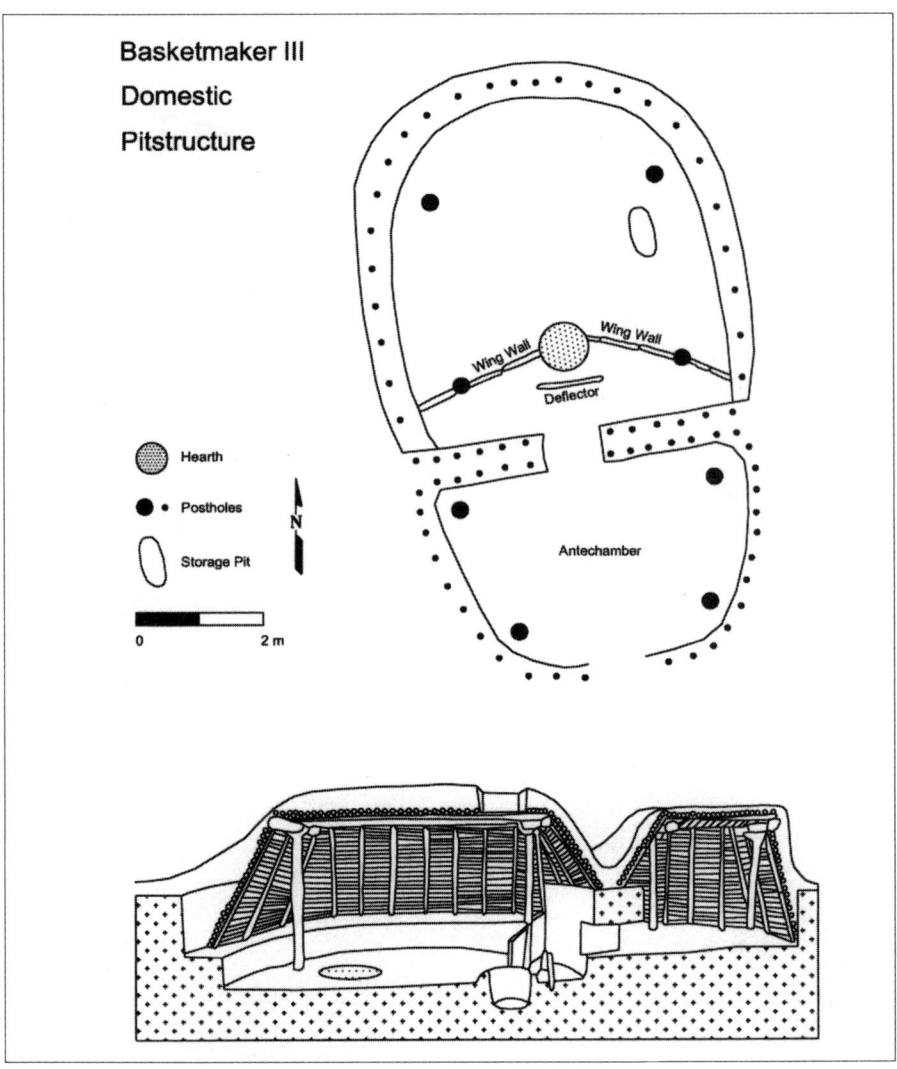

Figure 4.1. Plan of a Late Basketmaker III pitstructure, based on a drawing in Cassells 1983:117, figure 7.9.

sandstone overlooking the confluence of the Chaco and the Escavada washes. The Chaco Project recorded and partially excavated 29SJ423 (hereafter Site 423) in the 1970s (Windes n.d.a).

Shabik'eshchee is the center of a large Basketmaker III community comprising several sites and at least 100 pitstructures, stretching north-south for at least 4 km from Chaco Canyon across the top of Chacra Mesa and onto the plains to the south (Windes n.d.a). Shabik'eshchee Village proper con-

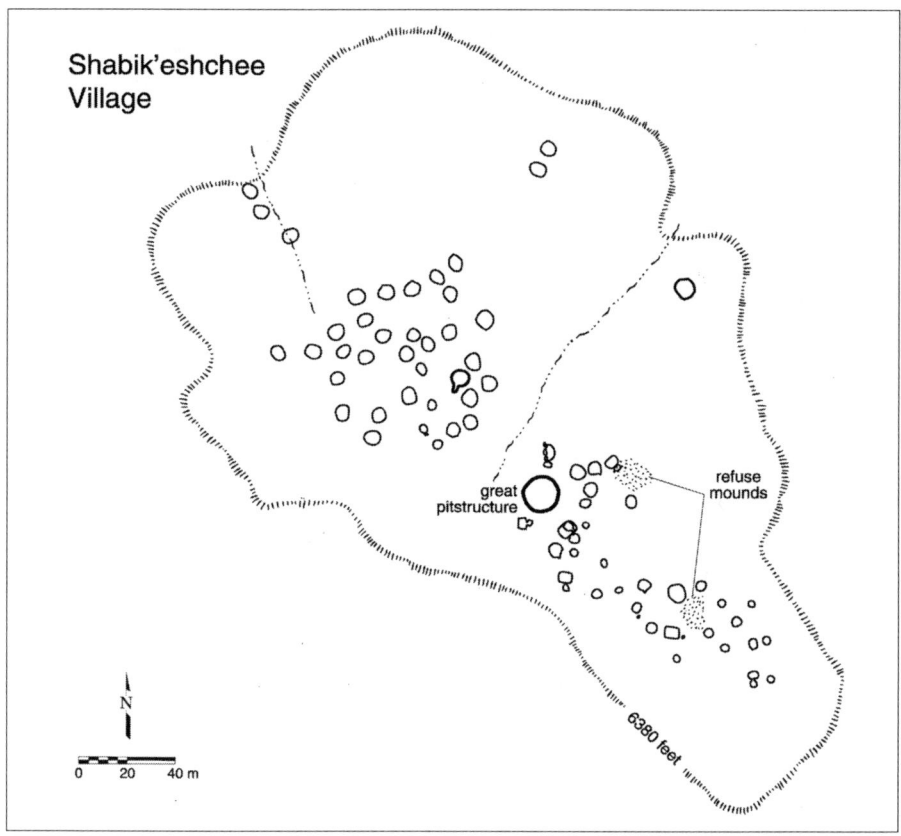

Figure 4.2. Plan of Shabik'eshchee Village, based on Roberts 1929 and Wills and Windes 1989:351, figure 3.

tains sixty-eight domestic pitstructures and forty-five cists arranged in a crescent opening to the east (figure 4.2). There are two refuse areas—one at either end of the crescent. The heart of the crescent is a great pitstructure with slab-lined bench and floor features and with plastered walls. Intriguingly, this layout suggests the same sort of dualistic symmetry that was formalized and elaborated in Classic Chacoan great houses five centuries later, although the pitstructures may not all be contemporaneous and Windes (n.d.a) cautions that there is no completely accurate map of Shabik'eshchee Village. Roberts' (1929) limited excavation identified two occupation episodes at the site. During the first occupation, the great pitstructure burned; during the second, the depression was used as a refuse dump. Newly revised tree-ring and archaeomagnetic dates indicate that Shabik'eshchee Village was inhabited between 550 and 700.

Figure 4.3. Site 423, the Basketmaker III village atop West Mesa.

Like Shabik'eshchee Village, Site 423 was the center of a much larger community of sites extending across West Mesa and the canyon bottom to the south for a distance of 3.5 km or more (figure 4.3). Site 423 itself contains at least twenty to twenty-five pitstructures, thirty slab-lined cists, a deep scatter of refuse, and a great pitstructure 10 m in diameter. Like the great pitstructure at Shabik'eshchee, this slab-lined, circular feature contained a bench and a number of floor features. The structure burned three times and was rebuilt twice—tree-ring dates indicate that these events took place between 521 and 557. Turquoise chips and a bead were found under the earliest roof supports.

These two large settlements are of exceptional size in the canyon, indeed in the San Juan Basin, suggesting that Chaco Canyon may have been an important hub of the Ancestral Pueblo world during the Basketmaker III period. At these and other Basketmaker III settlements, major elements important to an Ancestral Puebloan (and, later, Chacoan) worldview emerged—particularly visibility, communal ritual, and cyclical renewal.

The Basketmakers positioned their open-air settlements in high places, on ridges, bluffs, and mesa tops. Basketmaker builders chose site locations based on diverse factors including proximity to water and arable land, defensibility, and a clear view of the horizon. They positioned both Shabik'eshchee and Site 423 above confluences with good agricultural potential. In fact, at the Chaco/Escavada confluence below Site 423, a natural dam may have created a shallow lake (Force et al. 2002). But why build so high? Some scholars have suggested that Basketmaker III builders constructed their settlements in defensive locations (Chenault and Motsinger 2000; LeBlanc 1999), although evidence for conflict during this period is inconclusive at best (Vivian 2000:253–255).[3] Both Shabik'eshchee and Site 423 are perched near steep escarpments, but visitors can easily walk up to the sites from other directions.

A striking feature of these site locations is an exceptional view of surrounding terrain, both near and far. Visibility across the open expanses of the San Juan Basin is a key attribute of later Chacoan sites, and this trend can be seen half a millennium earlier at Basketmaker III settlements such as Shabik'eshchee Village and Site 423. From Shabik'eshchee Village, 45 m above the floor of Chaco Canyon, the Basketmaker III inhabitants' view extended approximately 4 km up canyon to the east and 3 km down canyon to the west, but visibility from the site does not extend beyond the canyon. The view from Site 423 is even more spectacular. Site 423 is situated approximately 100 m above the wash confluence below. Residents enjoyed a panoramic vista that extended at least 8 km east up Chaco Canyon, 3 km north up the Escavada Wash, and 4 km west down the Chaco River, past Peñasco Blanco. On the horizon, they could see the Chuska Mountains and Shiprock to the west and Huerfano Mountain, the La Plata Mountains, and the San Juan Mountains to the north. Clear views of the horizon might have been desired by Basketmaker agriculturalists, who would have been following the sun's cyclical and seasonal movements as they scheduled planting and harvesting. Distant landforms and oddly shaped peaks would have formed a backdrop for daily life—they likely had Basketmaker names and, perhaps, associated stories or other meanings.

Great pitstructures are good evidence for the importance of community gatherings and ritual practices during the Basketmaker III period. In addition to those at Shabik'eshchee Village and Site 423, archaeologists have identified at least eight great pitstructures in large Basketmaker III communities across the San Juan Basin (table 4.1; figure 4.4). These structures are sometimes called "great kivas" and "oversized pitstructures," but I prefer the term *great pitstructures*, which distinguishes them from later, Pueblo I and II period architectural developments. Great pitstructures are variable in size and morphology—some are circular, with full benches, and others are D-shaped or rectangular, with a partial bench and an antechamber. They are not necessarily deeper than associated domestic pitstructures but hold about four times the area, with diameters averaging 10 m. Some great pitstructures were burned, and some were repeatedly remodeled.

Figure 4.4. The great pitstructure at Shabik'eshchee Village. Photo by Frank H. H. Roberts (1929), published in Wills and Windes 1989:352, figure 4, reprinted by permission of the Smithsonian Institution.

The fact that Basketmaker III peoples built great pitstructures in large villages suggests that the activities carried out in them were important for social cohesiveness. Small-scale agriculturalists across the world frequently develop group ritual practices designed to assist in the healthy growth and harvest of crops, ensure rainfall and fertility, and promote community cohesiveness (Adler and Wilshusen 1990:138–143). These rituals are often held in multipurpose community spaces. In a large, circular space such as a great pitstructure, community members could have met to perform rituals, resolve disputes, discuss matters of concern, and conduct social or economic transactions. Although archaeologists have little in the way of physical evidence for specific Basketmaker III rituals, great pitstructures would have been suitable gathering places for these types of activities (Reed 2000:14).

Early farmers logically would have connected agricultural rituals with cyclical renewal as they observed the turning of the seasons and the sun's movements on the horizon. Ritual draws power from repetition (Moore and Myerhoff 1977). In ritual, the familiar is made new, as the same words, songs, dances, or gestures are repeated on multiple occasions, perhaps by different actors. Crown and Wills (2003) suggest that repeated kiva remodeling in later time periods is material evidence for the importance of ritual

Table 4.1 Basketmaker III (BM III) Great Pitstructures in Northwest New Mexico and Northeast Arizona

Site	Location	Dates (AD)	References
Shabik'eshchee Village	Chaco Canyon	550–700	Roberts 1929; Wills and Windes 1989; Windes n.d.a
29SJ423	Chaco Canyon	521–557	Windes n.d.a
Mexican Springs	Tohatchi Flats	640–700	Damp and Kotyk 2000:97–98
Twin Lakes	Tohatchi Flats	BM III	Gilpin and Benallie 2000:171
LA 80422	Tohatchi Flats	600–725	Kearns, McVickar, and Reed 2000:131
Tohatchi Basketmaker Village	Tohatchi Flats	BM III	Marshall et al. 1979:285–286; Peckham 1969
Electric Raven	Tohatchi Flats	701	Cunnar 1996; Kearns, McVickar, and Reed 2000:130–131
Broken Flute Cave	Red Rock Valley	623–635	Morris 1959, 1980
Juniper Cove	west of the Chuskas	650–675	Gilpin and Benallie 2000:162–167[1]
AZ E:12:5 (Lukachukai)	west of the Chuskas	691	Altschul and Huber 2000

1. Gilpin and Benallie (2000:167–169) and Reed and Wilcox (2000:86) discuss 11 more great pitstructures in the Red Rock Valley and northeastern Arizona, but I have not included them here. Tom Windes (personal communication, September 2005) contends that some of the unexcavated depressions may be eroded domestic pitstructures.

renewal in the Puebloan world. Similar processes may have been at work in Basketmaker III times. A number of great pitstructures, including the two in Chaco Canyon and at least four more outside the canyon, exhibit signs of multiple uses and reconstructions. At Shabik'eshchee, the great pitstructure burned and was later used as a refuse dump. At Site 423, the great pitstructure burned three times and was rebuilt twice. This latter circumstance, in particular, suggests repetitive ritual practices (Wilshusen 1986). If pitstructures were burned as part of ritual closure, then the great pitstructure at Site 423 may have been repeatedly closed and reopened in a cycle of ritual renewal.

Cyclicality also may have roots in the seasonal rounds followed by the Basketmakers' hunter-gatherer ancestors as they moved in repetitive patterns across the landscape to procure specific resources in season. Basketmaker III peoples continued to move away and reoccupy the same sites repeatedly, although chronological evidence is not fine-grained enough for us to know whether intervals between site occupations spanned seasons, years, or many decades. Those who returned may or may not have been the same people or the descendants of the people who left. In any case, the material traces of earlier occupations, including pitstructure depressions and refuse, would have been clearly visible on the ground surface. There are many examples of the remodeling or reuse of pitstructure depressions during secondary occupations (for example, Harriman and McVickar 1996).

Basketmaker peoples probably rebuilt on the same locations for a number of reasons, including the continuing attractions of nearby resources. Reexcavating or remodeling an abandoned pitstructure—using digging sticks and stone hoes—may have been easier than constructing a new one. Whether or not such practicalities figured into their decisions, the new occupants would have been fully aware that people had lived on this place before. Any reoccupation of an archaeological site always carries some symbolic ramifications. Those who resettled a site likely wove stories about previous inhabitants, whether they were still living, were held in the memory of the living, or were entirely fictive entities.

Collective stories and ideas about the past are an important component of social continuity and identity for all social groups. As the Basketmakers repeatedly touched the past through repeated remodelings of structures and reoccupations of sites, they were engaged in the construction of social memory. Hundreds of years later, during the Chacoan heyday, it was the Basketmaker past that figured prominently in the construction of Chacoan ideology and worldview as the Chacoans carried out their own practices of cyclical renewal.

The Pueblo I Crucible

By the end of the Basketmaker III period, several important aspects of what would become a Chacoan worldview, including the importance of visibility, communal ritual, cyclical renewal, social memory, and possibly dualism, were in place. The subsequent Pueblo I period (700–875) was a time of upheaval, population movement, aggregation, and social change. During this period, the concepts of visibility, communal ritual, cyclical renewal, social memory, and dualism continued to grow in importance. To understand these developments, we must look beyond Chaco to the area north of the San Juan River, which encompasses the Mesa Verde region, southeast Utah, and the Animas/La Plata valleys near Durango (figure 4.5). In Pueblo I times, the Chaco region was a relative backwater as thousands of settlers from across the Colorado Plateau aggregated in large villages in the northern

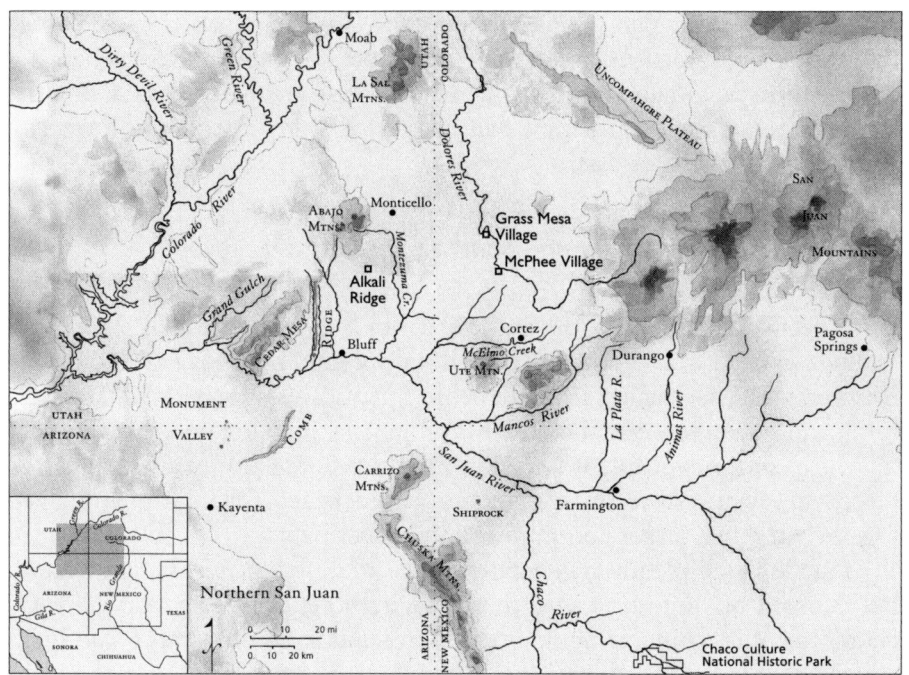

Figure 4.5. Locations of the northern San Juan Pueblo I–period sites discussed in the text. Drafted by Molly O'Halloran.

San Juan (Kohler 1992; Orcutt, Blinman, and Kohler 1990; Wilshusen and Blinman 1992). These villages were crucibles for the continued development of Puebloan ideas and worldviews. Aggregation on a large scale posed new social and logistical challenges, and villagers from diverse backgrounds likely brought a variety of rituals, ideas, and practices to the mix as they worked out ways to get along with one another and maintain social order. At the end of the Pueblo I period, around 875, many people migrated south, populating the San Juan Basin and Chaco Canyon, bringing with them the social seeds that would ultimately flower into Classic Bonito Chaco.

Archaeologists are only beginning to identify and understand the ways in which these large-scale movements and aggregations were related to developments at Chaco (Wilshusen and Van Dyke 2006; Windes n.d.a). Historically, many of us have treated the northern San Juan (including the Mesa Verde region) and the southern San Juan (Chaco) as two discrete study areas. We know a great deal about Pueblo I in the northern San Juan, thanks to major investigations such as the Dolores Archaeological Project. At present, we know considerably less about Pueblo I in the southern San Juan. But both regions were part of one Ancestral Puebloan landscape as people moved back and forth between them over time. My interpretations here are grounded in new data and ideas, which I will review before discussing the ways that a Puebloan worldview continued to develop during this formative period of the Chacoan past.

Settlement Patterns North and South of the San Juan River

Like their Basketmaker III predecessors, Pueblo I peoples continued to raise corn, beans, and squash, to hunt rabbits and deer, and to make grayware and whiteware pottery. Some of the most important changes that took place between the Basketmaker III and Pueblo I periods were economic, architectural, and social. More so than the Basketmakers, Pueblo I peoples were permanently and irrevocably invested in agriculture. Pueblo I peoples invested more energy in domestic architecture, used space differently, and lived together in much larger communities than ever before.

Pueblo I architecture is generally similar to Basketmaker III architecture, but Pueblo I builders organized their sites in more formally patterned ways. People spent less time living in pitstructures and more time in the slab-lined surface rooms behind them. Over time, arcs of connected surface rooms became pueblos, and pitstructures became kivas—specialized ritual rooms. This transition was gradual and somewhat piecemeal. Arcs of slab-footed surface structures were present in late Basketmaker III period sites, and it is not entirely clear when pitstructures began to be used for more specialized and less domestic functions. By the ninth century, Pueblo I sites consisted of a single or double row of contiguous masonry or slab-lined rooms forming a C shape. These arcs of rooms opened always toward the east, southeast, or south. In the plazas created by the roomblocks, builders positioned one or more pitstructures. They deposited refuse in middens on the far side of the plaza to the east, southeast, or south. The Pueblo I type site, site 13 at Alkali Ridge, is a sizeable village north of the San Juan in southeast Utah (Brew 1946). Site 13 consists of four large, linked crescents of slab-footed surface rooms opening toward the southeast to create four large plazas (figure 4.6). The Puebloans placed pitstructures in the plazas and in front of the roomblocks to the east and south, and they positioned large trash middens beyond the plazas.

The Northern San Juan, 700–875.

By the latter half of the ninth century, one-half to one-third of the known Ancestral Pueblo population—some 6,500 people—were living in the northern San Juan (Wilshusen and Ortman 1999:377–382). Alkali Ridge

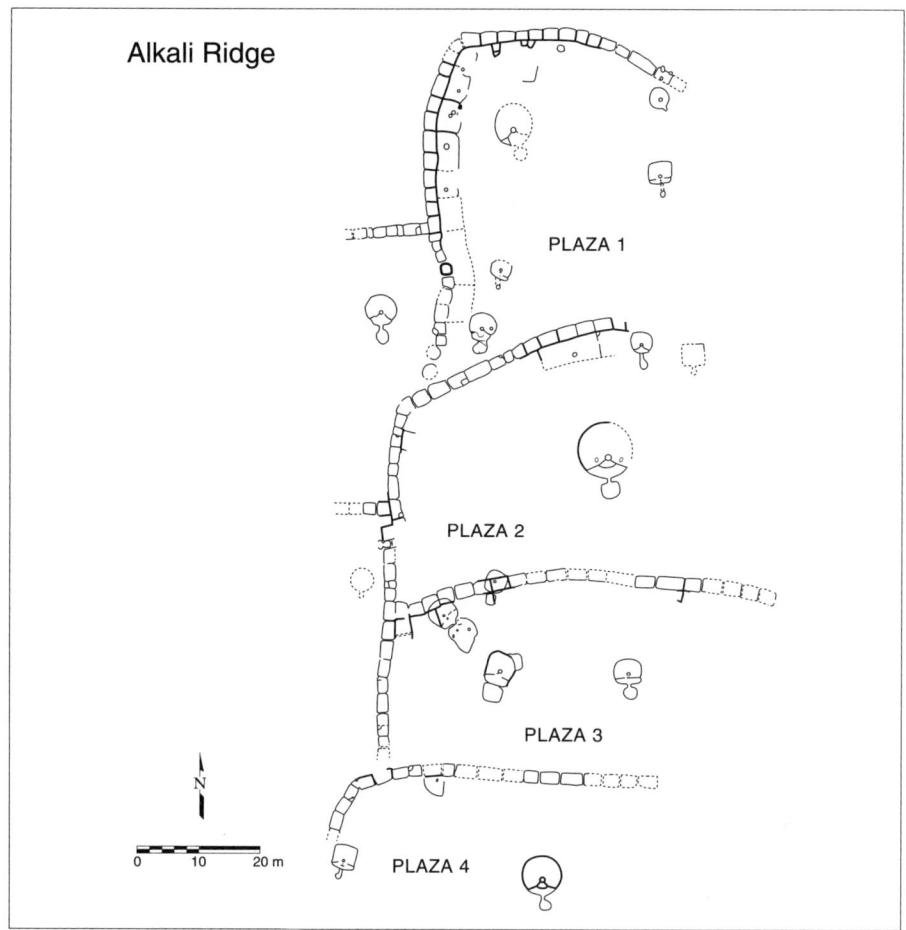

Figure 4.6. Plan of Site 13, Alkali Ridge, after Brew 1946:figure 27.

dates to an initial eighth-century period of Pueblo I aggregation (Orcutt, Blinman, and Kohler 1990). By 860, people were living in villages of a size similar to Alkali Ridge, from Mesa Verde to southeast Utah, with one important difference—the villages were now clustered into groups of three to seven, representing aggregation on an unprecedented scale. Although each of these village clusters was occupied only 25–40 years, each may have been home to as many as 1,000 people (Wilshusen and Varien 1996).

A number of later, Chacoan developments are foreshadowed by these northern Pueblo I villages. The northern villages involved the social integration of people from multiple backgrounds. Archaeologists working in the area argue that ritual activities in large, community structures helped create

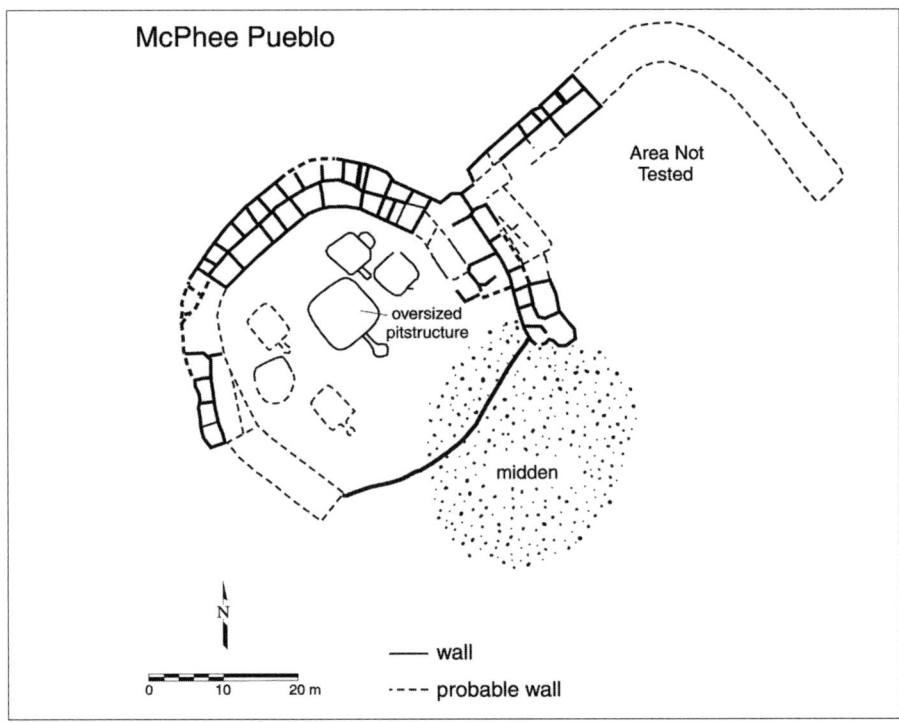

Figure 4.7. Plan of McPhee Pueblo, one of six pueblos with oversized pitstructures in McPhee Village, a cluster of sites on the west side of the Dolores River. Based on plans and information in Brisbin, Kane, and Morris 1988.

a sense of social cohesion. Wilshusen and Ortman (1999) propose that there were at least two kinds of Pueblo I community organization, based on patterned material differences between two village clusters in the well-studied Dolores area. They describe eight Pueblo I villages along the Dolores River—four on either side. On the west side of the river, McPhee Village contains paired, horseshoe-shaped roomblocks with enclosed plazas and restricted access (figure 4.7). On the east side of the river, by contrast, Grass Mesa Village has a long, slightly curving, nonsymmetrical roomblock with an open plaza.

McPhee Village resembles a later Chacoan great house in several respects. McPhee roomblocks were built of Type 1 masonry—horizontally stacked sandstone set in abundant mortar. Half a century later in the San Juan Basin, this masonry style was a defining characteristic of the earliest Chacoan great houses (Wilshusen and Van Dyke 2006; Windes n.d.a). Dualism—one of the most important spatial-organizing principles at Chaco—is everywhere in

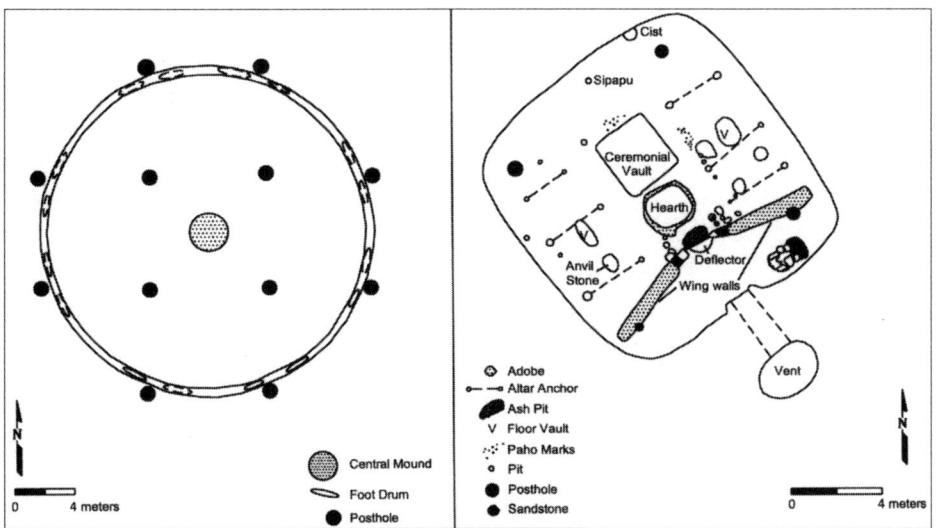

Figure 4.8. Comparison of a late Pueblo I great kiva and an oversized pitstructure from sites in the Dolores River Valley. The great kiva is from Grass Mesa Village (AD 760–840) and is based on a drawing in Kane 1986:411, figure 5.16. The oversized pitstructure is from Masa Negra (AD 840–910), a pueblo in McPhee Village, and is based on a drawing in Kuckelman 1988:434, figure 3.20.

evidence at McPhee. The village's layout is symmetrical, in the form of paired, horseshoe-shaped roomblocks. Some pitstructures feature paired floor vaults, paired sipapus, or paired male and female burials.[4]

"Regular" pitstructures 5–7 m in diameter are located in front of room arcs at both McPhee and Grass Mesa villages. Larger pitstructures, however, exhibit some important differences on either side of the Dolores River (figure 4.8). Archaeologists working in the northern San Juan categorize larger pitstructures into two varieties—"oversized pitstructures" and "great kivas" (Adler and Wilshusen 1990; Blinman 1989; Lightfoot 1988; Orcutt, Blinman, and Kohler 1990; Wilshusen and Wilson 1995). Oversized pitstructures are 9–11 m in diameter and, like some regular pitstructures, have special floor features called vaults or sipapus (Wilshusen 1989). Great kivas, by contrast, have diameters approaching 20 m or more and contain few distinctive floor features. Interestingly, oversized pitstructures are found at sites on the west side of the Dolores River, and great kivas are found on the east side. Oversized pitstructures, such as those at McPhee Village, tend to be located inside enclosed plazas. Great kivas, like the one at Grass Mesa Village, tend to be situated away from domestic architecture.

Oversized pitstructures and great kivas may represent two different attempts to ameliorate the tensions of village life and create a space for social integration. Members of the communities on both sides of the river may have participated in each others' ceremonies and may have even been members of each others' ritual societies, yet they retained some degree of separateness in terms of local social and ritual organization, as expressed by the architectural differences between oversized pitstructures and great kivas. Ritual participation at McPhee Village may have been somewhat exclusionary—oversized pitstructures, with their special floor features and relatively restricted spatial access, may have been used primarily for ritual activities, perhaps involving only certain segments of the community. Ritual at Grass Mesa Village, by contrast, may have been more accessible—freely approachable great kivas may have been flexible community spaces used for a variety of ritual and other activities (Lipe et al. 1988:134; Schachner 2001).

The intense Pueblo I occupation of the northern San Juan came to an end by 880. Social organization seems to have broken down, or perhaps the ritual system that helped hold these large villages together failed (Schachner 2001). At Grass Mesa Village, surface roomblocks were abandoned, and associated pitstructures were burned (Lipe et al. 1988:1,272–1,275). At McPhee Village, the oversized pitstructures, as well as some other pitstructures, were burned. In subsequent decades, the southern San Juan—the area Chacoanists refer to as the San Juan Basin—became the locus of the most intensive Ancestral Puebloan settlement. But before turning to those developments, we should look briefly at life in the southern San Juan Basin during the period of intense northern Pueblo I aggregation.

South of the River in the San Juan Basin, 700–875.

The San Juan Basin south of the river was far from empty between 700 and 875, but there were no large, aggregated village clusters like those in the northern San Juan. Rather, settlements were small and scattered across the landscape. Construction techniques and pottery styles differ slightly in the two regions, and the Pueblo I period is better studied in the north—two factors that have led archaeologists to misidentify or under-report sites dating from 700 to 875 in the southern San Juan (Windes n.d.a). Archaeologists working south of the San Juan River have expected Pueblo I pueblos to contain upright slab foundations and jacal walls, but in the relatively treeless San Juan Basin, Pueblo I builders did not use jacal—rather, they topped upright slabs with adobe "turtlebacks" and embedded sandstone spalls. In the shifting aeolian sands of the Basin, these sites can be virtually impossible to identify without excavation (for example, Loebig 2000). Differing pottery styles are another source of confusion. North of the San Juan River, the

Pueblo I period is signaled by the invention of neckbanded grayware pottery, but this marker does not correctly identify Pueblo I sites south of the river, where people did not use neckbanded pottery until the late 800s.

Pueblo I sites south of the San Juan River cannot match those north of the river in size and scope, but perhaps 2,000 people lived in small pueblos scattered across the San Juan Basin during this period (Wilshusen and Ortman 1999; Wilshusen and Van Dyke 2006). These settlements were home to 10–30 people. Clusters of small Pueblo I sites are found along the slopes of the Chuska Mountains, across the western Basin, on the South Chaco Slope, and along the Rio Puerco of the West.[5] In Chaco Canyon, Pueblo I roomblocks cluster at the mouth of nearly every major drainage on the south side of the canyon, from the Escavada Wash in the west to Shabik'eshchee Village in the east.[6]

Windes (n.d.a) documented one unusually large southern settlement, ceramically dated to ca. 800, approximately 8 km south of Chaco Canyon along the South Fork of the Fajada Wash. The South Fork community likely contained several hundred people—a size comparable to large, northern villages—but the population was not as densely packed. Rather, a string of 26 small pueblos was scattered across an area of 3.4 sq km. The community is of interest not only for its relatively large size but also because, like Basketmakers before them and Chacoans after them, South Fork inhabitants were interested in visibility. At the heart of the South Fork community, builders constructed two small pueblos with sandstone slabs set horizontally in mud. This early example of Type 1 Chacoan masonry resulted in buildings with greater vertical relief than the surrounding sites. All but two of the other sites in the community had a clear line of sight to these two sandstone structures. One of these—a horseshoe-shaped, upright slab enclosure with an excellent view of Fajada Butte—may have been linked to the Type 1 structures by a very early road segment. All the South Fork sites are also positioned with lines of sight to Hosta Butte, Huerfano Mountain, or Fajada Butte. Along the Kin Klizhin Wash, the next drainage to the east, is a second, similar community of ten small pueblos. All the Kin Klizhin Wash sites also are positioned within view of either Fajada Butte or Huerfano Mountain. Windes notes that these lines of sight would not have been present from other positions within the communities—rather, they appear to be intentional.

In the last decades of the 800s, as the large settlements north of the San Juan River succumbed to conflagration and collapse, people began moving south of the river back into the San Juan Basin. By 925, the aggregated villages of the north were essentially abandoned, giving way to new patterns of settlement in the south. Many areas of the San Juan Basin, including

Chaco Canyon, show evidence of a dramatic increase in settlement between 875 and 925, just as the villages north of the river were depopulated (Wilshusen and Ortman 1999; Wilshusen and Van Dyke 2006; Windes n.d.a).

Kidder originally assigned a range of 700–900 to the Pueblo I period, but this 200-year designation encompasses both the low-key Basin occupation of 700–875 and the concentrated new settlements founded by migrants from the northern San Juan after 875. As a result, there is some confusion about what archaeologists south of the San Juan River mean when we label a site Pueblo I. If we follow Kidder's Pecos Classification and assign a Pueblo I designation to both kinds of sites, then we hinder our ability to recognize important social changes and shifts in population. I propose that we keep the Pueblo I designation in the southern San Juan for the 700–875 period and consider large, post-875 "late Pueblo I" sites to herald the beginning of the Early Bonito phase.

The Rise of Proto-Great Houses and the Early Bonito Phase

By the early 900s, Ancestral Puebloan migrants had gathered in more than 30 large communities south of the San Juan River (table 4.2). These communities stretched from the La Plata Valley down the flanks of the Chuska Mountains, across the western and southern San Juan Basin, through Chaco Canyon, and into the Red Mesa Valley (figure 4.9). Although several major settlements were located in Chaco Canyon, the canyon was just one locality among many. But ideas that later became important at Chaco—the coming together of people from different backgrounds, the creation of links to the past, the visibility of specific topographic landmarks—were present in the tenth-century communities of the San Juan Basin.

Architectural data from 900s communities suggest that the northern San Juan migrants brought with them the two models for community organization developed at sites such as McPhee and Grass Mesa villages. In Chaco Canyon and in other scattered Basin locations, the McPhee model predominated, leading to the development of communities centered around proto-great houses. I have adopted the term *proto-great house* to distinguish this Early Bonito architectural innovation from later, Classic Bonito–phase great houses. Across the western Basin and into the Red Mesa Valley, by contrast, many tenth-century communities lack proto-great houses but are clustered around great kivas. In a few communities, such as Skunk Springs along the Chuskan slopes, Puebloans built proto-great houses *and* great kivas.

Early Bonito site chronologies are based on architecture, ceramics, and, in a few cases, tree-ring dates. Plain graywares, neckbanded graywares, and

Table 4.2 Proto-Great House and Great Kiva Communities in the San Juan Basin, AD 875–925

	Site[1]	Location	Early Bonito Dates (AD)	Proto-Great House?	Early Great Kiva?	Excavation Data?	Visible Landforms	References
1	Cedar Hill	Animas Valley	885–915	yes	yes	yes	none	Wilshusen and Wilson 1995
2	Morris 33	La Plata Valley	831	yes	yes	yes	Mesa Verde, Shiprock, Sleeping Ute Mountain	Marshall et al. 1979:303–304; Morris 1939:75–84
3	Squaw Springs (Morris 40)	La Plata Valley	"Pueblo I"	unclear	yes	yes	Hosta Butte, Huerfano Mountain	Marshall et al. 1979:304; Morris 1939:55–56
4	Hogback	Chaco River Valley	early 900s	yes	yes	no	Bennett Peak, Ford Butte	Marshall et al. 1979:241–245
5	Newcomb	Chuskan slopes	850–early 900s	no	yes	no	Bennett Peak, Ford Butte, Hogback, Huerfano Mountain, Shiprock	Gilpin, Dykeman, and Reed 1996; Morris 1959
6	Skunk Springs	Chuskan slopes	late 800s–early 900s	yes	yes	no	Bennett Peak, Ford Butte, Hosta Butte, Huerfano Mountain, Shiprock, Sleeping Ute Mountain	Gilpin, Dykeman, and Reed 1996; Marshall et al. 1979:109–113; Peckham 1969; Windes and Ford 1992:78–79
7	Great Bend	Chaco River Corridor	850–950	yes	no	no	Bennett Peak, Ford Butte	Marshall et al. 1979:33–36; Windes n.d.a
8	Willow Canyon	Chaco River Corridor	late 800s–950	yes	slab-lined enclosure	no	Bennett Peak, Ford Butte, Shiprock	Marshall et al. 1979:91–94; Windes n.d.a
9	El Llano	Chaco River tributary	875–925	no[2]	no	no	Bennett Peak, Ford Butte, Hosta Butte, Shiprock	Bradley and Sullivan 1994; Windes n.d.a
10	Casa Abajo (Indian Creek)	Chaco River tributary	875–1000	yes	no	no	Bennett Peak, Hosta Butte, Shiprock	Bradley and Sullivan 1994; Marshall et al. 1979:48–49; Windes n.d.a
11	Lake Valley	Chaco River Corridor	875–1000	yes	no	no	Hosta Butte	Marshall et al. 1979:73–75; Windes n.d.a
12	Kin Bineola	Chaco River tributary	890–1025	yes	no	no	Hosta Butte	Marshall et al. 1979:57–68; Van Dyke 2002; Windes n.d.a

Table 4.2 Proto-Great House and Great Kiva Communities in the San Juan Basin, AD 875–925 (continued)

	Site[1]	Location	Early Bonito Dates (AD)	Proto-Great House?	Early Great Kiva?	Excavation Data?	Visible Landforms	References
13	Kin Bineola South (29Mc291 and 261)	Chaco River tributary	890–1025	yes	yes	no	Hosta Butte, Bennett Peak	Van Dyke and Powers 2002
14	Casa del Rio	Chaco Wash (west)	late 800s– early 900s	yes	no	no	West Point	Windes n.d.a; Windes and Ford 1992:77
15	Padilla Well	Chaco Wash (west)	800s–950	yes	no[3]	no	West Point	Marshall and Sofaer 1988:76–82; Windes n.d.a; Windes et al. 2000:39
16	Peñasco Blanco	Chaco Canyon	860–900s	yes	no	no	29SJ423, Huerfano Mountain, West Point	Lekson 1986:99, 104–105; Van Dyke 2007; Windes and Ford 1992:77
17	South Gap: Pueblo Bonito	Chaco Canyon	860–935	yes	oversized pitstructure	yes	none	Judd 1964; Lekson 1986:127–132; Stein, Ford, and Friedman 2003; Windes 2003; Windes and Ford 1992:77, 1996
18	Fajada Gap: Kin Nahasbas	Chaco Canyon	late 800s– early 900s	yes	oversized pitstructure	yes	Fajada Butte, Hosta Butte	Luhrs 1935; Mathien and Windes 1988; Vivian and Reiter 1960:53–61; Windes n.d.a
19	Fajada Gap: Una Vida	Chaco Canyon	860–960	yes	no	no	Fajada Butte, Hosta Butte	Gillespie 1986; Lekson 1986:83, 90–91; Windes and Ford 1992:77
20	Fajada Gap: 29SJ1253	Chaco Canyon	early 900s– early 1000s	no	yes	no	Fajada Butte, Hosta Butte, Mount Taylor	Marshall et al. 1979:273
21	Chaco East	Chaco Canyon	875–950	yes	no	no	—	Windes n.d.a; Windes et al. 2000
22	Pueblo Pintado	Chaco Wash (east)	late 800s– early 900s	yes	no	no	—	Windes n.d.a; Windes et al. 2000:39
23	Guadalupe	east of Chaco Canyon	918–1050	yes	no[3]	yes	Cabezon Peak	Baker 1983; Baker and Durand 2003; Durand and Durand 2000; Pippin 1987; Washburn 1974
24	South Fork	south of Chaco Canyon	ca. 800	yes	slab-lined enclosure	no	Fajada Butte, Huerfano Mountain	Windes n.d.a

No.	Name	Region	Date			Landmark	References
25	Standing Rock	South Chaco Slope	860–960	yes	no	Hosta Butte, Huerfano Mountain	Bradley and Sullivan 1994; Windes and Ford 1992:177
26	Peach Springs	South Chaco Slope	late 800s–950	yes	no[3]	Bennett Peak, Huerfano Mountain	Gilpin and Purcell 2000; Marshall et al. 1979:91–94; Powers, Gillespie, and Lekson 1983:72, 86; Windes and Ford 1992:77
27	Dye Brush/Dzil Nda Kai	South Chaco Slope	"late Pueblo I–Pueblo II"	yes	no	Bennett Peak, Ford Butte, Huerfano Mountain, West Point	Marshall and Sofaer 1988:36–41
28	Los Rayos	South Chaco Slope	850–950	no	yes	Huerfano Mountain, West Point	Marshall and Sofaer 1988:42–45; Van Dyke 2003b
29	Coolidge	Red Mesa Valley	"Pueblo I"	no	yes	—	Marshall et al. 1979:293
30	Tse Bee Kintsoh	Red Mesa Valley	885–991	no	yes	—	Kantner 1996
31	Andrews	Red Mesa Valley	880–950	no	yes (2)	—	Van Dyke 1999a, 2001
32	Haystack D	Red Mesa Valley	"Pueblo I"	no	yes	Hosta Butte, Mount Taylor	Marshall et al. 1979:294
33	El Rito	Red Mesa Valley	860–950	yes	no	—	Powers, Gillespie, and Lekson 1983:216, 222–225
34	San Mateo	Red Mesa Valley	"Pueblo I"	no	yes	Mount Taylor	Marshall et al. 1979:295
35	Allentown/Whitewater	Rio Puerco of the West	"Pueblo I"	no	slab-lined enclosure yes	—	Marshall et al. 1979:289; Roberts 1939

1. This is not meant to be an exhaustive list. A number of communities with late Pueblo II great houses are reported to have early Pueblo II components: Bluff Great House (Cameron and Lekson 2000; Jalbert and Cameron 2000); Edge of the Cedars (Hurst 2000), and Wallace (B. Bradley 1974, 1993), all north of the San Juan; Morris 41, in the La Plata Valley (McKenna and Toll 1992; Powers, Gillespie, and Lekson 1983:147); Sterling, along the San Juan (Bice 1983; McKenna and Toll 1992; Powers, Gillespie, and Lekson 1983:139–141); and Cove, in Red Rock Valley (Reed and Hensler 1999). However, dates for these early great houses, where available, place them toward the middle 900s, so they are not included in this table. Also reported to have mid-900s great kivas are a number of communities with late Pueblo II great houses: Goodman Point and Mancos Canyon (Varien 1999), both north of the San Juan; Beth's Great Kiva/Figueredo Wash (Gilpin, personal communication, April 2003), on the South Chaco Slope; and Kin Lichee, Sanders (Fletcher 1994), Fort Defiance, Tse Chizzi, and Wide Ruins (Gilpin, personal communication, April 2003), all along the Rio Puerco or in eastern Arizona.

2. There is no clear proto-great house or great kiva in the El Llano community, but the aptly named House of the Giant Midden is unusual and indicates substantial occupation.

3. An unexcavated associated great kiva at this site is dated on the basis of surface ceramics to the Classic Bonito phase. However, it is possible that excavation would reveal an Early Bonito-phase component to the structure.

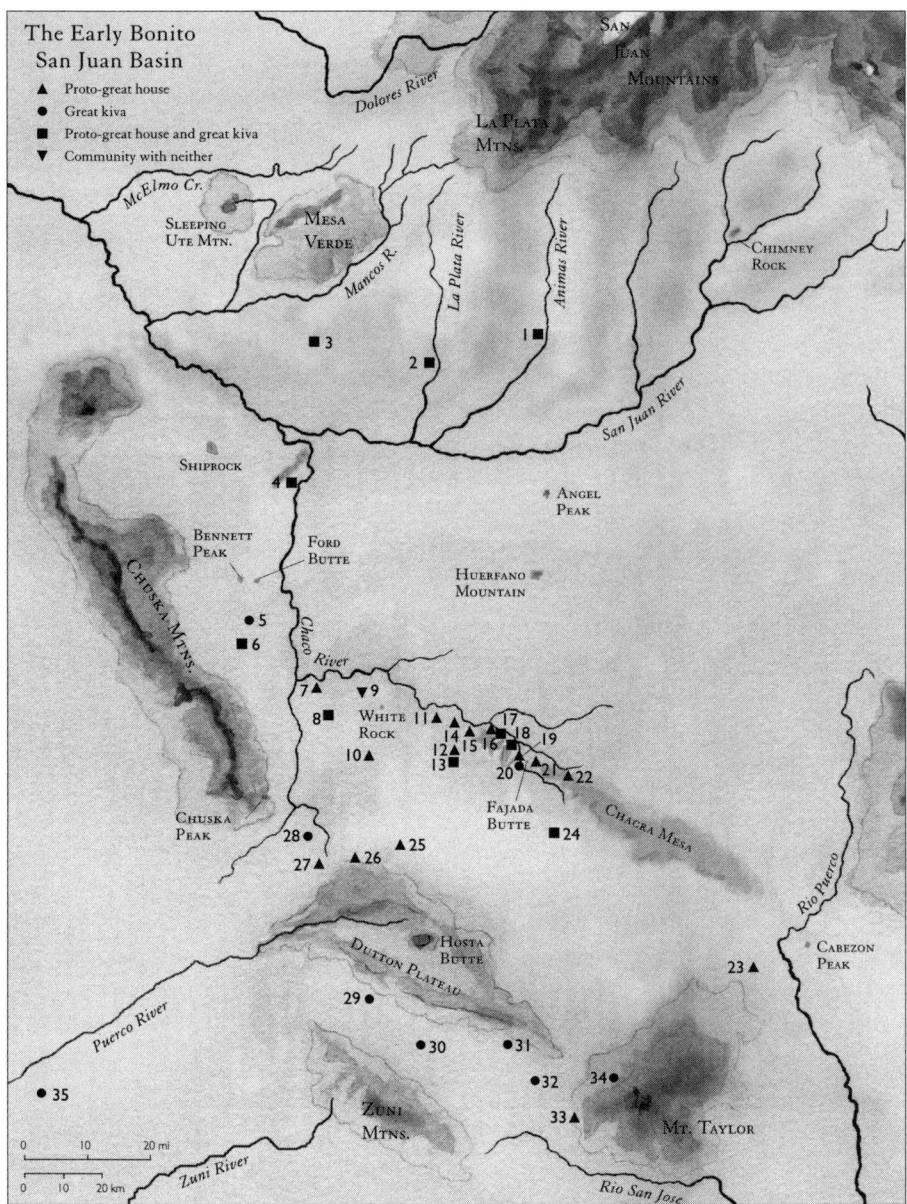

Figure 4.9. Early Bonito–phase communities in the San Juan Basin. The numbers correspond to the sites listed in table 4.2. Drafted by Molly O'Halloran.

Kiatuthlanna and Red Mesa Black-on-white dominate Early Bonito ceramic assemblages. At some communities, occupation ended at around 950. At others, occupation continued through the Classic Bonito phase and into the

82   The Chaco Experience

1200s. In many cases, Classic Bonito–phase Chacoan great houses were later erected on top of or near the proto-great houses. Classic Bonito great house builders sometimes incorporated the earlier structure, sometimes razed it and built over it, or sometimes chose to erect a completely new building nearby. These choices have important implications for archaeologists' ability (or lack thereof) to recognize Early Bonito structures that lie beneath or adjacent to unexcavated Classic Bonito buildings.

Early Bonito migrants positioned their new settlements near arable land and water, but emotional or symbolic connections to landscape also played a role in site locations. In particular, the ideas of visibility and social memory helped inform settlement choices. Migrants almost uniformly situated new communities in view of significant topographic landmarks such as Huerfano Mountain or Hosta Butte, and they frequently chose locations near ancestral Basketmaker III settlements. By the early 900s, common elements of an Ancestral Puebloan worldview were in play among communities that possibly had different kinds of internal social and ritual organization.

Early Bonito Settlements in the San Juan Basin and Chaco Canyon

With the invention of the proto-great house on the Chacoan landscape, we can consider that we have entered the Early Bonito phase. Early Bonito–phase settlements across the San Juan Basin contain approximately five to sixty small, discrete domestic pueblos. Most also include one or more large, central, community structures such as a proto-great house, great kiva, or slab-lined enclosure. Proto-great houses do not conform to the entire canon of formal attributes used to identify Classic Bonito great houses (Gladwin 1945), but they were prominent buildings in late 800s/early 900s community contexts.[7] Aggregated northern Pueblo I communities such as McPhee may have contained the seeds of the proto-great house idea, but the structure came into its own in the San Juan Basin several decades later, thanks in part, perhaps, to the ready availability of tabular sandstone (Windes n.d.a). Proto-great house builders employed sandstone slabs, as did earlier Pueblo I builders, but rather than place one row of slabs vertically into the ground as wall supports, they placed multiple slabs horizontally. The builders roughly shaped dark brown slabs of Menefee sandstone and stacked the slabs into Type 1 masonry walls, held together with abundant mortar and spall chinking. The resulting full-standing masonry structures were durable, highly visible features on the landscape. Proto-great houses were larger overall and contained larger rooms than did nearby, smaller domestic pueblos. Builders further enhanced the structures' prominence by situating them on rises or mesa tops.

Proto-great houses, situated in the center of a dispersed cluster of small sites, may represent a new way of thinking about community, developed in the wake of social upheaval that accompanied movement south from the aggregated pueblos of the northern San Juan (Wilshusen and Van Dyke 2006). It is not clear whether proto-great houses were the homes of important people or locations for communitywide events, or perhaps both. Archaeologists have excavated very few Early Bonito proto-great houses, but substantial associated trash middens suggest that they were domestic structures. However, proto-great house trash visible on the ground surface does not look different from the trash associated with nearby, smaller domestic sites. Further investigations are needed to clarify the social role of these prominent structures within Early Bonito communities.

Residents of some settlements constructed great kivas, either instead of or in addition to proto-great houses, as community focal points. Archaeologists in the San Juan Basin widely use the term *great kiva* for tenth-century circular depressions 10 m or more in diameter that are sometimes visibly lined with upright slabs. Because few of these features have been excavated, it is not clear whether the great kiva/oversized pitstructure distinction seen in the northern San Juan in the Pueblo I period continues to hold true south of the river during the tenth century. Two excavated great kivas in Chaco Canyon have floor features suggestive of northern oversized pitstructures (see table 4.1), so additional excavation may reveal important differences among circular, subterranean Early Bonito structures. Yet another type of community architecture—a large, subrectangular or horseshoe-shaped surface enclosure sometimes called a "dance court"—appears in several Early Bonito settlements. These enclosures are defined by double or single rows of upright slabs. The functions of the enclosures remain ambiguous.

Migrants from the northern San Juan region could have logically followed the river valleys of the San Juan, Animas, La Plata, and Chaco southwards as they spread into the San Juan Basin. In fact, many Early Bonito sites are located along this route (see table 4.2; see figure 4.9). In the Animas and La Plata valleys, Ancestral Puebloans founded Early Bonito–phase settlements at Cedar Hill, Morris 33, and Squaw Springs. Near the confluence of the Chaco and the San Juan rivers, they established Hogback. Continuing southwards along the eastern flanks of the Chuska Mountains, Early Bonito peoples founded Newcomb and created an extensive settlement at Skunk Springs.

Skunk Springs is a good example of a major Early Bonito settlement. The site was an important place in the Ancestral Pueblo world for four centuries, with occupation beginning in the late 800s and extending into the 1200s. The Early Bonito proto-great house perches high on a south-facing

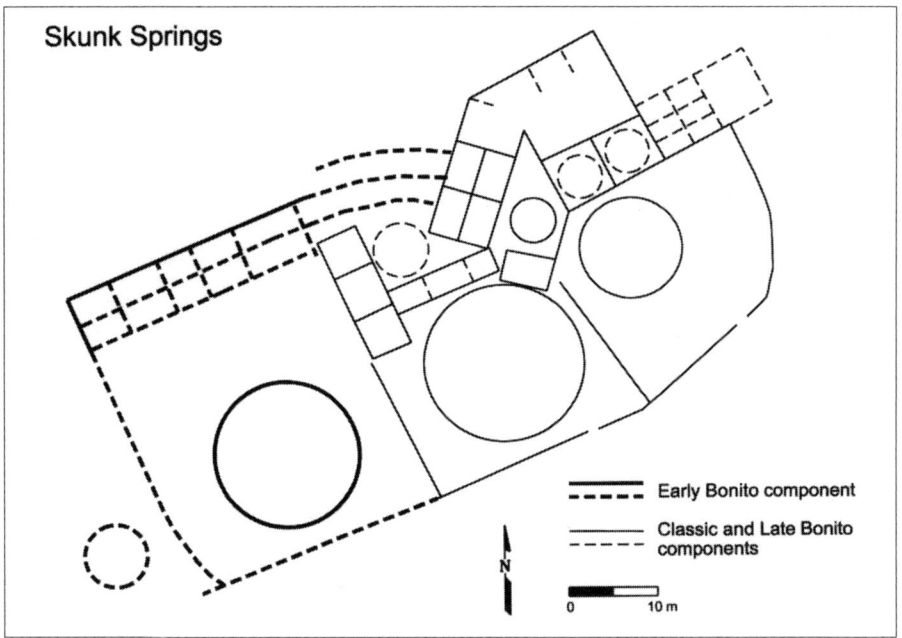

Figure 4.10. Plan of Early Bonito–phase Skunk Springs, after Marshall and others 1979:112.

escarpment of Grey Mesa, 60 m above a broad, well-watered valley. The proto-great house was built using upright slab foundations instead of Type 1 masonry, but it was quite large, containing a south-facing crescent of at least 20 rooms fronted by a 16-m-diameter great kiva within an enclosed plaza (figure 4.10). During later centuries, builders erected a Classic Bonito–phase great house on top and to the east of the proto-great house. An extensive and equally long-lived community of domestic pueblos stretches west of the great house for 13 sq km across the mesa top. A second large, unexcavated, late-ninth-century structure underlying several tenth-century small houses may represent a second proto-great house. None of these sites have been excavated.

Skunk Springs was a favored spot for Ancestral Puebloan settlement, in part because it offered access to a wealth of resources—wood, lithic raw materials, pottery temper, and big game in the Chuska Mountains and well-watered arable farmland. Skunk Springs is a likely locale for the production of trachyte-tempered Chuskan pottery, found in Early (and Classic) Bonito–phase communities from the Chuskan slopes to Chaco Canyon (V. King 2003; Mills, Carpenter, and Grimm 1997). Inhabitants also used an abundance of colorful Narbona Pass chert, which outcrops in the Chuska

Mountains 20 km to the southwest and, like trachyte-tempered pottery, appears in high frequencies at settlements across the western San Juan Basin (Cameron 1984, 2001; Ward 2004).

Situated well above most of the Basin floor, the Skunk Springs locale provided exceptional vistas to the north, east, and south. The view from the proto-great house encompasses Beautiful Mountain, Bennett Peak, Ford Butte, Shiprock, the Hogback, the La Plata Mountains, Hosta Butte, and the Dutton Plateau. A sweep of small pueblos are scattered in the valley below Grey Mesa. To the southeast, the eroded knob of White Rock connects Skunk Springs via line of sight to West Mesa in Chaco Canyon.

From Skunk Springs, Ancestral Pueblo migrants could have traveled downslope to the east, gradually descending into the Chuska Valley, encountering the "great bend" of the Chaco River after 20 km. By following the Chaco River to the south/southeast, our travelers would have arrived in Chaco Canyon after some 75 km of meanders. This "Chaco River Corridor" and its tributary drainages are loaded with Early Bonito communities, including Great Bend, Willow Canyon, El Llano, Indian Creek, Lake Valley, Kin Bineola, Casa del Rio, and Padilla Well (Windes n.d.a). The west end of Chaco Canyon is heralded by the sheer white cliffs of West Point—the west end of West Mesa—rising 165 m (540 ft) above the river. This visually stunning escarpment is visible from points across the San Juan Basin. After crossing the Chaco/Escavada wash confluence, travelers would have entered Chaco Canyon proper. Early Bonito–phase settlers built communities at five places where tributary drainages enter the canyon or create gaps through Chacra Mesa: the Chaco/Escavada wash confluence; South Gap; Fajada Gap; Wild Horse Canyon; and Pintado Canyon (Windes et al. 2000). All would have been excellent farming locales, and all are home to proto-great houses surrounded by communities of as many as sixty small sites (figure 4.11).

By 950, as many as 1,350 people may have been living in Chaco Canyon (Wilshusen and Van Dyke 2006). Because most of these sites later became major, Classic Bonito great houses, I will discuss them in some detail here, moving through the canyon as our migrants might have, from west to east. At the Chaco/Escavada wash confluence, Early Bonito peoples founded Padilla Well in a cul-de-sac below West Point, as well as Peñasco Blanco on a northeast-facing finger of West Mesa. Peñasco Blanco is best known as a Classic Bonito great house, but tree-ring dates place initial construction of the building in the 800s. Positioned 70 m above the confluence of the Chaco River and the Escavada Wash, Peñasco Blanco overlooks a large sand dune that may have created a shallow lake along the Chaco Wash during the early 900s (Force et al. 2002). By 915, the proto-great house consisted of a two-story, 120-m-long, arc-shaped structure of Type I masonry.

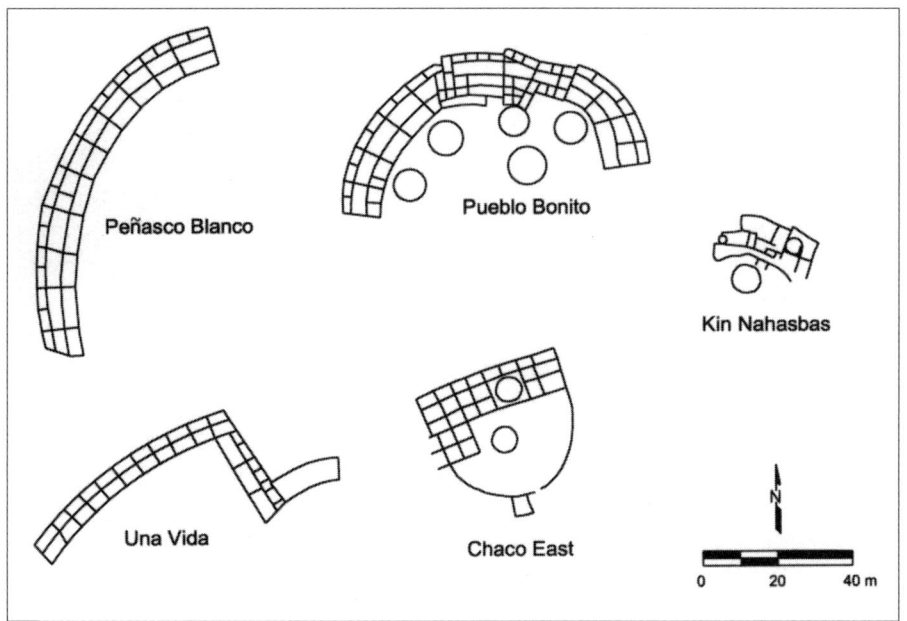

Figure 4.11. Plans of five Early Bonito–phase proto-great houses in Chaco Canyon. Peñasco Blanco, Pueblo Bonito, and Una Vida are based on plans in Lekson 1986. Kin Nahasbas is based on a plan in Mathien and Windes 1988:20, figure 5. Chaco East is based on a plan in Windes et al. 2000:49, figure 4.6.

At South Gap, approximately 5 km east of Peñasco Blanco, Ancestral Puebloans erected a second cluster of Early Bonito sites, including Pueblo Bonito (Lekson 1986:127–132; Windes 2003). Although Pueblo Bonito ultimately became the center of the Chacoan world and lent its name to the Bonito phases, tree-ring dates tell us that the structure began as a proto-great house during the mid-ninth century, with three small roomblocks dating to before the 860s, the 860s, and the 890s, respectively.[8] An eastern wing two and three stories high was added between 920 and 935. Domestic refuse and floor features associated with the earliest occupation of Pueblo Bonito indicate that at least part of the building was a residence. The eastern arc of 20–25 rooms contained living suites with domestic features, as well as "big-room suites" of uniformly large, empty rooms. In an arrangement that recalls the layout of McPhee Village, the horseshoe-shaped arc of roomblocks faced an oversized pitstructure.[9] Other South Gap sites on the canyon's south side were clearly domestic. Builders used puddled adobe or stacked sandstone to create roomblocks with habitation and storage rooms, all generally smaller than the rooms in Pueblo Bonito. The domestic sites also contain pitstructures, ramadas, and extramural living floors (McKenna 1984; Vivian 1990:194–202).

Another 5 km up the canyon to the southeast, Fajada Gap was home to a third cluster of Early Bonito sites, including two proto-great houses—Kin Nahasbas and Una Vida (Windes et al. 2000:39). Kin Nahasbas is atop a sandstone hill connected to the north escarpment of Chaco Canyon by a narrow ridge. Here, a block of rooms called the Old House exhibits Type I masonry. Directly south of the Old House, an oversized pitstructure contains floor features and artifacts—selenite wands, Narbona Pass chert, and iron concretions—similar to those found in oversized pitstructures north of the San Juan River (Wilshusen 1989). An unexcavated, Early Bonito great kiva (29SJ1253) perches on a colluvial ridge 1.5 km southwest of Kin Nahasbas amid scatters of small, domestic pueblos (McKenna 1984; Vivian and Mathews 1965; Vivian 1990:194–202; Windes 1993, n.d.a). A modern viewer looking northeast from the great kiva can just discern the traces of a ramp and a linear alignment connecting this structure with Kin Nahasbas. Although such features are notoriously difficult to date, this may be an early example of a road segment, perhaps used for processions between the proto-great house and the great kiva. East of Kin Nahasbas along the canyon face, Una Vida began during the 860s as a two-story arc of six rooms. Chacoans added an L-shaped wing of thirty two-story Type 1 masonry rooms between 930 and 950 and made a few more Type I additions between 950 and 960.

Approximately 14 km farther east up Chaco Canyon lies the fourth cluster of Early Bonito sites in the canyon—the Chaco East community (Windes et al. 2000). Here, settlers built a single-story, Type 1 masonry proto-great house on the south side of the canyon. The proto-great house contains 25 rooms and is surrounded by a community of 11 domestic sites. Most ceramic and lithic artifacts are of local origin (Windes n.d.a). The final Early Bonito settlement in Chaco is situated near the canyon's head another 8 km to the east, where Pintado Canyon slices through Chacra Mesa. At Pueblo Pintado, Windes (n.d.a) has identified two groups of seven domestic pueblos, 3 km apart, both ceramically dated to 875–925. Based on ceramic, lithic, and architectural differences, Windes suggests that the two site clusters represent two groups of migrants into the area—the east group from the northern San Juan and the west group from the Mount Taylor area to the south.

The pattern of Early Bonito settlements continues beyond Chaco Canyon to the east, south, and west, down the Fajada Wash and across the South Chaco Slope to the flanks of Lobo Mesa and the Dutton Plateau (see table 4.2). Guadalupe lies 30 km southeast of the east end of Chacra Mesa.[10] Dalton Pass provided southern passage into the Red Mesa Valley. At the Andrews community, population surges between 880–920 and 920–960 indicate that immigrants were moving into the area during the Early Bonito phase (Van Dyke 1999a, 2001).[11] Farther to the southwest, along the Rio Puerco of the West, are still more Early Bonito settlements. However, it is not clear that most or even all of the settlers in southern regions were arriving from north of the San Juan River. The southern Basin sustained a base population from Basketmaker III times onward and was home to the Loma Alta and White Mound–Kiatuthlana "subregional variants" of Ancestral Pueblo culture (Vivian 1990:136–153). Early Bonito–phase settlements in the southern Basin might represent aggregations of these local peoples or migrations from other areas, or both.

Proto-Great Houses and Great Kivas:
Two Models of Community Organization

Both proto-great houses and great kivas served as focal points for Early Bonito–phase communities across the San Juan Basin. Great kivas and great houses are closely associated in later, Classic Bonito–phase sites, but these two types of architecture do not uniformly co-occur in Early Bonito settlements. Tenth-century domestic pueblos are sometimes clustered around great kivas instead of proto-great houses (Eddy 1977; Martin and Rinaldo 1939; Powers, Gillespie, and Lekson 1983:26; Vivian 1990:174). A systematic examination of the distribution of proto-great houses and great kivas at thirty-one Early Bonito communities in the San Juan Basin reveals some interesting patterns (see table 4.2). At least twenty-four of the communities contain proto-great houses (see table 4.2), and at least nineteen contain some type of large, circular, community structure such as a great kiva, an oversized pitstructure, or a slab-lined enclosure. However, the overlap between proto-great houses and circular structures is not great (see figure 4.9). Only nine Early Bonito communities contain *both* proto-great houses *and* circular structures. In the absence of excavation data from most of these sites, gauging the strength of this pattern is difficult, but it is certainly provocative, particularly when one looks at the regional distribution of the various communities.

Many Early Bonito communities that contain great kivas but lack proto-great houses are located in the Red Mesa Valley and the southern part of the San Juan Basin. These sites include Los Rayos, Coolidge, Tse Bee Kintsoh, Andrews, Haystack D, and San Mateo. Proto-great houses without great kivas, by contrast, are concentrated in Chaco Canyon, the Chaco River Corridor, and the South Chaco Slope. These sites include Casa Abajo, Lake Valley, Kin Bineola, Casa del Rio, Padilla Well, Peñasco Blanco, Chaco East, Pueblo Pintado, Guadalupe, Standing Rock, and Peach Springs. If we consider that the two excavated, subterranean, circular structures at Pueblo Bonito and Kin Nahasbas more closely resemble the oversized pitstructures of the northern San Juan than they do great kivas, then the only good candidate for an Early Bonito–phase great kiva in Chaco Canyon is the unexcavated site 29SJ1253, in Fajada Gap.[12]

These patterns suggest to me that perhaps two models of community organization were in operation during the founding of Early Bonito–phase settlements in the San Juan Basin. One, centered around proto-great houses, may have taken hold in Chaco Canyon. Another model, centered around great kivas, may have been present in the Red Mesa Valley and some areas of the southern Basin. These two community configurations echo observations made by other researchers in related contexts. Remember, Wilshusen and Ortman (1999) tentatively identified two cultural groups living in the Dolores River Valley between 840 and 880—one great kiva–centered and one centered around horseshoe-shaped roomblocks. Perhaps when people moved south from the northern San Juan around 880, these two cultural groups maintained their distinctiveness. Proto-great house–centered groups may have moved into Chaco Canyon, but great kiva–centered groups did not. Recall that Windes and Ford (1992), as well as Wilshusen and Ortman (1999:391), see connections between McPhee Village and early Pueblo Bonito.

Alternatively, great kiva–centered communities may represent southern Basin integrative practices that have their own deep, historical roots in the area. The presence of a southern group of settlers is supported by Windes' (n.d.a) observations at Pueblo Pintado and by Vivian's (1990) identification of southern Loma Alta and White Mound–Kiatuthlana architectural patterns. Vivian (1989, 1990) follows Kluckhohn (1939) in arguing that two distinct ethnicities are present at Chaco—one northern, one southern—and that these ethnicities are traceable back into Basketmaker III times. A northern/southern distinction of some sort is also supported by distributions of nonlocal ceramics and lithics across the San Juan Basin; people along the Chaco River Corridor in the western Basin were part of different exchange networks than their neighbors to the south, along the Dutton Plateau and in the Red Mesa Valley (Van Dyke 1996, 2000). A strong southern pattern of great kiva–centered communities persisted into the eleventh and twelfth centuries at sites on the southern margins of the Chaco world, such as Tla Kii, Cothrun's, and Hough's (Herr 2001).

Ortiz (1969:29) describes how Tewa moieties came to exist as part of the journey south from the northern place of emergence. "In the very beginning we were one people. Then we divided into Summer people and Winter people; in the end we came together as we are today" (Tewa elder, quoted in Ortiz 1969:29). Eventually, the two moieties reunited at the center place.

Although it would be precipitous to link proto-great houses and great kivas to two different ethnicities, let alone moieties, this pattern in the regional proto-great house and great kiva data invites further investigation. A century later, during the Classic Bonito phase (1020–1100), ritual events at Chaco Canyon drew peoples from all over the greater San Juan Basin. At this point, Chacoans formalized the great kiva and incorporated it into the plazas of many Classic Bonito canyon great houses. If Early Bonito proto-great houses and great kivas do represent two kinds of community organization and if Early Bonito Chaco was settled primarily by proto-great house groups, then the incorporation and formalization of the Chacoan great kiva into canyon architecture during the 1000s might be interpreted as part of the social integration of great kiva–oriented communities into a larger, canyon-centric, Classic Bonito Chacoan world.

Memory, Visibility, and Sacred Geography in the Early Bonito Phase

As the trickle of late-ninth-century San Juan Basin settlers became a torrent, three key concepts—memory, visibility, and sacred geography—seem to have been critically important in the placement of Early Bonito buildings and settlements. These ideas had been part of a developing Puebloan worldview since the Basketmaker III period. On the sky-filled Basin landscape, Early Bonito sacred geography seems to have included distinctive landforms such as Hosta Butte, Fajada Butte, Bennett Peak, Huerfano Mountain, and Mount Taylor. Proto-great houses, great kivas, and enclosures were almost always positioned to create lines of sight with one or more of these high places (see table 4.2). Some of these landmarks—such as Bennett Peak, with its nearby cluster of Pueblo I period sites—may also have signified an association with ancestors. Landforms and ancestral sites may have figured as the locations of special events in myths and oral traditions, or perhaps they were held to possess particular qualities or powers. Many peoples attach special significance to points of dramatic landscape change, prominent topographic features, and places that afford panoramic vistas:

> *Often these are places where concepts of an upper world, a lower world, and the earth plain come together visually in a striking manner. These are places where the center of the world may be experienced, where an axis mundi is located (Eliade 1964, 1978; Ouzman 1998; Paper 1990), for it is at these places that it is claimed a powerful connection between different levels and states of existence can be encountered. [Taçon 1999:37–38]*

Social and emotional connections to landscape, in addition to more practical concerns, likely figured into Ancestral Puebloan migrants' decisions about where to relocate. Migrants typically move to places about which they have detailed knowledge (Cameron 1995; Cordell 1995; Duff 1998). Although the San Juan Basin was relatively empty during the Pueblo I period, it was not completely devoid of villages, and the distance between, say, the Pueblo I community at Bennett Peak and McPhee Village along the Dolores River is only 125 km as the crow flies. Migrants moving north of the San Juan River in the early 700s, as well as their descendants moving back south in the late 800s, would have been separated in time by five or more generations, but northerners may have maintained contact with those who stayed behind.

Early Bonito migrants may well have had a sense of emotional attachment to the landscape of the San Juan Basin, underscored by the long-range visibility of specific landforms. The horizontal topography of the Colorado Plateau, punctuated by volcanic plugs, mountain ranges, and mesas, extends the visible world across hundreds of kilometers. Landforms such as Sleeping Ute Mountain and the La Plata Mountains can be seen over great distances. The 2,188-m-high spire of Shiprock is one example of a landform that provides a visual connection between the north and south of the San Juan River. Shiprock is visible from the Pueblo I settlement of Alkali Ridge, 110 km north of Chaco Canyon, all the way to the southern edge of the San Juan Basin, 125 km southeast of Chaco. The plug's distinctive shape can also be seen from the Chuskan slopes and the uplands of Mesa Verde. The lands south of the San Juan River were not alien territory—rather, Ancestral Puebloans remained connected to northern homelands across miles of terrain by the intervisibility of sacred peaks.

Early Bonito migrants likely would have been familiar, to some degree, with the Basin as an ancestral landscape. Although no members of the original move north would have been alive during the Early Bonito phase, places inhabited by Basketmaker ancestors could well have figured in songs and stories. Even if no stories or memories of the southern San Juan had survived over the generations, when northerners arrived in the San Juan Basin, clear evidence for the previous occupation of specific locales would have been impossible to miss. The extensive Basketmaker III occupation in Chaco Canyon might have been one of the attractions for Early Bonito migrants, who would have recognized the archaeological footprints of Basketmaker ancestors in the pitstructure depressions and refuse at Site 423 and Shabik'eshchee Village. Scattered grayware and whiteware potsherds, lithic tools and debitage, and pitstructure depressions—some of them burned—are quite visible today at Basketmaker III sites in the Basin and would have been even more obvious only 150–200 years after their initial abandonment. These places would have been imbued with meaning for the returning Puebloans, whether as highly charged locations of specific, storied past events or as a more general landscape of ancestors, remembered or constructed (Van Dyke and Alcock 2003).

Once in the San Juan Basin, Early Bonito settlers founded communities along drainages and confluences, with access to water and to good farmland. But within these familiar ecological parameters, settlers had choices as to where to locate specific buildings. Decisions about where to found a settlement—particularly where to built a proto-great house, great kiva, or slab-lined enclosure—were informed, to some degree, by visibility and social memory. Ancestral Puebloans were likely developing a sense of sacred geography as elements of the landscape took on iconic significance for them.

Nearly all Early Bonito community buildings are positioned in high places, with lines of sight to one or more prominent, distinctively shaped Basin landmarks such as Hosta Butte, Huerfano Mountain, or Bennett Peak (see table 4.2). In several cases, Early Bonitians carefully selected building sites to frame a particular landform within view. Earl Morris (1939:76) noted this at Morris 33, where the Early Bonito structure was positioned to provide "a comprehensive panorama of the surrounding country," with Shiprock framed through a gap in the escarpment to the southwest of the site. Shiprock, Bennett Peak, and Ford Butte are all quite visible from Chuskan sites such as Newcomb and Skunk Springs (figure 4.12). One or more of these dramatic volcanic plugs can also be seen from many Early Bonito sites across the western San Juan Basin, even as far away as Peach Springs, at the base of the Dutton Plateau.

Community architecture at the Early Bonito settlement of Willow Canyon offers convincing evidence that line-of-sight connections to Shiprock, Bennett Peak, and Ford Butte were important to the settlers. Willow Canyon is located in an area of badlands along the Chaco River Corridor. Here, Ancestral Puebloans settled in an extensive community spread across a valley floor. They built a proto-great house and a large, slab-lined enclosure atop a nearby mesa. Visibility in the badlands is highly variable as a traveler dips and rises through numerous eroding shale ridges and swales amidst remnant mesas and spires of sandstone. However, the mesa top provides a vista up the valley toward the north/northeast. From this vantage point, the viewer's gaze is directed through a gap between nearby mesas and spires to focus directly on three dramatic landforms in the distance—Bennett Peak, Ford Butte, and Shiprock. These landmarks are not visible from the community on the valley floor below. At Willow Canyon, it is clear that the proto-great house and enclosure sites were situated purposefully within sight of these three volcanic landforms.

Figure 4.12. Bennett Peak and Ford Butte, as seen from atop Newcomb great house.

The builders of Skunk Springs positioned their settlement within sight of the familiar landmark of Shiprock. From Skunk Springs, a viewer could also see many other prominent Basin high places: ripple-backed Huerfano Mountain; Red Mountain, with its line-of-sight link to West Mesa; and Hosta Butte, rising sedately above the blue line of the Dutton Plateau. Bennett Peak, on the near horizon to the north, marked the dwellings of ancestors; three Pueblo I period sites (Bennett's Peak, Bennett's Peak #2, and Mitten Rock [Morris 1959]) cluster at its base.

Line-of-sight connections to ancestral sites and to prominent landmarks on the horizon figured into the location of Peñasco Blanco, high above the Chaco/Escavada confluence overlooking a possible tenth-century lake (Force et al. 2002). The confluence—with or without an ancient lake—would have been an excellent place for farming, but Peñasco Blanco builders need not have situated the new proto-great house atop this particular mesa finger. Rather, both memory and visibility seem to have figured into their decision. Builders chose a spot almost literally in the shadow of Site 423, the large Basketmaker III village located on a mushroom-shaped bench 300 m to the south (figure 4.13). Perhaps the builders deliberately intended to associate their new settlement with Basketmaker ancestors. The Early Bonito settlers may have constructed histories, myths, or other tales about those who had lived at the Basketmaker village. By erecting their proto-great house within sight of Basketmaker ancestors, the builders of

Figure 4.13. A view of Site 423 from Peñasco Blanco.

Peñasco Blanco could have been participating in a cycle of memory and renewal centuries in the making. They also chose a spot that provides spectacular views, particularly to the east and north. An Early Bonito viewer standing at Peñasco Blanco could look 10 km east up Chaco Canyon to the locations of three other proto-great houses: Pueblo Bonito, Kin Nahasbas, and Una Vida. Peñasco Blanco also can see and be seen from major basin topographic landmarks, including Huerfano Mountain, 40 km to the north, and the Chuska Mountains, 80 km to the west. The uplift of West Mesa blocks panoramic vistas to the south, but West Point and Site 423 are well within view.

Hosta Butte—the distinctive, flat-topped mesa that rises above the Dutton Plateau—is another highly visible landform important to the builders of Early Bonito proto-great houses. Hosta Butte looms on the horizon from the vantage points of nearly half of all Early Bonito proto-great houses and great kivas (see table 4.2). The Early Bonito structure at Kin Bineola is an excellent example of a proto-great house sited to frame a view of Hosta Butte. Kin Bineola is located along a tributary drainage south of the Chaco River, 15 km west of the river's confluence with the Escavada Wash. Here, an extensive community with at least three centuries of time depth extends for 3 km along the alluvial floor of the Kim-mi-ne-oli Valley. Kin Bineola is best known for its massive, E-shaped, Late Bonito–phase great house. The central wing of the E, however, contains Type I masonry and

Figure 4.14. The author looking out over Kin Bineola, with Hosta Butte on the horizon, June 2003. Photo courtesy of Randy McGuire.

tree-ring dates indicating that construction began in the early 900s. In the absence of excavation data, it is impossible to know just how extensive this earlier proto-great house may have been, but a small group of Early Bonito domestic pueblos clustered nearby. The Kin Bineola great house was positioned against a Cliff House sandstone escarpment at the head of the valley. Looking south down the valley, Hosta Butte, 45 km to the south, is neatly framed between the broad mesas that bracket the valley floor (figure 4.14). Approximately 3 km down the valley to the south, a second proto-great house (29Mc291) and an Early Bonito great kiva (29Mc261) rest amid another cluster of contemporaneous domestic sites. Hosta Butte is a prominent feature on the horizon from this locality as well. Population estimates derived from Powers' survey of the Kin Bineola community indicate that 500–600 people may have lived in the area during the early 900s (Sebastian and Altschul 2002).

Outside Chaco Canyon to the south, Early Bonitians situated many other proto-great houses with views of prominent high places. At the end of Chacra Mesa, beyond Chaco Canyon to the southeast, Guadalupe perches upon a small butte in the shadow of the great head of Cabezon Peak. Down the Fajada Wash south of Chaco Canyon, community builders' concerns with visibility date back to the Pueblo I period settlements of the early 800s, where Windes (n.d.a) documented line-of-sight connections between the sites in the South Fork and the Kin Klizhin Wash communities to Fajada Butte and Huerfano Mountain. Huerfano Mountain also can be seen from Peach Springs and Standing Rock, two communities 85 km south of Chaco at the southern edge of the South Chaco Slope. Still farther to the south, Mount Taylor and Hosta Butte hover on the horizons of Early Bonito communities in the Red Mesa Valley.

Visibility takes an interesting turn inside Chaco Canyon. As we have already seen, Peñasco Blanco, at the western edge of Early Bonito canyon settlements, was sited to provide spectacular visibility. Canyon walls and mesa rims curtailed, to some degree, the views from other Early Bonito settlements within the canyon. Despite these restrictions, all the settlements, with the major exception of Pueblo Bonito, seem to have been concerned with visibility in some fashion or another. Deep within the walls of Chaco Canyon, the Chaco East community was drawn together across rugged terrain through line-of-sight intervisibility with the proto-great house (Windes et al. 2000:45). Although long-distance views from Pueblo Pintado are blocked by Chacra Mesa to the south and by rising uplands to the north, the Pintado settlements were situated in relatively prominent positions on mesa flanks at least 30 m or so above the Chaco Wash. In Fajada Gap, Kin Nahasbas, Una Vida, and the great kiva 29SJ1253 all are positioned with excellent views of nearby Fajada Butte and distant Hosta Butte and Mount Taylor.

Interestingly, Pueblo Bonito is the only proto-great house in Chaco Canyon and, indeed, one of the few proto-great houses in the San Juan Basin where visibility does not seem to have been a factor in building location. Settlers in the vicinity of South Gap could have chosen to position Pueblo Bonito at the head of the gap, framing Hosta Butte on the horizon. Indeed, two centuries later, Pueblo del Arroyo was founded at this spot. During the Early Bonito phase, however, settlers positioned Pueblo Bonito several hundred meters too far to the east for this view. Perhaps they were more interested in siting the pueblo at a favorable spot for runoff from the northern canyon rim. Or perhaps an earlier, Basketmaker III settlement underlies this spot—the interpretive complications posed by subsequent centuries of construction at Pueblo Bonito make this difficult to know.

But Pueblo Bonito is the exception that proves the rule. We can only speculate about the specific meanings that volcanic plugs, buttes, mesas, and ancestral sites held for most Early Bonito builders, but the patterned positioning of community buildings where these features are visible indicates that special landforms and ancestors did, in fact, hold some kind of significance.

Emergence of the Center Place

One of the most basic and intriguing questions about Chaco concerns its location in the midst of the relatively arid and remote San Juan Basin. Why was the most complex era of the Puebloan past centered in Chaco Canyon, as opposed to the comparatively lush river valleys of the Animas and La Plata, 60 km to the north, or the eastern slopes of the Chuska Mountains, 75 km to the west? The river valleys offered permanent water, and the Chuskas offered timber, game, and ceramic raw materials. Yet, the most impressive standing masonry architecture in the prehispanic Southwest was erected in the middle of an agriculturally marginal, desolate canyon surrounded by scarps and dunes. Why?

During the century after the major migrations of the late 800s and early 900s, social and ideological forces continued to simmer across the San Juan Basin. At the advent of the Early Bonito phase, the settlements in Chaco Canyon were just a few examples among many as proto-great house and great kiva–centered communities sprang up like mushrooms along the major drainages of the San Juan Basin. A century later, as major building projects initiated the Classic Bonito phase, around 1020, Chaco was the ritual, social, and political center of the Ancestral Puebloan world—a central place for Basin-wide ritual gatherings and home to the elite Puebloans who presided over the ceremonies. How and why did this transformation take place? Chacoan scholars, myself included, too often dismiss the intervening decades as the century during which "not much happened" (for an exception, see Sebastian 1992), yet this was the formative period that resulted in the architectural florescence of the 1000s. The following scenario is admittedly speculative, but it fits the data.

Assuming that we accept the interpretation of Chaco Canyon as a central gathering place for ritual, we must address several critical tenth-century issues. Why did Ancestral Puebloans begin to gather together periodically, and why in Chaco? How did Early Bonito ritual leaders transform themselves into Classic Bonito political authorities? As inequalities intensified, why did people continue to agree to participate?

Redistribution was the Chaco Center's original explanation for why Ancestral Puebloans gathered. It continues to play a role in many scenarios, but I find it to be an unsatisfactory catalyst. Redistribution assumes that Basin residents were somehow organized into a coherent socioeconomic entity at the advent of the Early Bonito phase; the model also assumes that all (or most of them, anyway) recognized the potential instability of future crop yields and agreed to set up a complicated system of long-term sharing to be carried out at a central location.

By contrast, I see the tenth-century developments at Chaco as a gradual, piecemeal resolution of simmering social tensions that likely extended back into the Pueblo I period. Struggles among factions in the aggregated Pueblo I villages of the northern San Juan may have led to the conflagrations and population movements that resulted in dispersed Early Bonito settlements across the San Juan Basin. Despite the existence of social tensions, northern, Pueblo I period ceremonialism might have necessitated the participation of multiple social factions or sodalities, each holding disparate yet vital pieces of ritual knowledge. Perhaps the proper ceremonies for planting, rainfall, fertility, or harvest could not be completed with the participation of groups now scattered among various new communities. Furthermore, ritual gatherings in the northern San Juan would have been occasions for social interaction. Migrant settlers in dispersed communities across the San Juan Basin would have sought similar opportunities to connect with other Puebloans now scattered across the landscape. In coming together for periodic ritual gatherings, Early Bonito peoples may have been continuing a version of the ceremonial traditions that extended back to integrative rituals in the oversized pitstructures and great kivas along the Dolores River.

Initial gatherings were probably centralized at a number of locations, of which Chaco was but one. Early Bonito ritual gatherings need not have been of similar sizes, nor even for similar ceremonies or at similar times of year. Basin residents who had close ties with Chaco began to come to Chaco to celebrate some of the major events in the ritual cycle, such as solstices or equinoxes. These visitors would have included close neighbors from communities such as Casa del Rio, Kin Bineola, and Pueblo Pintado. Visitors also clearly included residents of communities along the Chuskas, such as Skunk Springs and Newcomb. We know that this is the case because there are high frequencies of Chuskan ceramics and lithics in Chaco Canyon in contexts dating from the 900s. There are also high frequencies of Chuskan ceramics at 900s sites along the Chaco Wash corridor between the two areas (Van Dyke 1997b). The social connections between Chaco Canyon residents and residents of the western slopes of the Chuskas may have preceded migration from the northern San Juan or may have developed during the 900s as canyon dwellers ranged to the west in search of wood for building homes and firing pottery.

These visitors and ritual participants did not envision what Chaco would become in the eleventh century. They were simply gathering at specific moments in the ceremonial cycle to perform rituals that ensured the continuance of life and the balance of the world. But slowly, over the course of the tenth century, the gatherings held at Chaco Canyon began to gain prominence over ceremonies held elsewhere. There are many possible, potentially overlapping and complementary reasons why Chaco Canyon emerged as a primary ceremonial center. Geography may have played a part. The canyon would have been relatively centrally located for Basin residents traveling from the north, west, and south—but this explanation is less than satisfactory because it assumes Basin-wide communication and social organization during the Early Bonito phase, when many settlers and social networks were perhaps still in flux. Economics have often been invoked as an explanation. If Force and his colleagues are correct about the natural dam at the confluence of the Chaco and the Escavada, then Chaco Canyon may have been an exceptionally good place to grow corn during the tenth century—perhaps canyon residents had enough agricultural surplus to throw really good parties. Sebastian (1992) has parlayed tenth-century canyon agricultural surplus into competition among leaders of great house communities. Perhaps some canyon community leaders were particularly charismatic or aggrandizing. Consider that the canyon was settled primarily by peoples who constructed proto-great houses similar to the spatially segregated Pueblo I village of McPhee on the Dolores River. Perhaps these proto-great house groups were heirs to several generations of competitive ritual displays and exclusionary tendencies such as those postulated for McPhee (Schachner 2001; Windes and Ford 1992). In Chaco Canyon, the ready availability of stackable tabular sandstone would have enabled proto-great house groups to construct domestic structures that were tall, massive, durable, and visually prominent. Proto-great house community leaders might logically have interwoven pueblo construction projects and competitive display with ritual.

Throughout the 900s, the ritual gatherings at Chaco gradually grew in size and prominence. Neighbors from places farther afield, such as the Red Mesa Valley, heard about them, and some decided to participate. The scale of the gatherings continued to escalate. Those who lived in the major buildings in Chaco were hosts to these increasingly elaborate ritual events and presided over the ceremonies. Intricate social rules may have developed around who could attend which aspects of what ceremonies and what they (participants or audiences) must contribute. During the tenth century, Chacoan leaders directed a series of formal additions to Peñasco Blanco, Pueblo Bonito, and Una Vida, transforming the structures into Chacoan great houses (Lekson 1986). Other canyon residents, as well as visitors from outliers, may have contributed most of the labor for these new construction enterprises.

As social inequalities increased between ritual leaders and other Ancestral Puebloans, why did people continue to participate? In my view, the most critical key to understanding the rise of Chaco over the course of the tenth century is ritual leaders' transformation of a shared Ancestral Pueblo worldview into a shared Chacoan ideology. Although Early Bonito–phase Puebloans were scattered across the San Juan Basin, they shared aspects of a worldview traceable back through the Pueblo I period and into the Basketmaker III period. This worldview emphasized landscape, visibility, dualism, balance, cyclical renewal, and social memory. For peoples holding these ideas in common, Chaco Canyon—homeland of ancestors, situated between two geologic zones, with prominent local topographic features and far-reaching vistas—would have seemed a logical *axis mundi*.

Chaco was a place of ancestors, the location of the two largest Basketmaker III villages in the San Juan Basin. The proto-great kivas in Shabik'eshchee Village and Site 423 indicate that Chaco Canyon was a place where ancestors had gathered for ceremonies in centuries past. For people who attached meaning to dramatic landforms and who wished to position themselves where such landforms were visible on the horizon, Chaco Canyon offered some of the best vistas in the Basin. Chacra Mesa, Fajada Butte, South Mesa, West Mesa, and the canyon's north rim provide excellent vantage points from which to observe the volcanic plugs, buttes, mountain peaks, and mesas that punctuate the sedimentary Basin horizons. And some of these landmarks, such as Shiprock, Huerfano Mountain, and the La Plata Mountains, were familiar connections back to the Pueblo I landscape of the northern San Juan. By the same token, the uplifts that form Chaco are visible for many kilometers across the southern and western Basin.

But Chaco Canyon was a low place as well as a high place, with hidden recesses between its overtly visible canyon rims. The canyon topography itself embodied opposing dualisms and a juxtaposition between visibility and invisibility. Perhaps the increasing cachet of Pueblo Bonito was due, in part, to the fact that the building could *not* be seen from outside the canyon. People perched atop South Mesa or West Mesa could see out toward distant peaks and other communities, but those outside could not see in. By the end of the Early Bonito phase, visibility at Chaco was no longer simply about long vistas in horizontal directions across the landscape—now, added to this was a new, vertical dimension. Chaco Canyon was not only the place that could be seen across the Basin and from which one could see across the Basin—it was also the place where a vertical axis of up and down intersected the horizontal planes of Basin topography.

Early Bonito ritual leaders appropriated these shared ideas to create a Chacoan ideology that supported their positions as ritual, social, and ultimately political authorities. Ideologies rely on the naturalization and universalization of beliefs so that they appear to be self-evident. Not only did it seem necessary to Ancestral Puebloans to perform periodic rituals to ensure agricultural success and to keep the world in balance, but also it now seemed necessary to perform these rituals in one symbolically laden, specialized location—Chaco Canyon. For Ancestral Puebloans in the Early Bonito phase, Chaco Canyon seemed to represent an obvious natural intersection, a balancing point, a center place in the geocentric world. This concept, encouraged by ritual leaders, would have made sense to visitors and ritual participants because it fit with aspects of shared Ancestral Pueblo worldview. Ideologies work because dominant and subordinate social factions share overlapping, partial understandings of power relationships. In the beginning, Chacoan ritual leaders, as well as visitors and ritual participants, likely contributed elements of ritual knowledge or different pieces of necessary ceremonies—everyone was invested in the success of Chacoan ritual endeavors. But by the end of the Early Bonito phase, visitors more often ended up contributing goods (pottery, lithics, turquoise, corn) and labor to the ceremonial enterprise, and canyon ritual leaders more often ended up contributing knowledge and supervisory expertise. As hosts and overseers of the ritual facilities, canyon leaders' prestige steadily increased with each ceremonial cycle, but participants' prestige may have been less consistent, varying with the quantity or quality of their material contributions. As the size and renown of ceremonies at Chaco increased, a social gap widened between the canyon great house leaders and everyone else. The stage was now set for the dramatic social and architectural developments of the Classic Bonito phase.

Notes

1. Basketmaker III sites in the San Juan Basin are sometimes subdivided into the La Plata, Sambrito, Lupton, and Sky Village variants (Plog and Wait 1982; Vivian 1990). There are Basketmaker III sites in the Mesa Verde and Ackmen-Lowry areas (Hayes 1964; Martin and Rinaldo 1939; O'Bryan 1950), in the La Plata Valley (Morris 1939; Toll and Wilson 2000), in the Navajo Reservoir District (Dittert, Eddy, and Dickey 1963; Eddy 1961), in the Cove–Red Rock Valley (Morris 1980; Reed and Wilcox 2000), along the slopes of the Chuska Mountains (Allen 1972; Biella 1974; Damp and Kotyk 2000; Wendorf, Fox, and Lewis 1956), on Tohatchi Flats (Kearns, McVickar, and Reed 2000; Marshall et al. 1979), and in the Red Mesa Valley (Stuart and Gauthier 1981).

2. Archaeologists also have documented smaller clusters of Basketmaker III pitstructures in Chaco Canyon, in Fajada Gap and South Gap (Windes n.d.a), but there is nothing else on the scale of the Shabik'eshchee and 423 communities.

3. Evidence for conflict includes the fact that some pitstructures are burned and some are surrounded by lines of postholes that may represent stockades (Rohn 1975; Wilcox and Haas 1994). Neither stockades nor burning appear consistently, however, nor does either provide conclusive evidence of violence. In many cases, burned pitstructures contain intact floor assemblages and foodstuffs, which countermands the likelihood of raiding. Walker (2002) and

Wilshusen (1986) suggest ritual closure as a more likely explanation for burned structures.

4. Wilshusen (Adler and Wilshusen 1990; Wilshusen 1988, 1989) has identified a three-tiered hierarchy of ritual pitstructure use, based on features and mode of abandonment. Pitstructures that contain much evidence for ritual use were burned at abandonment. Pitstructures that had some evidence for ritual use were not burned but were intentionally collapsed atop paired male and female burials on the floor. Pitstructures with little evidence of ritual use were left to collapse on their own.

5. Pueblo I settlements are recorded near Kin Ya'a and in the Crownpoint area (Stein and Roney 1987:174–175; Whitten 1982). In the Kim-mi-ne-oli Valley, three distinct clusters of habitation sites were ceramically dated to the 700–800 period by the Chaco Additions survey (Van Dyke and Powers 2002). Along the Chuskan slopes, Pueblo I sites include Bennett's Peak, Bennett's Peak #2, and Mitten Rock (Bannister, Robinson, and Warren 1970:13, 19; Morris 1959). On Tohatchi Flats, Red Willow Hamlet contained an arc of thirteen jacal rooms fronted by two deep pitstructures (Loebig 2000). Ceramics, radiocarbon, and archaeomagnetic dating place this site between 750 and 840. An underlying arc of six rooms is dated between 725 and 775. Less than 1 km to the northeast, a single pitstructure at Flowing Well Hamlet was dated by the same means to 750–830 (Loebig, Yost, and Van Dyke 2000). Near Mexican Springs, 10 km southwest of Tohatchi, six pitstructures at three multicomponent sites were dated by ceramics and archaeomagnetism to periods between the early 700s and the late 800s (Damp 1999). Up the Dye Brush Wash to the west of this area, a site in the Grey Ridge community contains seven pitstructures ceramically dated to the late 700s–early 900s (Dennis Gilpin, personal communication, April 2003). Along the West Rio Puerco drainage, Gladwin (1945) excavated White Mound Village, with twenty-five rooms in three roomblocks, as well as six pitstructures. The site is dendrochronologically dated between 780 and the early 800s.

6. Windes (n.d.a) reassessed and considerably downsized Hayes, Brugge, and Judge's (1981) picture of Pueblo I settlement in Chaco Canyon. Small Pueblo I roomblocks cluster at the mouths of drainages on the south side of Chaco Canyon at Shabik'eshchee Village, Fajada Gap, Marcia's Rincon, Weritos Rincon, South Gap, and the Padilla Wash (McKenna and Truell 1986; Windes n.d.a). The largest excavated Pueblo I sites are found in Marcia's Rincon and Weritos Rincon, on the south side of the Chaco Wash (McKenna and Truell 1986). Site 29SJ627 was occupied for one or more brief periods between 780 and 910. A small roomblock contains ten to fourteen small storage rooms and ramadas, and there are one to three associated pitstructures. Site 29SJ-724 dates between 760 and 820. It contains a nine-room pueblo, an isolated surface room, and a single pitstructure.

7. Wilshusen and Van Dyke (2006) term these "candidate great houses." I have subsequently decided that *proto-great house* carries fewer implications about the processes through which some, but not all, of these buildings were ultimately transformed into Classic Bonito great houses.

8. Dates and interpretations for early Pueblo Bonito are from Bustard 2003; Lekson 1986:127–132, 265; Stein, Ford, and Friedman 2003; Windes 2003; and Windes and Ford 1992, 1996. Windes' new tree-ring dates have established that a central block of eight rooms pre-dates the 860s, a western arc of approximately twenty-five rooms dates to the 860s, and another central block of nine rooms dates to the 890s (Windes 2003:20–22; Windes and Ford 1992, 1996). These new dates are for the areas Lekson (1986:109–143) designated as early 900s Stages 1B and 1C. From 920 forward, Lekson's (1986:127–132) dates hold.

9. Judd (1964:179, plate 23) partially excavated an unnumbered pitstructure beneath Kiva 2C. The 10-m-diameter structure is dated on the basis of stratigraphy and Type I masonry to 900–950. Lekson (1986:143) proposes that this structure may be a great kiva, based on its large size, but its interior features are ambiguous and it is probably better interpreted as an oversized pitstructure associated with the proto-great house.

10. Excavated by Cynthia Irwin-Williams and her students during the 1970s, Guadalupe is well dated by means of dendrochronology, archaeomagnetism, architectural styles, stratigraphy, and ceramic seriation (Baker 1983; Pippin 1987:92–128). Although this structure is well known as a Classic Bonito and post-Chacoan great house, initial construction began in the early 900s. The "Early Chaco" (918–1050) structure consisted of a nine-room, linear pueblo constructed of Type 1 masonry laid on basalt cobble foundations (Pippin 1987:100–105). Entryway and room size patterns indicate that the proto-great house was subdivided into room suites consisting of habitation and storage rooms (Pippin 1987:101). A large community spread on the valley floor below contains a substantial late Pueblo I/early Pueblo II component (Washburn 1974:315–316).

11. In the Andrews community, 80 km south of Chaco Canyon in the Red Mesa Valley, I have ceramically dated eleven small habitation sites and two great kivas to the period between 880 and 940. Four large trash middens near a Classic Bonito great house also date to this period, suggesting that a proto-great house may lie beneath the unexcavated edifice (Van Dyke 1999a).

12. Other scholars (Windes et al. 2000:39) have noticed the relative scarcity of Early Bonito great kivas in Chaco Canyon. However, only eight out of eighteen features identified as great kivas in Chaco Canyon have been excavated (Van Dyke 2007); future subsurface investigations into these depressions could change this interpretation.

5 The Center Place

When the journey of the Zuni people brought them close to the middle place, K'yan'asdebi, a water spider, assisted them in finding the exact center point, Itiwana. The water spider spread his legs out until he reached the four oceans in the east, west, south, and north, and also touched the zenith and nadir. When he had thus spread out to find the six cardinal directions, his heart was over the long-sought middle place.

—*from* A Zuni Atlas, *by T. J. Ferguson and E. Richard Hart (1985:23)*

During the Classic Bonito phase (1020–1100), social and architectural developments at Chaco reached their zeniths. Classic Bonito Chaco was the center of the Ancestral Pueblo world—a place where canyon and outlier dwellers bound by a shared Chacoan ideology gathered for periodic ritual events. Those who led these ritual events held unprecedented social power and prestige, and those who attended and participated contributed labor, resources, and allegiance. This shift toward hierarchy did not take place suddenly, nor is it attributable to a single causal factor. Rather, Chaco emerged as a center place and Chacoan ritual leaders gained social and political power as the result of the negotiation of ideas, landscape, and social history. Canyon and Basin residents shared a worldview that enabled leaders to develop a Chacoan ideology. The fully developed Chacoan ideology included elements of cosmography (directionality, balanced dualism, center place, cyclical renewal), sacred geography, visibility, movement, and social memory. Ritual leaders employed a Chacoan ideology to legitimate their prestige and power. Visitors and outlier dwellers participated in this ideology, blurring the boundaries between the obligatory and the desirable.

Architecture and landscape were central to this process as Chacoan leaders engineered multiple, overlapping intersections of spatial materialities, perceptions, and representations (Lefebvre 1991:38–46). Chacoan builders expanded the great houses at Una Vida, Pueblo Bonito, and Peñasco Blanco with carefully planned, massive new wings and upper stories. They constructed new great houses—Hungo Pavi, Chetro Ketl, Pueblo Alto, and Pueblo del Arroyo—and they added great kivas, earthworks, and road segments to the Bonito-style architectural suite. In Chaco Canyon, residents continued to build and occupy scores of small houses. And, across the San Juan Basin, Ancestral Puebloans erected Bonito-style architecture in more than 70 outlier communities.

There must have been many intersecting and overlapping sociopolitical factions at Chaco with complementary and conflicting agendas, resources, and positions. Archaeologically, it is easiest to talk (and to think) about the intentions of those who orchestrated the monumental Chacoan building projects, because we can see their intentions played out through the architectural remains. It is also possible, at least in broad terms, to talk and to think about those who contributed the labor and other resources and why they may have chosen to do so. In this chapter, I have constructed an interpretive explanation that fits the material evidence, but this is, of course, only one possible scenario. Some of my ideas are well supported by material evidence, some can and should be tested, and still others must remain more speculative.

Ritual Gatherings, Leaders, and Labor

By the end of the tenth century, Chaco Canyon had become the paramount location for periodic ritual gatherings in the San Juan Basin. The leaders of these gatherings ultimately became leaders of the Chacoan world. Early Bonito–phase ritual specialists may have been descendants of the founders of Pueblo Bonito and other Early Bonito canyon sites. At Hopi, "firstcomers" tend to have the most social prestige—they also tend to control the most important ceremonies, as well as the best farmland (Levy 1992). Chacoan ritual leaders may have infused periodic ceremonies with elements of exclusionism and competition, following trends traceable back to aggregated Pueblo I settlements such as McPhee Village (chapter 4). During the Classic Bonito phase, Chacoans transformed great houses into arenas for ritual, although leaders and their families continued to inhabit some suites of rooms. These leaders' primary responsibilities were to oversee ceremonies, construction projects, and other associated public activities. They and their families lived in the great houses, enjoying high social standing year-round and subsisting off the agricultural labors of others. These leaders' privileged status was legitimated by their naturalized position as the ancestral keepers of specialized ritual knowledge. Some of them were buried in Pueblo Bonito, where excavators recovered the remains of individuals interred with astonishing quantities of exotica, including thousands of pieces of turquoise and shell (Judd 1954:338–339; Pepper 1909, 1920).

Not all canyon residents were necessarily part of the elite leadership. Small house dwellers had much of the same ceramic and lithic material culture as great house inhabitants, but they were less well nourished and were not buried with exotica such as jet frogs and macaws. Small house dwellers may have been ritual participants instead of leaders.

Certain critical aspects of Chacoan ceremonial knowledge were likely the exclusive property of great house residents, passed from generation to generation. Other pieces may have been contributed by different sodalities, with sodality members drawn from canyon and outlier communities across the San Juan Basin.[1] Sodalities may have varied in prestige, as well as in ritual duties, with different groups responsible for different aspects of the ceremonial cycle. Complicated hierarchical or heterarchical social relationships may have existed among individuals and sodalities who controlled and participated in various ceremonies.

Many ceremonial participants did not live in Chaco but traveled to the canyon from outliers (chapter 7). Membership in Chacoan sodalities or participation in canyon ritual events undoubtedly would have had local social implications for outlier community dwellers. The ability to join certain societies might have been based on wealth, kinship, personal attributes, or some combination of the above. Perhaps Chacoan sodality members brought secret knowledge home to outlier communities, where they presided over local versions of the societies. Conversely, some outlier dwellers may have gained local prestige when they contributed ritual knowledge to Chacoan ceremonialism. Still other members of canyon and outlier communities might not have been ritual participants but simply gathered to witness the ceremonies, to join in associated games or social activities, and to contribute their goods and energy to the success of the undertakings. As ceremonies at Chaco grew, more and more people from communities farther and farther away began to make the trip. Ultimately, Chacoan ritual events might have brought together people who were from diverse ethnic backgrounds and spoke different languages. Chaco might have become a once-in-a-lifetime pilgrimage site for those who lived at the outer peripheries of the Chacoan world.

The archaeological evidence is largely silent regarding the exact nature of Chacoan ritual. We know that Chacoan ceremonialism predates the katsina cult, which emerged around 1300 (Adams 1991:120). In many Neolithic societies, ritual revolves around rain, fertility, and agricultural productivity. Perishable and unusual items recovered from Pueblo Bonito and Chetro Ketl offer a few clues. Caches of exotica from Pueblo Bonito include possible ceremonial paraphernalia such as wooden staffs, cylinder vessels, and clay pipes (Mathien 2003; Neitzel 2003a). Excavators found 37 adult macaw skeletons at Pueblo Bonito (Mathien 2003:129; Pepper 1920:194)—macaw feathers could have been incorporated into ritual costumes. Room 93 at Chetro Ketl contained a cache of carved and painted wooden objects, including many representations of birds. Gordon Vivian, the excavator, interpreted the materials to be dance paraphernalia or the remains of an altar (Vivian, Dodgen, and Hartmann 1978).

Archaeologists cannot glean much specific knowledge about the nature and meaning of Chacoan ceremonies from the study of material remains, however, nor should we necessarily try, for this might be considered inappropriate from the perspective of living Pueblo peoples. We can, however, make some broad, general observations. Like the ritual cycles of contemporary and historic Pueblos, the Chacoan ritual cycle possibly incorporated movements of celestial bodies. Ancestral Pueblo farmers since Basketmaker times likely observed solstices and equinoxes. Cardinal, solar alignments at Classic Bonito great houses suggest that periodic gatherings at Chaco followed the sun's movements. The Sun Dagger petroglyph atop Fajada Butte indicates that Chacoans marked solstices, equinoxes, and possibly lunar standstills (Sinclair, Sofaer, and McCann Jr. 1987; Sofaer 1997; Sofaer, Sinclair, and Doggett 1982; Sofaer, Zinser, and Sinclair 1979). The winter solstice—when the sun pauses on its southward journey and turns back on the horizon—was likely the ceremonial high point at Chaco. The winter solstice corresponds to critical events in many Pueblo ceremonial cycles (Parsons 1939:554). In Zuni cosmography, the winter solstice is associated with the middle place and the Zuni village itself (Young 1988:103–104).

Seasonal celestial phenomena would have been an ideal way to organize periodic ritual events that drew attendees from a large area. Outlier dwellers may have known that when the winter sunrise took place at a certain point on their local horizon, it was time to begin the journey to Chaco for winter solstice ceremonies. People who traveled to the canyon from outliers on the Chacoan periphery would have been gone from home for at least several weeks. Winter is a more likely time for major gatherings than summer because agriculturalists could not have absented themselves from their fields for long periods in summer. The long, dark nights of winter are ideal times for people to gather together to practice songs and prepare for ceremonies. If some gatherings did take place in the summer, these were likely smaller, more specialized affairs involving Chacoan leaders and select individuals from outliers who could afford to leave their fields.

In some Pueblo ceremonial cycles, it is important to coordinate solstice ceremonies with the full moon (Zeilik 1986). Lunar movements also appear to have been important at Chaco. Like solar orientations, lunar orientations would have emphasized the great houses of Chaco as center places around which celestial bodies seemed to revolve. Recent work by Anna Sofaer (1997, 1999) and others suggests that Chacoans observed phenomena known as "lunar standstills." Moonrise on the horizon shifts gradually from a northern to a southern extreme each month, and the width of this envelope expands and contracts over a cycle of 18.6 years. At the major lunar standstill, moonrise positions are at their maximum width—the moon swings exuberantly between its northern- and southernmost positions on the horizon. At the minor lunar standstill, moonrise positions are at their minimum width, shifting only within a narrow envelope. Chacoans could have obtained knowledge of major and minor lunar standstills by watching the moon rise and set on the horizon over 18.6 years. However, there are no ethnographic records of Pueblo peoples having observed the lunar standstills, and it is puzzling that the Chacoans would have paid attention to this phenomenon. The phases of the moon are well known and easily observed, but the moon's rising and setting positions on the horizon follow such a complex pattern, the Hopi say that the moon "has no home" (Phillip Tuwaletstiwa, personal communication, September 2001). The Maya were the only other ancient people in the New World known to have recorded lunar standstills (Aveni 1980).

Lunar standstill knowledge would have been of little practical utility to agriculturalists, although it might have constituted part of a body of esoteric ceremonial lore seen as the exclusive property of particular sodalities or individuals. Some have argued that Chacoan lunar standstill knowledge indicates a link between Chaco and Mesoamerica (Sofaer 1997:119). However, there may be a different, and much more interesting, explanation. As Chacoan ritual and political hegemony expanded across the San Juan Basin during the eleventh century, Chacoan leaders brought other, local forms of ceremonialism under the Chacoan umbrella. The Chacoan great kiva, discussed later in this chapter, is one example of this process. Lunar standstill knowledge may well be another—Chacoans could have imported this information from the outlier of Chimney Rock.

A fixed landmark is necessary to appreciate the importance of a lunar standstill moonrise. At Chimney Rock, along the Piedra River in southwest Colorado, a narrow ridge serendipitously provides an ideal location from which to view, and mark, the major lunar standstill (Malville 2004; Malville,

Figure 5.1. The major lunar standstill full moonrise at Chimney Rock, December 9, 2006. Photo courtesy of G. B. Cornucopia.

Eddy, and Ambruster 1991). During a major lunar standstill year, the moon rises at its northernmost position on the horizon for a few days every month, but the full moon coincides with this position only at the full moonrise nearest the winter solstice. The major lunar standstill moonrise nearest the summer solstice is a new moon and therefore invisible (Ron Sutcliffe, personal communication, December 2006). The major lunar standstill full moonrise nearest the winter solstice, however, rises dramatically between the twin pillars of Companion Rock and Chimney Rock, as seen from the vantage point of the ridge (figure 5.1). Ancestral Pueblo farmers occupied the area from the Pueblo I period onwards, so it is very likely that local peoples observed this phenomenon. Residents of the Chimney Rock area may have been the first Ancestral Puebloans to become aware of the major lunar standstill as they began to keep track of full moonrises between Chimney Rock and Companion Rock. These observances might have been the focus of local ceremonialism. As the Chacoan rituality expanded in the eleventh century, people from Chimney Rock may have brought knowledge of the lunar standstills to Chaco Canyon, and Chacoan leaders subsequently co-opted this knowledge into their own ceremonial sphere. In the 1070s and 1090s, Chacoans built an outlier great house on the prime lunar standstill viewing location, atop the ridge southwest of the twin pillars (chapter 7). The monumental architecture may have symbolized a Chacoan appropriation of the Chimney Rock lunar standstill phenomenon, along with attendant local ceremonialism.

As ceremonies at Chaco Canyon grew in size and scope across the eleventh century, so did the ritual facilities there. The major construction projects that characterize the Classic Bonito phase in Chaco include formal new great houses and numerous additions and changes to existing great houses. Chacoans had been creating massive structures of stackable sandstone throughout the Early Bonito phase. During the eleventh century, Chacoans transformed traditional, domestic pueblos into monuments, linking new meanings and contexts to the traditional meanings and practices of the past.

Whereas Early Bonito–phase great houses such as Pueblo Bonito were scaled-up domestic structures (Bustard 2003; Neitzel 2003b; Windes 2003), Classic Bonito–phase great houses were public spaces created through the organization and utilization of massive amounts of labor. With their many large, featureless rooms of uniform size, great houses inspire ongoing debates about their possible uses.[2] But the construction itself may have been the point—not the creation of functional spaces. The repetitive, highly visible forms of these structures bring to mind the easily recognizable, recurrent forms of liturgical symbols. Bonito-style construction, in itself, may have been considered a ritual activity.

Great house construction represents the large-scale organization of labor over long periods. Chacoan leaders may have orchestrated these periodic, formal, massive building events with specific moments in the ritual cycle. The constant additions and remodeling may have symbolized cyclical renewal—referencing something traditional from the past, but repeatedly revisiting it to make it new, according to a ceremonial calendar. The episodic nature of construction projects in Chacoan great houses fits not only with periodic gatherings during which people contributed labor but also with an ideology that held Chaco as the place where the world was made repeatedly new. Renewal happened metaphysically through ceremonies, and it happened physically, through remodeling and additions to Bonito-style architecture.

Major waves of great house construction took place in Chaco Canyon between 1010 and 1020, 1040 and 1050, and 1070 and 1080, with smaller building and remodeling episodes in intermittent decades. Classic Bonito builders expanded and remodeled curving tenth-century roomblocks at Peñasco Blanco, Pueblo Bonito, and Una Vida to create symmetrical, geometric shapes.[3] They also founded four new, symmetrical, bracket-shaped great houses—Hungo Pavi, Chetro Ketl, Pueblo Alto, and Pueblo del Arroyo (figure 5.2). Chacoans carried out the construction and expansion of each great house in a series of intermittent, patterned stages. Lekson (1986) provides

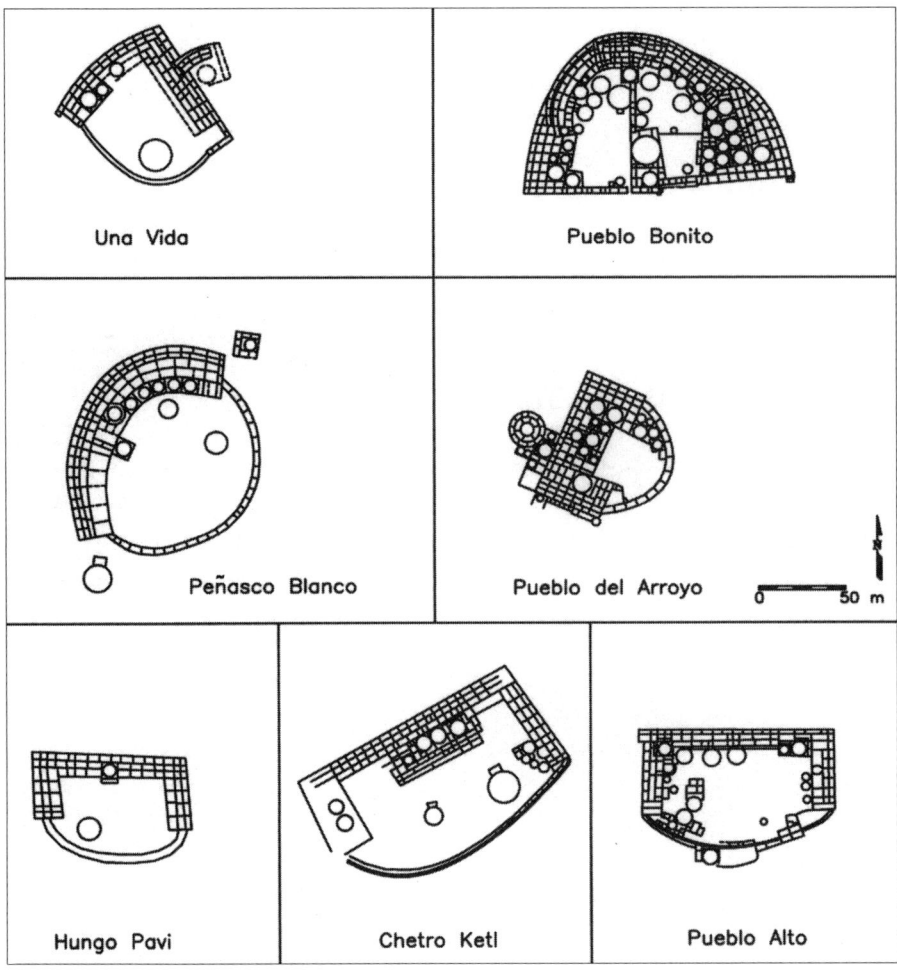

Figure 5.2. Plans of Classic Bonito canyon great houses, after Lekson 1986.

detailed accounts of these building sequences.[4] I briefly recount them here to demonstrate the well-orchestrated, patterned nature of the construction and the frequency and periodicity of the additions.

Between 1050 and 1095, builders made a series of additions to Una Vida that involved new stories, new kivas, a great kiva, and an extension to the north wing of the original L. After 1095, builders added an enclosing arc around the plaza (Gillespie 1986). Similarly, at Peñasco Blanco, Classic Bonito builders extended the original great house outward and upward into three stories in two building stages, between 1050 and 1065 and between 1085 and 1090. After 1090 they enclosed the plaza (Lekson 1986:94–109).

At Pueblo Bonito, Chacoans built up the great house in terms of height and overall coherence in two major building episodes, between 1045 and 1049 and between 1077 and 1082, and during several minor episodes in the 1050s and 1060s. Chacoans erected new rows of rooms around the building's exterior, topped the plaza-facing rooms of the old structure with a second story, added great kivas, and constructed parallel walls across the front of the plaza. They razed portions of the old east wing and replaced these with a new block of rooms that streamlined the pueblo's arc shape (Windes 2003:22–26). Extensive foundations to the north and east of Pueblo Bonito may represent additions that were later demolished or never completed (Judd 1964:151).

New great houses began as a single linear block of rooms, oriented east-west or northeast-southwest. Additions included perpendicular, symmetrical roomblock wings at either end of the original block, additional stories, particularly atop rear rows of rooms, and, around the early 1100s, a plaza-enclosing arc of either double walls or a single row of rooms (Vivian 1990:270–286). Builders erected Hungo Pavi, the first new great house, between 1006 and 1060 (Lekson, Windes, and McKenna 2006:79). First, Chacoans constructed a single-storied linear block of approximately thirty rooms. Then, they expanded this block into a bracket-shaped, symmetrical, 150-room structure three rooms deep and one to three stories high, with an elevated kiva in the center of the rear row of rooms, an arc of rooms enclosing the plaza, and a great kiva in the southwest corner of the plaza. Builders followed a similar sequence at Chetro Ketl between 1010 and 1115 (Lekson 1983, 1986:152–192).[5] They first erected a one-story-long, rectangular north block and then added a one-story east block and then a two-story west block. In the latter half of the eleventh century, builders added more stories, a great kiva, and small kivas and enclosed the plaza. As the structure grew, they raised the plaza surface until the original floor was subterranean.

Chacoans erected single-storied Pueblo Alto in a similar series of stages between 1000 and 1100. They began with the north roomblock, then added the west wing between 1020 and 1050 and the east wing between 1040 and 1060. Subsequent additional modifications included new kivas (Windes 1986).[6] Between 1078 and 1105, Chacoans erected Pueblo del Arroyo essentially in the same fashion. Pueblo del Arroyo began as a rear, western block of one- to two-story rooms. Builders then added north and south wings with sections from two to four stories high. The Chacoans subsequently made a few more modifications, added some new kivas, enclosed the plaza, and built a tri-wall structure behind the west wall (Judd 1959; Lekson, Windes, and McKenna 2006:79; Vivian 1959).[7]

Shaping and laying masonry was time-consuming and labor intensive, but the most "expensive" part of the construction process in terms of time and labor would have been harvesting and transporting the wood used for roofs and other features. Builders roofed great houses' high-ceilinged rooms in viga-and-latilla Pueblo style. They used massive wooden pillars to hold up great kiva roofs. Small kivas contained wooden beams inside masonry pilasters. Room 33 in Pueblo Bonito sported a wooden plank floor. Much of this wood was Ponderosa pine imported from the Chuskas and Mount Taylor (Durand et al. 1999; English et al. 2001).

Lekson (1986:257–263; Lekson, Windes, and McKenna 2006) provides a detailed look at the labor involved in great house construction events between 925 and 1140. Periodic Class I and II construction events took place throughout the Classic Bonito phase, with a few Class III and IV events toward the end of the eleventh century. Although we cannot know how many people were involved with each construction project or how many hours per day they worked, Lekson characterizes Class I events as involving 5,000–55,000 person-hours, Class II as involving 55,000–90,000 person-hours, Class III as involving 117,000–130,000 person-hours, and Class IV as involving 170,000–192,000 person-hours.

The phenomenal amount of labor represented by Chacoan masonry and wood construction events was likely contributed by people who did not reside in the great houses—namely, small site dwellers and visitors from outliers (Lekson, Windes, and McKenna 2006:82–83). In some cases, different veneer styles exist side by side, suggesting that discrete groups of masons worked to complete interlocking portions of a single master plan. Canyon leaders may have directly overseen the engineering of these construction projects, and the projects could have served multiple, overlapping purposes. Great houses were not only elite residences but also settings for ritual events. Visitors to Chaco received ritual knowledge and the benefit of participation in important ceremonies. In return, some could have contributed food, ceramics, lithics, or turquoise; others, lacking such material resources, could have contributed labor. Working together on construction projects could have fostered a sense of common cause or solidarity among visitors from different communities (and perhaps even different language groups or ethnicities). Construction events could have been part of initiation into adulthood or into particular Chacoan sodalities. At Chaco, participating together in ritual societies, feasting together as part of ceremonial events, working together on construction projects, people from around the San Juan Basin may have felt a sense of community. Regardless of ethnic background or language, participants were part of a larger, common Chacoan identity.

The forms that the new architecture took clearly embody the familiar principles of a shared Ancestral Pueblo worldview. In this way, those directing construction also created spaces that reflected and legitimated experiential dimensions of a shared Chacoan ideology. Chacoans designed Bonito-style architecture to give visitors spatial experiences that confirmed the position of Chaco Canyon as center place. Designers paid special attention to how buildings would be viewed and to how people would move across the landscape, into the canyon, and through the buildings.[8] But the visitors' understandings of these experiences were only partial. Because visitors resonated emotionally with the elements of Puebloan worldview experienced in Chaco, it seemed right and good to lend their labor to Chacoan construction projects and to contribute resources such as food, pottery, lithics, wood, and turquoise. At the same time, their participation legitimated the authority of those who ran the ceremonies, contributing to their status and prestige. In this way, ritual leaders transformed the ceremonial into the political and rendered aspects of an Ancestral Pueblo worldview into a Chacoan ideology.

Bonito-Style Architecture and Chacoan Ideology

Classic Bonito canyon leaders planned monumental architecture and modified the canyon landscape to emphasize the canyon as the balancing point of the cosmos, the appropriate place in which to conduct ceremonies. Under leaders' direction, builders constructed spatial metaphors for the ideas that bound them together as a community. When people viewed, approached, and moved through Classic Bonito great houses, their senses confirmed the importance of these ideas and the significance of Chaco as center place.

A Chacoan ideology worked because it was grounded in ideas shared by all Ancestral Puebloans. Classic Bonito leaders directed architectural construction that not only embodied core ideas but also created aesthetic experiences encouraging people to perceive of Chaco Canyon as the center place. Chacoans saw the social and spiritual worlds as a series of interlocking, nested, balanced divisions associated with highly visible elements of the natural landscape. The juxtaposition of opposites such as north and south, vertical and subterranean, visible and hidden, created balanced dualisms. These opposing divisions or directions intersected at a center place, the point of cyclical renewal and balance. The human body spatially experienced these ideas through visibility, movement, and memory. Builders carefully designed great houses, great kivas, and earthworks to embody and promote these aspects of a Chacoan ideology. This architecture and its attendant ideology traveled outwards along roads and lines of sight into the surrounding landscape (chapter 6) and into the Classic Bonito outlier communities of the San Juan Basin (chapter 7).

Great Houses

Repetitive, shared, iconic design elements characterize the Classic Bonito Chacoan great house (Stein and Lekson 1992). Builders constructed the monumental edifices according to "precepts of order, formality, standardization, and symmetry" (Vivian 1990:268). Formal, patterned, highly visible architectural elements are ideal for communicating symbolic meanings (Carr 1995:195–198). Great houses materially represented the ideas of dualism, directionality, center place, and cyclical renewal. Visitors perceived great house spaces through visibility, movement, and a lens of social memory.

As Fritz (1978) noted decades ago, dualism is perhaps the most obvious feature of every Classic Bonito great house. Hungo Pavi, Chetro Ketl, Pueblo Alto, and Pueblo del Arroyo typify the ideal Classic Bonito great house. All four of these new, eleventh-century structures are symmetrical, bracket-shaped great houses. As builders constructed additions, they carefully balanced wings, stories, and enclosed kivas to reflect balanced dualism. Chacoans also converted Una Vida, Peñasco Blanco, and Pueblo Bonito into fair approximations of symmetrical buildings (plate 7; see figure 5.2). The standardized, easily recognizable layouts of these buildings resemble the repetition and formality found in liturgical order.

Great house forms are standardized in terms of not only symmetry but also orientation. All Chacoan great houses are oriented to open toward the east, south, or southeast. All seven Classic Bonito canyon great houses face between 115 and 180 degrees east of true north. A southeast orientation is not unique to great houses—it is a long-standing pattern common to most Ancestral Pueblo sites. The southeast orientation takes best advantage of the low, southern winter-sun angle, keeping rooms warm and light during colder seasons and allowing prevailing winds to move midden odors away from the pueblo. Over time, as functional practices become traditional, they grow laden with memory. Basketmaker III settlements such as Broken Flute Cave consist of long arcs of pitstructures situated in southeast-facing rockshelters, and subsequent southeast-facing Ancestral Pueblo roomblocks might reference this ancestral tradition (John Ware, personal communication, July 2004).

Not surprisingly, the original structures at Peñasco Blanco, Pueblo Bonito, and Una Vida faced southeast. This orientation might have been a nod to the ancestors—a reference to traditional ways of organizing space. During the Classic Bonito phase, however, Chacoan great houses began shifting to face due south. Builders began to emphasize a north-south "meridian" alignment in great house orientation (Fritz 1978; Lekson 1999; Sofaer and Sinclair 1987; Stein, Suiter, and Ford 1997; Williamson, Fisher, and O'Flynn 1977). Early tenth-century additions at Pueblo Bonito converted the great house into a structure facing due south (Windes 2003:20). Builders oriented the new great houses of Hungo Pavi and Pueblo Alto to face due south. This new emphasis on cardinality appeared in the 1000s and grew stronger over time, reaching its greatest elaboration during the early 1100s (chapter 8).

Cardinality is related to dualism and to center place—Chaco is the point of balance between north and south. Cardinality also references solstices, equinoxes, and the movements of the sun. Chacoans, like their Ancestral Puebloan forebears, would have been well aware of cardinal directions because they lived on an open landscape interposed with topographic landmarks and because the sun's movements were important to their agricultural livelihood. North bisects the daily, as well as the biannual, route of the sun. At midday, when the sun is halfway across the sky, any shadow is cast along a north-south meridian. On solar equinoxes, when the sun rises and sets at its midpoint on the horizon, there is no midday shadow at all. North also represents a fixed point in the night sky around which the stars revolve.

The three Classic Bonito great houses oriented to face due south—Pueblo Bonito, Pueblo Alto, and Hungo Pavi—are aligned to the noonday sun's zenith. Sofaer (1997) and others (Farmer 2003; Stein, Suiter, and Ford 1997) have pointed out that Pueblo Bonito showcases patterns of shadow and light that correspond with the equinox—the midpoint of the sun's journey on the horizon—reinforcing the idea of Pueblo Bonito as a center place within the turning of the heavens. Animated time-lapse imaging in Sofaer's (1999) film, *The Mystery of Chaco Canyon*, demonstrates this well. On the equinox, the sun rises and sets along the east/west front wall at Pueblo Bonito, and the sun's shadow disappears along a perpendicular north/south wall bisecting the plaza. The walls of Pueblo Bonito mark the midpoint of the sun's passage through the day, as well as its northern- and southernmost positions through the year. The great house becomes the symbolic center place—the point at which these oppositions intersect, the fulcrum around which they cyclically revolve.

Sofaer (1997, 1999) argues that the orientations of noncardinal canyon great houses, including Chetro Ketl, Pueblo del Arroyo, Una Vida, and Peñasco Blanco, relate to major or minor lunar standstills. It is difficult to know whether all these alignments represent intentional relationships. The rear wall of Chetro Ketl is one of Sofaer's most convincing examples, for it aligns precisely with the rising full moon at the minor lunar standstill. A line drawn along the major lunar standstill perpendicular to Peñasco Blanco is less convincing because Peñasco Blanco is an arc that can be bisected in several places.[9] If Chacoans did orient some great houses to embody lunar standstill knowledge, then this would have been one more way to construct an experience of the canyon as center place—the location around which the moon, as well as the sun, revolves.

Chacoans designed Classic Bonito great houses to represent and reinforce a Chacoan ideology, so these structures and their messages are highly visible. Classic Bonito builders were clearly attempting to maximize visibility among canyon great houses and also from afar. Intended viewers may have been neighbors, visitors, and ritual participants. The shape of Pueblo Alto on the horizon draws the eye of travelers approaching Chaco from the north, and Pueblo del Arroyo greets those entering Chaco through South Gap (chapter 6). The fact that Chacoans built so many highly visible great houses in close proximity might be interpreted to indicate competition among various canyon factions (Sebastian 1992)—perhaps different canyon groups sponsored each great house in an attempt to attract followers. Builders seem to have developed the canyon landscape as one holistic entity (chapter 6), however, and I think it more likely that canyon great houses were hierarchically organized under the leaders of Pueblo Bonito—clearly most central of buildings at the center place. Different canyon great houses might have been associated with, or sought to attract, visitors and outlier dwellers from specific outlier communities or ritual sodalities.

In a study of Andean monumental architecture, Moore (1996) found that clear forms, contrasting backgrounds, exaggerated height, and exaggerated mass enhance visibility. As should be evident from the preceding discussions, Classic Bonito great houses had clear forms. In Chacoan times, they also had contrasting backgrounds. Although today great house sandstone walls seem to emerge organically from the canyon cliffs behind them, there is some evidence to suggest that, in the past, the structures were coated in white plaster (Lekson 1986:29, 173).[10] In the bright Colorado Plateau sunlight, the white walls would have created a striking effect against the dark brown sandstone cliffs of Chaco Canyon. Multi-storied canyon great houses exhibit exaggerated heights, commonly attaining three and four stories, towering above single-storied, domestic, small sites. Where Chacoans did not use multiple stories to emphasize great house height, they employed topography—they built Pueblo Alto, the only one-story Classic Bonito great house in Chaco Canyon, in an elevated location.

Great houses are larger edifices than small, domestic pueblos in terms of height, areal footprint, and room count, but great houses are not simply taller, wider stacks of pueblo rooms. Chacoan builders went to impressive lengths to exaggerate the mass of these buildings, "bulking up" great houses with unusable interstitial spaces, empty, featureless rooms, and high ceilings (Fowler and Stein 1992).[11] Core-and-veneer masonry, necessary for multi-storied walls, also added extra heft. Comparing the seven Classic Bonito

Table 5.1 Estimated Height, Footprint, Room Counts, and Mass for Seven Classic Bonito Canyon Great Houses and One Small House
(Measurements Derived from Lekson 1986)

Classic Bonito Great House	Estimated Original Height (m)	Areal Footprint (sq m)	Number of Classic Bonito–Phase Rooms	Mass (cu m)[1]
Pueblo Bonito	10.0	4,762	695	26,700
Chetro Ketl	9.0	3,423	580	13,428
Peñasco Blanco	9.0	3,989	215	12,691
Pueblo del Arroyo	5.3+	2,103	290	8,792
Pueblo Alto	3.5	2,163	130	7,571
Hungo Pavi	6.1	2,011	150	7,418
Una Vida	5.8	2,260	160	6,296
Bc 51 (small house)	2.1	680	45	1,360

1. For these great houses (and for others in chapters 7 and 8), I calculated mass by multiplying the heights of each section of the building by its corresponding area. I used actual heights where known; otherwise, I assumed a height of 1.8 m for each story.

great houses with Bc 51, the largest excavated small site (table 5.1), the monumental scale of the Bonito-style architecture becomes evident. Classic Bonito great houses occupy three to seven times the areal footprint of Bc 51 and four to twenty times as much mass as the small site.

Clearly, Chacoan great houses were meant to be highly visible structures. But Classic Bonito great houses also represent exclusive knowledge—meanings that would have been hidden from casual users, available only to designers and builders. This dualistic tension between the visible and the hidden is carried out on many levels across the Chacoan landscape. Some aspects of Chacoan architecture, such as banded veneers, were deliberately hidden from public view. During the Classic Bonito phase, banded facing styles were developed, using alternating layers of thin, tabular and massive, bun-shaped Cliff House sandstone, both of which occur side by side in the canyon walls.[12] Banded veneers represent a structural improvement over Early Bonito Type I masonry (figure 5.3). The very tight coursing leaves "very little mortar exposed to action of wind, rain, and frost" (Morris 1939:52) and enhances strength and stability, transferring the load from the weaker core to the stronger, outer facing (Lekson 1986:23; Reiter 1933:67). However, banding was not necessary to achieve these benefits—a later Classic Bonito veneer style, Type IV, also maximizes stone-on-stone contact

Figure 5.3. Banded, Type III Chacoan masonry.

but lacks the striped appearance of Types II and III. Nor did building material determine banding (Powers, Gillespie, and Lekson 1983:317). Rather, banded veneers were a deliberate construction choice subsequently hidden under coatings of mud or plaster. The presence of banding and any attached symbolism would not have been visible to the casual visitor—rather, the banding would have been known only to designers, builders, or others who had been present during wall construction.

This tension between the visible and the hidden, the accessible and the restricted, is played out in multiple ways inside great houses. Until builders added enclosing walls near the end of the eleventh century (chapter 8), Classic Bonito great houses were easy to enter, with open plazas facing south or southeast. However, the interior spaces of great houses were more restrictive (Bustard 2003; Cooper 1995). The building block of Early Bonito great houses had been the room suite, with a large front room, a large middle room, and one or two small rear rooms arranged in a row (Lekson 1986:62). This domestic-looking organization shifted by the 1030s into a linear pattern of four or more rooms of the same size, arranged in a row (Lekson 1986:64). Access to the "deepest" rooms in the structure is, in space syntax terms, "asymmetrical" and "nondistributed" (Hillier and Hanson 1984). Great houses thus embody a dualistic opposition between the visible and the hidden. Although great house plazas were likely open, publicly accessible spaces, the activities within interior rooms and kivas would have been restricted from the gaze of outsiders. Inside the plaza at Pueblo Bonito, there is a spatial opposition between the open plaza, with its soaring four-story walls, and the impenetrable, closed nature of what could be transpiring inside the pueblo behind those walls (plate 8). Pueblo Bonito may have had nested layers of access, with some individuals allowed into the innermost sanctums, some allowed into the great house plaza or great kivas, and some perhaps not allowed into the great house at all.

At least two areas within Pueblo Bonito—enclosed kivas and burial areas—probably were not accessible to all comers. Enclosed or blocked-in kivas could have easily been camouflaged entirely from view. On average, Classic Bonito–phase great houses contain one enclosed kiva for every fifteen rectangular rooms (Van Dyke 1998: table 4.3). This 1:15 kiva/room ratio is quite different from the 1:6.5 ratio that characterizes kivas found in domestic pueblos, used by households or extended families (Lipe 1989:59, 64). Chacoan enclosed kivas may have been the exclusive meeting places of particular sodality members.

Great house builders sought to create continuity with the past—to construct social memories representing eleventh-century sociopolitical organization as a seamless extension of all that had come before. This was likely one motivation for iterative great house additions and remodelings. Periodic changes and expansions to buildings that were decades or centuries old entail a form of cyclical renewal in which the past is repeatedly touched and made new. Crown and Wills (2003) noticed the Chacoan propensity to frequently replaster and restructure great house kivas, often offsetting the new kiva slightly, and installing new floors, benches, and walls (Crown and Wills 2003; Judd 1964:194; Smith 1952:17). For example, at Pueblo Bonito, Chacoans remodeled twenty-two of thirty kivas excavated by Judd (1964). At Chetro Ketl, they rebuilt Kiva G eight times (Crown and Wills 2003:519).

Cyclical renewal likely contributed to a larger, more politicized process —the construction of social memory. Aspiring leaders frequently employ connections with the people and events of antiquity to legitimate power and to consolidate social identity (Van Dyke and Alcock 2003). Several clusters of rooms in the earliest sections of Pueblo Bonito were used as northern and western elite burial areas during the latter half of the eleventh century (Akins 2003). Remodelers carefully preserved the original core of ninth-century rooms at Pueblo Bonito, and Classic Bonito builders erected a screening wall that shielded the northern roomblock core from the gaze of people in the plaza (Ashmore 2007).

The Classic Bonito reuse of ninth-century rooms for eleventh-century elite burials may have been a deliberate attempt to make a connection with an ancestral past. The individuals placed in Room 33 and adjacent rooms in Pueblo Bonito were interred during the late eleventh century, in rooms that were nearly 200 years old at that time. The burials' placement in the oldest part of the central great house in Chaco Canyon is likely to have had special meaning. Such a connection could have helped naturalize and legitimate the increasing social power of Chacoan ritual leaders, symbolizing that the source of the leaders' power was time-honored, ancestral, and therefore above question. Conversely, it might have entailed a removal or forgetting of these individuals' power, sending them out of sight, back to the ancestors.

The Chacoan Great Kiva

The Chacoan great kiva—another formal, monumental hallmark of the Classic Bonito phase—is deeply implicated in the construction of social memory, the legitimation of power, and the consolidation of social identity. During the eleventh century, Classic Bonito builders erected one or more great kivas in association with all canyon great houses except Pueblo Alto and Pueblo del Arroyo, and they built several "isolated" great kivas on the south side of Chaco Canyon. These circular, semisubterranean structures were likely venues for ritual events. Chacoan great kivas embody familiar ideas of balanced dualism and directionality, with floor features and niches in symmetrical arrangements and with primary axes located along either cardinal or northwest/southeast orientations. Great kivas also represent another spatial means through which canyon leaders sought to convert the ritual to the political. In a study of prehistoric British monumental architecture, Bradley (1998:132–146) notes that as sociopolitical hierarchy increased, communal spaces were appropriated and converted to exclusionary venues. Chacoan architects were engaged in a similar process when they brought formal great kivas into the Bonito-style repertoire. The Chacoan great kiva represented an imagined continuity with the ritual structures of the Basketmaker III past and an imagined solidarity with Basin-wide, great kiva–centered outlier communities.

Although great kivas were a focal point of many Early Bonito communities across the San Juan Basin (chapter 4), the circular structures are relatively scarce within Chaco Canyon before the Classic Bonito phase (Windes et al. 2000:39). Rather, proto-great houses were the most common form of Early Bonito communal architecture in the canyon. At around 1040, however, Classic Bonito architects began building a highly standardized type of great kiva as part of the suite of Bonito-style features. At least fourteen of the seventeen known canyon great kivas date from the Classic Bonito phase (table 5.2;

Table 5.2 Great Kivas in Chaco Canyon

Location	Dates (AD)	Above Bench Diameter (m)	Excavated?	Sources
Pueblo Bonito, Kiva Q	1040–1050	14.6	Judd, 1924	Judd 1925, 1964:207–211; Lekson 1986:142–143; Vivian 1940:127–130; Vivian and Reiter 1960:62–66
Pueblo Bonito, SW Plaza	1050–1060	19.4	Judd, 1924	Judd 1964; Lekson 1986:142; Roberts 1927:40–41; Vivian and Reiter 1960
Pueblo Bonito, Kiva A	1100+	17	Judd, 1921	Hewett 1936; Judd 1922, 1964; Lekson 1986; Martin 1936; Vivian and Reiter 1960
Chetro Ketl	1060–1090?	16.5	SAR, 1921, 1929–1933	Bradfield 1921; Chapman 1921; Hawley 1934; Hewett 1921, 1922, 1936; Leinau 1934; Lekson 1983, 1986; Miller 1937; Reiter 1933; Vivian and Reiter 1960
	1090?–1120	18.4		
Chetro Ketl, Court Kiva (converted)	1060–1120	10	SAR, 1934	Hawley 1934; Lekson 1983, 1986; Vivian and Reiter 1960; Woods 1934
Kin Nahasbas	1030–1070 1060–1100+	15.5	SAR, 1935	Luhrs 1935; Mathien and Windes 1988; Vivian and Reiter 1960
Una Vida, Great Kiva 1	930–950	17	no	Gillespie 1986
Una Vida, Great Kiva 2	1050–1095	18	no	Gillespie 1986
Hungo Pavi	1060–1080	15	no	Lekson 1986
Peñasco Blanco, Plaza Great Kiva 1	1000–1100?	13	no	Lekson 1986
Peñasco Blanco, Plaza Great Kiva 2	1000–1100?	15	no	Lekson 1986
Peñasco Blanco, Plaza Great Kiva 3	1000–1100?	17	no	Lekson 1986
Peñasco Blanco, NW Great Kiva	1000–1100?	23	no	Lekson 1986, personal observation
Casa Rinconada	1060–1109	19.5	SAR, 1930–1931	Vivian and Reiter 1960
Fajada Gap: 29SJ1253	900–1050	20	no	Marshall et al. 1979
Across from Wijiji: 29SJ1642	900–1100	17	minor testing by Vivian	Marshall et al. 1979; Gwinn Vivian, personal communication, 2001
Chaco Additions: 29SJ2557	1000–1225	13	no	Van Dyke and Powers 2002

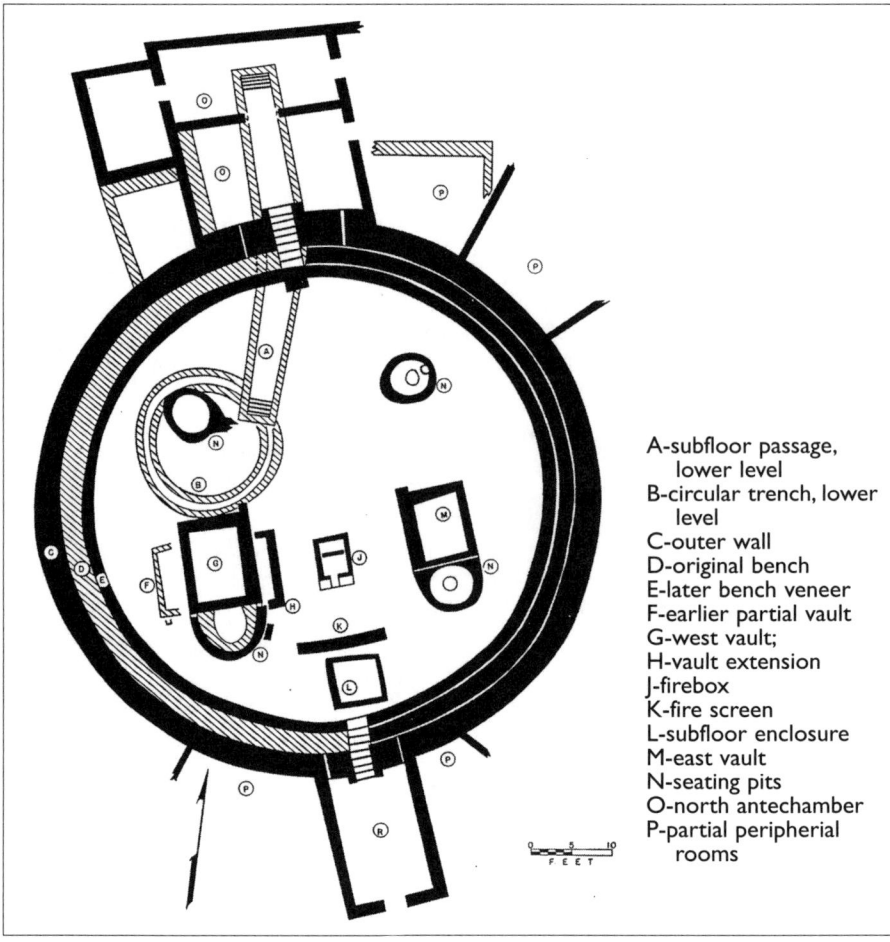

Figure 5.4. Plan of Casa Rinconada, from Vivian and Reiter 1960:10, figure 4, by permission of SAR Press.

A-subfloor passage, lower level
B-circular trench, lower level
C-outer wall
D-original bench
E-later bench veneer
F-earlier partial vault
G-west vault;
H-vault extension
J-firebox
K-fire screen
L-subfloor enclosure
M-east vault
N-seating pits
O-north antechamber
P-partial peripherial rooms

Van Dyke 2007; Vivian and Reiter 1960).[13] Some of these structures are well known; others remain unpublished. Most canyon great kivas are unexcavated, bowl-shaped depressions. Excavated great kivas include one from Kin Nahasbas, two from Chetro Ketl, four from Pueblo Bonito, and the "isolated" great kiva Casa Rinconada (Vivian and Reiter 1960). "Isolated" great kivas are located more than 100 m from a great house, often in the midst of clusters of small sites.

Like other aspects of Bonito-style architecture, Chacoan great kivas are highly formalized in their construction, shape, size, symmetry, orientation, and associated features (figure 5.4). Classic Bonito great kivas are lined with banded masonry, and the aboveground portions of the walls are of core-and-veneer construction. Great kiva diameters can range from 10 to 20 m, but most measure from 15 to 17 m (Van Dyke 2002). The structures are oriented on either a cardinal or a northwest/southeast-trending axis. Entry is often by means of an antechamber to the north; sometimes a southern entry is present as well. When associated with a great house, these subterranean or semisubterranean structures are located in an open space or plaza to the south or southeast of the great house. Chacoan builders roofed great kivas by means of four wooden pillars that supported a four-log framework surrounded by radial beams and overlain with layers of smaller posts, bark, and earth. They aligned antechambers and interior features with cardinal directions or with the primary orientation of the great house. The north/south kiva axis expresses bilateral symmetry, with patterned wall niches, paired masonry-lined floor vaults, and two pairs of masonry-lined roof support pits with basal stone discs. Other formal interior features include an encircling masonry bench and a central elevated masonry firebox, sometimes protected by a deflector.

Religious architecture tends to be conservative, incorporating repetitive, iconographic material symbols easily recognized by ceremonial participants and observers (Rowlands 1993). In a cross-cultural analysis of integrative spaces, Adler and Wilshusen (1990) argue that great kivas' standardized sizes, layouts, features, and orientations suggest liturgical order, concluding that the structures were venues for specialized ritual activities. Great kivas were ideal performance spaces, and much evidence indicates that they were used for ceremonial events. Great kivas possess acoustic properties ideal for songs, chants, and dances. Floor vaults may have been used as foot drums, overlain with wooden planks that would make a booming noise when people jumped or danced atop them. A subterranean passageway leading into a screened area in the great kiva at Casa Rinconada would have facilitated surprise entrances at dramatic moments.

Caches of turquoise, beads, and other items found in sealed wall niches, under remodeled floor vaults, and under the seating discs for roof columns in some great kivas seem to represent votive deposits (Hewett 1936:87–93). Chacoans placed similar votive caches inside hollowed-out spaces in radial beam pilasters in small kivas (Lekson 1986:54). In the great kiva at Chetro Ketl, the northeast roof column–support pit contained four massive sandstone seating discs; beneath the lowest disc, a leather bag containing pulverized turquoise was covered with alternating layers of lignite and adobe. These deposits undoubtedly held symbolic meanings.

Great houses and great kivas balance each other on the landscape at several levels of increasing scale—a nested arrangement reminiscent of Puebloan cosmography. Like great houses, great kivas possess internal, standardized features that represent dualism and directionality. The pairing of great kivas with great houses might be interpreted as representing oppositions: circular and rectangular, subterranean and vertical, hidden and visible, accessible and restricted, and possibly even female and male. Just as great houses are visible and vertical edifices, great kivas are hidden and subterranean. Great houses have partible, restrictable interiors, whereas great kiva main chambers are open spaces. Great houses and great kivas might represent opposing dimensions of a vertical axis, with great houses extending in a celestial direction and great kivas, in a subterranean direction; the plaza is the center place in which they meet. A male/female dualism can also be imagined, albeit tentatively, in the great house/great kiva pairing. At Zuni, for example, kivas may carry female, lunar, uterine associations.[14] Great houses could be considered somewhat phallic, by contrast.

The great house/great kiva opposition can be extended across the canyon landscape to encompass "isolated" great kivas. "Isolated" great kivas are located on the south side of Chaco Canyon, whereas most great houses are located on the north side. For example, Casa Rinconada is located 700 m south-southeast from Pueblo Bonito, directly across the Chaco Wash. Casa Rinconada is aligned with the gap between Pueblo Bonito's East Mound and West Mounds. It is likely that a path or road segment originally connected the two buildings (figure 5.5). These structures may represent a paired opposition, with Casa Rinconada as a circular, southern, subterranean space balanced against Pueblo Bonito as a rectangular, northern, vertical space. This pattern reiterates the dualistic and directional balance between north and south, vertical and subterranean, with the central canyon itself as the point of intersection. These architectural dualities replicate still larger landscape constructions that emphasized Chaco Canyon as a center place created by the intersection of opposing directions (chapter 6).

Like the enclosed kivas in great houses, Chacoans frequently dismantled, remodeled, and reconstructed great kivas. This is well illustrated by Vivian and Reiter's (1960) review of multiple construction episodes in the excavated great kivas of Chetro Ketl, Kin Nahasbas, and Casa Rinconada. At Chetro Ketl, for example, Chacoans constructed a great kiva and then extensively remodeled it within several decades. During the late eleventh century, they added features to transform the Court Kiva, a 10-m-diameter kiva in the central plaza of Chetro Ketl, into a great kiva (Vivian and Reiter 1960:50). At Pueblo Bonito, Chacoans built at least three successive great kivas over the life of the pueblo. Stein, Suiter, and Ford (1997) contend that a new great kiva was built near the start of every major construction phase at Pueblo Bonito. The repetitive, episodic nature of great kiva construction and remodeling suggests that, like great house additions and

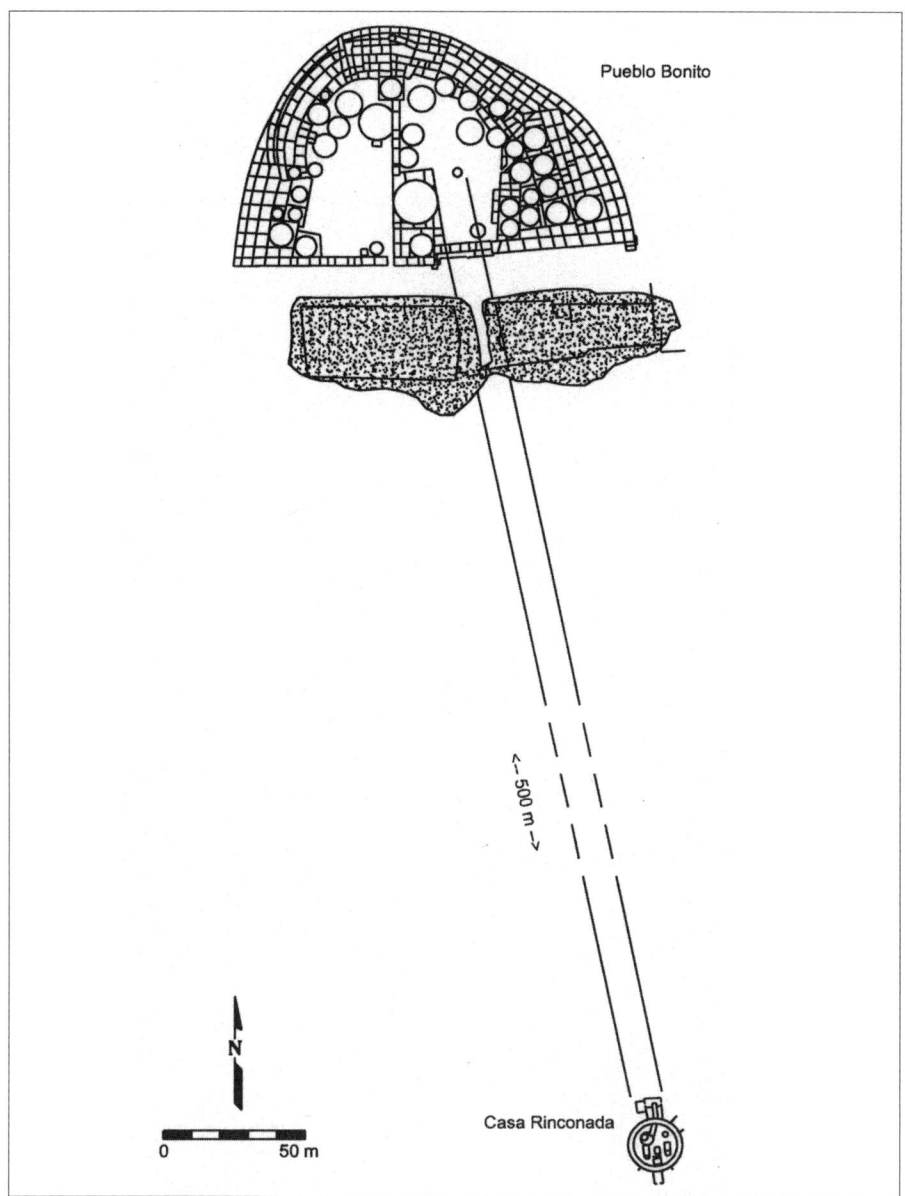

Figure 5.5. A possible processional route between the Pueblo Bonito mounds and Casa Rinconada. Based on a drawing in Stein and Lekson 1994:54.

remodeling events, Chacoans may have undertaken work on great kivas at periodic intervals as part of a cycle of ritual renewal. When Chacoans sealed turquoise behind walls, in niches, and under floor features, they may have been engaging in ritualized "forgetting," creating knowledge restricted to those who witnessed the deposits (Mills n.d.).

Great kivas may have been an especially potent way to integrate outlier dwellers from diverse community backgrounds into one social whole, with a shared ideology and shared, imagined ancestral traditions. As with Chimney Rock's lunar standstill, Chacoan leaders tended to appropriate and incorporate the ritual practices of others. Some visitors to Chaco likely came from great kiva–centered communities. Classic Bonito leaders may have instituted the formal Chacoan great kiva as part of an effort to attract people from great kiva–centered outlier communities to ritual activities at Chaco, thereby accruing more labor, more resources, and the allegiance of more Ancestral Puebloans.

When Chacoan leaders erected great kivas, they also may have been connecting themselves to a real or an imagined communal ethos of Basketmaker III forebears. Social memories of an imagined, shared past also are used to construct common identities among peoples of different backgrounds. Great kivas echo the forms of the ancestors' great pitstructures at the Basketmaker III villages of Shabik'eshchee Village and Site 423 (Lightfoot 1988:617–618; McLellan 1969:178). Imagined continuity with the communal ritual practices of the past would have helped naturalize and legitimate Classic Bonito great kiva ceremonialism, ultimately supporting the leaders' unequal access to specialized knowledge, authority, resources, and social prestige.

Regardless of these associations, it is unlikely that Chacoan great kivas were, in fact, spaces for communal events open to all. Although the circular interior space facilitated interaction, not everyone necessarily had access to great kivas. Ceremonies in the great kivas must have been somewhat restricted, based on space limitations. Using an estimate of 1 sq m of floor space per person, approximately 250 people could fit in a great kiva with an 18-m-diameter floor, such as Casa Rinconada, but this discounts the area taken up by the floor features and leaves no room for activities inside the structure. A more realistic estimate may be derived by imagining a row of spectators shoulder to shoulder around the circumference. In this scenario, approximately 75 people could stand around the 56-m circumference of an 18-m great kiva, leaving room for activities in the center. Ceremonies in great house plazas, however, would have been highly visible to spectators in the plaza or on rooftops.

Great kivas embody a particular kind of ritual space, nested within a hierarchical, dualistic arrangement of features. They represent several major tenets of Chacoan ideology. Great kivas symbolize continuity with peoples of the past and peoples in distant communities yet, in practice, entail conversion of the communal into the exclusive.

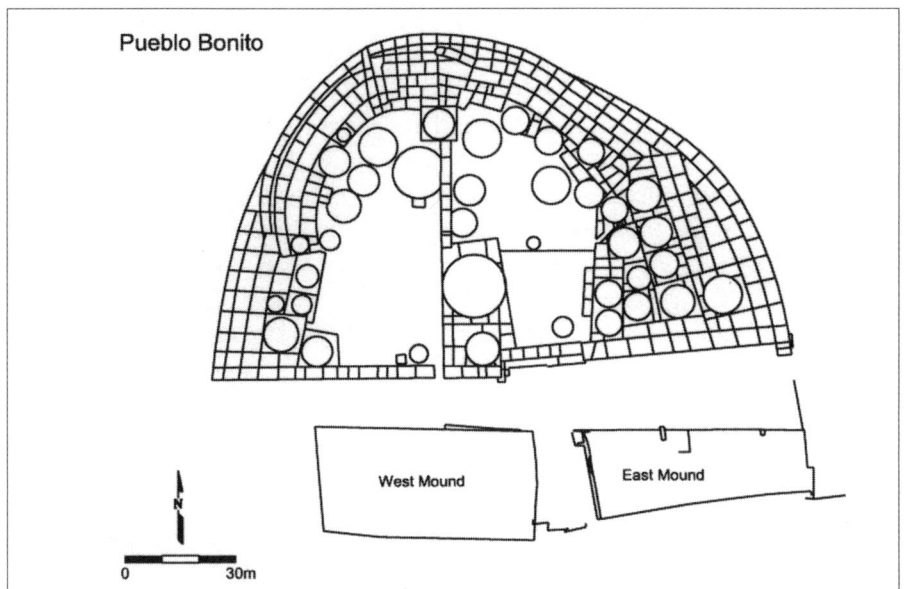

Figure 5.6. Plan of Pueblo Bonito, showing the East Mound and West Mound. Based on drawings in Lekson 1986:111, figure 4.17, and Judd 1964, figure 23.

Figure 5.7. Peñasco Blanco, as approached from the east within Chaco Canyon. Notice the large mound in front of the great house to the left.

Earthworks

Formal mounds or earthworks are a third major type of Classic Bonito monumental construction. Earthworks are associated with Peñasco Blanco, Pueblo Alto, Pueblo Bonito, and Chetro Ketl (Cameron 2002; Lekson 1986:74; Stein, Ford, and Friedman 2003; Stein and Lekson 1992; Wills 2001; Windes

1987:561–667) (figures 5.6 and 5.7). Chacoans erected most canyon earthworks between 1050 and 1100, although some of the deposits may have been there earlier (Windes 1987:664). The Pueblo Bonito mounds are rectangular masonry enclosures 2 m high and are filled with rubble, artifacts, and sand (Judd 1964:125–176, 212–222). The Pueblo Alto mound stratigraphy suggests intermittent episodes of intense deposition and contains an unusually high concentration of broken utility jars, providing strong evidence for periodic feasting (Toll 1985, 2001; Windes 1987; but see Wills 2001 for a different view).[15]

The earthworks are located to the south or southeast of great houses, where trash middens would normally be situated. It is possible that earthworks were meant to represent large midden deposits. Trash middens were part of the formal spatial arrangement of Ancestral Pueblo habitation sites from at least the ninth century onward, when occupants began routinely placing their garbage in front of dwellings to the southeast. Ancestral Puebloans often interred human burials within domestic middens (for example, Akins 1986; Roberts 1939). For contemporary Pueblo peoples, trash middens are sacred space, and shrines are often located there. Refuse must be carefully returned to the earth and treated with respect (Cameron 2002; Ellis 1966; Ortiz 1969).

Earthworks at great houses are strewn with trash on the surface, but where the mounds have been excavated, the stratigraphy does not resemble domestic midden deposits. To Ancestral Puebloans familiar with the traditional spatial positioning for trash deposits, however, great house mounds might have appeared to represent giant middens—exaggeratedly large quantities of trash that indicate an exceptionally long period of occupation (John Roney, personal communication, April 1999). In this way, great house earthworks might have represented artificially constructed histories or imagined social memories. Deep histories, of course, lend legitimacy to existing social configurations.

Great house earthworks also would have been ideal staging areas for public events. Stein and Lekson (1992; Lekson 1986:143–144; Stein, Ford, and Friedman 2003:52) interpret the Bonito mounds as paved platforms (but again, see Wills 2001 for a different perspective). Standing atop them, with the great house and the north face of Chaco Canyon towering behind, ritual leaders would have been a very impressive sight. Ceremonies performed atop the mounds would have been highly visible to masses of people who, perhaps, did not have access into the great house itself.

Earthworks positioned in front of Pueblo Bonito helped control great house access and visibility. Chacoans would not have approached Pueblo Bonito as modern visitors do, along a park service trail that breaches the rear wall of the building. Rather, the formal Chacoan approach to Pueblo Bonito would have necessitated passing through or around the two mounds (see figures 5.5 and 5.6). To gain some idea of the perspectives shared by Chacoan visitors, I walked from the middle of Chaco Canyon north toward Pueblo Bonito and the twin earthworks. Although the East Mound and West Mound are eroded today, the 2-m-high rectangular earthworks may have been encircled by adobe embankments, steps, and masonry retaining walls in Chacoan times (Judd 1964:13).[16] The two mounds create a sense of perspective that shifts with the context of the viewer. As I approached Pueblo Bonito from the south, the mounds loomed much larger than the great house, and motion toward the great house seemed logically directed through the gap between them. When I reached this interstitial space, I could still barely see the great house because the West Mound obstructs the western end of Pueblo Bonito. The gap between the mounds encourages motion forward into the plaza. As I emerged into the Bonito plaza, this sheltered yet public space opened before me, with high interior walls of the great house encircling and looming against the canyon face. Turning back toward the pueblo entrance, I found myself looking directly back out, through the gap between the two mounds, at Casa Rinconada. These sensations of juxtaposed openness and confinement, of visibility and concealment, are similar to those I experienced walking along road segments toward the canyon (chapter 6).

Summary

Inside Chaco Canyon during the Classic Bonito phase, leaders directed the careful construction of great houses, great kivas, and earthworks. These highly standardized, large-scale buildings and features represented aspects of an ideology shared by Chacoan leaders and by Ancestral Puebloans who participated in Chacoan ceremonialism.

Balanced dualism is expressed in Bonito-style architecture through the symmetrical forms of great houses and great kivas and through the juxtaposition of opposing elements of spatial experience and representation. Great houses and great kivas are paired opposites representing dualisms, including the vertical and subterranean and the visible and hidden. Balanced dualism is also represented by the juxtaposition of the visible and the hidden in Bonito-style architecture. Great houses are highly visible structures, with clear forms, exaggerated mass, exaggerated height, and contrasting backgrounds. However, great house architecture also contains hidden dimensions such as banded veneers. Great houses embrace accessible, open plazas, but they also conceal interior rooms, burial areas, and enclosed kivas.

Opposing directions represent another kind of dualism also evident in great houses and great kivas. Cardinal and solar alignments juxtapose north and south, east and west. Solar and lunar alignments emphasize great houses as the fulcrum around which the celestial bodies revolve. Dualisms create a point of intersection or balance between two opposing directions or ideas. This point of balance, represented by the great house plaza in microcosm and by Chaco Canyon in macrocosm, was a center place around which social and ritual life revolved.

The periodic return to center place involves cycles of repeated ritual renewal represented architecturally by periodic additions to great houses and by repeated remodeling of great houses, kivas, and great kivas. A related idea, social memory, involves the construction of connections with a real or an imagined past. The Early Bonito–phase burial rooms at Pueblo Bonito, the construction of earthworks to resemble artificial middens, and the southeast orientations of some great houses are ways in which Bonito-style architects constructed social memory. Classic Bonito builders also referenced the past through the revival and incorporation of formal great kivas into the Bonito-style architectural repertoire.

When Chacoan leaders, other canyon dwellers, outlier leaders, and outlier dwellers came together at Chaco for ritual gatherings, every aspect of their spatial experiences emphasized Chaco Canyon as the point of balance, the place of renewal, the home of ancestors, the center place around which all in life revolved. A shared Chacoan ideology supported Classic Bonito leaders as orchestrators of ritual, keepers of exclusive ceremonial knowledge, and directors of building projects. It also framed participants as contributors of some ceremonial knowledge, economic resources, and labor. Carefully constructed spatial experiences at Chaco legitimated and naturalized the leaders' authority by emphasizing aspects of a shared Ancestral Pueblo worldview. The Chacoan experience reinforced the notion of Chaco Canyon as center place and Chacoan leaders as the true and natural arbiters of necessary rituals there. This idyllic vision of a world in balance is captured in the Acoma story of Kashkahtruutih, which may well represent Chaco:

> *When the people arrived at the place and time known as Kashkahtruutih, they found that it was ideal. There was nothing to want, all conditions and circumstances were perfect and good. Nobody lacked for anything —not food, clothing, or shelter. Sacred spirit helpers-protectors, who were very much like human beings, lived among them.... Animals and plants could talk to each other, and the people could talk with the animals and plants; there was only one language, and all things communicated in this language.... Anytime they needed rain, they would just ask their friends*

and neighbors the sacred beings to bring rain from the west, and the rain would fall to nourish their corn plants.... This is the way it was at the beautiful place and time of Kashkahtruutih. [Ortiz 1994:65–66]

By the late 1000s, Chaco had become an aesthetic experience. Ritual leaders and visitors alike shared elements of a common ideology that explained how the world stayed in balance through ceremonies in the canyon. Social, ritual, and political organization fit together as parts of a nested, interlocking, hierarchical whole. Visitors were swept up in an emotionally charged experience that resonated with their worldview and legitimated leaders' power. Ultimately, people were willing to come, lend their labor, bring food, and contribute resources to the events at Chaco because the rituals and spatial experiences there confirmed and reinforced their ideas about the way the world works. Everything about the visitors' experience, from their initial walk into Chaco Canyon, to the architecture and landscape elements they encountered, to the rituals they witnessed, reciprocally confirmed for them the rightness of their participation and the rightness of Chaco as center place.

Notes

1. In an interesting twist on this idea, John Ware (2001, 2002) suggests that Chaco evolved out of the social tension around the separation of sodalities, or ritual societies, from the matrilineal descent groups that had formerly been responsible for ceremonialism.

2. In the absence of specific evidence for habitation or other activities, great houses have been suggested to represent storage facilities and military barracks. See Bernardini 1999, Lekson and Cameron 1995, Wilcox 1993, and Windes 1984, 1987, for additional discussions.

3. Kin Nahasbas was also repeatedly remodeled during the Classic Bonito phase, although it was never transformed into a massive, multi-storied formal great house on the order of the others discussed here. A symmetrical addition called the New House, built to the east of the Old House, contains 13 rooms and exhibits masonry dating from the late AD 1000s to the early 1100s. Between 1030 and 1070 (based on masonry styles), a formal great kiva was built on the site of the tenth-century great pitstructure. The great kiva was extensively remodeled at some point between AD 1062 and 1090 and was used into the early 1100s (Luhrs 1935:27, 30; Mathien and Windes 1988:32, 40–69; Vivian and Reiter 1960:53–61). Chacoans formally linked the great kiva with the Old House via a small northern antechamber and a three-step masonry stairway.

4. Lekson's (1986:109–144) thorough overview of great house building sequences remains generally valid today, although some of his reconstructions have been honed and improved by new tree-ring dates. Windes (2003; Windes and Ford 1996) and Stein, Ford, and Friedman (2003) provide the most recent dates and discussion for eleventh-century construction at Pueblo Bonito.

5. Much of Lekson's interpretation is based on the work of Hewett and his students. Hewett excavated much of the great house and the two great kivas as a joint venture between the School of American Research (SAR) and the Museum of New Mexico in the 1920s and 1930s (Hawley 1934; Hewett 1936; Leinau 1934; Miller 1937; Reiter 1933; Vivian, Dodgen, and Hartmann 1978; Vivian and Reiter 1960:27–50).

6. Pueblo Alto was excavated by the Chaco Project (Mathien and Windes 1987; Toll 1985; Wills 2001; Windes 1986, 1987).

7. Judd (1959) excavated Pueblo del Arroyo. Lekson (1986:209–223) describes construction sequences in detail. Lekson's dates have been updated by more recent tree-ring data (Lekson, Windes, and McKenna 2006). Vivian (1959) described the tri-wall structure. These enigmatic features, known from only a few locations across the San Juan Basin, consist of three concentric, circular walls partitioned into two series of long, narrow rooms.

8. Sound also would have been part of the experience. Canyon acoustics at this point are such that loud sounds emanating from Casa Rinconada or other places in this general vicinity reverberate back and forth between the canyon walls (Stein, personal communication, July 2002). John Stein and Rich Friedman conducted experiments in which they learned that sounds originating on the canyon's south side are thrown back so that they seem to be emanating from the north face. The Pueblo Bonito plaza is a good place, acoustically, for public spectacle.

9. Sofaer believes that lunar alignments extend beyond Chaco Canyon to position the orientations of outliers such as Pueblo Pintado and Kin Bineola. I consider connections on this scale to be unlikely, for two reasons. First, Kin Bineola and Pueblo Pintado were founded in the early 900s, but in Sofaer's conception, they are linked along lunar angles to the fulcrum of Chetro Ketl, which was laid out at least 100 years later. Chacoans often did connect buildings across time, but Sofaer's scenario supposes that Chetro Ketl, indeed the entire Chacoan landscape, was planned from the early 900s. I view the Chacoan landscape as a palimpsest that evolved, along with changing sociopolitical organization, over centuries. Second, the Chacoan landscape was built to be experienced—Chacoans used roads and shrines to create connections across landscape, but invisible alignments connecting buildings 18–27 km away could not have been experienced by anyone (although, admittedly, such alignments could have constituted esoteric knowledge).

10. Preserved wall plaster has been documented at Chetro Ketl (Lekson 1986:173), Aztec (Morris 1928:120, 272–273, 289, 294), Bis sa'ani (Marshall 1982:185, 187), Casamero (Sigleo 1981:3), Guadalupe (Pippin 1987), Morris 39 (Morris 1939:52), and Salmon Ruin (Irwin-Williams et al. 1975:52, 120). Ethnographic evidence from Zuni also supports the practice of plastering Pueblo walls (Mindeleff 1989[1891]:137–138).

11. Piling behavior in the pursuit of mass is known from many locations around the prehispanic Southwest in other times and places. At the post-Chacoan site of Big House near Manuelito Canyon, Fowler, Stein, and Anyon (1987:61–66; Fowler and Stein 1992:111) note that a massive masonry facade was extended across the natural cliff face to create the appearance that the structure is 20 m or ten stories tall. At Meddler Mound in the Tonto Basin of central Arizona, the Salado built rubble- and earth-filled cubicles that, although resembling pueblo rooms, were merely a construction technique contributing to the overall massive size of the platform mound (Craig, Holmlund, and Clark 1998).

12. Classic Bonito veneers include Types II–IV (refer to figure 2.3, this volume; Lekson

1986:17–19). Types II and III exhibit clear banding of alternating sandstone varieties, and Type IV consists of repeated layers of stones of relatively equal size.

13. Dating often rests heavily on stratigraphic relationships, with absolute dates obtained through dendrochronology, associated ceramics, or masonry styles. Dates for unexcavated great kivas are based primarily on associated ceramics.

14. Clowns at a Zuni summer rain dance in 1969 walked on the roof of a kiva to imitate astronauts landing on the moon. According to the Zuni who related the story, the clowns' purpose was to criticize the astronauts, who showed disrespect for the moon-mother by walking on her and piercing her with probes (Young 1988:114).

15. The Pueblo Alto mound contains thick layers of cultural material and sand deposited intermittently over a relatively short time, probably between 1050 and 1100 (Windes 1987:609). The cultural material does not resemble domestic trash, containing little in the way of vegetal material, corncobs, ash, charcoal, and burials (Morris 1924:221–225; Roberts 1939:252; Stein and Lekson 1992:96; Windes 1987:612–613). Rather, cultural layers contain unusually high densities of ceramics, including high frequencies of imported Chuska grayware (Toll 1984, 1985) and intentionally broken bowls (Toll 2001; Windes 1987:602) and high densities of imported Narbona Pass chert (Cameron 2001). These materials are often interpreted as evidence for periodic social gatherings involving feasting and votive deposition (Cameron 2001; Renfrew 2001; Toll 1985, 2001; Windes 1987:616), although Wills (2001) disputes this interpretation.

16. See also the results of Wills' current, ongoing excavations.

6 Connections

How does vision, this tyrant of the senses, draw someone to a piece of earth? What do the eyes rest upon—mind disengaged, heart not—that combines senses and affections into a homeland?

—*from* The Anthropology of Turquoise *by Ellen Meloy*

All around in the sacred directions of the Earth

a Mountain is standing. Look!

And look from all the sacred directions of the Earth

we are standing here. Look!

—*from "Look to the Mountain," by Simon Ortiz (2002:88)*

Landscapes are experienced through the senses, particularly the sense of sight. The Chacoans inhabited a country where boulders gather at the gray-green skirts of sandstone mesas and the fantastical forms of eroded plugs and hoodoos pierce the sky. In the open, sky-filled San Juan Basin, the human eye is drawn to the unusual—jagged, distant mountain peaks or oddly shaped volcanic plugs. Here, where meandering canyons dissect broad, level mesas, the topography itself juxtaposes the seen and the unseen, the visible and the hidden.

In earlier chapters, I argue that far-reaching vistas and sacred geography were of interest to Ancestral Puebloans. During the Classic Bonito phase, the Chacoans not only built great houses and great kivas but also modified the landscape to express a Chacoan ideology emphasizing the canyon as center place. Chacoans built two kinds of connections—lines of sight and physical alignments—radiating out from Chaco Canyon. Significant Chacoan lines of

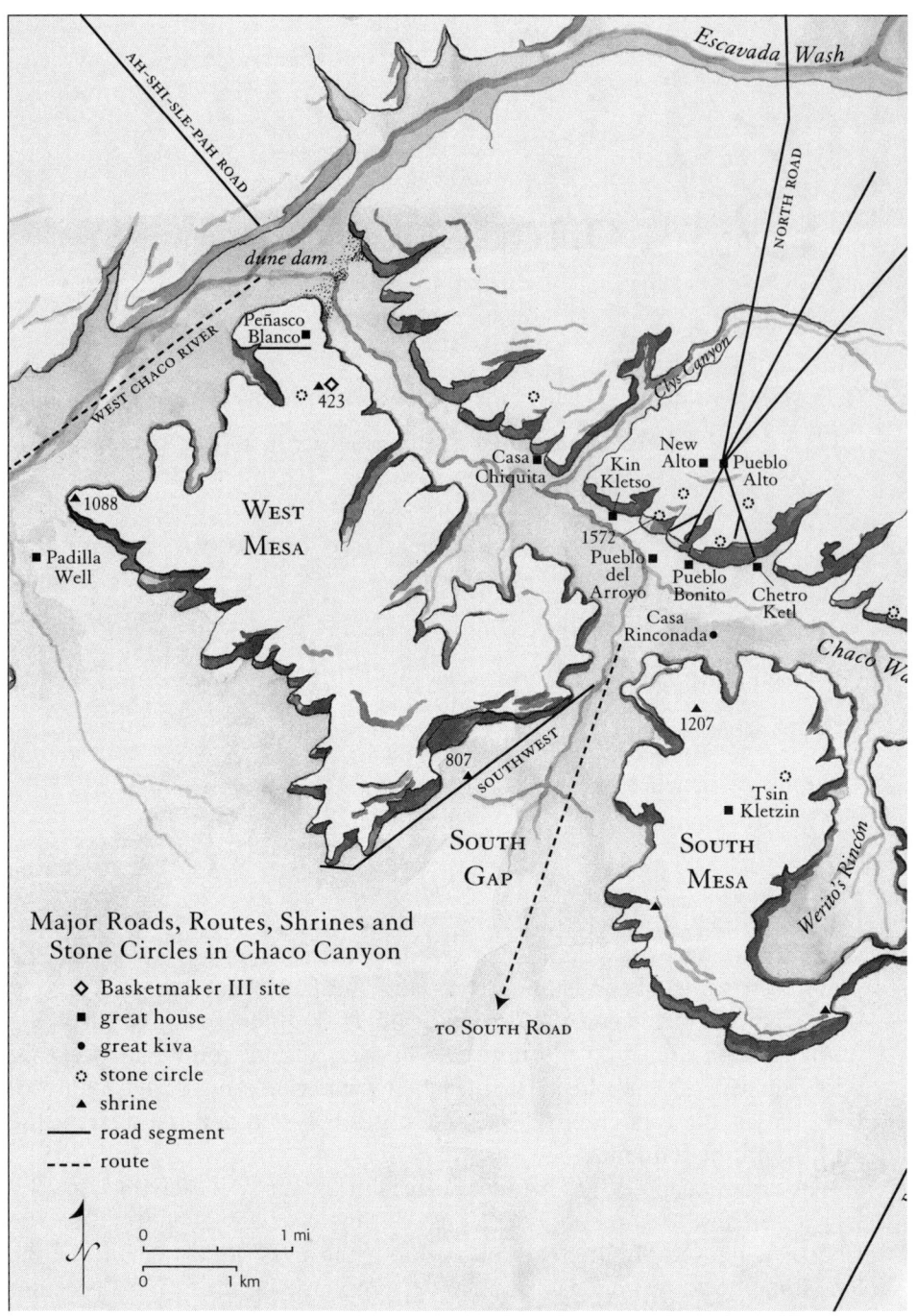

Figure 6.1. Major roads, routes, shrines, and stone circles in Chaco Canyon. Based on maps in Drafted by Molly O'Halloran.

138   The Chaco Experience

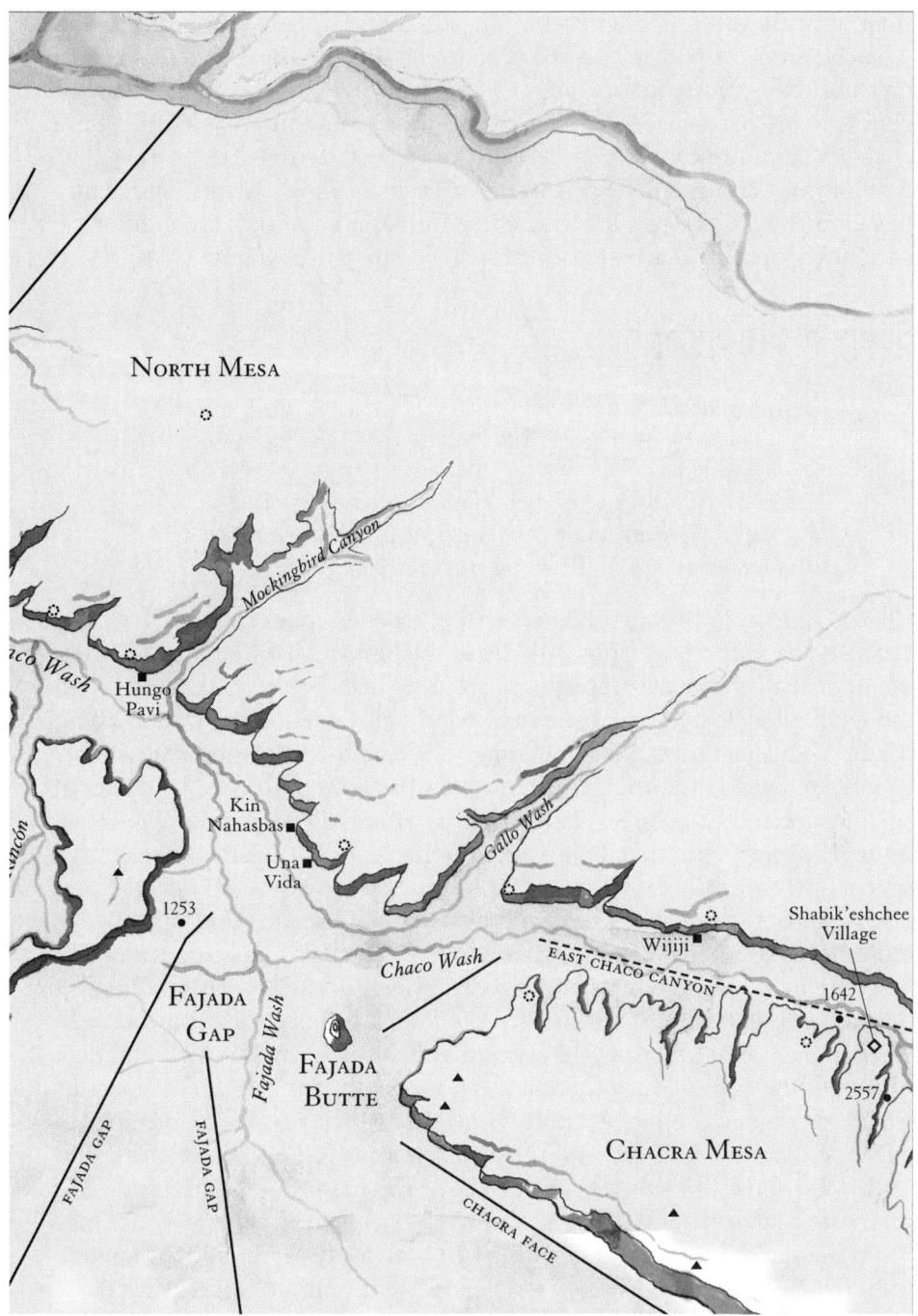

Vivian 1997b:12, figure 2; Windes 1978:2, figure 1; and Hayes and Windes 1975:145, figure 17.

sight are delineated by intervisible shrines, stone circles, great houses, and other features on high places. Chacoan roads are physical alignments that link not only places but also ideas. These connections encouraged participation in a Chacoan ideology in several ways. Shrine networks may have enabled communication between the canyon and Chacoan participants. Both shrines and roads helped inscribe dualism, directionality, and center place on the landscape. Roads acted as formal access routes, conditioning specific aspects of Chacoan visitors' spatial experiences (figure 6.1).

Sacred Geography

> *It is, perhaps, more than a little significant that the boundaries of [the Chacoan] world form the horizon line seen from certain elevated landmarks in the Chaco Core.... [P]erched on the mesa above Chaco Canyon, one is encircled by a world whose edges are punctuated by the shapes of Mount Taylor, Hosta Butte, Roof Butte, and the La Plata peaks set against the skyline. [Vivian 1990:35]*

Chaco Canyon is ideally situated to be a center place, and not simply because it is in the geographic middle of the Basin's Ancestral Pueblo settlements. In the natural landscape of the San Juan Basin, Chacoans found topographic elements that represented and substantiated their ideas about balanced dualism, directionality, center place, and cyclical renewal. Highly visible, unusual landforms in the San Juan Basin seem to have held special significance for Chacoans. Places such as Huerfano Mountain and Hosta Butte may have represented particular directions or boundaries or may have been associated with particular myths or histories. We cannot know the precise meanings these places held in the past, but Chacoans positioned some buildings and other features to create lines of sight with specific landforms and they marked these high places with shrines.

In a way, Chaco Canyon itself represents a balanced dualism between vertical and subterranean, between highly visible and entirely hidden. Although the name *Chaco Canyon* suggests depth, the mesas that form its walls are some of the highest points in the San Juan Basin. The precipitous edges of Chacra Mesa and its fragments—Fajada Butte, South Mesa, and West Mesa—rise from 90 to 180 m above the Basin floor. Chacra Mesa is intervisible with many locations across the San Juan Basin and with landforms along the Basin's edges, 50–100 km away. Huerfano Mountain, Cabezon Peak, Mount Taylor, Hosta Butte, and Shiprock punctuate Basin horizons. The Basin's periphery is demarcated by the La Plata Mountains in the north, the Sierra Nacimiento in the east, the Dutton Plateau in the south,

Table 6.1 Line-of-Sight Visibility from Classic Bonito Great Houses in Chaco Canyon

Great House	Visible Major Buildings and Landforms
Peñasco Blanco	Pueblo Alto, Pueblo Bonito, Pueblo del Arroyo, Una Vida, Casa Rinconada, Site 423, Site 1088, Huerfano Mountain
Pueblo del Arroyo	Hungo Pavi, Chetro Ketl, Pueblo Bonito, Peñasco Blanco, Casa Rinconada, Hosta Butte
Pueblo Bonito	Chetro Ketl, Hungo Pavi, Una Vida, Pueblo del Arroyo, Peñasco Blanco, Casa Rinconada
Pueblo Alto	Peñasco Blanco, Fajada Butte, Hosta Butte, Huerfano Mountain, Mount Taylor
Chetro Ketl	Una Vida, Pueblo Bonito, Pueblo del Arroyo, Casa Rinconada
Hungo Pavi	Una Vida, Pueblo Bonito, Pueblo del Arroyo, Fajada Butte, Mount Taylor
Una Vida	Hungo Pavi, Chetro Ketl, Pueblo Bonito, Peñasco Blanco, 29SJ1253 (Fajada Gap great kiva), Fajada Butte, Hosta Butte

and the Chuska Mountains in the west. We know that many of these places were significant to the Chacoans, because they marked them with shrines and rock art. They also carefully situated particular sites to create line-of-sight connections among these high places.

Classic Bonito Chacoans played upon these visual connections in a number of ways. They situated great houses to be intervisible with one another and with prominent Basin landmarks (table 6.1). Where Classic Bonito great houses could not see one another directly, Chacoans established line-of-sight connections by means of shrines on intervisible high places. All Classic Bonito canyon great houses are intervisible with one or more others. Peñasco Blanco and Pueblo Alto, both situated in high places, are intervisible with each other and are highly visible to people traveling toward Chaco Canyon.

Shrines are Chacoan landscape features located atop prominent peaks or other high places with excellent visibility (Hayes and Windes 1975; Windes 1978). Most shrines are box-shaped, low-walled masonry enclosures that sometimes contain turquoise beads, turquoise chips, or other exotica. Some shrines are J-shaped or comet-shaped. Barrel-shaped cairns constructed of Bonito-style architecture may also have functioned as shrines. Hayes and Windes (1975) recognized the importance of Chacoan shrines for intervisibility. Their investigations, focused on canyon shrines, indicated that line-of-sight connections with other shrines and with great houses were critical factors in these features' locations. Chacoans did not always put shrines on the highest point of a landform. Rather, Chacoans positioned shrines in strategic locations to facilitate intervisibility. Because shrines have few associated artifacts, they are difficult to date precisely, although reasonable guesses for indirect dates can be made, based on the sites these features visually connect. The Chacoans appear to have established the shrine network during the Classic Bonito phase and expanded it during the Late Bonito phase (chapter 8).

From an archaeological perspective, Chacoan shrines perform at least two functions—they mark places that held some special meaning for Chacoans, and they create a visual network that links places in the Chacoan world. Two shrines on Chacra Mesa and South Mesa bracket Fajada Butte, iconic symbol of central Chaco and home of the Sun Dagger petroglyph. Fajada Butte is visible for at least 25 km down the Fajada Wash to the southeast and for a similar distance to the northeast. Fajada Butte also is intervisible with other prominent Basin peaks, including Huerfano Mountain, Mount Taylor, and Hosta Butte. All these landmarks are prominently visible from multiple locations at Chaco, and all are topped with shrines (see table 6.1). Chacoans also erected shrines on places inhabited by ancestors. The first shrine discovered in Chaco Canyon was a Classic Bonito–phase, J-shaped feature erected atop Site 423, the Basketmaker III village above Peñasco Blanco (Hayes and Windes 1975)—more evidence that Classic Bonito Chacoans created meaningful connections to real or imagined Basketmaker forebears.

Shrines create a line-of-sight connection with every great house along the Chaco Wash, from Casa del Rio, 6 km west of the Chaco/Escavada wash confluence, to Pueblo Pintado, 40 km away at the east end of Chaco Canyon. These connections likely extended for some distance into the San Juan Basin, linking outlier communities to the canyon (Windes, personal communication, January 2003). Windes suggests that the features may have functioned as a communication network; this possibility is a subject of current investigation (Robinson, Van Dyke, and Windes 2007). Experiments with signal fires and mirrors have demonstrated that shrines could have been used for communication,[1] although there is currently no archaeological evidence to corroborate this. Shrines are documented above many outlier great houses. In some cases (at Kin Bineola, for example), a shrine created a line-of-sight connection back to Chaco. Cabezon Peak, above the outlier of Guadalupe, is topped by a shrine, and although this "giant head" is not visible from Chaco Canyon, it is well within sight of the east end of Chacra Mesa and connections back to Chaco. Mount Taylor, easily visible from Chaco, can be seen from a host of outliers in the Red Mesa Valley. A Farmington middle school student used mirrors to demonstrate that Huerfano Mountain could have linked Pueblo Alto to the outlier of Chimney Rock, 140 km to the northeast (Lekson 2002a). These line-of-sight connections can help us investigate interactions between specific outlier communities and Chaco Canyon.

It is tempting to view the shrine network as one means for Chacoan leaders to call people together for ceremonies. However, the shrines could have just as easily functioned as symbolic umbilicals, linking participant outlier communities to Chaco through sight. Perhaps it was symbolically meaningful to be able to see certain sites or to establish a visual connection with Chacoan landmarks, whether or not one actually used these vantage points to communicate with neighbors or with Chaco Canyon.

In my dissertation research (Van Dyke 1998, 1999b), I was somewhat skeptical of the notion that Chacoans had managed to integrate most outliers into a coherent system. I still contend that outlier–canyon interactions were variable over time and space (chapter 7), but I became convinced of the scope of Chaco's reach when I visited the west end of West Mesa, where the slender promontory of West Point overlooks the confluence of the Kin Klizhin Wash and the Chaco Wash.

The Chacoans marked the western tip of West Point with a dozen barrel-shaped shrines and a circular masonry enclosure (29SJ1088, hereafter Site 1088) (plate 9). The easternmost shrines along the mesa's edges are collapsed piles of stone, spaced every 10 m or so. At the point's extremity, five standing barrels can be clearly seen from the Chaco Wash, 150 m (500 ft) below. The westernmost of these is one of the best preserved. This solidly circular mass of stacked, tabular, brown sandstone is approximately 1.3 m in diameter and 1.2 m high, although limited rubble attests to a slightly taller original height. At the edge of the mesa, the sandstone caprock has begun to fracture, its surface crazed with deep and dangerous-looking cracks. Across one of these, below the barrel-shaped shrines, is a low-walled, circular enclosure with an opening to the southeast. The tabular, brown, Bonito-style masonry is the same as that used to construct the shrines. The enclosure was partially excavated by Peter McKenna and Tom Windes in the 1970s (Windes, personal communication, June 2005). Very few artifacts are associated with any of these features, but both Tom Windes and Gwinn Vivian are convinced that they represent Bonito-style masonry.

From West Point, it is possible to see most of the western half of the San Juan Basin—a region that contained nearly 60 Classic Bonito–phase outlier communities. From West Point, the peripheries of the Chacoan world are marked by Mount Taylor to the southeast, the Dutton Plateau to the south, the Chuska Mountains to the west, and the La Plata Mountains to the north. Looking south, the dark cavities of Borrego Pass and Dalton Pass erode the flanks of the Dutton Plateau, with Hosta Butte and Little Hosta presiding above. Looking west, the long blue rise of the Chuska Mountains is punctuated by Chuska Peak and Narbona Pass. More than 150 m directly below, the sandy white ribbon of the Chaco Wash stretches around the squat, gray-and-rust-skirted badlands at the head of the Kin Klizhin Wash. Close by on the valley floor are the outliers at Padilla Well and Kin Klizhin, and Casa del Rio's prominent midden of ground stone marks the river's first major bend. Between the bend and the Chuskan horizon lie colorfully dissected Menefee shale badlands, where a dozen outliers sleep along the confluences of Indian Creek. The volcanic spires of Bennett Peak and Shiprock jut upwards in front of Beautiful Mountain to the northwest. Looking to the northeast, Peñasco Blanco reclines atop the northern finger of West Mesa. Although Pueblo Alto is hidden behind the rising terrain, a prominent uplift northeast of Pueblo Alto marks the south bank of the Escavada, and Huerfano Mountain ripples above the horizon.

If someone standing on West Point can see most of the Chacoan world, then it follows that Ancestral Puebloans living in some 60 Classic Bonito outlier communities could also see West Point (and therefore Chaco). Did this matter? I think, clearly, it did. Outlier dwellers in view of Site 1088 were literally under the gaze of Chaco. There is no evidence that Chacoans sought to visually dominate or surveil outlier communities in a Foucaultian sense, nor could they have, from such a distance. But an outlier resident living within sight of West Point or another iconic Chacoan high place may have felt an emotional connection with Chaco, as a place where important events or ceremonies had occurred in the recent past and would soon occur again. In addition to West Point, Pueblo Alto, Fajada Butte, and Chacra Mesa are some of the most visible high places in the San Juan Basin. These landmarks could have reinforced perceptions of Chaco Canyon as center place, situated at the intersection of major directions, at the juxtaposition of the vertical and the subterranean. By the mid-1000s, the Chacoans went a step further, formally inscribing aspects of their ideology onto the physical landscape through the construction of road segments.

The Roads to Chaco

> *Mythic roads lead us beyond ourselves.*
> *It doesn't matter where they lead.*
> *We are there on them heading beyond.*

They could be returning or leaving.
We could be leaving or returning.
—from "Epic," by Simon Ortiz (2002:65)

Chacoan road segments represent some of the clearest expressions of a Chacoan worldview or cosmography. Road segments also channeled visitors' access and movement, helping create spatial experiences that emphasized facets of Chacoan ideology. Like shrines, roads are notoriously difficult to date—the best methods involve absolute dates gleaned from articulated endpoints such as great houses (Vivian 1997b:14). Although some scholars believe that Chacoans were experimenting with roads during the Pueblo I period (for example, Windes n.d.a), most indications are that road construction began in earnest in the Classic Bonito phase. In the canyon, despite the effects of ranching, erosion, and other recent disturbances, road segments are associated with all Classic Bonito–phase canyon great houses (Vivian 1983, 1997b). Windes (1987:529–555) determined that fourteen segments in Chaco Canyon date between 1050 and 1140.

At least eight road segments extend outward from Chaco Canyon (Vivian 1997b), but the roads do not connect all or even many outliers to Chaco. The extent of the road network outside Chaco Canyon was greatly exaggerated in the 1980s, when Chaco Center scholars drew roads extending from Chaco to outliers, like the spokes of a wheel (Lekson et al. 1988). However, subsequent ground-verification efforts by the Bureau of Land Management (BLM) in many cases came to naught (Kincaid 1983; Nials, Stein, and Roney 1987). Roney (1992) pared down the road database to confirmed segments, demonstrating that the road network is not as complete or extensive as once thought. Roney confirmed approximately 305 km of ground-verifiable Chacoan roads and road segments at forty-one locations across the San Juan Basin. The four longest segments verified by Roney are the North Road (50.5 km), the South Road (51.0 km), the Ah-Shi-Sle-Pah Road (11.5 km), and the Coyote Canyon Road (11.5 km). The first three radiate out from Chaco Canyon, and the latter connects the Peach Springs outlier to the Pueblo I-period Grey Ridge community (figure 6.2). Most road segments, however, are less than a mile in length, originating or terminating at great houses or great kivas, then quickly disappearing into difficult terrain.[2]

Road construction minimally involved the clearing of stones and earth out of the roadbeds. Engineers sometimes created staircases, causeways, ramps, and grooves. Roads usually average about 9 m wide, but width can range from 3 to 12 m. Formal surfacing is rare, and road depressions may be as shallow as 30 cm. Chacoan roads consist of straight segments. Wide,

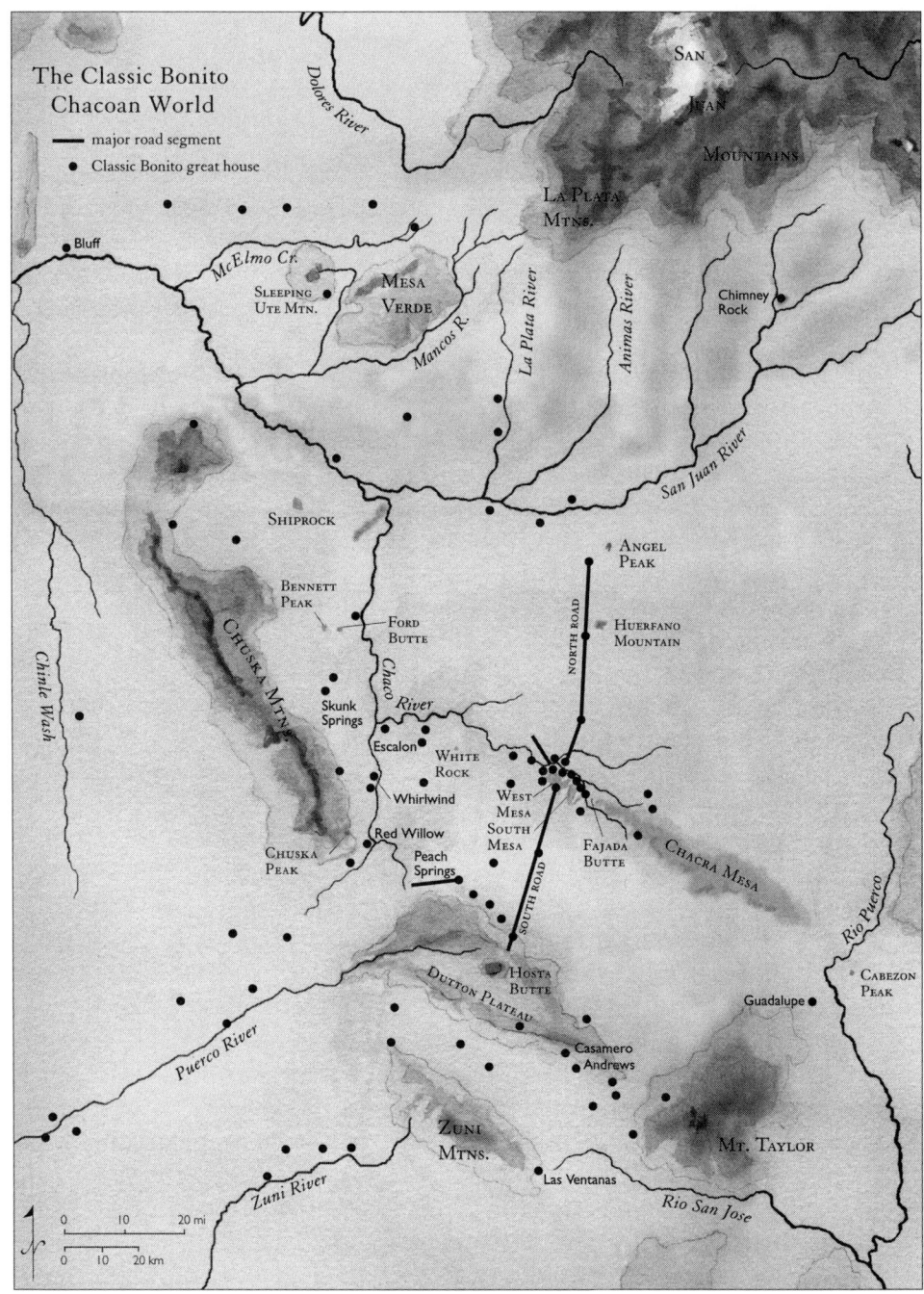

Figure 6.2. The Classic Bonito Chacoan world. Drafted by Molly O'Halloran.

Figure 6.3. Dave Ayers walks along a Chacoan road segment in the western San Juan Basin, September 1991.

major segments sometimes split into narrow "spur roads." Major directional changes are angular and occur at points of topographic change, intersections, or sites. Chacoan engineers could have maintained the roads' alignments using simple survey techniques such as backsighting (Lekson 1999:117–118; Nials 1983:6–27). *Herraduras* are a road-related feature often found atop major topographic breaks with good visibility. These horseshoe-shaped, low-walled masonry structures range from 5 to 7 m in diameter and open to the east (Lekson 1999:117–118; Nials, Stein, and Roney 1987). J-shaped "Windes' shrines" are often found along Chacoan roads (Kincaid, Stein, and Levine 1983:20; Windes 1991:118).

Embedded in the very term *road* is the idea of transportation. Many archaeologists originally assumed that the roads functioned to facilitate travel for economic, ritual, or political purposes (for example, Judge 1979; Judge et al. 1981; Powers, Gillespie, and Lekson 1983:262; Schelberg 1984; Vivian 1983; Wilcox 1993). The roads' relatively compacted surfaces do provide easier walking than the stabilized dunes that compose much of the Basin floor (figure 6.3). However, trails would have functioned just as effectively to ease pedestrian movement. The straight, wide, overengineered road segments are anomalous within a cultural context that included neither pack animals nor the wheel. And the most intensive construction efforts occur near Chacoan buildings, *not* in areas of difficult terrain.

Connections   147

By the early 1990s, Chacoan scholars recognized that roads probably had multiple functions (Windes 1991). The preponderance of evidence suggests that roads were not built primarily to facilitate transportation. There is little archaeological indication of roadside camping (Kincaid, Stein, and Levine 1983). Linear, roadside sherd scatters do not seem to represent pot drops (Hancock 1990). Chacoans clearly maintained thriving interactions with communities on the Chuskan slopes 90 km to the west, yet the best-elaborated road is the North Road, which does not connect the canyon to the Chuskas. A GIS-based "cost-path" analysis conducted by Kantner (1997) suggests that travel along roads would not have contributed to economic efficiency. Roney (1992) suggests that the short road segments commonly associated with outliers are not *meant* to go anywhere. Rather, the segments are part of the complex of Bonito-style architecture that includes great houses, great kivas, and earthworks. Chacoan "roads" were symbolic alignments meant to express Chacoan cosmographic principles.

Nevertheless, after the features were built, people almost certainly walked on them. The two functions are not mutually exclusive (Vivian 1997a; Windes 1991). We often think of Chacoan roads as moving outward, connecting Chaco Canyon to surrounding outlier communities. However, it is equally likely that the roads were important connections moving inward, prescribing formal routes of access for visitors and pilgrims into Chaco Canyon. The tracks may have been used for ceremonial races or ritual processions (Judd 1954:350; Judge 1989). Roads were particularly likely to have been used as routes of travel at the final stage of approach to Chaco and to outlying great houses, where they are best elaborated. The roads condition the approaches to Chaco Canyon and to specific buildings within and outside the canyon (Schelberg 1982:108; Ware and Gumerman 1977). Roads may have been yet another way Chacoan leaders manipulated the landscape to encourage visitors to participate in a Chacoan ideology. Classic Bonito engineers likely used the roads to symbolize aspects of an Ancestral Pueblo worldview and to prescribe access routes that directed visitors toward specific spatial experiences.

Roads and Cosmography

The two major road segments—the North Road and the South Road—represent directionality and dualism and construct the idea of Chaco Canyon as center place. Roads also created connections with sacred landmarks and ancestral sites.

The North Road constitutes perhaps the best evidence for a Chacoan concern with cardinal directions (Lekson 1999; Marshall 1997; Marshall and Sofaer 1988; Sofaer 1999; Sofaer, Marshall, and Sinclair 1989). The North Road bears north from Chaco for 50.5 km, extending from Pueblo Alto past the outliers of Pierre's and Halfway House to the badlands at the edge of Kutz Canyon (Sofaer, Marshall, and Sinclair 1989:367–368; Stein 1983). En route are jogs, gaps, and parallel segments. The last clear evidence for the road is at the canyon's edge, where there is an earth and juniper log stairway. Upper Twin Angels mound, a prominent, symmetrically shaped pinnacle topped with a shrine, is nearby (Sofaer, Marshall, and Sinclair 1989), and the Late Bonito–phase Twin Angels outlier is on the canyon rim 6.5 km to the northwest (Carlson 1966).

The northern terminus of the North Road is subject to debate. Some archaeologists believe that it continued down Kutz Canyon to the outlier of Salmon Ruin on the San Juan River. Lekson (1999) and others (Stein and McKenna 1988) contend that the road then headed north from Salmon Ruin to the Aztec outlier on the Animas River. The North Road as a link from Chaco Canyon to Aztec is a major lynchpin of Lekson's (1999) argument in *Chaco Meridian*. Currently, no physical evidence or aerial imagery substantiates these claims, but any evidence for a road in the canyon badlands would have long since eroded away. Also, the areas around Salmon and Aztec have been heavily farmed and otherwise modified over the past century, potentially obliterating road evidence there.

The North Road might be better interpreted not as a physical path linking settlements, but rather as a symbolic statement of the importance of the direction north for Chacoans (see also chapter 3). Keresan emergence stories describe a sipapu to the north, where the people came forth into this world. The people then migrated south to find the center place (White 1942:177, 1960:89). For the Tewa (Harrington 1916:166, 167), the sipapu can be represented on the landscape by an unusual landform such as a lake, cave, or mountain peak, linked to the center place by a path. Puebloan pilgrimages to the place of emergence frequently involve votive deposits at shrines (Ellis and Hammack 1968). For the Hopi, a road to the sipapu also represents life's journey (Parsons 1939:310). Infant souls travel along this path from the sipapu to the center place at birth, and souls return along this path to the sipapu at death. In Tewa tradition, parallel life paths exist, and mortuary rituals may involve breaking ceramic vessels (Ortiz 1969:54, 57). At Acoma, offerings that represent the soul of a deceased person are deposited in a canyon or crevice in the north (White 1973[1932]:137).

Building on these ideas, Marshall (1997) and Sofaer, Marshall, and Sinclair (1989) have interpreted the North Road as a symbolic pathway linking Chaco Canyon, and more specifically Pueblo Alto, with a place of emergence represented by or near Kutz Canyon or the San Juan Mountains beyond (plate 10). Early Bonito–phase settlers likely moved to the San Juan Basin from southwest Colorado, migrating from the north to Chaco. Parallel segments of the North Road might represent the parallel paths taken by different clans or moieties on their journey south to the center place. Shrines along the way may have been places for pilgrims to pray or leave votive deposits. North might have been the direction of death, as well as emergence, as humans completed a cyclical life journey. The large volume of smashed ceramic vessels in the mound at Pueblo Alto has been interpreted as the detritus from feasting (Toll 1985:369–406). Another possibility is that some of these vessels may have been broken in mortuary rituals as the souls of the dead began their journey back to the sipapu along the North Road. Perhaps Chacoans believed that the pots, brought to the canyon at important ceremonial times and ritually deposited, contained the souls of the dead. Perhaps Chuskan vessels were deemed uniquely suitable for this purpose, or perhaps a great many people came from the Chuskas bearing them.[3]

In balanced dualism with the North Road, the South Road extends for 51 km from Chaco Canyon south-southwest toward the Dutton Plateau. The BLM Roads project traced a total of 39 km along the South Road, beginning just south of the park service boundary and extending past Bee Burrow and Kin Ya'a. The South Road stops 5 km short of Hosta Butte, a prominent landmark on the southern horizon rising 300 m above the Dutton Plateau (Marshall 1997:71; Nials, Stein, and Roney 1987:18). The fact that the South Road does not trend directly south does not preclude its interpretation as the balanced, directional counterpart to the North Road. In contemporary Pueblo cosmography, features associated with directions need not be oriented precisely along cardinal axes. More important than creating a true southerly orientation may have been the desire to connect the canyon symbolically with Hosta Butte.

Many scholars, especially Marshall (1997), Sofaer (1999; Sofaer, Marshall, and Sinclair 1989), and Lekson (1999), have recognized that the North and South roads not only express a Chacoan concern with directionality but also fix Chaco Canyon as a center place. The North Road and the South Road counterpose not only north and south but also the subterranean and the vertical (Marshall 1997:71).[4] The North Road begins at a high place—Pueblo Alto, on Chaco Canyon's north rim—and leads to a low place—Kutz Canyon. By contrast, the South Road begins at a low place—Pueblo del Arroyo, on the floor of Chaco Canyon—and leads to a high place—Hosta Butte. Not only do the two roads form opposing pairs of north/south and down/up, but they are also of equal length, balancing the canyon like a fulcrum between them, intersecting at Chaco Canyon—the center place.

Thus, the roads inscribe Chaco Canyon as the center place, the intersection of north and south, up and down. Chaco Canyon itself may represent an east-west opposition. Some evidence exists for an East Road and a West Road, but, in general, these directions seem to have been less formally elaborated on the landscape. Certainly, the Chaco Wash was a logical conduit for movement both east and west out of central Chaco Canyon. An East Road may have run down the length of the canyon for approximately 25 km from Fajada Butte to Pueblo Pintado (Windes et al. 2000:42–43). Although there is no well-defined, continuous West Road, there are several short segments near Peñasco Blanco and the outliers of Lake Valley and Escalon (Hancock 1990; Nials, Stein, and Roney 1987; Windes 1987:97).

Other road segments do not exhibit clear directional associations but rather connect Chaco Canyon to unusual landforms or springs (Sofaer, Marshall, and Sinclair 1989). The Ah-Shi-Sle-Pah Road, 11.5 km long, originates at Peñasco Blanco (Nials, Stein, and Roney 1987:120–126; Stein 1983). A stairway leads north into the Chaco/Escavada wash confluence below Peñasco Blanco, and a matching modified path known as Vivian's Staircase climbs up the north side of the confluence. From the north rim of the wash, a road extends to a series of bedrock tanks (Los Aguajes), then can be traced through sherd scatters over slickrock to a masonry ramp descending into the Ah-Shi-Sle-Pah Wash. An additional 2 km are visible past this point, and the northern terminus of the road is thought by some to be a shrine-like site at Black Lake (Marshall and Sofaer 1988; Roney 1992). Chacoans intensified the practice of constructing roads as links with symbolically significant locations during the Late Bonito phase (chapter 8).

Approaches to Chaco

Classic Bonito builders not only engineered roads to symbolize elements of a Chacoan ideology but also constructed roads as formalized approaches into Chaco Canyon. There are many possible ancient routes of access into the core area of the canyon. On the south side, the canyon may be easily entered through the two major breaks in Chacra Mesa—Fajada Gap and South Gap. On the north side, tributary washes create many entries. Fairly easy descents are possible through the Gallo Wash (the modern park service road), through Mockingbird Canyon, or at the west end of the canyon through the Escavada Wash. Steeper descents are possible through Clys Canyon and other smaller, unnamed tributary canyons. The canyon also may be entered at its east and west ends. Any or all of these may have been used in daily life by inhabitants and visitors to Chaco, but Classic Bonito Chacoans constructed road segments, ramps, staircases, and shrines to direct travelers' movements along specific routes. Formal approaches employed the natural topography to enhance the contradictions inherent in the canyon landscape, maximizing the visibility of specific Chacoan buildings or other features as visitors neared the canyon. The Chacoans may have designed these formal routes for processions (Barclay and Harding 1999; Barrett 1994; Tilley 1994:173–200). These routes may have been one way that Chacoan leaders created specific spatial experiences for pilgrims arriving in Chaco.

During July 2002, with research permits from the Navajo Nation and Chaco Culture National Historic Park, I walked six major formal approaches into the canyon. From east, to north, to west, to south, these are the North Road, the Ah-Shi-Sle-Pah Road, the West Chaco River, the South Road, Fajada Gap, and East Chaco Canyon (see figure 6.1). Along the way, I paid special attention to sights, sounds, and other sensations. I am under no illusion that these phenomenological experiments allowed me to replicate the Chacoan spatial experience—my sensual interactions with the canyon landscape are culturally conditioned, and the canyon landscape has not persisted unchanged across a millennium of history. Nevertheless, I learned much through these experiments about the ways Chacoan visitors would have experienced the journey into the canyon and about the ways the road segments formalized their spatial perceptions, emphasizing certain sights and sensations while minimizing others.

The North Road.

The North Road linking Pueblo Alto and Kutz Canyon is famous for its length (more than 50 km) and direction (true north). However, the North Road is not actually one continuous road segment, nor do the segments point precisely north. Along the route are gaps in the road as long as 12.5 km and areas of double and occasionally quadruple parallel segments. Five small masonry shrines are located on pinnacles or ridge crests along the route (Stein 1983). From Pueblo Alto, the road heads toward the Escavada Wash at a bearing of 13 degrees east of north. From this point, the road runs within half a degree of north to the buildings at Pierre's outlier, 16 km distant. Pierre's is a substantial outlier community with two clusters of Bonito-style buildings atop and at the base of a prominent isolated butte (Harper et al. 1988; Powers, Gillespie, and Lekson 1983:95–133). The last 31 km of the road, between El Faro and Kutz Canyon, bear 2 degrees east of true north.[5] Along this stretch, Halfway House is a small, core-and-veneer great house situated on a knoll above a tributary to the Gallegos Wash (Powers, Gillespie, and Lekson 1983:183–186).

As the North Road traverses the Chaco Plateau's gradual, 90-m northern uplift, distinctive Chacoan landforms, including Chacra Mesa, West Point, South Gap, and Hosta Butte, remain intermittently visible until the plateau begins to drop toward Kutz Canyon. Fajada Butte is visible from many vantage points northeast of Chaco, including Nageezi at 30 km, Crow Mesa at 44 km, and Huerfano Mountain, at 46 km distance, but Fajada Butte is not visible from along the North Road—the high bluffs along the Escavada Wash block the line of sight.

On a clear summer morning, I walk the final 3.5 km of the North Road from the Escavada Wash to Pueblo Alto. Chacoan residents of communities along the Escavada Wash could have entered Chaco Canyon by following the wash to its confluence with the Chaco below Peñasco Blanco. The formal route, however, leads up out of the wash and over a dune-covered expanse toward the low mounds of Pueblo Alto and the two-story walls of the Late Bonito great house New Alto, beckoning on the skyline. When I begin, the two Altos are quite visible, but as I set out across the dunes, I find that distances are deceiving and perspectives are constantly shifting. Atop high dunes, Pueblo Alto seems just within reach, but in troughs, I can see nothing beyond a sea of sand and scrubby vegetation. The Chacoan road alignment would have helped travelers keep their bearings in this deceptively difficult terrain. Amid the rabbitbrush and saltbush, I stay on course by following a compass bearing, keeping a sharp lookout for intermittent, telltale swales and sherd scatters.

A little more than 1 km north of Pueblo Alto, the North Road crosses the headwaters of Clys Canyon, a small northern tributary draining into Chaco Canyon. Clys Canyon provides easy access to the canyon interior and was the location of a now abandoned park service road. It is difficult not to give in to gravity and shift downhill to the west toward this logical canyon access point, but I hold to my course. I pass Rabbit Ruin, a Late Bonito building on a terrace above Clys, 100 m to the west. The formal route I follow directs me toward the massive edifice of Pueblo Alto, looming ever larger atop the undulating sea of brush-covered dunes. The totemic landforms of the southern Chacoan horizon remain largely hidden from view.

At last I reach Pueblo Alto, where as many as 12 Chacoan road segments converge (Windes 1991: figure 11.4). But the road does not take me directly to the great house. A low masonry wall extends 143 m to the east of Pueblo Alto, connecting the great house with the twelve-room East Ruin (Windes 1987:80). Three road segments meet at this wall, where a 1-m-wide opening or "gate" allows access through the wall (Ware and Gumerman 1977). The opening may have controlled access or slowed traffic, perhaps to ensure that everyone passing into Pueblo Alto took full notice of the views from this location. But the Pueblo Alto gate is more than a major threshold for physical admission into the Alto complex. It is also the point at which I first catch sight of Fajada Butte, as well as the other major topographic landmarks of the southern Chaco horizon, including Mount Taylor, the Dutton Plateau, Dalton Pass, Hosta Butte, and South Gap.

Pueblo Alto is the only one-story great house in Chaco Canyon, but the builders created a powerfully vertical monument by siting Pueblo Alto in this high place. From Pueblo Alto, as from West Point, I can see much of the Chacoan world. To the north lie the snow-capped La Plata Mountains and, less distant, Huerfano Peak. To the northwest, the folded stone sails of Shiprock protrude above the horizon, and the Carrizo Mountains are visible beyond. To the west are the Chuskas, with Beautiful Mountain, the creases of Narbona Pass, and the pyramidal footnote of Chuska Peak. The Dutton Plateau forms the southern horizon, with Hosta Butte peeping above. To the southeast, I can see Mount Taylor, and to the east, the Sierra Nacimiento near Cuba, New Mexico. The other great houses of Chaco Canyon, however, remain hidden inside the canyon.

From Pueblo Alto, a Chacoan could have proceeded down into Chaco Canyon along several formal routes, dropping over an upper bench before descending the canyon's north face (Windes 1991). A road segment extends from the west side of Pueblo Alto across the broad benches of the north mesa down a set of masonry steps. This segment then splits into two "spur" roads, one heading toward Pueblo del Arroyo, the other toward Pueblo Bonito. Southeast of Pueblo Alto, two parallel road segments drop over the first cliff edge and cross the slickrock. The two roads then narrow and diverge. One leads to a set of ramps and stairways that descend to the Talus Unit, behind Chetro Ketl. The other drops into the main canyon via ramps and stairs in a small rincon northeast of Chetro Ketl (Gwinn Vivian, personal communication, November 2006; Windes 1991:117). Still farther to the east, Jackson Staircase links the upper bench of the north mesa to a small side canyon behind Chetro Ketl. Although a Chacoan standing at the head of the Jackson Staircase would have glimpsed part of Chetro Ketl below, this approach to Chaco does not seem particularly designed for dramatic effect.

The modern park service trail from Pueblo Alto to Pueblo Bonito parallels the Bonito spur of the westernmost road from Alto. As I make my way down along this trail, Tsin Kletsin, Peñasco Blanco, South Gap, and Fajada Butte slowly come into view, but the great houses on the canyon floor remain hidden under the edge of the mesa until I am almost directly above them. The road segment disappears at the canyon edge above Pueblo Bonito. Chacoans would have descended via a staircase behind Pueblo Bonito, but I follow the park service trail west along the canyon rim.

Along this area of the north rim, South Gap is visible to the southwest across the canyon below, and Hosta Butte presides over the southwestern horizon. As I move west along the canyon rim, I visit one of the most spectacular and potentially symbolically significant spots in Chaco. The Chacoans constructed a stone circle (29SJ1572) at the point along the north rim where Hosta Butte is framed in the center of South Gap. From the circle, Pueblo del Arroyo, South Gap, and Hosta Butte are in perfect alignment along the trajectory of the South Road (plate 11).

Like shrines, stone circles are an enigmatic Chacoan landscape feature that flirts with visibility. Chacoans nearly always constructed them on slickrock, on high points or benches that provide good vantage points (Windes 1978). Although termed *circles*, the features actually tend to be ellipses of compound, core-and-veneer, or upright slab masonry. During the Chaco Project, Windes (1978) identified sixteen stone circles on the north rim and four on the south mesas of Chaco Canyon. Windes and other researchers have located additional circles at outliers across the San Juan Basin, including Andrews, Grey Hill Spring, Kin Bineola, Las Ventanas, Pierre's, and Twin Angels (Van Dyke 2001; Windes 1978). Stone circles range in size, from 9–32 m along a long axis to 7–20 m along a short axis. Most stone circles contain one or more circular or rectangular basins pecked or ground into the interior slickrock. Although ceramics are scarce, associated sandstone abraders are common. Windes speculates that these abraders might have been used to smooth wood, hides, or the sandstone surfaces of the circles themselves. On the basis of sparsely associated ceramics, the stone circles are dated between 1000 and 1150. In Chaco Canyon, viewsheds from stone circles always include one or more great kivas, but the closest great houses are usually hidden beneath the canyon rim. Stone circles are carefully sited to achieve these effects—if the features were moved only a few meters, sometimes to more level terrain, then these dual attributes of visibility and invisibility would be lost. Windes suggests that the dual visible/invisible quality of circles might have made them ideal places for the manufacture of ritual items or preparation for ceremonies. Whatever practical or symbolic functions it may have served, the stone circle above South Gap marks a dramatic visual connection replicating the physical alignment embodied by the South Road.

The Ah-Shi-Sle-Pah Road.

The Ah-Shi-Sle-Pah Road is a formal access route into Chaco Canyon that terminates at the Chaco/Escavada confluence (Nials, Stein, and Roney 1987:120–126; Stein 1983). The other end of this road segment is thought to be Black Lake, 4 km northwest of the Ah-Shi-Sle-Pah Wash (Marshall and Sofaer 1988; Roney 1992). A masonry ramp leads out of the wash, and the road can be traced through sherd scatters over slickrock to Los Aguajes—a series of bedrock tanks. Between Los Aguajes and Chaco Canyon, the Ah-Shi-Sle-Pah Road is a cleared, linear alignment marked by swales and sherd scatters. With the help of aerial photographs provided by John Stein, I join the road segment approximately 3 km northwest of Chaco Canyon.

As along the North Road, the terrain between Los Aguajes and Chaco Canyon consists of undulating aeolian sand dunes topped with rabbitbrush and four-wing saltbush. The road alignment is difficult to see on the ground, and I keep myself on track with a compass bearing, the aerial photo, and periodic glimpses of artifacts along the swales. Here, as along other Chacoan road segments, dense, linear sherd scatters appear at intervals along the road's edges. Whiteware jars are most common (Windes 1987, 1991).

As I follow the Ah-Shi-Sle-Pah Road to Chaco, I learn two important things. First, I am surprised by how physically difficult it is to walk among the stabilized dunes. Morenon and Amick (1977) found walking on Chacoan roads to be a more efficient use of caloric energy than walking on the adjacent natural terrain, and the tired muscles in my calves support their conclusions—the ancient roadway provides a slightly more compact (and therefore easier) walking surface than the spongy dunes. Second, I am surprised by the way that visibility and perception are constantly shifting among the dunes. Some landmarks I expect to see remain hidden, and others are revealed. Huerfano Mountain, Pueblo Alto, a bluff along the Escavada north of Pueblo Alto, and West Mesa guide me on the horizon for much of the way, but at times I slog across the sand seeing nothing but higher dunes on all sides. From a dune crest approximately 2 km out, West Mesa is extremely prominent—behind it, Hosta Butte and Dalton Pass are visible. To the west are dunes and distant badlands, and behind, the long blue line of the Chuska Mountains. To the east, the gleaming white braid of the Escavada Wash stretches in the sun. However, I cannot see Peñasco Blanco or anything else inside Chaco Canyon.

At last, I crest the final dune before dropping to a broad slickrock bench above the Chaco/Escavada confluence. Now I am confronted with a spectacular vista (plate 12). Directly across the Chaco, Peñasco Blanco gleams golden in the late afternoon sunlight, and Site 423, capped with its Classic Bonito shrine, rises above. The road aligns with the stretch of Chaco Canyon between the Escavada Wash and South Gap so that, as I look toward the canyon, the Chaco Wash appears to be an extension of the path I have been walking. Below me, the broad white expanse of the Chaco/Escavada confluence beckons, dotted with the tiny forms of a few sultry cows. The end of the road is marked by twin cairns atop Vivian's Staircase, a relatively easy descent down a series of slickrock benches and rock and masonry steps into the Escavada Wash. Directly across from Vivian's Staircase is the rock-cut stairway leading up to Peñasco Blanco.

The Ah-Shi-Sle-Pah Road likely had both practical and symbolic functions. The segment may have been a processional pathway leading out of Chaco Canyon to shrines at Black Lake. The road segment would have facilitated travel into Chaco Canyon—the cleared alignment would have helped keep travelers on course across the dunes, and the wide road would have enabled two or more people to walk abreast. However, travelers on this road, unlike those who arrived via the West Chaco River and other access routes, were probably not outlier dwellers—there are no outliers in the area immediately northwest of Chaco, where the terrain degenerates into the inhospitable Bisti badlands. Neither is the Ah-Shi-Sle-Pah Road a logical route of access into Chaco Canyon from the northwest—access would be more easily gained via a small tributary canyon on the north side of the Escavada 1 km farther northeast. The Ah-Shi-Sle-Pah Road does give the pedestrian traveler a dramatic and relatively sudden canyon vista directed at Peñasco Blanco, Site 423, and the Chaco Wash. Perhaps this vista was the point—the road may have been intended for processions emphasizing one or more of these locales. The Ah-Shi-Sle-Pah Road also is provocatively tied into the shrine network that provides visual connections up and down the canyon—Vivian's Staircase, at the end of the road, is positioned in the only place where the north face of the Escavada Wash can be seen from the shrine at 29SJ1207 atop South Mesa. Another possibility is that, like the North and South roads, the Ah-Shi-Sle-Pah Road forms the northwest half of a pair of directional alignments intersecting in Chaco Canyon. Ah-Shi-Sle-Pah is on the same axis as Chacra Mesa. There may have been a road paralleling Chacra Mesa along its southern slope (Vivian 1972). This Chacra Face road would have trended toward the direction of Cabezon Peak—a high, southeast place balancing the low, northwest place of Black Lake. However, road scholars disagree regarding the antiquity of a Chacra Face road (Roney 1992:125; Vivian 1997b:18).

West Chaco River.

The Chaco River is probably one of the oldest access routes into Chaco Canyon, traversed by Early Bonito migrants as they made their way into the canyon from the western Basin and the slopes of the Chuska Mountains in the mid-800s (chapter 4). During the Classic Bonito period, outlier communities stretched along the major drainages of the western Basin like beads on strings, reaching toward the Chuska Mountains 70 km away. Ceramics, lithics, wood, and corn poured into Chaco Canyon from the west, providing solid material evidence that many, many Ancestral Puebloans walked this way (Snygg and Windes 1998; Toll 2006). Trachyte-tempered Chuskan ceramics are found in abundance in Chaco Canyon and in sites all along the route (Toll 1985:439–451; Van Dyke 1997b).[6] Skunk Springs was the likely locus of production for Chuskan gray ware, which makes up 30 percent of the total ceramic assemblage in the trash mound at Pueblo Alto (V. King 2003; Toll 1984:115).

It is 67 km as the crow flies from Skunk Springs to West Point. If Chacoan roads were built primarily to facilitate travel, then the clearest road should extend from the canyon to the west, linking Chaco with Chuskan communities and resources. Evidence for a formal west road, however, is minimal. A short (0.1 km) road segment heads west from the area of Peñasco Blanco (Windes 1987:97), a segment (2.1 km) is present in the vicinity of Lake Valley (Nials, Stein, and Roney 1987:116–117), and a segment (3.1 km) is visible near Escalon (Hancock 1990), but researchers' attempts to find a coherent, ground-verifiable western connection have thus far been unsuccessful.

Nevertheless, Ancestral Puebloans undoubtedly traveled this way for hundreds of years. The Chaco River provides a logical route for the stretch between West Mesa and the Great Bend, where the Chaco turns north. Travelers likely made their way across 20 km of downward-sloping terrain between Skunk Springs and the Great Bend of the Chaco River, then followed the river into the canyon. The packed sand of the wide river bottom serves as a natural trail; its level walking surface is easier for pedestrians to traverse than the surrounding badlands and dunes. Six outlier communities are located at intervals along this corridor, potentially providing overnight stopovers and other resources for travelers. The river would have provided the most critical resource for the traveler—water. Even when the Chaco is not running, in modern times the water table is rarely more than a few feet below the riverbed.

On another bright July morning, I begin my pedestrian journey into the canyon from the Chaco River approximately 2 km west of West Point and 5 km from Peñasco Blanco. The riverbed is a natural and open highway, and walking in the hard-packed sand is easy. Sheer rock canyon walls rise to the north. The shrines at Site 1088 along the edges of West Point loom like eerie sentinels against the sky, and I feel myself under the gaze of Chaco. Were these barrel-shaped shrines meant to serve as beacons or boundary markers for travelers approaching the canyon? I detour over to Padilla Well, an outlier situated directly under West Mesa on the south side of the Chaco River. From Padilla Well, the West Point shrines appear as a row of jagged jack-olantern teeth. After I pass West Point, however, I note that the shrines are no longer in view. If the shrines were meant as welcoming beacons for travelers entering Chaco Canyon, then I expect there to be more of them lining the cliffs on either side as I near the Chaco/Escavada confluence, but there are not.

The shrines' primary audience seems to have been distant viewers instead of Chaco River travelers. Although West Point is visible from many high points in the western Basin, it cannot be seen from the twisting bends of the river bottom until the last 10 km of the approach. West Point becomes more visible farther west and south in the San Juan Basin, particularly toward the eastern foothills of the Chuskas, and along the northern flanks of the Dutton Plateau. Perhaps the shrines were situated to signal outliers that could not otherwise see one another. West Point can be seen from both Padilla Well and Casa del Rio, but these two outliers are not intervisible around the bend in the Chaco Wash.

Back along the Chaco River, I round West Point and sight the broken form of Peñasco Blanco on a West Mesa terrace 3 km away. The white ribbon of the Chaco points directly toward the great house. The confluence with the Escavada creates a wide and shimmering sandy plain. To access Peñasco Blanco directly, I could climb the stairs cut into the steep sandstone cliff on the south side of the wash. Instead, I choose to continue down the wash into the central part of the canyon, traversing the south edge of the major sand dune that blocks the Chaco Wash just east of the Escavada confluence. If this dune did, in fact, dam the Chaco Wash during the Classic Bonito phase (Force et al. 2002), then an Ancestral Pueblo traveler at this point would have been skirting a reservoir. Today, a series of intermittent, stagnant pools lie under the cliff edge, and I tramp my way through a dense, brushy, bug-besotted thicket, startling the same few cows. It is a relief to emerge again into the open, 500-m-wide expanse of canyon bottom. From here, Pueblo Bonito is fewer than 5 km away along the canyon bottom.

South Gap and the South Road.

South Gap—the break between South Mesa and West Mesa—was cut by an unnamed wash that drains the South Chaco Slope between Kin Klizhin and Fajada washes. South Gap is a natural conduit for traffic into and out of central Chaco Canyon. Small Basketmaker settlements dot the slopes along the west side of the gap (Hayes 1981:24–25), and Early Bonitians built Pueblo Bonito at the confluence of the gap with Chaco Canyon. From inside Chaco Canyon, South Gap frames Hosta Butte on the horizon. This topographic coincidence likely did not go unnoticed by early settlers. Classic Bonito builders clearly considered the South Gap–Hosta Butte relationship to have special significance, modifying the landscape and erecting structures and features to emphasize the connection. Chacoans constructed the South Road along the South Gap–Hosta Butte alignment. Pueblo Bonito is slightly offset to the east, so Chacoans built Pueblo del Arroyo at the mouth of South Gap, in direct alignment with Hosta Butte. They also constructed the stone circle (29SJ1572) atop Chaco Canyon's north rim, at the spot where Pueblo del Arroyo, South Gap, and Hosta Butte are in visual alignment.

From Pueblo del Arroyo, the South Road stretches toward the distant horizon of the Dutton Plateau, punctuated by Dalton Pass, Hosta Butte, and Little Hosta Butte. Like many Chacoan roads, the alignment today is more visible from the air than on the ground. The BLM Roads project traced the South Road from the south end of South Gap, just outside the park boundary. The project defined segments following bearings ranging from 184 to 220 degrees east of true north (Nials, Stein, and Roney 1987:32–51; Roney 1992:126). Inside South Gap, a segment follows the west side of the gap to the south edge of West Mesa, disappearing at the point where Kin Klizhin becomes visible (Gwinn Vivian, personal communication, November 2006). In July 2002, John Stein, Rich Friedman, and I spent a day looking for traces of the South Road inside South Gap. Our search on the valley floor was inconclusive because the area where the road would be has been extensively disturbed by old park service two-tracks and historic Navajo occupation. We found and examined 29SJ807, a shrine related to the segment that extends along the west side of South Gap. From the shrine, we could clearly see Pueblo del Arroyo and Pueblo Bonito, but Pueblo Alto and New Alto were hidden behind the west face of South Gap.

Like the North Road, the South Road is composed of discontinuous segments. West Mesa and South Mesa are intermittently visible from points all along the South Road. Along the way, the road passes the outliers of Upper Kin Klizhin, Bee Burrow, and Kin Ya'a before disappearing atop Lobo Mesa south of Crownpoint. Kin Ya'a is intervisible with a shrine site on South Mesa (29SJ706) (Hayes and Windes 1975:153). On another sun-seared July morning, I set out to walk the final 7 km of the South Road's projected alignment, entering Chaco Canyon through South Gap. I join the South Road amid the rolling dunes near the break between the Kin Klizhin and South Gap wash drainages. I will gain approximately 35 m in elevation over the next several kilometers. As on the Ah-Shi-Sle-Pah Road and the North Road, landmarks such as West Mesa, South Mesa, Chacra Mesa, and the Chuska Mountains are now visible, now hidden, as I make my way across the dips and rises of dunes and dissecting washes. Approximately 4 km from South Gap, I top a rise to be greeted with the sight of the two Altos, on the mesa

Figure 6.4. Entering Chaco Canyon through South Gap. From this point, Pueblo del Arroyo appears on the canyon floor on the right side of South Gap. New Alto is centered on the horizon, and Pueblo Alto is the low mound on the horizon to the right of New Alto.

top, and Pueblo del Arroyo, framed through the gap straight ahead.

As I enter South Gap, I move from the relatively expansive space of the dunes to a more restrictive visual environment. The gap directs my gaze toward the most prominent features on the landscape—Pueblo del Arroyo, New Alto, and Pueblo Alto. Pueblo del Arroyo is centered in my field of vision, with Pueblo Bonito and Kin Kletso off to the east and west sides, respectively. On the north mesa above Chaco, New Alto rises directly behind Pueblo del Arroyo, and Pueblo Alto is offset to the east (figure 6.4). As I emerge through the mouth of South Gap into Chaco Canyon, two small sites are positioned on either side. Today, the Chaco Wash is deeply entrenched, but in the eleventh century I would have been able to walk directly up to the south wall of Pueblo del Arroyo.

Very probably, Pueblo del Arroyo was constructed to be framed within South Gap. It is an impressive terminus to the South Road and, like Pueblo Alto, is situated to make an impression on visitors entering the canyon through a formal route of access. Pueblo Bonito was not positioned to take full advantage of the framing effect of South Gap. The construction of Pueblo del Arroyo in the 1070s must have been, at least in part, a result of Chacoan leaders' desire to formalize the spatial experiences of people moving into the canyon through South Gap. The juxtaposition of this great

Figure 6.5. Entering Chaco Canyon along SR 57, through Fajada Gap. Fajada Butte lies straight ahead, and Huerfano Mountain is visible on the horizon.

house against the north rim of the canyon 200 m distant, with West and South mesas flanking it on either side, exaggerates the building's proportions. The formal approach through South Gap may have been used for ritual processions, or it may have been for the benefit of travelers from the south, or perhaps both.

Fajada Gap.
The Fajada Gap route to Chaco is familiar to modern visitors who have traveled to the canyon on Route 57, turning north from Navajo 9 at Seven Lakes. The modern road traverses clay hills and outcrops along the west side of the Fajada drainage. Fajada Butte is visible at many points along Route 57 (figure 6.5) and for at least 35 km southeast of Fajada Gap as the terrain rises 275 m to meet the Continental Divide near modern Hospah. From these vantage points, the long, low form of Chacra Mesa to the east directs the gaze northwards toward Fajada Butte. For a pedestrian traveler to Chaco Canyon, Fajada Butte would have loomed larger and larger between undulating hills, just as it does today for a motorist following Route 57 into the canyon. Beyond Chaco, Huerfano Mountain hovers on the northern horizon.

Although there are large Pueblo I settlements along the South Fork of the Fajada Wash (Windes n.d.a), there are few Classic Bonito outliers directly south of the canyon. Most travelers arriving in Chaco from southern outliers would have been more likely to follow the South Road from the Kin Ya'a area into South Gap. Nonetheless, road researchers have identified a number of floating, southeast road segments pointing toward Fajada Gap (Kincaid 1983; Obenauf 1980; Vivian 1983). These segments are in dispute, however, because ground-verification of roads identified on aerial photographs is difficult (Nials, Stein, and Roney 1987:67; Roney 1992). For example, the Chacra Face Road is a floating segment paralleling the southern slope of Chacra Mesa, pointing between Fajada Butte and Cabezon Peak. This road is clearly visible on aerial photographs (Obenauf 1983:4/14), although some researchers consider it to be historic (Roney 1992:125). The Chacra Face Road might have symbolically balanced the Ah-Shi-Sle-Pah Road, opposing the intercardinal directions of northwest and southeast. Or it might have symbolically pointed to Cabezon Peak, a sacred, shrine-topped high place.

I decide to walk the last few kilometers of Fajada Gap into Chaco Canyon in the general vicinity of the wash, where these roads would have entered the canyon. It is slow going through the stabilized dunes. The wash itself is deeply entrenched, so I stay high to either side. As I approach Fajada Gap, Fajada Butte dominates my field of vision, with its colorfully stacked layers of Menefee shale and Cliff House sandstone rising 430 m from the canyon floor. As I enter the gap, Una Vida and Kin Nahasbas (plate 3) come into view. Kin Nahasbas particularly draws attention, highlighted against the canyon wall in a direct line with the north-trending wash. I turn to look south through Fajada Gap and see Mount Taylor and Hosta Butte on horizons to the southeast and southwest, respectively.

East Chaco Canyon.

A 22-km stretch of Chaco Canyon between Fajada Gap and Pintado Canyon creates a natural conduit to the east. Travelers approaching Chaco Canyon from the east would have been coming from the Chaco East community, Pueblo Pintado, and Guadalupe. Intermittent features, such as a 100-m-long road segment near Chaco East, suggest that an East Road may have existed in the canyon bottom (Windes et al. 2000). Another 400-m-long road segment leaves Pueblo Pintado and extends toward Chaco Canyon (Roney 1992:125–126; Windes 1991). Erosion could have obscured additional traces of an East Road, or perhaps this road never was continuous. In any case, the canyon itself prescribes the best eastern approach to central Chaco.

The Chacoans may have modified the east end of the canyon route to enhance the visibility of the outlier great house Pueblo Pintado. Although Pueblo Pintado is built on a rise, the building is not particularly prominent when approached from the south (as modern tourists do, by car). But travelers from central Chaco would have exited the canyon toward Pueblo Pintado by a series of large steps cut into the canyon wall. From the vantage point of the canyon staircase, "Pintado looms like a medieval castle… because it is built on top of the rise that pushes the whole structure skyward" (Tom Windes, personal communication, June 2005).

I turn my boots to face downtown Chaco, and in afternoon sunlight, I walk the final 4.5 km of the east canyon route between the isolated great kiva 29SJ1642 and Fajada Gap. The canyon here is slightly narrower than downstream in the vicinity of the Classic Bonito great houses. The Chaco Wash is deeply eroded, and the canyon bottom is choked with low, brushy vegetation, so I keep to the trail in the center of the canyon. By contrast with the open vistas of the North Road or some other approaches, my visibility is restricted to several hundred meters in all directions by the gently twisting canyon walls. My world is a linear, sandy track through the brush, bounded on all sides at a brief distance by brown Menefee and Cliff House sandstone. I pass the photogenic ruins of the Late Bonito great house Wijiji (chapter 8). Just after Wijiji disappears behind me, Fajada Butte begins to emerge, approximately 1.5 km east of the canyon's confluence with the Gallo Wash. The butte is invisible, then visible—at first, Fajada Butte looks like part of Chacra Mesa, but as I move closer, it separates into a discrete pillar. I pass several small sites in the area of the Gallo Wash confluence, but Una Vida remains hidden from view until I come abreast of Fajada Butte. For travelers along this eastern route, traveling to Chaco might have been like emerging from a long tunnel with restricted visibility into the light, space, and monumentality of the central canyon.

Discussion and Summary

During the Classic Bonito phase, as the scale of participation in Chacoan ceremonialism increased, connections between Chaco Canyon and the surrounding San Juan Basin became more and more significant. Visible and physical connections between Chaco and the surrounding terrain helped hold the Chacoan world together while expressing key elements of the Ancestral Pueblo worldview. Chacoans already placed importance on the visibility of natural landforms like Hosta Butte. Classic Bonito great house locations, shrines, and stone circles emphasized the visible connections between Chaco and dramatic high places, and road segments created physical connections with specific places and ideas. The North Road and the South Road represented directionality and balanced dualisms and, as a pair, defined the canyon as a center place. Roads also provided visitors to Chaco with particular spatial experiences.

The great houses of Chaco juxtaposed high visibility with hidden interior spaces. They embodied dualism, directionality, center place, and cyclical renewal, creating spatial experiences for visitors that reciprocally confirmed aspects of a shared Ancestral Puebloan worldview (chapter 5). Chacoans sited several great houses on the landscape to further emphasize these ideas. All Classic Bonito great houses had line-of-sight connections with one or more others, and a shrine network facilitated intervisibility down the length of the canyon. Shrines signal the importance of unusually shaped landforms and high places such as Fajada Butte, Huerfano Mountain, Shiprock, Cabezon Peak, Mount Taylor, Hosta Butte, and West Point. From the shrines on West Point, Chaco Canyon was intervisible with Chacoan outliers across the western and southern Basin. Visual connections held the Chacoan world together.

Some roads were guided approaches to Chaco that maximized the visual impact of specific great houses and played with the juxtaposition of the visible and the hidden. The North Road leads to Pueblo Alto, intermittently visible from nearly 20 km away. The South Road frames Pueblo del Arroyo in South Gap for the last few kilometers of the approach. At its southern end, the Ah-Shi-Sle-Pah Road points to Peñasco Blanco. Interestingly, these three are the longest and clearest of all identified Chacoan road segments. Neither the North Road nor the Ah-Shi-Sle-Pah Road provides the easiest or the most logical access into the north side of Chaco Canyon.

In all three of these instances, the road/great house association seems constructed especially to heighten the drama of the approach. At Pueblo Alto and Pueblo del Arroyo, both sited during the Classic Bonito phase, Chacoan builders employed the natural topography to emphasize the structures' visibility. The roads direct movement toward the great houses, ensuring that a traveler keeps them in sight. The great houses loom ever larger as the traveler approaches. Although the west route into Chaco undoubtedly saw very high traffic during the Classic Bonito phase, the approach to Peñasco Blanco from the west is not as formal as the others. The Chaco Wash itself points toward Peñasco, originally sited in the mid-800s. Perhaps the Ah-Shi-Sle-Pah Road was constructed as a formal approach to Peñasco Blanco, but this would not have been a logical point of access for outlier dwellers. All these factors, taken together, suggest that the major roads into Chaco were intended less as practical paths for travel and more as formal procession routes that led travelers to specific views and spatial experiences, including the visual impact of a specific great house when first glimpsed from each direction. Still another purpose might have been a reminder of balanced dualisms represented by the roads as they extended north and south, traveling to high and low points, meeting at the center place.

Another aspect of Chacoan travelers' experiences might have involved the juxtaposition of the visible and the hidden. As I followed formal road segments over the undulating dunes to Chaco, I was acutely aware of the ways in which visual perceptions alter with movement (De Certeau 1984:91–130; Tilley 1994:27–31). The approach to Pueblo Alto particularly highlights the interplay of visible and hidden elements. Pueblo Alto, visible from afar, begins to appear and disappear within the last few kilometers of the approach. Although this great house on a high place can be seen from across the Chaco Plateau, the great houses inside Chaco Canyon remain hidden from view. At the same time, Pueblo Alto offers some of the most spectacular 360-degree vistas of any Chacoan great house.

Visual and road connections, of course, extend in two directions—from the canyon outwards and from the Basin inwards. Similarly, highly visible structures or landmarks are also vantage points from which to gaze across the surrounding terrain. Some great houses, such as Pueblo del Arroyo in South Gap, seem to have been positioned primarily to be viewed. Moore (1996) investigated the ways different vantage points on the Andean landscape seemed constructed for different audiences. Similarly, different Chacoan features seem to have been intended for different kinds of Chacoan audiences, and different roads for different kinds of movements. Chacoans sited Pueblo Alto and Pueblo del Arroyo to be viewed by people approaching along specific access routes laden with multiple layers of cosmographic meaning—in both cases, viewers could have been outlier dwellers coming to the canyon or ceremonial participants engaged in processions. However, neither the North Road nor the South Road seems to have been created primarily to facilitate access into the canyon. Rather, these formal tracks directed pedestrians—whether outlier dwellers or members of ritual processions—to engage in particular spatial experiences.

The Ah-Shi-Sle-Pah Road was probably not a conduit for pilgrims from outliers. Rather, the Ah-Shi-Sle-Pah Road seems most likely to have been primarily for ritual processions or movement between the canyon and Los Aguajes or Black Lake. We do not know who participated in these processions or how exclusive or inclusive they may have been. By contrast, the West Chaco River was probably a practical route of travel into Chaco Canyon for outlier dwellers from the Chuskan slopes and the western San Juan Basin. This route heads toward Site 1088 and Peñasco Blanco but does not direct the traveler toward any unusual drama. Site 1088 is visible at distances of several kilometers or more from Chaco, but the shrines are not visible as the pedestrian passes under them. Rather, the intended viewers of Site 1088 seem to have been people from afar, supporting the idea that the shrines were intended to function as communication or line-of-sight connections with outliers across the Basin.

Many of the people who attended and participated in Chacoan ceremonialism lived in outlier communities scattered across the greater San Juan Basin. Ideas such as dualism, directionality, center place, and cyclical renewal were shared, to some extent, by many Ancestral Pueblo peoples, which is why visitors to Chaco felt such a strong emotional and aesthetic resonance through their experiences in the canyon. At the same time, visitors from the outliers carried home specific ideas from their journey to the center place—and these ideas influenced the shapes of local landscapes. Through participation in Chaco, through colonization, and through emulation, Bonito-style architecture spread to more than 70 Classic Bonito–phase communities in the San Juan Basin and to additional communities in peripheral areas. In the following chapter, I examine expressions of dualism, directionality, center place, cyclical renewal, and social memory as inscribed on outlier landscapes. I argue that the appearance of Bonito-style architecture in outlier communities resulted from a number of specific social processes, some of which were similar to processes taking place in Chaco Canyon and some were quite different.

Notes

1. Gwinn Vivian and Doug Palmer recently used mirrors to demonstrate line-of-sight connections between Pierre's outlier and both Pueblo Alto and Tsin Kletsin. Vivian suggests that the Chacoans may have used selenite, an abundant mineral in the Basin, for signaling between high places (Gwinn Vivian, personal communication, November 2006).

2. It is important to distinguish Chacoan road segments—straight, wide, linear alignments that often point to cardinal directions or natural features on the horizon—from other road segments at the periphery of Chacoan time and space. Some roads, particularly those in southeast Utah, seem to be a slightly different animal, articulating with great houses but curving across the landscape to link sites and settlements (Till 2001). At the Bluff great house in southeast Utah, gaps in the southeast and northwest sides of an encircling berm articulate with a road segment that passed between the great house and the great kiva, then headed north up the Cottonwood Wash toward the Cottonwood Falls great house (Cameron 2002; Till 2001).

3. Toll (2006) has suggested that the "missing" population of Chaco Canyon can, in fact, be found in the Chuskas—that during the Bonito phase, people moved regularly back and forth between the two locations. A strong connection between Chaco and Chuskan outliers such as Skunk Springs and Newcomb is indisputable. Perhaps the "missing" burials of Chaco are located on the Chuskan slopes, and only the symbolic referents for those individuals—corrugated jars—were ever meant to be deposited at Chaco.

4. Interestingly (and perhaps problematically) for this argument, however, the association of north with down and south with up is the opposite of the dualism embodied in great houses and great kivas.

5. Sofaer, Marshall, and Sinclair (1989) note that this section points toward the shrine-topped

Upper Twin Angels mound on the edge of Kutz Canyon and remark upon the close resemblance between this mound and El Faro.

6. Classic Bonito outliers positioned along the Chaco Wash on a direct line from Skunk Springs include Great Bend, Cuatro Payasos, Escalon, Lake Valley, Casa del Rio, and Padilla Well. Still others, such as Whirlwind, Indian Creek, and Kin Bineola, are located just slightly farther to the south. All these communities contain high quantities of Chuskan wares, but Chuskan ceramic frequencies diminish abruptly as one moves onto the South Chaco Slope.

7 The Classic Bonito Chacoan World

The great house is the central and dominant element in a Chaco era landscape …usually constructed in an imposing situation where it can be seen from some distance. The structural mass of the great house is disproportionate to its "footprint," creating an illusion of verticality and overall size.… The effectiveness of this design has diminished somewhat over the centuries, but its characteristic form on the skyline can still lure archaeologists from a considerable distance.

—*from "Architecture and Landscape," by John Stein (1987:80)*

On an August afternoon at Skunk Springs, I stand atop a jumbled pile of dark sandstone masonry at the edge of the aptly named, sparsely vegetated Grey Mesa (figure 7.1a). The surrounding dunes are dotted with small rubble mounds, denoting a large Ancestral Pueblo community. Diminutive figures move about the Navajo settlement in the valley 60 m below. Behind me to the west rise the blue Chuska Mountains with their offerings of cool trees and colorful chert. The horizons before me are punctuated by distinctive and familiar landforms—Bennett Peak, Ford Butte, Shiprock, Huerfano Mountain, Hosta Butte. The air is absolutely still. I look east toward White Rock, a prominent badlands peak south of the Chaco River, directly in line between Skunk Springs and West Point. I imagine Ancestral Puebloans traveling from Skunk Springs to Chaco Canyon, following the Tuntsa and Sheep

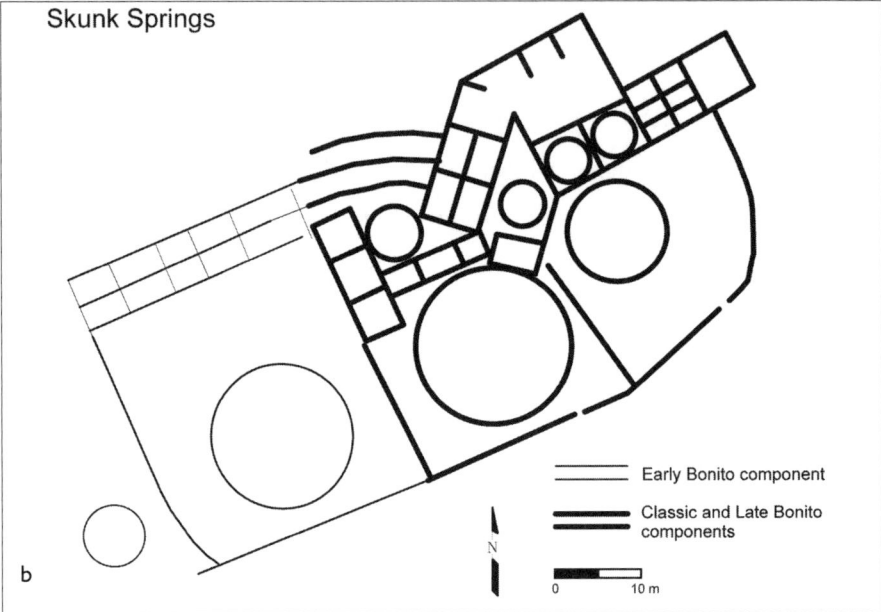

Figure 7.1. (a) Skunk Springs great house, looking east, and (b) plan of the Classic Bonito–phase Skunk Springs great house, after Marshall and others 1979:112.

Springs washes downslope to the Chaco River, then walking the west Chaco River Corridor the rest of the way, stopping to distribute Chuskan wares and Narbona Pass chert and to gossip at places like Great Bend, Cuatro Payasos, Lake Valley, and Casa del Rio. The 90-km journey (as the river bends) would likely have taken at least a few days, maybe more, depending on stops.

The ancestral, Early Bonito–phase settlement at Skunk Springs grew to be one of the largest and most important of several Classic Bonito outliers along the Chuskan slopes. During the eleventh century, builders expanded the original, crescent-shaped great house and great kiva, adding two new sections—a central roomblock and an eastern roomblock. The new great house was at least two stories high and contained several enclosed kivas. Each new roomblock had its own attached plaza and great kiva (see figure 7.1b) (Marshall et al. 1979:109–113; Peckham 1969).[1]

Skunk Springs is one of approximately seventy eleventh-century outliers dotting the terrain across the western and southern San Juan Basin (figure 7.2; refer to figure 6.2). Archaeologists define Chacoan outliers by the presence of Bonito-style architecture (Fowler, Stein, and Anyon 1987; Kantner and Mahoney 2000; Marshall et al. 1979; Powers, Gillespie, and Lekson 1983). The Bonito-style elements are usually in the midst of a community of thirty to forty small habitation sites. Like canyon great houses, outlier great houses are massive, core-and-veneer buildings with large rooms, symmetrical layouts, enclosed kivas, and high visibility. Builders often placed a formal, Chacoan great kiva to the east, south, or west of the great house. Frequently, they further modified the surrounding topography by constructing earthworks and road segments.

Some Classic Bonito outliers have a long and venerable history, with proto-great houses, great kivas, or communities occupied from the mid-800s onward. Others were established wholesale during the eleventh century. Doyel, Breternitz, and Marshall (1984) termed these "ancestral" and "scion" outliers, respectively; I prefer to think of these as "ancestral" and "colonial," for reasons I will discuss below. Some ancestral outliers emerged out of tenth-century proto-great house communities, and others evolved from great kiva–centered communities. Some colonial outliers, such as Casamero in the Red Mesa Valley, have extensive communities; others, such as Salmon along the San Juan River (chapter 8), appear to have none.

Bonito-style architecture in outliers represents, at a minimum, shared participation in key Chacoan ideas. Who built Bonito-style architecture in outlier communities, and why? In some ancestral outliers, local residents may have developed Bonito-style architecture in tandem with Chaco Canyon. At others, local residents may have imported Bonito-style architecture as they began to participate in Chacoan ritual. In colonial outliers, people from Chaco or from other outliers set up great houses in new areas. What are the boundaries of the Chacoan world? Not all communities necessarily interacted with Chaco, and not all large pueblos represent public architecture. Internal or hidden architectural variables, line-of-sight connections through shrines, and ritual landscape features help separate Chacoan participants from Chacoan emulators. Which aspects of Chacoan worldview and ideology were expressed by the construction of Bonito-style architecture in outliers, and to what ends? Outlier great houses and great kivas

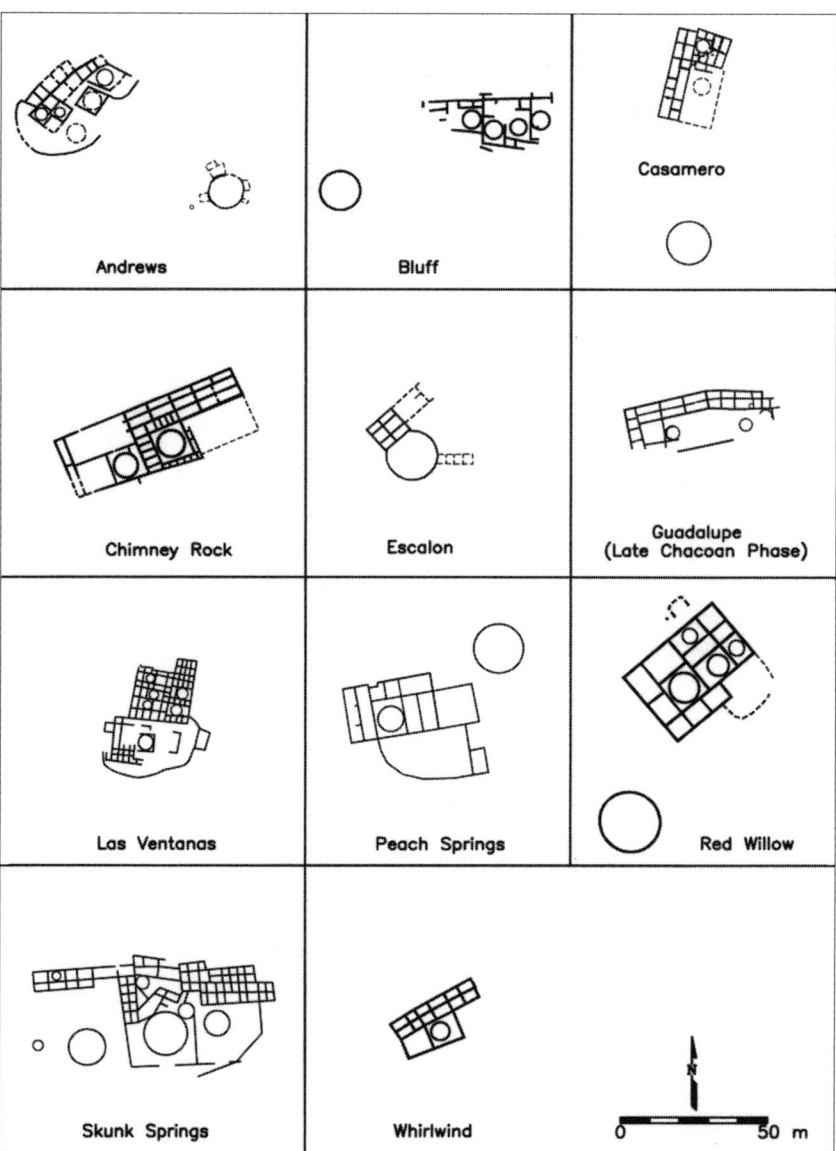

Figure 7.2. Plans of Classic Bonito outlier great houses discussed in the text. Andrews is based on a map by Van Dyke 1999a:61, figure 4. Bluff is based on a map provided by Cathy Cameron and drafted by Phil Geib and Jonathan Till. Escalon is based on an unnumbered map in Marshall and Sofaer 1988. Guadalupe is based on a map in Pippin 1987:31, figure 13. Peach Springs is based on a map in Powers, Gillespie, and Lekson 1983:69, figure 22. Casamero is based on a map in Harper and others 1988:116. Chimney Rock is based on a map in Jeancon 1922:plate XII. Las Ventanas, Red Willow, Skunk Springs, and Whirlwind are based on maps in Marshall and others 1979.

represent, in microcosm, the same aspects of an Ancestral Pueblo worldview that these structures embody in Chaco Canyon. Dualism and memory seem especially important. Directionality, center place, and cyclical renewal are less evident in outliers, perhaps because these ideas legitimated periodic gatherings in Chaco Canyon. Bonito-style architecture at outliers emphasizes visibility and access, suggesting that the buildings symbolized Chacoan identity and were venues for local community rituals and events.

Ancestral and Colonial Outliers

Although all Classic Bonito outliers contain some kind of Bonito-style architecture, they are tremendously variable in terms of great house sizes, numbers, and locations, great kiva numbers and locations, and configurations of roads or earthworks. Surface ceramics and architecture tell us that in some instances, as at Skunk Springs, eleventh-century people constructed Bonito-style architecture in an existing community. In other instances, they erected new outlier great houses in previously unoccupied places. But who were these people—were they colonists from Chaco, or locals, or some combination of the two? Archaeologists have spilled much ink over the past decade in an attempt to understand these relationships (for example, Hurst 2000; Kantner 2003a; Van Dyke 1999b, 2003a).

What went on, socially and politically, inside outlier communities? Despite much recent work on Chacoan outliers, our understanding of internal community social dynamics remains murky (Duff 2006; Gilpin 2003; Mahoney 2000). Part of the problem is that relatively few outlier great houses, and still fewer outlier small sites, have been excavated. As in Chaco Canyon, local community leaders may have been descendants of the first settlers who controlled the best agricultural land in the area. Aside from the architecture itself, however, there is little evidence for social differentiation in outlier communities. Early Bonito settlers across the San Juan Basin seem to have organized their communities in a variety of ways, around proto-great houses, great kivas, both, or neither (chapter 4). If Classic Bonito outlier residents (or some subset of outlier residents) regularly contributed time, labor, and other resources to regional gatherings at Chaco Canyon, then Bonito-style architecture likely represents some level of participation in Chacoan ceremonialism. On a local level, however, it is unclear whether Classic Bonito outlier great houses functioned primarily as residences or as venues for community events, or both.

The construction of Bonito-style architecture in ancestral proto-great house communities, in ancestral great kiva communities, and in previously unoccupied areas probably resulted from several different kinds of processes.

The following three scenarios are among the most likely: (1) Local residents of ancestral communities may have developed Bonito-style architecture in interaction with, and at the same time as, Chaco Canyon. (2) Local residents of ancestral communities may have adopted Bonito-style architecture during the eleventh century as they began to participate in events at Chaco. (3) Chacoan colonists may have established new Bonito-style buildings in areas that previously lacked community centers or that were relatively uninhabited.[2] These three scenarios offer a necessarily simplified view of what were undoubtedly complicated events—the three processes need not have been mutually exclusive, nor did one necessarily always happen in proto-great house communities, the second in great kiva–centered communities, and so on. They merely provide a starting point for thinking about the different kinds of relationships outliers had with Chaco Canyon, as well as the different social avenues through which Bonito-style architecture spread during the eleventh century.

Bonito-Style Architecture as a Concurrent Development with Chaco

Proto-great house communities such as Skunk Springs may have had the closest relationships with Chaco Canyon during the tenth century. Building on a shared history in the northern San Juan, residents of proto-great house communities likely were neighbors, kin, and trading partners with one another and with the communities in Chaco. Proto-great houses may have been the residences of community leaders and also gathering points for community-wide ritual events. Members of Early Bonito proto-great house communities were probably the first to participate in periodic, larger gatherings at Chaco. Bonito-style architecture might have appeared almost organically in these communities, evolving along with Bonito-style architecture in Chaco Canyon. Outlier dwellers who visited Chaco may have worked on the construction of canyon great houses, then returned home to direct construction of their own, local versions.

Peach Springs, like Skunk Springs, is a good example of an ancestral proto-great house community that was transformed into a Classic Bonito–phase outlier (Gilpin and Purcell 2000; Powers, Gillespie, and Lekson 1983:55–93). The Peach Springs community is clustered around a spring along the foothills of Lobo Mesa. Many of the twenty-five small sites in the eleventh-century community have occupations that extend back into the tenth century. On a sandstone ridge just south of the spring, Ancestral Puebloans erected a formal, Classic Bonito great house with an adjacent great kiva, an encircling berm, and an associated road segment (figure 7.3 and plate 13). Although Peach Springs is unexcavated, looters have exposed

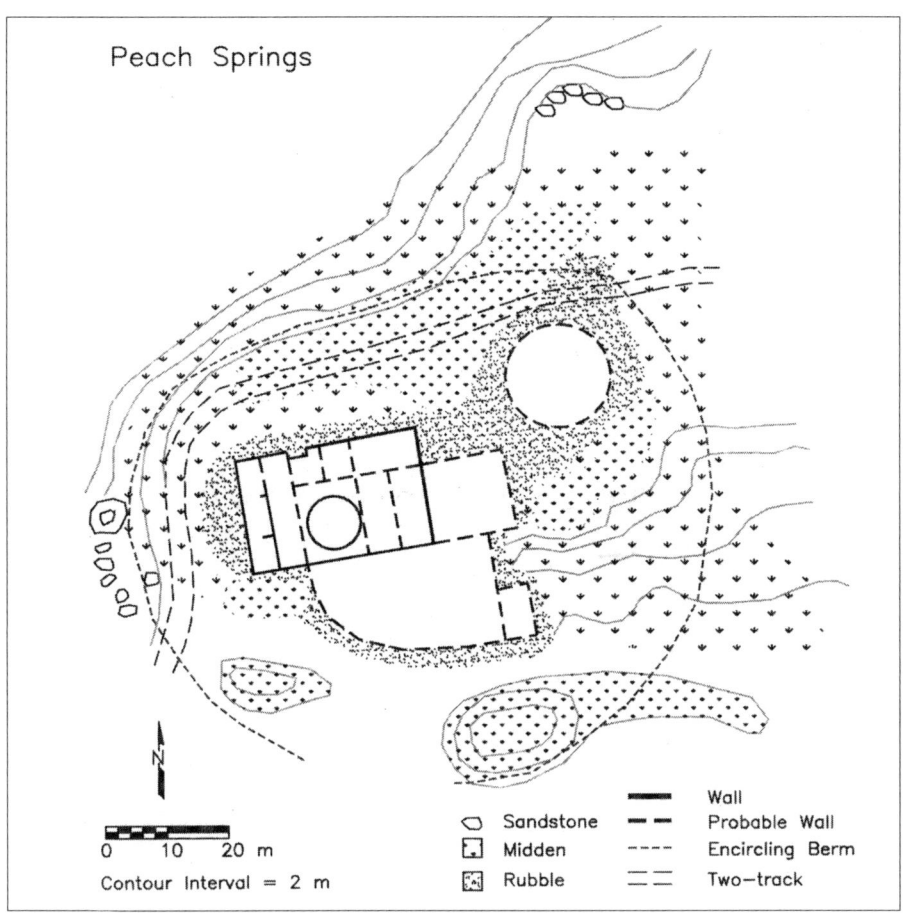

Figure 7.3. Peach Springs great house environs, based on a map in Powers, Gillespie, and Lekson 1983:69, figure 22, with modifications by the author.

Type 1 masonry walls at the rear of the great house, indicating the structure's tenth-century origins.

In ancestral communities, the individuals or factions who controlled and directed construction of local Bonito-style architecture may have been those who played highly visible roles in ceremonial activities both at Chaco and at home. Induction into specific sodalities at Chaco Canyon may have become a great privilege. Initiates could have brought their secret knowledge home to outlier communities, where they presided over local versions of the sodalities, who met in Bonito-style facilities. Possibly, this led to increased social inequalities in outlier communities, based on differential access to ritual knowledge.

Bonito-Style Architecture Imported by Locals from Chaco

As Chacoan ceremonialism spread in popularity, residents of some ancestral communities may have adopted Bonito-style architecture as a badge of membership or participation. Some ancestral communities were likely participating in events at Chaco as they developed across the tenth century, but others may not have joined until the Classic Bonito phase. People in great kiva–centered communities probably shared many aspects of an Ancestral Pueblo worldview but may not have participated regularly in events in Chaco Canyon until the Classic Bonito phase, when the Chacoans incorporated formal great kivas into the Bonito-style suite of features.[3] As members of these communities decided to take part in Chacoan ceremonialism, community leaders or members may have returned home from the canyon bearing Bonito-style architectural knowledge. Alternatively, emissaries from Chaco may have visited these communities—many of which are in slightly more distant locales, such as the Red Mesa Valley—to try to persuade locals to participate in canyon gatherings. In these communities, Ancestral Puebloans built Classic Bonito–phase great houses and great kivas to replace tenth-century great kivas.

At the Andrews outlier, in the Red Mesa Valley, this shift is readily apparent. During the tenth century, Andrews was an insular community clustered around two great kivas along a series of finger ridges at the base of an unnamed mesa. In the early 1000s, Ancestral Puebloans erected a great house and a new, Bonito-style great kiva on a ridge northwest of the tenth-century great kivas (Van Dyke 1999a) (figures 7.4 and 7.5). This new focal point for the Andrews community exhibits all the characteristics of a Chacoan ritual landscape.

Bonito-Style Architecture in Chacoan Colonies

Still other outliers are better interpreted as Chacoan colonies. At these outliers, people from Chaco Canyon, or people who had participated extensively in Chaco Canyon, founded new outlier communities with all the architectural elements associated with Chacoan ideology and ceremonialism—great houses, great kivas, earthworks, and road segments. Chimney Rock is an excellent example of a colonial outlier (Eddy 1977; Jeancon 1922; Jeancon and Roberts 1923, 1924; Malville 2004; Roberts 1922). Here, in the foothills of the San Juan Mountains 150 km northeast of Chaco Canyon, two spectacular vertical stone pillars—Chimney Rock and Companion Rock—reach more than 400 m above the surrounding terrain (refer to plate 5 and figure 5.1). Chimney Rock great house is an L-shaped, two-story great house on the bedrock crest of a narrow ridge southwest of

Figure 7.4. Andrews great house, with California State University–Fullerton students, John Kirby and Jodi Dalton, June 2000.

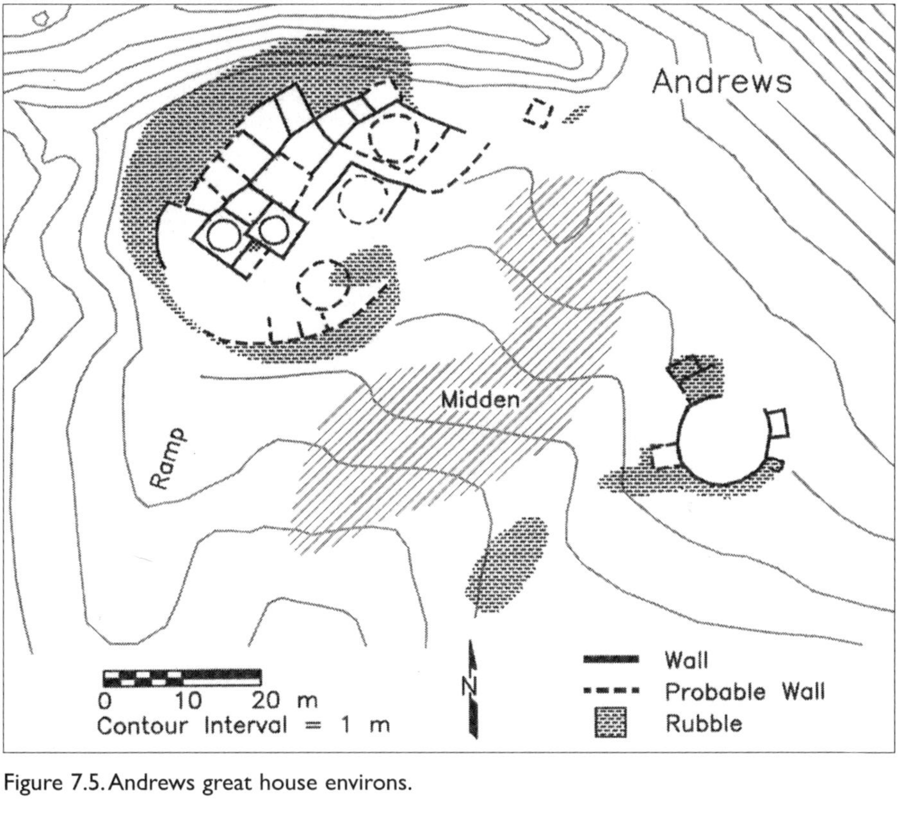

Figure 7.5. Andrews great house environs.

The Classic Bonito Chacoan World 177

the pillars. The surrounding community includes a great kiva and a number of small houses. The great house provides spectacular panoramic 360-degree vistas that include the San Juan Mountains to the north and the Piedra Valley toward the south. Although Chimney Rock is situated far from the mainstream of the Chacoan world, it is linked back to Chaco via a line-of-sight connection across Huerfano Mountain. The major lunar standstill phenomenon may have attracted Chacoans to this area, constructing the great house as a platform for ritual events associated with the winter solstice full moonrise (chapter 5). Clusters of tree-ring dates in the 1070s and 1090s correspond with major lunar standstills in 1076 and 1093. People gathering to participate in standstill events might also have provided labor and resources for construction of the great house.

After 1080, Chacoan colonial expansion accelerated. Colonists built Salmon in the 1080s and Aztec, Lowry, and other outliers in the northern San Juan during the early 1100s (chapter 8).[4] They also built new outliers in the Cibola area and the Rio Puerco Valley to the south and southwest of the San Juan Basin, respectively. Founders of these colonial outliers had in-depth knowledge of Chacoan architectural precepts. The leaders of these new communities may have been Chacoans who struck out into new areas to expand agricultural production for the canyon. Alternatively, they may have been emigrants from Chaco, carving out their own niches in competition with the canyon.

Boundaries of the Chacoan World

At both colonial and ancestral outliers, Bonito-style architecture was likely planned by people who had intimate knowledge of canyon construction methods, through participation or observation, or both. But not all large, multi-storied pueblos in the centers of communities, or all great kivas, were necessarily built by people participating in Chaco. During the Pueblo II period, Ancestral Puebloans constructed great kivas in communities north of the Mogollon Rim in eastern Arizona (Herr 2001). They built large, great house–like pueblos in the northern San Juan (Varien 1999), southeast Utah (Hurst 2000), and northeast Arizona (Fowler, Stein, and Anyon 1987). The pattern of very large pueblos intensified through the Pueblo III period, driven by post-Chacoan changes to the Pueblo world. But during the eleventh century, some of the people responsible for these large pueblos may have been emulating Chaco, rather than participating in Chaco. Emulators might have been competing with Chaco or with one another, following Renfrew and Cherry's (1986) peer–polity interaction model (Kantner 1996; Kintigh 1994). Alternatively, emulators might have been engaging in a form of Taussig's (1993) mimesis, copying the "other" to bring it into comprehension and under control. We can identify outliers with close relationships to Chaco on the basis of shared "internal" great house attributes, shrines and line-of-sight connections, and ritual landscapes.

Architectural Attributes and Chacoan Emulators

In Chaco Canyon, builders erected great houses in a formal, patterned manner (chapter 5). The overall shapes and configurations of these highly visible structures would have been apparent to any visitor, but hidden, internal architectural attributes would have been apparent only to those who designed, built, or used the great houses. Because internal attributes would not have been immediately visible to outside observers, these are good indicators of participation in common learning frameworks (Dobres 2000; Lechtman 1977; Lemonnier 1986). The presence of Chacoan internal attributes at outlier great houses suggests construction by people intimate with canyon great houses; conversely, the absence of internal attributes suggests construction by people who sought to emulate Chaco but did not have firsthand knowledge of canyon building designs and techniques. In two comparative studies that included 55 and 188 outlier great houses, respectively, I used internal variables to investigate relationships between outlier great houses and Chaco Canyon, based on the assumption that visible architectural characteristics could be emulated but that invisible characteristics must be acquired through shared learning. Three of the most useful attributes included banded veneers, core-and-veneer masonry, and enclosed kivas (Van Dyke 1998, 1999b, 2003a).

Banded Type II and III veneers characterize Classic Bonito masonry in Chaco Canyon. Because outlier great house veneers, like those in Chaco, were covered by plaster, banding likely would have been known only to initiates of Chacoan building techniques. Canyon masons created banding by alternating rows of blocky and tabular sandstone. Banded veneers are found in some form at many outliers.[5] Sometimes builders went to great trouble to create banding when tabular sandstone was unavailable. At Casamero, builders created banding with white limestone and red sandstone. At Aztec West, they incorporated a broad band of green sandstone into the west wall of the brown sandstone building.

Core-and-veneer masonry allowed Chacoans to construct massive walls capable of supporting multi-story architecture. This innovation may have been inspired by the availability of stackable tabular sandstone in many areas of the San Juan Basin. However, it is not a necessary technique for the construction of large pueblos and would not have been visible behind the great houses' coatings of plaster. Nearly all Classic Bonito great houses in the San Juan Basin are built of core-and-veneer masonry.[6] In adjacent regions such as eastern Arizona, southwest Colorado, and southeast Utah, however, only about half (45–55 percent) of late Pueblo II period large pueblos contain core-and-veneer masonry. The availability of stackable sandstone does not easily explain the presence or absence of core-and-veneer masonry. Rather, like banding, it seems to be a technique shared by Chacoan builders.

Enclosed kivas are another internal characteristic of outlier great houses. These rooms would not have been externally visible to outsiders. Access was probably restricted to members of specific societies who used the enclosed kivas as meeting places. In Chaco Canyon, Classic Bonito great houses contain one enclosed kiva for approximately every fifteen rooms, for a kiva/room ratio of 1:15. Most outlier great houses have a similarly low or lower kiva/room ratio. This pattern is in stark contrast with non-Chacoan, domestic pueblos, where kiva/room ratios are as high as one kiva for every 6.5 rooms (Lipe 1989:56, table 1). In my comparative studies, I concluded that large pueblos with more than one kiva for every ten rooms are unlikely to be true Chacoan great houses (Van Dyke 2003a).

If a large Pueblo II or early Pueblo III period pueblo contains banding, core-and-veneer masonry, and a low kiva/room ratio, then that structure is most likely a great house, built by people familiar with Chacoan building tenets. By the same token, the absence of banding and core-and-veneer masonry coupled with a high kiva/room ratio suggests that a large pueblo was probably *not* built by Chacoan insiders. Such a structure may be a domestic pueblo or may have been constructed by emulators—people who had not directly observed or participated in construction events at Chaco.

The Shrine Network

The shrine network offers another way to think about the issue of outlier relationships with Chaco Canyon. Perhaps, in some sense, intervisibility defines the boundaries of the Chacoan World. Participation in Chacoan ceremonialism might have involved construction of a line-of-sight connection back to the canyon. Shrines on high places and above outlier great houses in many areas of the San Juan Basin may have been built for practical purposes of communication or may have created symbolic linkages to Chaco (chapter 6). In either case, these would have been meaningful connections.

Nearly all the outliers discussed in this chapter have line-of-sight connections either directly to Chaco or to prominent peaks visible from Chaco (table 7.1). Much of the Chaco Plateau north of the canyon is intervisible with Pueblo Alto. Most of the southern and western San Juan Basin is visible from

Table 7.1 Classic Bonito Outliers Discussed in the Text

Outlier Great House	Type	Mass (cu m)	Foot-print (sq m)	Region & Distance from Chaco[1]	Visible High Places	Visibility to Chaco	Primary References
Andrews	Ancestral great kiva	1,981	616	Red Mesa Valley, 70 km	(From stone circle) Goat Mountain, Hosta Butte	Hosta Butte to Site 1088	Marshall et al. 1979; Van Dyke 1999a, 2000
Bluff	Colonial	2,112	715	Northern San Juan, 190 km	—	—	Cameron 2002; Jalbert and Cameron 2000
Casamero	Colonial	1,070	580	Red Mesa Valley, 65 km	—	—	Harper et al. 1988; Marshall et al. 1979; Sigleo 1981
Chimney Rock	Colonial	3,694	1,510	Piedra Valley (Northern San Juan), 150 km	San Juan Mountains, Huerfano Mountain	Huerfano Mountain to Pueblo Alto; Huerfano Mountain to Site 1088	Eddy 1977; Jeancon 1922; Jeancon and Roberts 1923, 1924; Malville 1990, 2004; Roberts 1922
Escalon	Colonial	718	473	West Chaco River Corridor, 35 km	(from Escalon atalaya) Bennett Peak, Ford Butte, Hosta Butte, White Rock	White Rock to Site 1088	Bradley and Sullivan 1994; Marshall and Sofaer 1988
Guadalupe	Ancestral great house	1,818	909	Rio Puerco of the East, 90 km	Cabezon Peak	Cabezon Peak to Chacra Mesa; Cabezon Peak to Mt Taylor to Site 1088	Baker 1983; Durand and Durand 2000; Irwin-Williams and Baker 1991; Pippin 1987; Washburn 1974
Las Ventanas	Colonial	1,208	693	Red Mesa Valley, 105 km	Goat Mountain, Mt Taylor	Hosta Butte to Site 1088; Mt Taylor to Site 1088	Marshall et al. 1979
Peach Springs	Ancestral great house	2,296	1,303	South Chaco Slope, 55 km	Bennett Peak, Huerfano Mountain	Huerfano Mountain to Pueblo Alto; Huerfano Mountain to Site 1088	Gilpin and Purcell 2000; Obenauf 1980; Powers, Gillespie, and Lekson 1983
Red Willow	Colonial	2,510	1,036	South Chaco Slope, 75 km	Huerfano Mountain	Huerfano Mountain to Site 1088	Marshall and Sofaer 1988; Van Dyke 2003b
Skunk Springs	Ancestral great house/ great kiva	3,854	1,683	Chuskan slopes, 80 km	Shiprock, Ford Butte, Bennett Peak, Beautiful Mountain, White Rock, Hosta Butte	White Rock to Site 1088	Marshall et al. 1979; Peckham 1969
Whirlwind	Colonial	612	379	West Chaco River Corridor, 50 km	Shiprock, Ford Butte, Bennett Peak, White Rock, Huerfano Mountain	White Rock to Site 1088	Kearns 1996; Marshall et al. 1979

1. Linear distance from Fajada Butte

Chacra Mesa, South Mesa, and West Mesa. West Point, in particular, seems to be an important spot for intervisibility. The dozen barrel-shaped shrines at Site 1088 may be positioned to facilitate lines of sight with particular Basin shrines, landmarks, or outliers (Robinson, Van Dyke, and Windes 2007).

Further investigations into an intervisible shrine network could help us develop a more nuanced picture of the various kinds of possible relationships between outliers and Chaco Canyon. Some outliers, such as Casamero and Bluff, contain great houses with core-and-veneer masonry, banding, low kiva/room ratios, and indisputably Chacoan layouts, yet they lack line-of-sight connections to Chaco. Perhaps these colonial outliers had less direct or less intense connections to canyon ceremonialism. They may have been offshoots of other colonies, for example.

The shrine network might also help us determine whether any areas of the San Juan Basin remained isolated or independent from Chaco during the 1000s. Archaeologists "lured from a distance" by great houses on the Basin landscape may well have overlooked the presence of eleventh-century small site communities that lack Bonito-style architecture altogether. One of these settlements might be represented by the Blackbird Site—a Pueblo II hamlet I excavated as part of a pipeline project 10 km west of Yah-ta-hey, at the southern end of the Chuska Mountains (Yost and Van Dyke 1996). Although there were at least two contemporaneous small sites in this area, there is no nearby great house. The nearest outlier is Toh-La-Kai, 12 km to the east over rugged terrain. If Bonito-style architecture is a badge of membership in Chacoan ceremonialism, perhaps Ancestral Puebloan communities lacking great houses or great kivas were excluded by Chaco, or chose not participate.

Ritual Landscapes

Co-occurrence of internal architectural attributes and intervisibility with Chaco Canyon can help delineate the scope of Chaco's reach. But the Chacoan landscape is more than a set of architectural traits or visual connections. Outlier dwellers who participated in Chaco arranged their monumental spaces in ways that resonated with the worldview they shared with Chaco Canyon, albeit on a smaller scale and with some important differences. They positioned Bonito-style architecture on high places, overlooking surrounding communities of small sites. They established shrines and stone circles with lines of sight to prominent peaks. They constructed earthworks and berms, controlling access into the great house/great kiva complex and structuring the spatial experiences of those who approached the structures.

No two outliers are exactly alike, yet all outlier landscapes unmistakably echo the ideas of sacred geography, dualism, visibility, and social memory so important in Chaco Canyon. Stein and Lekson (1992) used the term *ritual landscape* to describe the shared, iconographic messages communicated by outlier Bonito-style architecture. Archaeological visitors to these outlier communities today experience these spatial resemblances to Chaco as more than the sum of their constituent parts. Throughout the following discussion, I draw upon a few key outlier examples to illustrate the ways in which outlier landscapes represent participation in a Chacoan ideology (see table 7.1).

Bonito-Style Architecture and Chacoan Ideology

Whether introduced by Chacoans or carried home from Chaco by outlier residents, whether developed in tandem with events at Chaco or founded late in the eleventh century, outlier landscapes embody many of the same ideas found in Chaco Canyon. In some cases, Bonito-style architecture might have been directed by local leaders who participated in events at Chaco and had intimate knowledge of Chacoan architectural techniques, symbolic meanings, and ritual practices. In other cases, the builders themselves may have been Chacoan. Outlier dwellers were the people who contributed labor and resources to Chaco Canyon. Local versions of canyon great houses, great kivas, and other features symbolized this participation. Local leaders could have manipulated construction and use of these buildings in various ways to enhance or legitimate their own prestige.

Outlier great houses, great kivas, and earthworks represent many of the same core ideas found in Chaco Canyon, especially balanced dualism, center place, and social memory. The presence of these shared ideas communicates shared participation in a Chacoan ideology and in canyon ceremonialism. Like canyon great houses and great kivas, outlier great houses and great kivas might have been sites for periodic local ritual or other community events. Outlier great houses are highly visible, and access to the buildings is often structured, formal, and public. Local Bonito-style architecture may have been intended to provide a spatial experience that emphasized some of the same ideas as canyon architecture. Like the canyon landscape, outlier landscapes juxtapose the visible and the hidden and create intervisible connections with sacred landmarks and ancestral locations.

Form

In most Classic Bonito outliers, Bonito-style architecture centers around a massive, core-and-veneer great house paired with a formal, Chacoan great kiva. As in Chaco Canyon, great houses and great kivas represent balanced opposites on several levels. Great houses are highly visible structures yet also contain hidden features such as banded veneers and enclosed kivas. The upright form of an outlier great house is counterposed against the subterranean form of an associated great kiva, creating a vertical axis that intersects at a center place—the great house plaza. Like their canyon counterparts, outlier great houses share similarities in layout and orientation. They are planned structures with large rooms and enclosed kivas, built in symmetrical shapes facing the east, southeast, or south (see figure 7.2). Builders erected the rear spine of the structure first, then added wings. Like canyon great houses, nearly all outlier great houses are oriented between 90 and 180 degrees east of true north; few face due east or south. Rather, most great houses follow the ancestral southeast pattern (Van Dyke 1998:254–257, 308–328).

Like canyon great kivas, Classic Bonito outlier great kivas are standardized in size. Although outlier great kiva diameters range between 12 and 22 m, most fall between 15 and 17 m. The coefficient of variation for a sample of forty-four Classic Bonito–phase outlier great kivas is a conservative 0.20 (Herr 1994). The same uniformity in orientation, symmetry, and interior features found in excavated great kivas in Chaco Canyon characterizes excavated outlier great kivas at Village of the Great Kivas (Roberts 1932), Fort Wingate (Peckham 1958), Aztec West (Morris 1921), Salmon (Marshall et al. 1979: 304), and Lowry (Martin 1936). As with canyon great kivas, archaeologists have interpreted this standardization to represent liturgical order (Adler and Wilshusen 1990). Great kivas likely represent a space for community ritual, and architectural attributes likely carried specific meanings, such as balanced dualism.

Visibility

As Stein suggests in the opening to this chapter, Chacoans positioned outlier great houses to maximize their visibility from the vantage points of external viewers. As in Chaco Canyon, outlier great houses were constructed of formal, repetitive, easily recognizable elements. Great house builders used exaggerated mass, height, topographic elevation, and associations with dramatic landforms to create highly visible structures. Many outlier great houses were built at mesa's edge or teeter precipitously atop badland spires. Still others are on slightly elevated terrain above the surrounding community. Smaller, single-storied great houses tend to be positioned in high places; larger great houses achieve high visibility with multiple stories and exaggerated mass. The natural settings of Chacoan great houses often juxtapose upper and lower elements to "create illusions of exaggerated verticality" (Stein 1987:77).

Figure 7.6. Cabezon peak, as seen from Guadalupe great house.

Guadalupe is a good example of a Classic Bonito outlier great house built in a highly visible, elevated topographic situation. Ancestral Puebloans erected the Guadalupe great house on an isolated sandstone butte high above the Rio Puerco of the East, approximately 90 km southeast of Chaco Canyon. During the eleventh century, builders transformed an Early Bonito–phase domestic structure into a symmetrical, Bonito-style great house (Baker 1983; Pippin 1987). They situated a great kiva to the southeast of the great house, on a lower spur of the butte. Although only one story high, the great house commands a 360-degree view of the surrounding terrain, including Cabezon Peak (figure 7.6) and a community of some thirty to forty small sites on the valley floor below.[7]

Some outlier great houses dazzle not by virtue of elevated setting, but by a combination of mass and topography. Stein (1987:80) observes, "The great house is…largely an illusion…. [E]xceptional 'mass' in conjunction with the open settings where many of these structures are located contributes to their high visibility."

At Peach Springs, builders used structural mass in combination with natural topography to produce a strikingly visible outlier. The Peach Springs great house consists of a symmetrical, two-story roomblock with an enclosed kiva, fronted by an elevated plaza. A single-story roomblock is attached to the east side of the core edifice. Ancestral Puebloans erected the great house atop the south end of a natural sandstone ridge, creating an optical illusion—the two-story great house stands approximately 7 m above the surrounding terrain, but some portion of this is actually the ridge foundation (see figure 7.3 and plate 13). In front of the great house to the southeast, large trash middens are incorporated into an aureole or encircling berm, further confusing the relationship between the natural topography and the built environment. The great house represents 2,296 cu m of mass on a 1,303-sq-m footprint, yet it dominates the surrounding community of small habitation sites.

Outlier great house sizes are extremely variable—floor areas range from 145 sq m at Halfway House to 8,320 sq m at Salmon Ruin (Powers, Gillespie, and Lekson 1983:313–315). Although most outlier great houses are considerably smaller than canyon great houses (Powers, Gillespie, and Lekson 1983:313–315), like canyon great houses, they are quite massive compared with surrounding small sites. The Andrews great house, for example, with two stories, twenty rooms, and a 616-sq-m footprint, is not particularly large compared with canyon great houses, yet it dwarfs the local small sites. The average Classic Bonito small site at Andrews is one story high, has four to six rooms, and has a footprint of less than 30 sq m. Great house builders at Andrews worked to create additional ways to enhance Andrews' dominance over the community. The Andrews great house is elevated only about 10 m above the surrounding topography but looks down upon the small sites from a ridgetop in the midst of a highly modified landscape.

Outlier builders frequently sited great houses in association with unusual or highly visible landforms. The Andrews great house was positioned directly below a highly visible geologic juncture in the mesa behind it, where smooth red Wingate sandstone meets the blocky brown sandstone of the Entrada formation. This positioning served primarily to enhance the local visibility of the great house. In other situations, such as the construction of Chimney Rock great house beneath twin pillars, Chacoans erected a structure to appropriate a natural feature that likely held significance for them already.

Unusual peaks provided line-of-site connections between most outliers and Chaco—particularly to Site 1088 atop West Point (see table 7.1). Peach Springs, for example, is too near Lobo Mesa to see Hosta Butte, but the Peach Springs great house provides a surprising view of Huerfano Mountain on the opposite side of the San Juan Basin, 95 km to the northwest. At Andrews, no dramatic peaks are visible from the great house, but Hosta Butte is visible from a stone circle on the escarpment above (LA 13801). A "floating" road segment in the valley below is on a direct line between the stone circle and Hosta Butte, increasing the likelihood that this line of sight held significance for Andrews builders.⁸ Guadalupe and Las Ventanas are good examples of outliers in sight of unusual landforms that not only emphasize the position of the great house but also create line-of-sight connections back to Chaco Canyon.

Guadalupe's position as the lone outlier far to the east of Chaco has occasioned much speculation among scholars. Perhaps the settlement was an outpost for the procurement of Cerrillos turquoise, although Guadalupe is 104 km from the turquoise source (Sebastian 1992:95). The community is in a well-watered location with excellent farmland, which may have been part of the original tenth-century attraction for the proto-great house builders. A continuous connection with people and events in Chaco Canyon probably led to the eleventh-century adoption of Bonito-style architecture. Guadalupe's unusual views of distinctive landforms such as Cabezon Peak and Mount Taylor probably contributed to Chacoan interest in the area. Although distant from downtown Chaco, Guadalupe is not as isolated as it appears. Like Chimney Rock, the great house is visually linked back to Chaco Canyon. Nearby Cabezon Peak is visible from points on Chacra Mesa 30 km to the northwest.

Las Ventanas, also known as Candelaria, is located at the edge of a vast lava flow called the Malpais, approximately 105 km south of Chaco Canyon near Grants, New Mexico. Las Ventanas illustrates the importance of dramatic natural features in the construction of an outlier landscape. Located on a high, red sandstone ridge that blocked the flow of lava from the west, the great house looks toward the nearby cone of Mount Taylor. The great house seems positioned at the intersection of lava, sandstone, and sky. There is an associated great kiva, a community of small sites, a shrine, and a stone circle (Marshall et al. 1979:187–193). The stone circle and the shrine are located on two prominent overlooks at the edge of the sandstone escarpment above the Malpais. The stone circle is constructed of upright, rectangular, sandstone cobbles surrounded by rubble. The great house cannot be seen from the circle, but Mount Taylor is very prominent. The shrine is a horseshoe-shaped structure located on a high, red sandstone knob. The 1-m-diameter structure is constructed of three to four courses of stacked sandstone cobbles. It opens to face Mount Taylor (figure 7.7).

Lines of sight within and between neighboring outlier communities shed light on differences in local community dynamics. Andrews and Casamero, two neighboring outliers, contain highly visible great houses, but each seems intended to be viewed by members of the immediate community. By contrast, at the outlier of Whirlwind, the intended audience for the great house seems to have been visitors approaching the area from a distance, instead of immediate community members.

Figure 7.7. Mount Taylor, as seen from a shrine in the vicinity of Las Ventanas.

Andrews and Casamero present an interesting situation in which two great houses could have been positioned to be intervisible with each other, but they were not. The two contemporaneous Red Mesa Valley great houses are separated by only 5 km across the Casamero Valley. Like Andrews, the Casamero great house is located on a colluvial ridge below an escarpment, overlooking a community of small sites (Harper et al. 1988; Sigleo 1981). As at Andrews, builders positioned Casamero at a highly visible spot against the escarpment face. Casamero is located just beneath a pair of unusual, eye-shaped, red sandstone alcoves (figure 7.8). The alcoves and the cliff between them resemble an owl's face, which is why the place is known locally as "tecolote" (Gwinn Vivian, personal communication, December 2006). But even though they are only a few kilometers apart, the two great houses are not intervisible with each other. The jutting edge of the mesa above Andrews blocks the line of sight between them. Deviation of just a few meters in either direction would have created a visible link between the two great houses. The avoidance of intervisibility suggests an effort at creating separation or reinforcing social distance between the two communities. Kantner (1996) has suggested that outlier community leaders in the Red Mesa Valley may have been constructing Bonito-style architecture to compete with one another for followers. The positioning of the Andrews and Casamero great houses belies this interpretation. If great house builders were creating high-visibility architecture to compete with one another, then they would have erected these structures within sight of their neighbors. Rather, the intended audience for each great house seems to have been the local community.

In other situations, however, the intended audience for great houses in high places may not have been the local community, but neighbors or other

Figure 7.8. Casamero, with the "tecolote" alcoves behind the great house.

Figure 7.9. Whirlwind great house, looking west.

visitors approaching from a distance. At Whirlwind Lake, above a broad valley in the western Basin south of the Chaco River, a community of approximately twenty habitation sites is strung along the valley floor, and the great house perches above, on the narrow point of an unnamed mesa (figure 7.9) (Kearns 1996; Marshall et al. 1979:87–89). The compact, one- to two-story great house is built of dark brown, tabular sandstone. Whirlwind great house has line-of-sight connections to Shiprock, Ford Butte, Bennett Peak, the Chuska Mountains, White Rock, and Huerfano Mountain. Many of the community sites are clustered at the base of the mesa, but the great house is not intervisible with these. The Whirlwind great house is set 150 m back from the mesa edge, and a 20-m escarpment precludes direct line of sight with small houses near the cliff edge. However, the great house is visible from distances of 2–3 km at the edge of the valley from the north, west, and southwest. Perhaps the intended audience for the Whirlwind great house was not the immediate community, but visitors entering the valley from other parts of the western Basin.[9]

Access

Not only did builders create outlier Bonito-style architecture to symbolize many key aspects of Chacoan ideology, but they also arranged the outlier architecture to structure spatial experiences similar to those in Chaco Canyon. Although Bonito-style architecture is highly visible, the natural topography restricted access to some outlier great houses. To reach the Chimney Rock great house, for example, it is necessary to climb a steep, eroded, narrow ridge. At other outliers, berms and road segments created formal entrance routes. As in Chaco, outlier approaches often created a dualistic balance between visible and hidden elements.

Although the Guadalupe great house can be clearly seen from the community below, the structure can be reached only by climbing a steep trail up the south side of the butte. Access to the great house along this trail could have easily been limited to certain members of the community. The climb to Guadalupe could have involved a highly visible procession, but once atop the butte, any activities undertaken within the great house would have been hidden from viewers in the valley below. These activities are likely to have been both ritual and domestic. An analysis of Guadalupe avifauna suggests that the great house may have been the site of ritual practices involving birds (Durand 2003; Roler 1999). Room and doorway configurations at Guadalupe suggest that the structure was a domestic pueblo with several discrete but equivalent households (Van Dyke 1999c). Perhaps residents were community leaders with exclusive access to specialized ritual knowledge.

Escalon is another outlier with restricted access to specific features. The Escalon community clusters around a tall, mushroom-shaped butte amid the badlands of the Indian Creek drainage, 35 km west of Chaco (Bradley and Sullivan 1994; Marshall and Sofaer 1988:46–70).[10] At Escalon, as at Guadalupe, Bonito-style architecture is found both on the valley floor and on the isolated butte. On the valley floor, a single-storied core-and-veneer great house consists of six large rooms and an attached great kiva.[11] The butte, a brown sandstone cap resting atop a column of gray shale in the center of an open valley, provides a natural stage. Atop the butte is an "atalaya" —a series of fourteen compound or core-and-veneer masonry enclosures. To access the top, Ancestral Puebloans constructed a massive platform and stairway complex 8–10 m high against the butte's south face (plate 14).[12] The builders of Escalon could have used a ladder, but instead they constructed a public, formal route for ascending the butte. Processions may have been staged to proceed up the stairway. Any activities taking place atop the butte, however, would have been hidden from the view of spectators immediately below by the steep angle of the butte's edge.

Most outlier great houses are in less topographically extreme situations, but builders used road segments, ramps, and earthworks to delineate particular approaches. Earthworks of sterile soil, trash, and construction debris are found in association with at least thirty-four outlier great houses (Cameron 2002; Fowler and Stein 1992; Fowler, Stein, and Anyon 1987; Marshall and Sofaer 1988; Stein and Lekson 1992:95). Earthworks often take the form of discontinuous, encircling berms with breaks to admit ramps or road segments. Stein and Lekson (1992:97) argue that encircling berms are *nazha*, a Navajo word meaning "to surround spiritually." They argue that the nazha demarcate space, separating great houses from the world beyond or perhaps representing, in microcosm, the encircling walls of Chaco Canyon. The berms are not wide or high enough to have been effective as fortifications. The approach to the Andrews great house, for example, was defined by the construction of a southwest/northeast-trending ramp (see figure 7.5). Dense trash and dark soil cover the east side of the ramp, indicating either a trash-covered berm or the use of trash deposits as part of the earthwork.

Social Memory and Cyclical Renewal

Social memory and cyclical renewal are expressed at outliers through periodic architectural modifications, earthworks, site superposition, and the construction of "roads through time." As in Chaco, outlier builders remodeled rooms and kivas and added new wings. However, these activities did not happen with the same frequency as construction events in Chaco Canyon. For the fifteen or so outlier great houses where excavation or standing walls have provided us with construction sequences, it appears that builders erected outlier great houses in bursts of activity that encompassed relatively few stages. At Chimney Rock, for example, two construction events—1076 and 1093— correspond to lunar standstill years (Malville 2004). Bluff, a colony great house on the San Juan River, was erected in two or three stages (Jalbert and Cameron 2000). Clearly, organization of labor would have figured prominently into the timing of outlier construction. Intermittent bursts of activity may represent the periodic gathering of residents from several communities for local ritual events and construction. Tree-ring dates may cluster because groups of Puebloans may have made periodic, labor-intensive timber-cutting forays, then stockpiled the wood for gradual use by locals as they slowly erected a great house. Memory would have been woven into community identity, as the outlier great house would have embodied the memories of group labor, gatherings, and associated events leading up to its completion. Where extensive remodeling is found at outlier great houses, however, it often appears related to a shift in the structure's function. Just as Early Bonito structures such as Skunk Springs and Peach Springs were converted to great houses in the eleventh century, Classic and Late Bonito great houses such as Guadalupe, Salmon, and Aztec were converted to domestic structures during the late 1100s and 1200s, when Chaco was essentially over.

Ancestral Puebloans also used earthworks, site superposition, and "roads through time" to construct social memory within outlier landscapes. In ancestral communities such as Skunk Springs, Peach Springs, and Guadalupe, new great houses incorporated earlier proto-great houses. This shift may have involved transforming the structures from domestic to public space. At Peach Springs and in many other outliers, builders integrated tenth-century, Type 1 masonry rooms into massive, formalized, eleventh-century great houses. At Andrews, builders sited the new great house in the vicinity of five large, tenth-century middens—excavation could determine whether the new great house is superimposed on tenth-century structures. At Peach Springs, many Classic Bonito small sites are atop Early Bonito habitations. As in Chaco Canyon, older rooms and earlier sites may have been associated with ancestors or may have held other kinds of special importance.

Does site superposition actually represent an attempt to create a meaningful association with the past? Alternatively, this practice might simply represent remodeling or reconstruction during continuous occupation, or it might result from environmental concerns. Other archaeologists, however, have observed the same phenomenon and have concluded that, at least in some cases, new buildings constructed atop old structures likely held cultural significance. Toll and Wilson (2000:33–43), for example, observed this phenomenon during excavations in the La Plata Valley, where four out of five Basketmaker III or early Pueblo I pitstructures were overlain by Pueblo II components. Toll and Wilson consider several possible explanations for this pattern, including similarities in environmental conditions and subsistence strategies. Ultimately, they conclude that the Pueblo II inhabitants of the La Plata Valley deliberately wanted to associate themselves with the Basketmaker inhabitants: The "superimposition of Pueblo II habitations on

Basketmaker structures is so regular...that there can be little question that this was intentional" (Toll and Wilson 2000:33). The multicomponent sites of the La Plata Valley carried multiple layers of meaning for Pueblo II builders because these had been inhabited in the past. This pattern of deliberate Pueblo II superposition atop earlier sites is also known from southwest Colorado, Second Mesa at Hopi (Sebastian 1985:50–55), and the Quemado area (Bullard 1962:26–27).

The construction of memory—a social relationship to a real or an imagined past—was an integral part of the eleventh-century Ancestral Pueblo worldview. Earthworks represent one way in which Puebloans incorporated social memory into outlier landscapes. As in Chaco, earthworks may represent large, formalized, "fake" refuse deposits—the literal construction of a past where none existed before. This may have been particularly important at colonial outliers, where great house builders sought to establish a Chacoan presence in a new area. Limited excavations in berms support this interpretation. At the outlier of Bluff, in southeast Utah, for example, an encircling berm consists of an array of trash, ash, sterile earth, stone spalls, and construction debris (Cameron 2002).

Some outlier road segments represent the construction of social memory. The Red Willow–Los Rayos road is an excellent example (Van Dyke 2003b).[13] The Red Willow great house is an eleventh-century, Bonito-style complex, complete with great house, great kiva, and encircling earthwork (figure 7.10). It is situated atop an unnamed mesa overlooking the broad expanse of Tohatchi Flats, approximately 75 km southwest of Chaco (Marshall and Sofaer 1988:142–143). The great house was constructed in the late eleventh century in the midst of an early tenth-century community, perhaps on top of an earlier building. A trash-covered berm encircles the great house, and a great kiva is immediately to the southwest. The collapsed building retains a topographic relief of 4 m, and the rubble mound is visible for several kilometers to the east and south across Tohatchi Flats. An opening on the southeast side of the encircling berm becomes a ramp slanting downslope off the mesa edge to the east. This ramp leads down to a road segment that extends across the valley for 2.5 km, climbs a neighboring mesa, and ends at the Los Rayos great kiva, an early tenth-century structure (Marshall and Sofaer 1988:42–45; Van Dyke 2003b) (figure 7.11).

The fact that the road articulates with the eleventh-century berm surrounding the Red Willow great house argues strongly for an eleventh-century road construction date. The Classic Bonito–phase great house builders seem to have deliberately constructed a physical link with the early Pueblo II great kiva across the valley. The builders of Red Willow could have been referencing the past to create the illusion of continuity or to suggest the

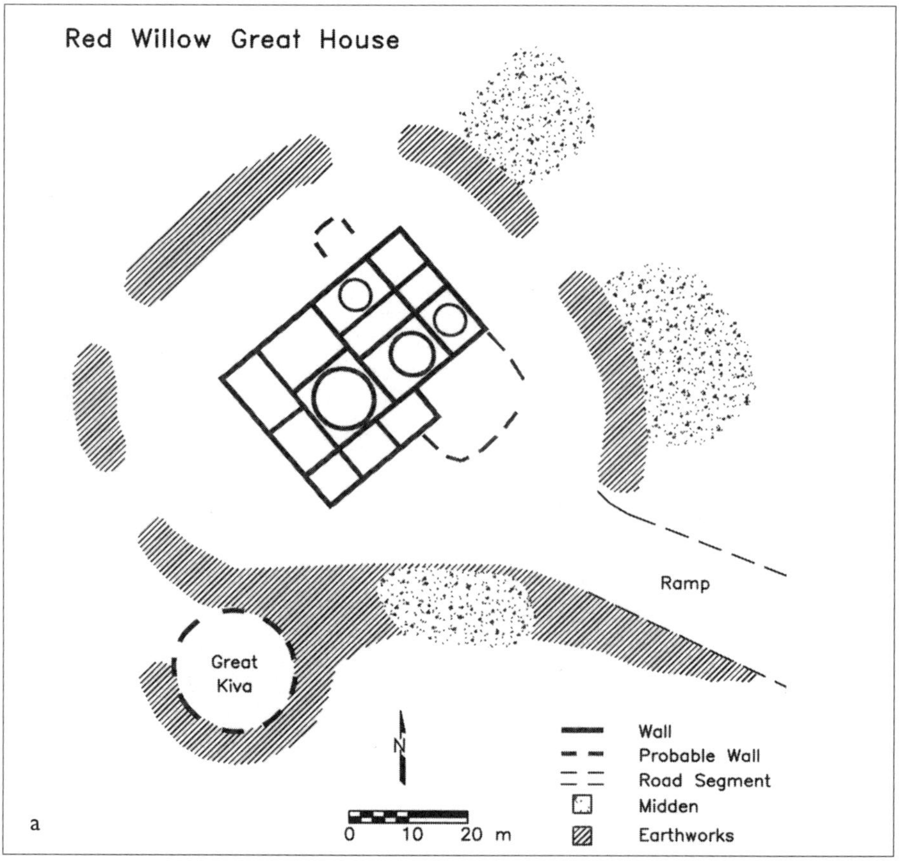

Figure 7.10. (a) Red Willow great house environs, based on an unnumbered figure in Marshall and Sofaer 1988, with modifications by the author, and (b) Red Willow great house, looking west.

194   The Chaco Experience

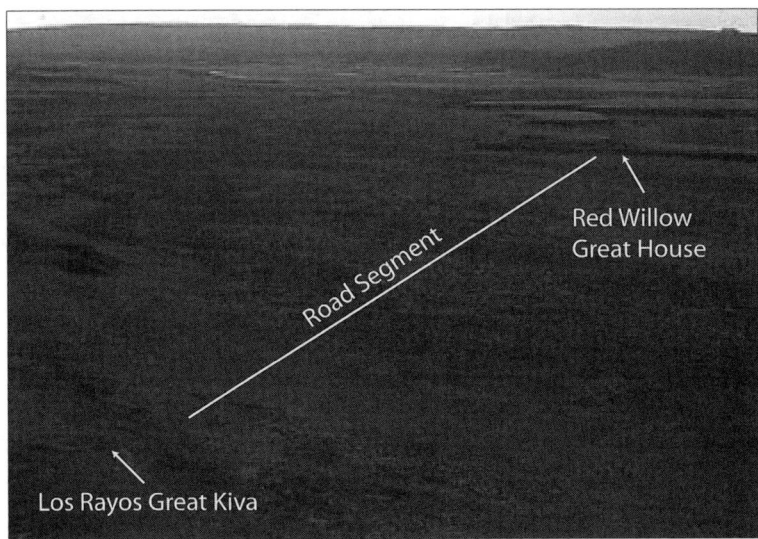

Figure 7.11. The road connecting Red Willow great house and Los Rayos great kiva, in the western San Juan Basin.

continuation of ancestral communal practices represented by the great kiva. This could have helped to naturalize the authority of Red Willow leaders. The road segment could have been used for processions across Tohatchi Flats between the two structures. The rubble mound of the Red Willow great house is quite visible from Los Rayos. Ritual participants could have set out from the great house and processed to the great kiva and back again, or perhaps processions originated in Los Rayos and ended at Red Willow. The ramp provides formal access to Red Willow from the valley below. In the climb up the mesa from the valley floor, the great house drops from view, then re-emerges at the top of the ascent in a route reminiscent of the spatial experiences provided by the North Road, the Ah-Shi-Sle-Pah Road, and the South Road in Chaco Canyon (chapter 6).

Summary

Bonito-style architecture in outlier communities indicates a close relationship with Chaco Canyon. Inhabitants of outlier communities likely participated in periodic gatherings at Chaco and contributed their labor to build Bonito-style architecture there and at home. Undoubtedly, there was a wide range of relationships between outlier residents and Chaco Canyon. Settlement patterns suggest at least three major scenarios for the appearance of Bonito-style architecture in outliers.

In some cases, as at Skunk Springs and Peach Springs, local residents of ancestral communities likely had close relationships with Chaco Canyon that extended back into the Early Bonito phase. In these communities, locals transformed tenth-century proto-great houses (perhaps leaders' residences) into eleventh-century public facilities. Local social organization may have been undergoing a shift toward greater inequality. For example, some residents may have held secret ritual knowledge gleaned from initiation into canyon sodalities. Bonito-style architecture was a badge of membership in Chaco and also may have served similar local functions involving public ceremonialism that heightened inequalities within outliers.

In other cases, as at Andrews, local communities originally may have been more insular, with great kivas serving as foci for relatively egalitarian, community-wide gatherings. During the eleventh century, when these communities decided or were enticed to participate in ritual events at Chaco, locals or Chacoans erected new, Bonito-style buildings to represent this association, to serve as a new community focal point, and perhaps to facilitate smaller, local versions of Chacoan rituals. As with proto-great house ancestral communities, local social organization probably shifted toward greater inequality. At colonial outliers, people from Chaco Canyon or people from other outliers who were intimately part of Chaco established new, Bonito-style buildings. Some of these colonies, such as Chimney Rock, represent outposts selected by Chacoans for specific meanings or topographic features. Others, such as Whirlwind, may represent new community centers constructed in areas that were sparsely occupied in earlier times.

In still other parts of the greater San Juan Basin, some local communities built large pueblos that emulated Chacoan great houses in certain respects, but these builders did not have a close relationship with the canyon. And some eleventh-century communities may not have participated in Chaco at all. Several architectural lines of evidence can help delineate the boundaries of the Chacoan world. Participation in Chacoan ceremonialism is highly probable when an outlier exhibits the presence of specific, internal architectural characteristics, shrines creating visual links to Chaco, and the overall suite of Bonito-style features that constitute a Chacoan "ritual landscape."

Although Classic Bonito outlier architecture encompasses much variability, the Chacoan themes of dualism, visibility, and social memory are present at each. As in Chaco Canyon, outliers frequently pair great houses with formal great kivas, creating a balanced opposition. Great houses and great kivas may represent a vertical axis setting high against low, visible against hidden, or other possible dualisms. Outlier great houses and great kivas may represent a local version of the center place where these opposites meet and are balanced. Formal platforms and procession ways at sites such as Escalon and Andrews suggest that Bonito-style architecture provided a setting for local ritual activities.

Visibility is a particularly important characteristic at outlier great houses. Many great houses, including Skunk Springs, Chimney Rock, Guadalupe, Whirlwind, and Red Willow, are sited on high places. At others, including Peach Springs, Andrews, and Casamero, builders used natural topographic elements to enhance great house visibility. Many great houses provide line-of-sight connections to unusual landforms, such as Hosta Butte or Huerfano Mountain. In all the cases discussed here, either the great house or a nearby shrine provides a line-of-sight connection that links the outlier back to Chaco Canyon. Site 1088, in particular, may be of critical importance in a line-of-sight network across the Chacoan world (Robinson, Van Dyke, and Windes 2007).

Outlier great houses not only are highly visible but also generally have restricted or formalized means of access. As at Chaco, ramps and stairways may have structured the spatial experiences of people approaching the great houses. These features also would have provided routes for public processions. Processions or other public events at great houses may have been spectacles observed primarily by the local community, or they may have been meant for more distant viewers. At Escalon, Guadalupe, Andrews, and Casamero, great house visibility is limited to the surrounding community. At Whirlwind, by contrast, the great house is not visible to most of the local community. Rather, the intended viewers for Whirlwind may have been visitors approaching the valley from a distance.

Outlier Bonito-style architecture illustrates the Ancestral Pueblo concern with social memory. Classic Bonito builders incorporated ancestral, Early Bonito structures into new great houses. They erected earthworks that may represent artificial middens—the literal construction of a past. And, at Red Willow, they built a "road through time," linking a late-eleventh-century great house with an early-tenth-century great kiva. This physical connection with an ancestral space may have also been a metaphorical connection with real or imagined ancestral beliefs or practices.

By the late eleventh century, at least seventy outlier communities were integrated into periodic ritual activities at Chaco Canyon. The internal dynamics of these communities likely varied, but in all cases, community members adopted Bonito-style public architecture. Outlier great houses, great kivas, earthworks, and road segments represented shared participation in Chacoan ideology. Outlier landscapes embodied aspects of this ideology, including balanced dualism, center place, visibility, and social memory. Bonito-style architecture resonated with the same ideas and provided similar spatial experiences to those in Chaco Canyon. Smaller-scale rituals at outliers may have contributed to local ritual leaders' prestige. Bonito-style architecture and local rituals also kept outlier residents involved with the ideology that fostered periodic grand and glorious gatherings in the center place—Chaco Canyon.

Notes

1. This style of great house is known from other outliers found along the Chuskan slopes and in the western Basin, such as Newcomb, Sanostee, Tocito, Toh-La-Kai, and Escalon (Marshall et al. 1979).

2. There are many possible variations on these patterns. For example, Chacoans could have acted as missionaries, carrying Bonito-style architecture into existing communities. Or Chacoans could have established new Bonito-style architecture on the site of recently abandoned tenth-century communities. The current archaeological resolution is not such that we can distinguish among all possible variations, so I have left this picture in broad brushstrokes for the time being.

3. Better dating of multiple great kivas could help confirm whether this scenario is correct. Where Classic Bonito outlier communities contain multiple great kivas, some should date to the tenth century, and one should be associated with the Classic Bonito great house.

4. Although some of these outliers were technically founded during the Classic Bonito phase, I discuss them in chapter 8 with the Late Bonito phase because the preponderance of their occupation and importance lies with events and processes of the late 1000s and early 1100s.

5. Banded veneers are present at 20 out of 38 Classic Bonito outlier great houses in the San Juan Basin (Van Dyke 1999b:491–492). Archaeologists have uncovered evidence for plastered walls at the excavated great houses of Salmon (Irwin-Williams et al. 1975:52, 120), Bis sa'ani (Marshall 1982:185, 187), Aztec West (Morris 1928:120, 272–273, 289, 294), Morris 39 (Morris 1939:52), Guadalupe (Pippin 1987), and Casamero (Sigleo 1981:3).

6. For references to the ubiquity of core-and-veneer masonry at outliers, see Marshall and others 1979:15; Morris 1919:105; Powers, Gillespie, and Lekson 1983:16; Roberts 1932:29; Roys 1936; Vivian and Mathews 1965.

7. Interestingly, there is a second possible great house—the Eleanor site—on the valley floor. Like Guadalupe, it was constructed of banded, core-and-veneer sandstone from a source several kilometers to the south. Surrounding domestic sites are built of simple, locally available basalt cobble masonry (Proper 1997).

8. Segment 192 is visible on aerial photographs (Nials, Stein, and Roney 1987:133, map 50; Roney 1992:127) and was verified on the ground by Van Dyke (2001). The enigmatic, 2-km-long segment appears to be floating between the Andrews and Casamero great houses, but, contrary to Kantner's (1997) assumptions, it does not connect either of those two structures.

9. The Skunk Springs great house is in a somewhat similar situation with respect to viewshed. A community of 65 small sites is scattered along Grey Mesa to the west of the great house and off the edge of the mesa in the valley below. The structure would have been highly visible from other sites on the mesa and from sites outside the valley but would have been blocked from view at sites on the valley floor close to the mesa's edge.

10. The El Llano community, 2 km to the southeast, was occupied during Basketmaker III

and Pueblo I times. Escalon, however, does not appear to have a proto-great house or 900s great kiva, so it is considered here a colonial community. By the Pueblo II period, the focus of settlement shifted to the Escalon community, where 13 sites date between AD 1000 and 1050.

11. Standing walls exceed 1.5 m in height, and mound elevations extend up to 2 m. The great kiva is appended to the structure's northeast side, and a linear segment of four rooms abuts the great kiva. An additional four to six rooms were originally present on the east side of the roomblock, but vandals have removed these walls. Two middens and a pile of sandstone spalls are found on the north and east sides of the great house. The great house represents at least 718 cu m of mass on a 473-sq-m footprint.

12. Platform and stairway complexes are known from a few other Chacoan locations. For example, there is a similar ramp on the Ah-Shi-Sle-Pah Road (Nials, Stein, and Roney 1987:124). The platform-staircase and atalaya structures resemble Toyee Rock on the South Chaco Slope, where a massive Bonito-style platform leads to a summit containing low rock enclosures (Marshall and Sofaer 1988).

13. Three other possible cases of Classic Bonito "roads through time" include a road linking the eleventh-century Padilla Well great house with a tenth-century great kiva (Marshall and Sofaer 1988:76–82), a road linking the late-eleventh-/early-twelfth-century Kin Nizhoni great house with the late-tenth-/eleventh-century Lower Kin Nizhoni great house (Nials, Stein, and Roney 1987:127–128), and a road linking Upper Kin Klizhin, an early-tenth-century great house, with Casa Patricio, an early-ninth-century great kiva (Kincaid, Stein, and Levine 1983:77).

8 The Late Bonito Phase

At the still point of the turning world. Neither flesh nor fleshless;
Neither from nor towards; at the still point, there the dance is,
But neither arrest nor movement. And do not call it fixity,
Where past and future are gathered. Neither movement from nor towards,
Neither ascent nor decline. Except for the point, the still point,
There would be no dance, and there is only the dance.

—*from "Burnt Norton," by T. S. Eliot (1991 [1935]:177)*

By 1080, Chaco Canyon was the still point of a turning world—the central place around which revolved a highly formalized ritual dance. Great houses such as Pueblo Bonito, Pueblo Alto, and Chetro Ketl housed religious elites and formed the core of a ritual landscape. People from communities across the San Juan Basin and beyond gathered periodically in the canyon for festivities coordinated with astronomical events such as solstices, equinoxes, or lunar standstills. Visitors moved through a landscape that enhanced and communicated shared aesthetic ideas such as visibility, directionality, balanced dualism, center place, cyclical renewal, and social memory. The social power of Chaco religious leaders was at its apogee. Leaders organized labor to build venues for ritual activities, to manipulate visitors' experiences, and to celebrate elements of the belief system. They orchestrated and presided over ritual events, deriving a great deal of status and prestige from these roles.

But Chaco was never a static entity. Both the social and the architectural landscapes were continually changing, with new social configurations emerging from the old, just as new buildings referenced older constructions. During the Late Bonito phase (1100–1140), the role of Chaco Canyon within the Ancestral Pueblo world peaked, then began to decline. As new outlier settlements grew in the northern San Juan, Chaco and its core outliers in the central San Juan Basin changed in response, which effected more change in the northern San Juan. Ultimately, this process led to the demise of Chaco as a ritual center.

In the early 1100s, Chaco's influence continued to expand outwards as outliers proliferated across the San Juan Basin and adjacent areas (Kantner 2003b; Kantner and Mahoney 2000) (figures 8.1 and 8.2). In the canyon and at outliers, Chacoans manipulated landscape on a more formal scale than ever before, legitimating and perpetuating Chacoan ritual practices and beliefs. They erected six new great houses in the canyon—Casa Chiquita, Headquarters Site A, Kin Kletso, New Alto, Tsin Kletsin, and Wijiji. People in the canyon had close ties to communities in the northern San Juan—the two areas shared a new "McElmo" architecture style and black-on-white pottery decorated with organic paint. During the early 1100s, a new outlier grew to rival and briefly eclipse Chaco as a ritual gathering place—Aztec, on the banks of the Animas River 85 km to the north. By 1130, builders ceased construction of new great houses in Chaco Canyon, and the focus of most Ancestral Pueblo activity shifted to the northern San Juan. Those who continued to live in Chaco built more small sites and eventually turned portions of some great houses into domestic habitations, depositing trash in abandoned rooms (Judge 1989:246; Toll 1985:483–489). In this chapter, I examine these social and architectural developments within and outside Chaco Canyon.

Chaco's Northern Expansion

During the last decades of the eleventh century, Chaco's influence continued to spread rapidly outward. As Chacoans and local Ancestral Puebloans constructed new colonial outliers such as Chimney Rock, Red Willow, and Las Ventanas to the north, west, and south of Chaco Canyon (chapter 7), the area north of the San Juan River also became a particular focus of new settlement. The major population shifts of the late 800s never entirely depopulated the Four Corners region, and by the late 1000s, this area began to experience a surge in growth, with at least thirty-six major community centers dated to 1050–1150 (Varien 1999). Archaeologists consider some of these centers, including Edge of the Cedars and Lowry, to be Chaco outliers,

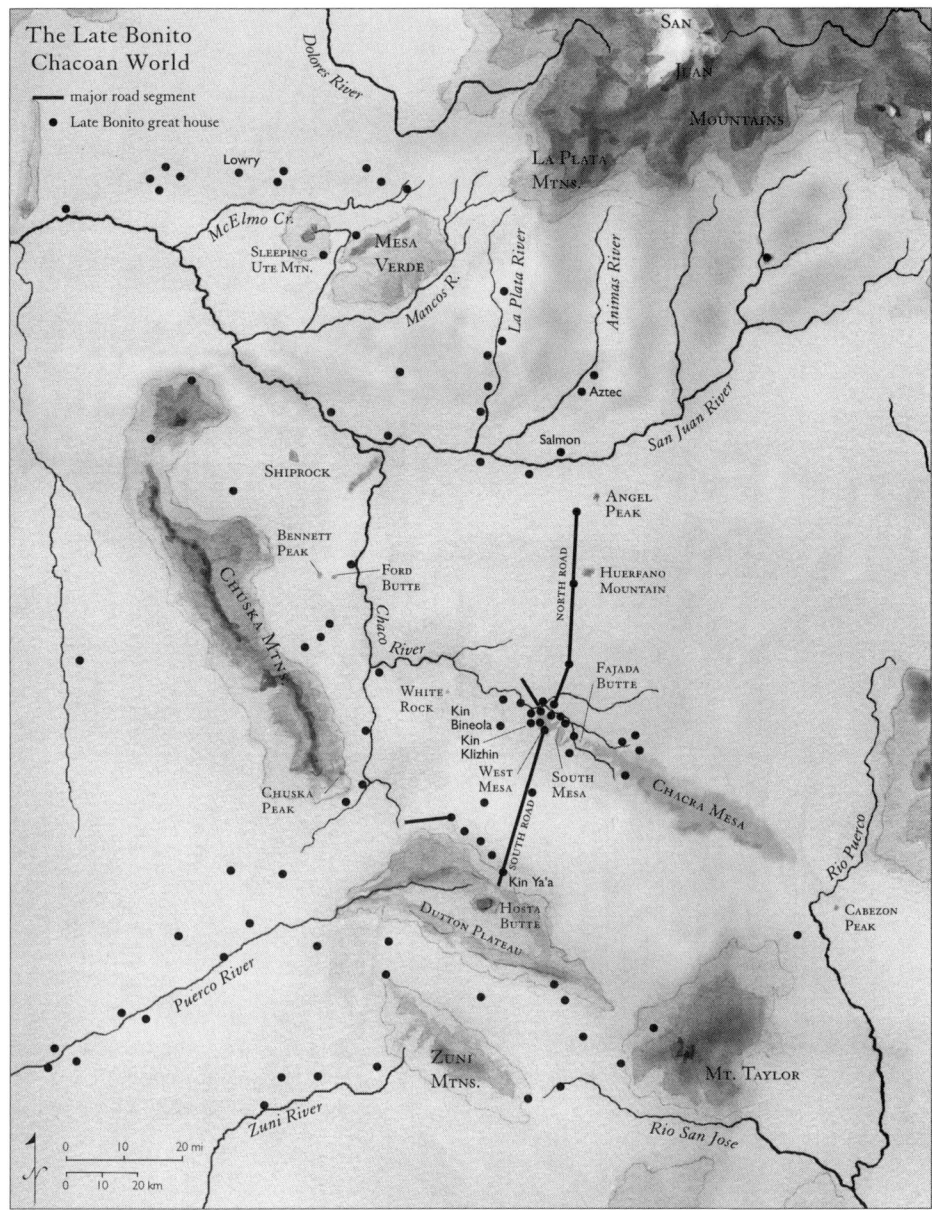

Figure 8.1. The Late Bonito Chacoan world. Drafted by Molly O'Halloran.

based on great house layout and site organization. Edge of the Cedars was likely built by local people who had begun to participate in Chaco and sought to integrate themselves into the Chacoan world (Hurst 2000). Lowry was likely built by colonists from the canyon.

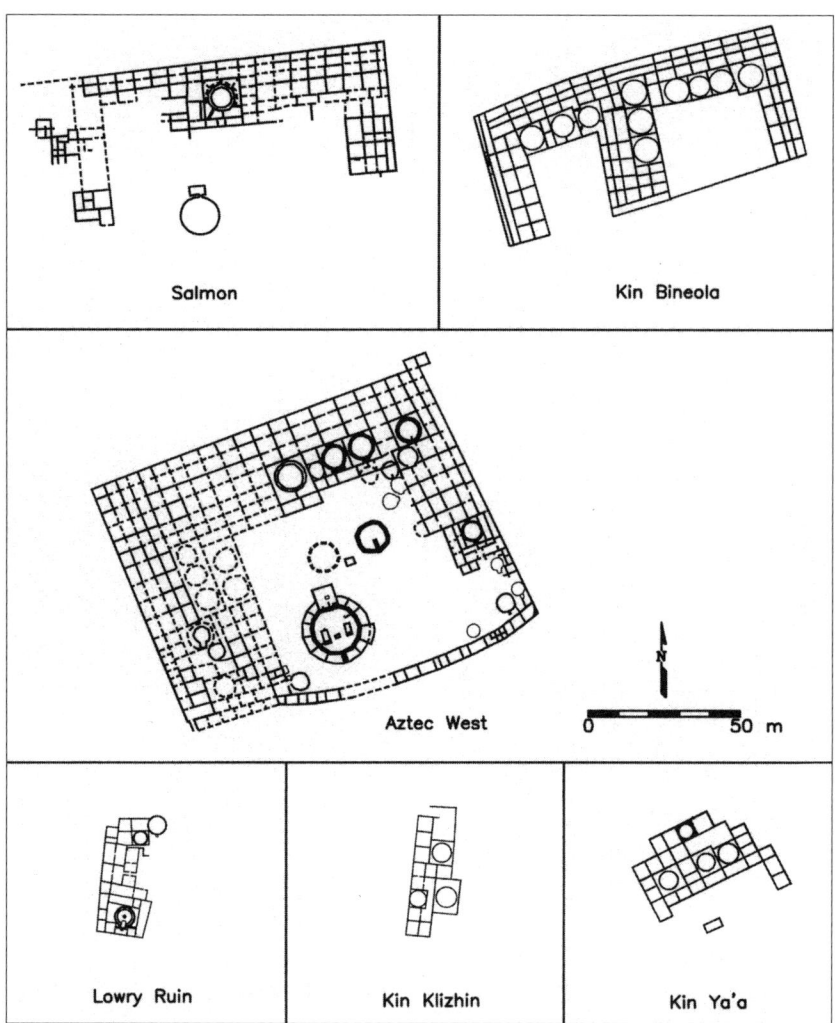

Figure 8.2. Plans of Late Bonito outlier great houses described in detail in the text. Salmon is based on a map in Reed 2006b:3, figure 1.2. Aztec West is based on a map in Morris 1924:145. Lowry Ruin is based on a map in Martin 1936:1, map 1. Kin Bineola, Kin Klizhin, and Kin Ya'a are based on maps in Marshall and others 1979.

The Lowry site complex is a good example of a colonial outlier near the northern edge of the Chacoan world. Lowry builders constructed a formal landscape that expresses balanced dualism, symmetry, center place, directionality, visibility, and social memory (figure 8.3). Located in southwest Colorado 190 km north-northwest of Chaco Canyon, Lowry contains two Chacoan great houses, a large post-Chacoan pueblo, a great kiva, road seg-

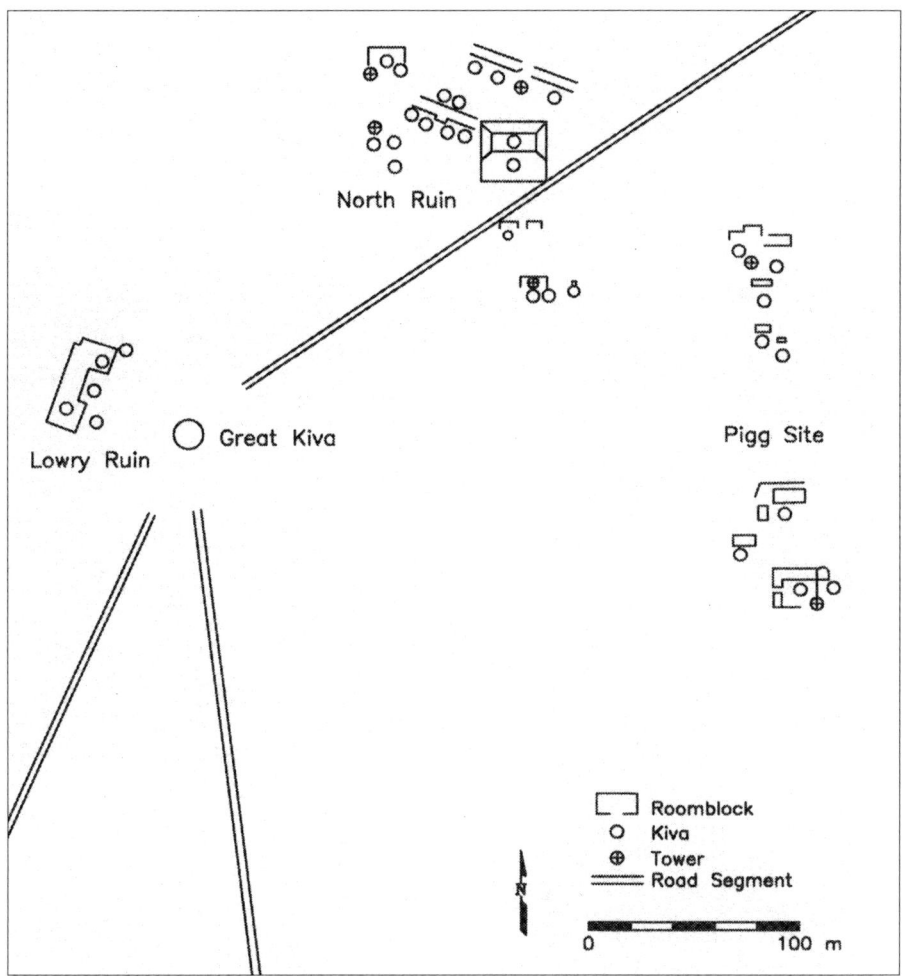

Figure 8.3. The Lowry landscape, after Kendrick and Judge 2000:121, figure 9.7.

ments, and a surrounding community of at least sixty contemporaneous, small domestic sites (Kendrick and Judge 2000). Ancestral Puebloans constructed Lowry Ruin, an 870-sq-m core-and-veneer great house, between 1086 and 1106 (Martin 1936). The rooftops of Lowry offer a sweeping, 360-degree vista punctuated by highly distinctive peaks and mesas, including Sleeping Ute Mountain. Lowry Ruin faces east. Approximately 200 m to the northeast, a second great house, the North Ruin, faces south. The North Ruin, a multi-storied, unexcavated great house with two elevated, enclosed kivas, may predate Lowry Ruin. The Pigg Site is a post-Chacoan pueblo southeast of the North Ruin. Builders used these three major architectural elements to create a highly structured landscape. In the midst of the open space in front of Lowry and the North Ruin is a great kiva with at least one associated road segment (Roney 1992:128). The site complex exhibits the core tenets of the Classic Bonito worldview. The Chacoan complex at Lowry represents the founding of a new community center in an area that previously supported a more dispersed, smaller population.

This pattern characterized many late eleventh-century outliers on the Chacoan periphery. The Totah region, where the Animas and La Plata rivers empty into the San Juan, was a particular focus of new settlement by the 1080s.[1] Over the subsequent half-century, population, new construction, and ritual importance shifted from Chaco Canyon to the Totah, and more specifically to Aztec (Judge 1989; Lekson 1999; Toll, Windes, and McKenna 1980). Both social and environmental pulls and pushes paved the way for this transformation.

The Totah landscape was not empty, physically or conceptually, for Chacoans. Migrants from the northern San Juan into the central Basin and Chaco Canyon had passed this way in the late 800s, establishing proto-great house communities at Cedar Hill (Wilshusen and Wilson 1995). Places on this landscape are likely to have figured into Chacoan migration stories or other oral traditions. At canyon gatherings, northern visitors may have told inhabitants of the central San Juan Basin about the verdant northland. Occupation of the Totah had been constant, but at a small scale, across the tenth and eleventh centuries (McKenna and Toll 1992:133–135). The Totah contained several Classic Bonito outliers, including Sterling, Jaquez, and Morris 41. Sterling and Jaquez are great houses on the south bank of the San Juan River (Wheelbarger n.d.). Morris 41, a site complex overlooking the La Plata River, contains two great houses and at least forty other sites dated between the Basketmaker III and Pueblo III periods (Morris 1939; Toll n.d.).

The Totah would have been particularly attractive to Chacoans during the 1090s, when a prolonged drought led to a sharp downturn in agricultural production in the central San Juan Basin (Sebastian 1992:135). Chaco was always a marginal place for agriculture, even in the best years, and the Animas, La Plata, and San Juan rivers offered pastures that were literally greener. Perhaps new northern outliers were a Chacoan attempt to establish farming communities along permanent watercourses, with the aim of counteracting central Basin food shortages. But this environmentally driven scenario alone does not explain the rise of Aztec; the drought in the central Basin ended just as Aztec got off the ground. Rainfall and agriculture rebounded to reach previously unprecedented levels at Chaco between 1100 and 1130.

The environmental problems of the 1090s may have exacerbated social tensions in Chaco toward the end of the Classic Bonito phase. Burial evidence indicates that material and nutritional differences between great house and small site inhabitants were at their most extreme at the end of the eleventh century (Akins 1986, 2003). Perhaps ritual leaders were attempting a more coercive style of management and met with some resistance. Today, Pueblo society tends to be intolerant of individual aggrandizement—this may be in reaction to past leaders who overstepped their bounds. Or if Chacoan ceremonialism was supposed to ensure agricultural productivity, then a decade of extremely low corn production might have shaken the populace's faith in the leadership. Intriguingly, one of the two men buried with thousands of exotics under the floor of Room 33 in Pueblo Bonito met a violent end, with chop marks on his left parietal, temporal, and femur (Akins 2003). He was interred as a person of great importance—did he perish in an internecine conflict? Was he an aggrandizer removed by disaffected followers, who nevertheless buried him with pomp because they feared his power? Perhaps, as social and environmental problems mounted, rival factions began to emerge in Chaco Canyon. Some continued to uphold Chaco as center place for regional ritual gatherings. One or more other groups may have set out for the Totah to build a new center place in a more socially and environmentally hospitable environment.

Salmon

Salmon Ruin is a major new outlier constructed on the banks of the San Juan River during the 1080s and 1090s (Reed 2006b). The great house was established near the confluence of the river with Kutz Canyon, 15 km northwest of the North Road at Kutz Canyon's edge. The builders of Salmon were intimately familiar with the tenets of Chacoan great house construction. In fact, Salmon is a near duplicate of Hungo Pavi in Chaco Canyon. Although construction at Salmon proceeded in phases, builders conceived the structure as an architectural whole. The bracket-shaped great house contains an estimated 175 rooms within two to three stories (table 8.1). An elevated, second-story "tower kiva" is centrally located in the rear linear roomblock, and a great kiva is situated in the southwest plaza.[2]

Like canyon great houses, Salmon embodies balanced dualism, expressing nearly perfect bilateral symmetry and juxtaposing the great house's vertical space against the subterranean space of the great kiva in the plaza to the east. The great house is divided into two halves by the "tower kiva" in the rear roomblock. This is the only enclosed kiva in the original Chacoan configuration of Salmon, and its placement seems highly significant.

Table 8.1 Estimated Floor Area, Height, and Room Counts for Six Late Bonito Outlier Great Houses (Based on Powers, Gillespie, and Lekson 1983:Table 41)

Great House	Estimated Floor Area (sq m)	Number of Stories	Estimated Number of Rooms
Aztec West	15,030	1–3	405
Salmon	8,320	2–3	175
Kin Bineola	8,225	1–3	230
Kin Ya'a	2,395	1–4	44
Kin Klizhin	1,905	1–3	18
Lowry	870	1–2	34

Builders incorporated similar central, elevated kivas into other great houses, including Aztec West, Hungo Pavi, and Pueblo del Arroyo. Some archaeologists have taken to calling these features "orbiter" kivas because the rest of the great house appears to revolve around them. Architecturally, an orbiter kiva is a center place—a point of intersection between each half of the pueblo and between vertical and subterranean space.

Tree-ring dates suggest that construction at Salmon may have coincided with lunar events. Builders undertook the first major construction between 1089 and 1090, but a few earlier tree-ring dates, from the east wing, are from 1068 to 1072 (Baker n.d.; Windes n.d.b). Baker believes that initial planning and woodcutting for Salmon may have begun in the late 1060s, in connection with the minor lunar standstill of 1066. The back wall of Salmon is aligned to the minor lunar standstill. A second major construction episode dates to 1094–1095, coinciding with a major lunar standstill. The third and final Chacoan construction events at Salmon date from 1105 to 1106 (Windes n.d.b).

Salmon expresses the key themes found in all Chacoan architecture and was likely designed by colonists from Chaco. But who supplied the labor for its construction? Archaeologists have not located a surrounding community of small sites, although San Juan River flooding may have obscured any traces. The Totah area was not densely settled at this time, but scattered domestic pueblos and other great houses did exist in the area. Sterling, Jaquez, and a small pueblo called the Tommy Site are clustered 15 km downriver to the west (Wheelbarger n.d.). Some elements of the local populace likely shared Chacoan ideology and participated in canyon ritual, so perhaps they were willing to lend their labor to construction of a new, local ritual center. Lunar standstills could have been occasions to call people together for work parties in combination with local ceremonial events. A great number of people would not necessarily have been required. Windes and McKenna (2001:134–136) estimate that a crew of ten people working ten-hour days could have harvested and processed the wood for Salmon in a little more than 35 days.

Reed (2006a:267) believes that Salmon served as a residence for Chacoan colonists. Lekson (1999:137) contends that Chacoan colonists meant Salmon to become a new center place but when the San Juan River proved subject to turbulent floods, they relocated their efforts to the banks of the Animas. Chacoans likely did inhabit the Salmon great house, but I think it probable that builders intended Salmon as a regional gathering place for people living in the Totah. By contrast, builders designed Aztec to rival, if not replace, Chaco Canyon as center place for the Ancestral Pueblo world. It is possible that the two outliers were conceived at roughly the same time, perhaps by two groups of Chacoan colonists.

Aztec

Aztec is a highly formalized, planned landscape constructed in several stages (McKenna and Toll 1992; Stein and McKenna 1988). Not only did the builders of the Aztec complex emphasize the familiar concepts of a Chacoan worldview, but they also went further, creating a landscape that replicates the core spatial relationships of Chaco Canyon (figure 8.4). The complex contains three great houses—Aztec North, which sits on the edge of a mesa overlooking the Animas Valley, and Aztec West and Aztec East, which mirror each other and sit on the northern bank of the Animas. Farther to the southeast, trending roughly east-west, runs the Animas River. These spatial relationships are exactly the same in general orientation and layout as the relationships between Pueblo Alto (represented by Aztec North), Pueblo Bonito (represented by Aztec West), Chetro Ketl (represented by Aztec East), and the Chaco Wash (represented by the Animas River). A road segment bisects Aztec East and Aztec West, climbs the bluff north of the two great houses, passes just west of Aztec North, and extends northwest for at least 4.5 km—this road segment is in the same relative position as the North Road above Pueblo Alto. Standing atop Aztec North and looking down over Aztec West and Aztec East toward the southeast, it is clear that the builders of Aztec had these Chacoan relationships in mind. Colonists planned the buildings and their spatial relationships in toto. The positions of the mesa, the northern river floodplain, and the river itself presented builders with a topographic space in which to re-create the core Chacoan landscape.

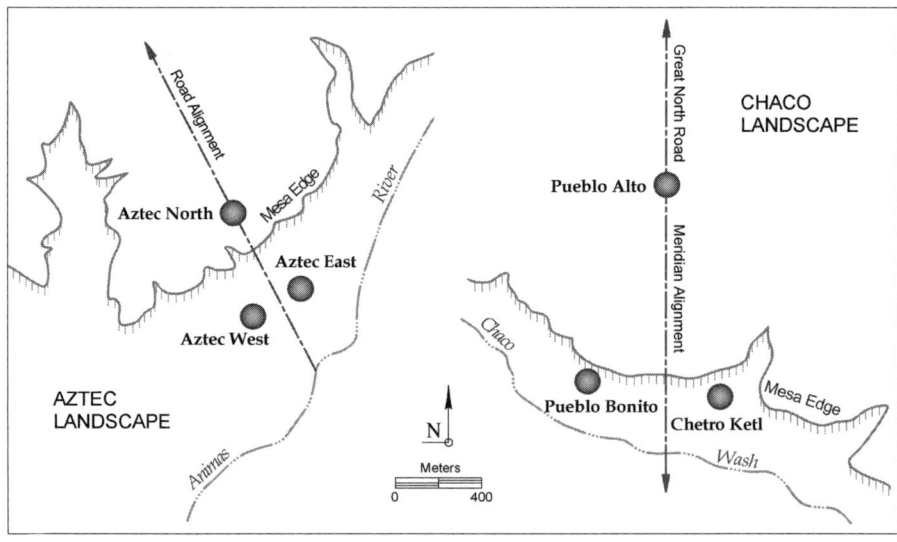

Figure 8.4. A comparison of the Aztec and Chacoan landscapes. Drafted by Catherine Gilman, courtesy of the Center for Desert Archaeology.

Builders initiated construction of the Aztec landscape with Aztec North in the late 1000s, continuing with Aztec West in the early 1100s and later with Aztec East into the 1200s.

Aztec North is the earliest and possibly the largest of the three great houses, probably founded in the 1080s (McKenna and Toll 1992; Stein and McKenna 1988). The cobble-and-adobe structure is represented by a large rubble mound. Because Aztec North is unexcavated, we have no detailed understanding of its interior spaces. Adobe is an unusual choice of great house construction material, but Chacoans employed it for at least one other outlier great house, Bis sa'ani (Breternitz, Doyel, and Marshall 1982). Perhaps engineers directing initial construction at Aztec North lacked the labor force to quarry the building stone for the structure. Aztec was founded in a previously unoccupied space (Lekson 1999:135; Stein and McKenna 1988:4), and it may have taken a few years or decades for Chacoans to convince others to participate in the building projects. Blocky and tabular sandstone are not readily available at Aztec and must be carried from at least several kilometers away; adobe and cobbles from the nearby Animas may have been an expedient alternative. The end result was not as durable as a great house built of stacked sandstone, but plastered over, it may have looked like a reasonable facsimile.[3]

Aztec West—the major ruin that forms the focus of Aztec National Monument—is an exceptionally large great house, second only to Pueblo

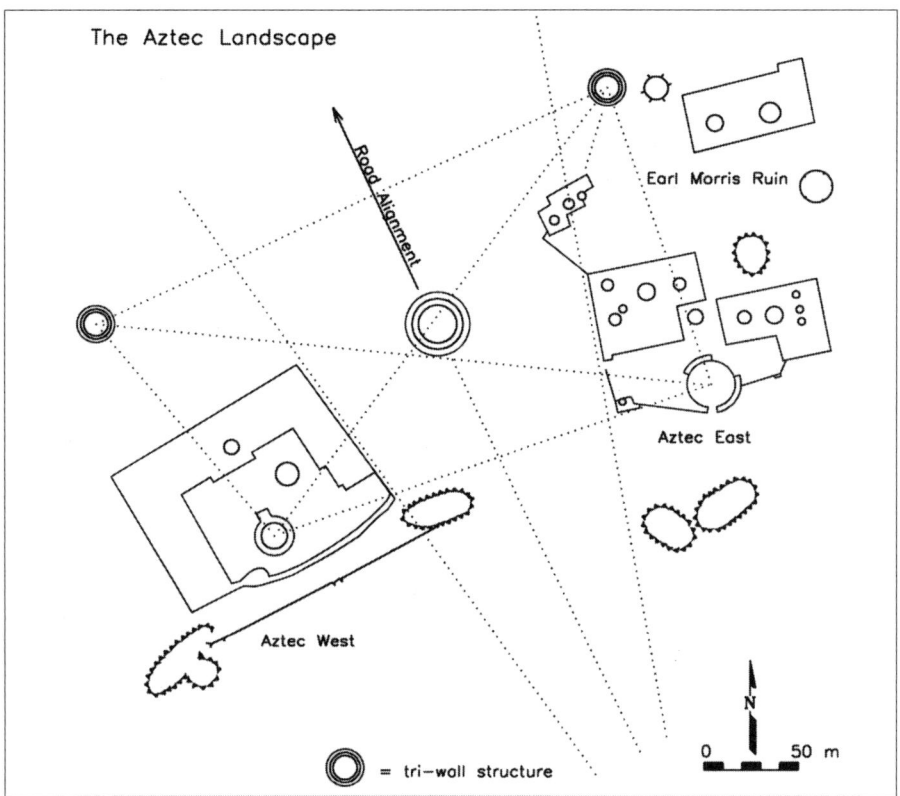

Figure 8.5. The Aztec landscape, after McKenna and Toll 1992:136, figure 11-4.

Bonito and Chetro Ketl in floor area (see table 8.1) (Powers, Gillespie, and Lekson 1983:313).[4] It embodies familiar Chacoan spatial themes, including balanced dualism and center place. In its earliest design, Aztec West closely resembles Salmon Ruin, with a symmetrical, bracket-shaped layout pivoting around an elevated orbiter kiva and a southeast-facing plaza enclosing a great kiva (see figure 8.2). Builders used dark green sandstone to create banding along some brown sandstone walls (Morris 1928:316). As in Chaco Canyon, builders carved a hollow space into the hidden end of some radial-beam kiva pilasters and filled the space with beads or other votive offerings (Gary Brown, personal communication, April 2006).

Aztec East completes the balanced, symmetrical landscape layout of the Aztec complex (McKenna and Toll 1992:136) (figure 8.5). It consists of two compact, McElmo-style buildings oriented to face a great kiva.[5] Aztec East is unexcavated, but standing sandstone walls give us an idea of overall building layouts. Chacoans designed and began construction of Aztec East in the Late Bonito phase, but changes in wood procurement and treatment, as well as later clusters of tree-ring dates, indicate that other builders completed the great house generations later. Construction episodes date to 1115, the 1190s, the 1210s, and the 1240s, with some additions as late as 1270 (Brown, Windes, and McKenna n.d.; McKenna and Toll 1992).

Tri-wall structures are another enigmatic feature of the Late Bonito Chacoan landscape. These circular features consist of three concentric low walls subdivided by multiple crosswalls (Judd 1959; Reyman 1985; Vivian 1959). Three tri-wall structures on the Aztec landscape are behind Aztec West to the north, behind Aztec East to the north, and halfway between Aztec West and East. It is not clear what activities went on inside these structures, but each is situated at a point of symmetrical balance on the landscape.

Although the Aztec landscape was clearly designed by builders who were knowledgeable about Chaco, at least part of the labor was likely undertaken by locals. Local Ancestral Puebloans living in dispersed communities may have coalesced around the Aztec project. There are at least ninety small pueblos within a 2.5-m radius of the Aztec complex. Perhaps, for a variety of reasons, local Totah residents were eager, or at least willing, to lend their efforts to construct public structures at Aztec. Windes (n.d.b) has observed two kinds of viga-finishing techniques found side by side in the same roofs—one typically Chacoan, the other expedient. This suggests that at least two different work parties—perhaps Chacoans and locals—cooperated on roof construction. The builders of Aztec West began stockpiling timbers during 1110. In 1113, they began construction in the north and east wings; they continued work on the great house with a second major construction episode in 1119 (Brown, Windes, and McKenna n.d.; Windes and McKenna 2001:133–134). Windes and McKenna (2001:134–136) estimate that the initial construction episode at Aztec West could have taken as little time as 42 days and the second episode, a little more than 52 days. If it had been spread over several years rather than undertaken all at once, then this would not have constituted an unreasonably demanding amount of labor. Windes and McKenna envision a small workforce organized along the lines of historic Pueblo work societies, involving extended or fictive kin.

The builders of Aztec clearly sought to replicate Chaco in the design and layout of the three great houses on the north bank of the Animas. They may have sought to attract followers to a new ritual order grounded in the old Chacoan traditions. The formalization of old Chacoan ideas on a new landscape encouraged Ancestral Puebloans to envision Aztec as a new cosmographic, social, and ritual gathering place. To some degree, over the long term, the leaders of Aztec were successful. By the late 1100s, Aztec had become an important center of the post-Chacoan world (Judge 1989:247;

Lekson 1999:140–141). However, a Chaco-to-Aztec transition did not happen wholesale, nor did it happen quickly. Between 1100 and 1140, Chaco Canyon and Aztec may have competed with each other for the role of ritual center of the Ancestral Pueblo world.

Late Bonito Chaco Canyon

The first few decades of the 1100s were among the wettest ever in Chaco Canyon. If the drought years of the 1090s had weakened Puebloans' confidence in ceremonies at Chaco, then renewed times of plenty could have restored their faith. One way for canyon leaders to cope with competition from Aztec might have been to initiate new building projects that celebrated a renewed world order yet provided a familiar sense of continuity with the preceding centuries. The canyon leaders needed to assure followers that Chaco Canyon was still the center place and the most important location in which to conduct ceremonies to keep the world in balance. They may also have wanted to attract new followers. For these purposes, the Late Bonito Chacoans initiated a new construction program firmly grounded in old ideas yet slightly different. They formalized aspects of the Chacoan ideology as never before, from the ground up, making symbolic connections to the past order but reinstating directionality and duality with the placement of new buildings. The new order was based on the old, but with even more clarity, to encourage confidence in its strength (Van Dyke 2004b).

During the Late Bonito phase, a new set of great houses was established in Chaco. Although these structures exhibited clear architectural continuity with existing great houses, they also represented something new and distinctive. The new great houses may have served a variety of practical functions, but on a symbolic level, they presented people with something both novel and familiar, recalling the meanings represented by older Classic Bonito great houses. Chacoan great houses, shrines, and road segments continued to emphasize visibility, balanced dualism, directionality, center place, and cyclical renewal. Late Bonito builders sought to remake the Chacoan world but at the same time to link themselves directly to the Classic Bonito heyday of their parents and grandparents' experience.

New Canyon Great Houses

Chacoan builders erected six new Late Bonito great houses—Casa Chiquita, Headquarters Site A, Kin Kletso, New Alto, Tsin Kletsin, and Wijiji (table 8.2, figures 8.6 and 8.7). The new architecture elegantly, cleanly, and expediently exemplifies the tenets of the Chacoan worldview that were so important

Table 8.2 Estimated Height, Footprint, Room Counts, Mass, and Visibility for Six Late Bonito Canyon Great Houses
(Measurements Derived from Data in Lekson 1986 unless Otherwise Specified)

Great House	Number of Stories	Areal Footprint (sq m)	Ground Floor/Total Rooms	Mass (cu m)	Visible Major Buildings and Landforms
Casa Chiquita	1–3	381	34/59	1,122	Pueblo del Arroyo, Casa Rinconada
Headquarters Site A	*	780	39/39	*	29SJ1253 (Fajada Gap great kiva), Fajada Butte, Hosta Butte
Kin Kletso	2–3	999	57/132	4,422	Peñasco Blanco, Pueblo Bonito, Pueblo del Arroyo, Casa Rinconada
New Alto	1–2	507	32/58	1,688	Peñasco Blanco, Pueblo Alto, Tsin Kletsin, Shiprock, Hosta Butte, Huerfano Mountain, Fajada Butte, Mount Taylor
Tsin Kletsin	1–2	1,444	55/89	3,696	Pueblo Alto, New Alto, Kin Klizhin, Shiprock, Huerfano Mountain
Wijiji	1–3	1,161	104/206	4,146	29SJ1642 (isolated great kiva)

*Measurements derived from site form. No reliable estimate because the building consists only of foundations.

throughout the Classic Bonito phase. "Late Bonito Chacoan architecture strongly reflected the ancient precepts of order, formality, standardization, and symmetry, and the concept of a master plan" (Vivian 1990:374). But this new construction reaches beyond simple continuity with the forms and ideas of the preceding century. Chacoans sited new buildings in carefully balanced topographic locations. Alignments between buildings along Chaco's central axis made reference to the old Classic Bonito order. The new buildings encouraged viewers to appreciate the potency of Late Bonito leaders, and they brought to mind the longevity and past importance of Chaco ceremonialism and beliefs.

By contrast with Classic Bonito–phase buildings, which were modified in planned stages, Late Bonito great houses represent self-contained units of design (Lekson 1986:64). Chacoans erected Late Bonito great houses in one

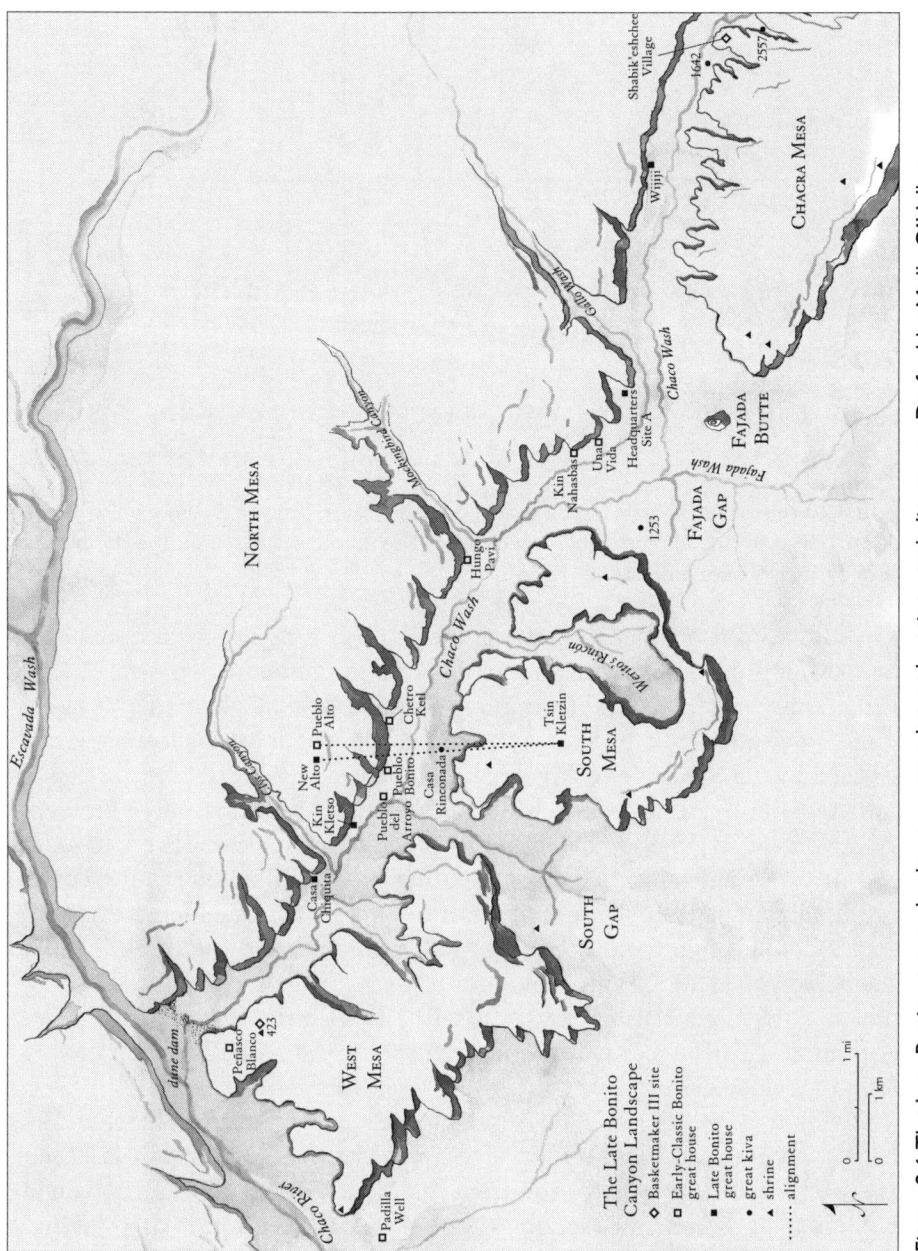

Figure 8.6. The Late Bonito canyon landscape—great house locations and alignments. Drafted by Molly O'Halloran.

The Late Bonito Phase

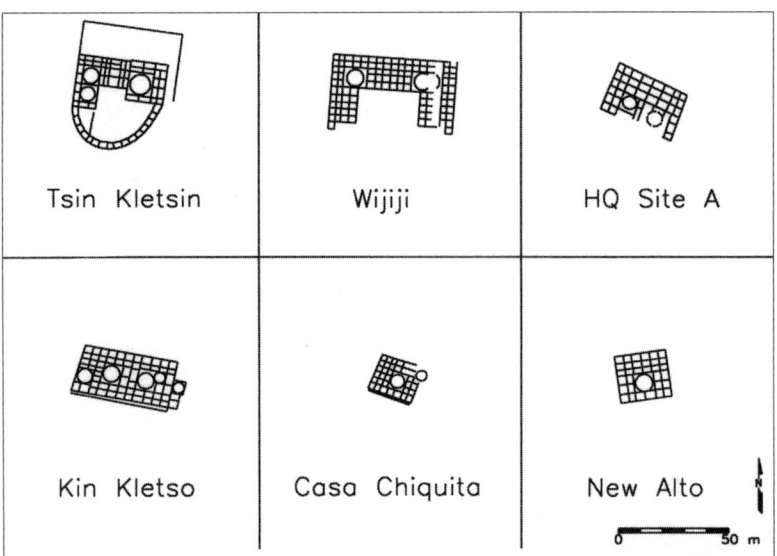

Figure 8.7. Plans of Late Bonito–phase great houses in Chaco Canyon. Based on plans in Lekson 1986, with the exception of Headquarters Site A, which is based on the site plan drawn by Tom Windes and Dabney Ford.

or two brief, well-planned construction events. Late Bonito great houses are one to three stories high and contain one or two symmetrical blocks of uniform rooms, each block surrounding a single kiva. Unlike their Classic Bonito forebears, Late Bonito great houses do not have enclosed plazas, associated great kivas, or earthworks.

Late Bonito great houses feature core-and-veneer masonry. Builders used Type III, Type IV, and McElmo veneer styles (Lekson 1986:17–21). Type III veneers exhibit distinctive banding produced by alternating layers of thin, tabular sandstone with layers of massive sandstone blocks. Type IV veneers contain tightly coursed, thin, tabular sandstone. At Wijiji, in east Chaco Canyon, Late Bonito builders used veneer Types III and IV. At the other five new Late Bonito canyon great houses—Kin Kletso, Tsin Kletsin, Headquarters Site A, Casa Chiquita, and New Alto—builders employed McElmo-style masonry.

McElmo veneers consist of rows of pecked, bun-shaped blocks. The *McElmo* moniker was bestowed by Vivian and Mathews (1965), who believed the style to represent an intrusion from the Mesa Verde region. They named McElmo architecture after McElmo Canyon near Cortez, Colorado. McElmo structures represent a specific architectural template shared by builders in Chaco Canyon, the Totah, and other parts of the northern San Juan. Symmetrical, compact, uniform McElmo structures found both inside and outside

Chaco Canyon are a recognizable and discrete class of buildings (Lekson 1986:269–272; Vivian 1990:375–376). However, McElmo structures might just as easily have developed in Chaco Canyon and spread northward in the early twelfth century.

Each of the five McElmo-style great houses in Chaco Canyon consists of one or two "McElmo units"—compact, symmetrical squares or rectangles of approximately thirty rooms arranged in a grid-like fashion around an enclosed kiva. Room sizes vary, from 2.5 sq m (New Alto second story) to 9.4 sq m (Kin Kletso), but are fairly uniform within each great house. Although Wijiji lacks McElmo masonry, it appears to have been constructed at the same time as the five McElmo great houses—the building has a single published tree-ring date of 1110c (Lekson 1986:224–231; Shiner 1959; Vivian 1990:286 –288). Wijiji is also larger than the others, with a configuration transitional between Classic Bonito and McElmo-style layouts. Like Classic Bonito great houses such as Hungo Pavi, Wijiji is bracket-shaped. Like its Late Bonito brethren, each half of Wijiji centers around an enclosed kiva, essentially creating an expanded version of the kiva-centered McElmo unit.

Kin Kletso, located against the north wall of Chaco Canyon northwest of Pueblo Bonito, is the only excavated McElmo great house (Vivian and Mathews 1965). As a result, interpretations made at Kin Kletso are often applied to the other McElmo sites. Kin Kletso consists of two adjacent McElmo units, with a small addition later added to the east end of the structure. Construction of both halves took place over a short span between AD 1118 and 1125 or between 1125 and 1130. Some eleventh-century tree-ring dates likely represent reused beams (Bannister 1965; Lekson 1986: 238–246; Vivian and Mathews 1965:53–54).

Like Kin Kletso, Tsin Kletsin consists of two buildings. A McElmo unit on the east is attached to an L-shaped roomblock on the west, with an enclosed plaza in front to the south. Although Tsin Kletsin may represent two separate construction events, the building was completed over a short span of time between AD 1110 and 1115 (Bradford 1981; Lekson 1986: 231–238; Mayer 1971).[6] Tsin Kletsin is the only Late Bonito great house with associated refuse, although the light scatter of spalls and artifacts enclosed by a masonry wall south of the great house does not resemble domestic trash (Windes 1987:642–644).

Casa Chiquita and New Alto closely resemble each other in size and layout, each consisting of one symmetrical McElmo unit. Casa Chiquita is northwest of Kin Kletso, at the mouth of Clys Canyon (Lekson 1986:246–251; Voll and Mayer 1964).[7] New Alto is atop the north side of Chaco Canyon, west of the Classic Bonito great house Pueblo Alto (Lekson 1986:251–256; Morris and Kayser 1966; Vivian 1947).

Headquarters Site A is a smaller version of Wijiji, located in a cul-de-sac on the north side of Chaco Canyon just northwest of the Gallo Wash (Lister and Lister 1981:252–253; Vivian and Mathews 1965:81; Vivian 1990:350, 365, 425). This little-known structure is represented by a series of foundations largely buried by alluvial wash—either it was never completed, or building stone from the upper courses was reused elsewhere. Headquarters Site A is dated to the Late Bonito phase on the basis of McElmo-style masonry.

In addition to these new Late Bonito great houses, builders continued to make modifications to the existing great houses—Peñasco Blanco, Pueblo Bonito, Chetro Ketl, Pueblo Alto, and Pueblo del Arroyo (Lekson 1986).[8] Many of these modifications employed McElmo-style masonry, although some involved Type III or IV veneers. Common additions included plaza-enclosing arcs of rooms, blocks of small rooms, firepits, second-story kivas, and remodeled kivas and great kivas (Hawley 1934:25–30; Lekson 1986; Windes 2003). Late Bonito builders experimented with new forms, erecting a colonnade-like feature at Chetro Ketl (Lekson 1986:192) and a tri-walled structure behind Pueblo del Arroyo (Judd 1959; Vivian 1959). They laid McElmo masonry foundations for Hillside Ruin, an ambiguous and never-completed structure east of Pueblo Bonito (Jackson 1878:442; Judd 1964:146–147; Stein, Ford, and Friedman 2003:55–56; Windes 2003:31). East of Wijiji, they laid out foundations for another unfinished McElmo structure—Roberts' Small Pueblo (Roberts 1926–1927).

Size- and masonry-based distinctions between great house and small sites began to blur (Truell 1986:145–146). In addition to the buildings described above are at least 20 smaller McElmo-style structures in Chaco Canyon dating to the Late Bonito phase (Hayes 1981; Lister and Lister 1981:252–254; McKenna and Truell 1986; Vivian and Mathews 1965; Vivian 1990:423–429). Some of the better-known include Rabbit Ruin, northwest of Pueblo Alto (Windes 1987:85–90); Lizard House, east of Chetro Ketl (Vivian and Mathews 1965:135, 137); and an isolated McElmo unit on a platform northeast of Peñasco Blanco (Lekson 1986:95, 109). At Pueblo Bonito, sometime in the early 1100s, Puebloans moved into portions of the great house and transformed certain rooms into domestic spaces. They erected room dividers, sealed doorways, constructed new small kivas, and dumped domestic trash in empty rooms (Windes 2003:26–27). Although Chacoans continued to formalize and modify the landscape to emphasize the canyon as center place, the architectural and social fabric of Chaco was changing.

During the Classic Bonito phase, Chacoan architects likely were able to draw upon a large labor pool when Basin residents visited to attend ritual events. However, there are some indications that the Late Bonito leadership had less labor at its disposal, perhaps because an increasing number of outlier residents were shifting allegiance to Aztec. Late Bonito builders seem to have been concerned with maximizing both labor and resources. Lekson (1986:257–269) considers McElmo-style buildings to represent "Class II" construction events, which required 55,000–90,000 person-hours, or approximately one-half to one-third as much labor as Classic Bonito–phase construction events. McElmo structures such as Hillside Ruin and Roberts' Small Pueblo may have been left unfinished because of resource or labor shortages. At least three characteristics of McElmo great houses suggest that builders were concerned with expediency: blocky veneers, recycled roof timbers, and compact, standardized layouts.

By contrast with the banded masonry that characterized most eleventh-century construction, McElmo masonry uses only large, pecked sandstone blocks and omits the alternating bands of shaped, thin tabular sandstone. Sources of blocky sandstone were immediately on hand near most great houses, but builders would have had to bring tabular sandstone from slightly farther away. Furthermore, wide, fat sandstone blocks may have been faster to shape and stack than small pieces of tabular sandstone (Gwinn Vivian, personal communication, January 2003).

Beam transport was the most time-consuming of the various activities involved in great house construction, but builders saved time and labor by recycling wood from older structures. Anomalous tree-ring dates from Casa Chiquita and Kin Kletso suggest the use, or re-use, of beams harvested during the Classic Bonito phase. The smaller rooms found in McElmo structures required less timber for ceilings and roofs, which would have also saved labor.

The compact, standardized McElmo template facilitated speedy and straightforward construction of multiple buildings. With footprints ranging between 381 and 1,161 sq m, Late Bonito great houses are considerably smaller than Classic canyon great houses, which range between 2,011 and 4,762 sq m.

The structures are symbolically potent; in fact, builders may have intended symbolism as their primary function. The practical uses for McElmo great houses have long been debated. The structures lack trash middens or other physical evidence for occupation. Lekson (1986:269–272) contended that McElmo buildings were specialized structures built for administration and storage. Vivian (1990:375–376) challenged Lekson's interpretation, arguing rather that McElmo structures were built to be apartment-like habitations for an increasing canyon population. Whether the great houses were used for either or both of the above, they make strong symbolic statements. They are more than simple facades—they contain rooms and also kivas with floor features—but their design and appearance seem to have been at least as important as their functionality.

Chacoan Themes on the Late Bonito Canyon Landscape

Late Bonito builders incorporated Classic Chacoan themes—particularly visibility, balanced dualism, directionality, and social memory—into the fabric and form of Late Bonito great houses. They also carefully sited the new structures with attention to topography and existing architectural elements, creating compositions that formally illustrated the Chacoan worldview on the larger canyon landscape and emphasized the canyon as the center place around which space and time revolved.

Despite their smaller sizes, Late Bonito great houses carried visual impact comparable to that of Classic Bonito great houses. Chacoans made Late Bonito great houses look larger than they were, employing visual tricks to emphasize mass and height. For example, they constructed secondary, externally faced, parallel walls along the south sides of Casa Chiquita and Kin Kletso (Vivian and Mathews 1965:44; Voll and Mayer 1964:7). Crude, unfaced, internal crosswalls turned the space between the walls into small, 150- by 50-cm cells.[9] Vivian and Mathews speculate that these walls may represent "buttresses" or "defensive devices." The walls and the spaces they define have no clear structural or functional purpose, however. These partitioned, empty spaces may simply represent added mass.

One of the most prominent features of Kin Kletso is Kiva A, a two-story kiva built atop a large boulder that looms above neighboring rooms. Lekson (1986:245) speculates that architects intentionally chose to construct Kin Kletso around and atop the boulder so that it could be used to elevate the kiva; the overall effect is one of a more imposing building. Alternatively, Chacoans may have located this kiva atop a boulder to heighten its symbolic significance. The Tewa, for example, consider boulders to be shrines (Parsons 1939:195, 307). When Chacoans reused roof timbers in Late Bonito great houses, this may have had symbolic significance, as well as practical utility. Builders may have intended certain timbers to reference practices or events that took place in the past, in the beams' original structures.

All six Late Bonito great houses express balanced dualism in the form of bilateral symmetry. Builders created symmetrical structures with the juxtaposition of two adjacent McElmo units (Kin Kletso, Wijiji, Headquarters Site A), the juxtaposition of two balanced sections (Tsin Kletsin), or the bisection of a single McElmo unit (Casa Chiquita, New Alto). Builders did not balance Late Bonito great houses against an associated great kiva, but they inserted a single enclosed kiva in the center of each McElmo unit, which would have created a similar kind of vertical/subterranean juxtaposition.

Late Bonito builders carefully located great houses within the larger topographic and existing architectural elements in the canyon to formally

Figure 8.8. Tsin Kletsin, the Late Bonito great house atop South Mesa.

express the themes of visibility, directionality, balanced dualism, and social memory. These intersecting ideas are apparent in the positioning of Tsin Kletsin (see figure 8.6).

Intervisibility with other great houses was one major consideration in the siting of Tsin Kletsin high atop South Mesa (figure 8.8). From Tsin Kletsin, a viewer can see Pueblo Alto, New Alto, Kin Klizhin, Bis sa'ani, and a site in the Kin Bineola community (29SJ1578), as well as Huerfano Mountain and the more distant ranges of the La Plata and Chuska mountains. Tsin Kletsin also is a critical link in a line-of-sight network created by the careful positioning of several shrines along South Mesa and West Mesa.[10] The line-of-sight network connects all twelve canyon great houses, as well as the outlier great houses of Kin Klizhin, Kin Ya'a, and Kin Bineola. If any of the shrines were situated beyond a very confined diameter, then the network of intervisibility would not be possible (Hayes and Windes 1975:153). Hayes and Windes consider that visual connections may have been part of the rationale behind the location of later great houses. "Many of the big pueblos, such as Bonito…show long occupation before the Bonito phase, and obviously were rebuilt and added to…[b]ut some of those which appear to have been built and used only during the last period may have been put where they were to fit them into an interconnected network of visual contact" (Hayes and Windes 1975:154). Not only Tsin Kletsin but also Wijiji may have been positioned to fit in to the shrine network.

Linking the shrine network was not the Chacoans' sole concern in the siting of Tsin Kletsin, for rising dunes block the view of the Chaco Slope to the south. Better intervisibility would have been afforded by construction of Tsin Kletsin on the true high point of South Mesa, some 700 m to the southwest and 50 ft higher, along the old park service boundary fence. From this spot, a viewer can see nearly all the landmarks and features listed above and also the vast expanse of the Chaco Slope, including the outlier Kin Ya'a and a third shrine, 29SJ2113 (Hayes and Windes 1975). Why was Tsin Kletsin not constructed here, with vistas to the south, as well as to the west, north, and east?

The builders of Tsin Kletsin were concerned not only with intervisibility but also with directionality. They sited Tsin Kletsin directly south of the Classic Bonito great house Pueblo Alto, which sits atop the north side of Chaco Canyon. The Pueblo Alto–Tsin Kletsin alignment is "so familiar it evokes little comment in the vast Chacoan literature" (Lekson 1999:82). Fritz (1978) and Sofaer (1997) consider the alignment to be the north-south axis of a directional cross, with the east-west axis formed by Pueblo Bonito and Chetro Ketl. The alignment places Tsin Kletsin and Pueblo Alto in dualistic opposition on either side of the canyon.

It is important, however, to note that the north-south relationship between Pueblo Alto and Tsin Kletsin is an alignment not only through space but also through time. Occupation of the site of Pueblo Alto dates from the early 1000s, and modifications to the great house continued through the early 1100s (Windes 1987). But the major construction and use of this great house—including the controversial smashing of many imported Chuskan jars (Toll 1985; Wills 2001)—occurred during the Classic Bonito phase. When Late Bonito builders erected Tsin Kletsin in the early 1100s, they symbolically connected themselves to the past ritual order and to past ritual activities conducted at Pueblo Alto. The importance of this relationship was further emphasized by the construction of a road segment leading due north from Tsin Kletsin, pointing toward Pueblo Alto (Stein and Lekson 1992:90; Vivian 1997b:12,14,15). The Pueblo Alto–Tsin Kletsin alignment was part of the construction of social memory—a deliberate and conscious link to the Classic Bonito–phase world order. Similar "time bridges" between noncontemporaneous sites are known from outliers dating from the late eleventh century onwards (Fowler and Stein 1992:116–118; Van Dyke 2003b; see also Lekson 1999:130).

In constructing Tsin Kletsin, Late Bonito builders successfully referenced the rituals, beliefs, and power structure of the preceding generation. The next step was to invoke a new order, grounded in the old but separate.

Like the old order, the new framework was concerned with balance, with dualism, with directionality, with visibility. Late Bonito builders continued these traditions but wanted to establish themselves as separate from, more formal than, and, perhaps, more powerful than those who had come before. So they built New Alto. They did not situate New Alto due north of Tsin Kletsin, but rather at 3 degrees west of true north, 3.7 km away. The importance of this alignment is emphasized by a second road segment leading north from Tsin Kletsin to the edge of South Mesa, pointing directly to its early 1100s neighbor, New Alto. The positioning of New Alto with respect to Tsin Kletsin created a new north-south axis, a new meridian, based on the old but slightly different (see figure 8.6). This new axis travels across Casa Rinconada and bisects the space between Pueblo Bonito and Pueblo Alto, referencing these earlier structures and perhaps legitimating the new Late Bonito alignment through associations with the past.

The Pueblo Alto–Tsin Kletsin–New Alto alignments are elegant examples of Late Bonito Chacoan ideas expressed on the landscape. But all six Late Bonito great houses operate at still more levels to convey symbolic meaning. Late Bonito builders reformalized the Chacoan landscape to express and restate vertical directionality and dualism. This was accomplished within the buildings themselves and through the positioning of the great houses on the landscape.

As we have seen, Tsin Kletsin, Pueblo Alto, and New Alto form two north-south axes over the core of Classic Bonito–phase Chaco, one an alignment to the past, one to the present. East-west directional patterning is evident in the paired opposition of four Late Bonito great houses on the canyon floor, on either side of this meridian. Kin Kletso and Casa Chiquita extend an arm of the axis to the west, and Headquarters Site A and Wijiji extend the axis to the east. All six structures are symmetrically balanced against one another, with the core of the old Classic Bonito canyon as its center place.

Not only the horizontal but also the vertical dimension was important in the concept of six sacred directions and a center place. Tsin Kletsin and New Alto are highly visible, and intervisible, structures. These buildings may represent the high, the light, the vertical direction. However, the edges of Chaco Canyon block views from Tsin Kletsin and New Alto to the other McElmo-style great houses. These two high buildings exist on their own upper plane, in opposition with the buildings on the canyon floor, which exist on a different, lower plane. In the canyon below, Casa Chiquita, Kin Kletso, Headquarters Site A, and Wijiji may represent the low, the dark, the subterranean direction. The positions of the six great houses create a balance of low against high, subterranean against celestial.

Another related duality revolves around the visible and invisible. This opposition is strongly expressed in the positioning of Late Bonito great houses. As mentioned, Tsin Kletsin and New Alto are highly visible but not from within the canyon. Most Classic Bonito canyon great houses are intervisible with at least one other great house, and some with as many as eight. For example, from Peñasco Blanco, a sweeping vista eastwards down Chaco Canyon includes most of the central canyon great houses. Pueblo Bonito was probably not originally sited with a concern for visibility, yet nearly all the central canyon great houses, from Peñasco Blanco to Kin Nahasbas, are within sight of its walls. Even Hungo Pavi, all alone at the mouth of Mockingbird Canyon, is connected through line of sight with three other great houses.

Interestingly, Headquarters Site A and Wijiji are the *only* canyon great houses that lack a line-of-sight connection to any other great house. Both were deliberately positioned in cul-de-sacs or around canyon corners, just out of sight of others. However, both are within sight of a great kiva (see table 8.2). Just as the siting of Tsin Kletsin and New Alto suggests a deliberate concern with visibility, the positions of these sites suggest a deliberate concern with *in*visibility. Paradoxically, these structures were built to be seen…but not from other great houses. Perhaps builders intentionally connected them with the hidden, subterranean spaces represented by great kivas.

Visibility, directionality, balanced dualism, and social memory are Classic Bonito concepts that would have been familiar to Late Bonito viewers. Elegantly and directly, Late Bonito leaders restated these Classic themes on the landscape. Late Bonito great houses in Chaco Canyon form a patterned, nested series of relationships emphasizing Chaco Canyon as the nexus of a larger universe. Reiteration of these Classic ideas tied the Late Bonito phase into the beliefs and practices of an earlier era.

Late Bonito Chacoans lived in a world they perceived to be logical and coherent, grounded in a landscape their ancestors had occupied, and modified considerably, over preceding centuries. Like the Classic Bonito landscape, Late Bonito architecture expressed aspects of a worldview designed to be experienced by subjects moving in and among the buildings, conveying meaningful ideas, offering spatial experiences that resonated with a traditional Chacoan aesthetic. Late Bonito leaders continued to erect great houses to look imposing and to convey symbolic messages, even though builders had less labor at their disposal. The structures celebrated themes that helped keep the world in balance. Late Bonito leaders bolstered confidence in a new world order, using tangible references to the earlier, Classic Bonito landscape.

The Late Bonito Phase in the Central San Juan Basin

Chacoans continued to emphasize visibility, balanced dualism, directionality, and social memory in new building projects at Late Bonito outliers. They built upon these familiar themes to reinvigorate landscape and architecture in outliers in the core area to the west and south of Chaco Canyon. At some outliers, such as Kin Bineola, the scale of Late Bonito great house construction surpassed anything seen before. At Kin Klizhin and Kin Ya'a, builders came up with an innovation—the true tower kiva. As in Chaco Canyon, Late Bonito outlier architecture represents increased formalization and innovative restatements of familiar Ancestral Pueblo spatial themes.

Kin Bineola

At the outlier of Kin Bineola, 18 km southwest of Chaco, Late Bonito builders transformed an early building into a massive structure rivaling Aztec, Salmon, and the Classic Bonito great houses in Chaco Canyon (Marshall et al. 1979:69–72; Van Dyke and Powers 2002). Kin Bineola is on the Kim-mi-ne-oli Wash, a tributary drainage south of the Chaco River. A central roomblock, with Type I masonry and a cluster of tree-ring dates from 942 to 943, dates from the Early Bonito phase. Between 1111 and 1120, builders used Type IV masonry to expand Kin Bineola into a massive, E-shaped, three-story edifice (see table 8.1). This expansion project is contemporaneous with major building episodes at Aztec West and with McElmo great houses in Chaco Canyon.

The Late Bonito great house of Kin Bineola visually dominates its surroundings, and its layout embodies balanced dualism. Builders positioned the great house on open terrain facing the southeast (plate 15). The structure is so large that, upon approach, it can appear to be an isolated sandstone butte. The great house covers an area of 4,167 sq m and contains at least 230 rooms. The E shape is actually composed of two adjoining open rectangles, each surrounding a plaza, each containing an enclosed second-story kiva. As at Casa Chiquita and Kin Kletso in Chaco Canyon, the builders of Kin Bineola used a double-walled technique to "bulk up" the structure's visual impact. Along the west exterior wall of the great house, two massive core-and-veneer walls are separated by crosswalls into 55- to 75-cm-wide cells. Ancestral Puebloans positioned Kin Bineola to face Hosta Butte, which rises prominently above the Dutton Plateau on the southern horizon.

South and southeast of the great house are four large mounds. Some may be middens. The most prominent mound, measuring 50 by 11 m, is so large that it was originally given its own site number (29SJ2531). However, artifact density atop the mound is relatively low—29SJ2531 appears to be an earthwork containing primarily sandstone spalls and construction debris (Sebastian and Altschul 2002:15). The Kin Bineola mound may be another example of the construction of social memory on an outlier landscape. The earthwork appears to represent a deep, dense midden deposited over centuries, but the feature may have been deposited within the short span of Late Bonito construction.

Kin Bineola is an ancestral outlier that likely maintained close ties with Chaco throughout the Early, Classic, and Late Bonito phases. Approximately 3 km south of the great house, an Early Bonito community clusters around a tenth-century great kiva. Surface ceramics date at least 38 small sites along the wash to the Classic and Late Bonito phases. Ceramics, lithics, architecture, and line-of-sight shrine connections indicate that Kin Bineola had strong ties with Chaco. The valley may well have provided corn for residents of Chaco, given the excellent agricultural potential afforded by the Kim-mi-ne-oli Wash.

Kin Bineola is an unusual Late Bonito great house, primarily because of its massive size—only Aztec West and Salmon Ruin are larger. Pueblo Pintado, 22 km from downtown Chaco at the east end of the canyon, is the only other outlier great house in a comparable class. Both Kin Bineola and Pueblo Pintado were almost certainly designed by architects from Chaco. Both represent Type IV, early 1100s great house construction in ancestral areas with good farmland. There could be several reasons Chacoans invested such energy into massive, nearby outlier great houses during the Late Bonito phase. Perhaps the boom years of 1100–1130 saw renewed interest in colonial expansion—but this explanation is at odds with the notion that canyon builders were struggling to find the labor and resources to build new great houses there. Perhaps, like Salmon and Aztec, Kin Bineola and Pueblo Pintado represent the interests of Chacoan factions striking out on their own...but the outliers are so near the canyon, this does not seem likely. Many outlier residents, particularly west and south of Chaco, likely continued to visit Chaco for ritual gatherings, and more distant outliers to the south and west still had strong canyon connections throughout the Late Bonito phase. Finally, perhaps the overly massive Kin Bineola represents an attempt to demonstrate the continuing power of Chaco—overbuilding in a time of uncertainty to quell any popular notion that Chaco's resources and influence were under threat. Perhaps one reason less labor was invested in canyon great houses was that leaders were directing more labor into the nearby colossal edifice of Kin Bineola.

Tower Kivas: Kin Klizhin and Kin Ya'a

During the Late Bonito phase, builders provided some outlier great houses with dramatic visibility through the addition of a tower kiva. Tower kivas consist of a series of as many as four enclosed kivas vertically stacked on top of one another. Only two true tower kivas are definitely known to have existed in the Chacoan world—at Kin Klizhin and Kin Ya'a.[11] Conceptually, tower kivas may be related to elevated or second-story kivas and circular rooms found at some canyon and outlier great houses, including Chetro Ketl, Kin Kletso, Kin Bineola, Salmon, and Aztec West. Elevated kivas are not the same as tower kivas—the differences are nicely illustrated by Marshall and others (1979:18). True tower kivas contain three or four circular rooms stacked one atop another, and elevated kivas are built atop boulders or second stories.[12]

The Kin Klizhin great house (plate 16) is located along the ephemeral Kin Klizhin Wash 6 km southwest of West Mesa. Kin Klizhin is a small but imposing structure located on a sandy knoll. The dark ruins of the tower kiva protrude against the sky like a hitchhiker's thumb and lend the structure its Navajo name, "black house." Kin Klizhin is visible from a number of shrines atop West Mesa and South Mesa. Investigations at the 472-sq-m ruin have included tree-ring dating, stabilization, examination of associated irrigation features, and a survey of the surrounding community.[13] Tree-ring samples collected by Florence Hawley in 1932 indicate that the great house was constructed around 1087 (Bannister, Robinson, and Warren 1970:24). The great house faces east-southeast and has standing walls of banded, core-and-veneer masonry reaching two to three stories high (see table 8.1). Marshall and others (1979:70) described the tower kiva in detail. There are three stacked kivas built within a rectangular enclosure measuring 6.5 m north-south by 6 m east-west. The circular interior has a diameter of 5 m and standing walls that reach 9 m above the modern ground surface. Although the upper kiva floors have collapsed and the lower kiva floor has yet to be excavated, three ledges and a number of viga holes suggest that a succession of interior floors and benches may have once existed.[14]

In a broad alluvial valley southeast of Crownpoint, the standing walls of Kin Ya'a rise dramatically from the center of a low mound (Marshall et al. 1979:201–206). *Kin Ya'a* means "standing-up house" or "tall house" in Navajo. The builders of Kin Ya'a used banded, core-and-veneer masonry to erect this multi-storied building (figure 8.9). The great house faces the southeast, and a tower kiva is centered in the rear of the structure, flanked by second- or possibly third-story rooms. Standing masonry indicates that the tower kiva originally stood four stories high, probably reaching an original height of

Figure 8.9. The Kin Ya'a tower kiva.

12 m (see table 8.1). Marshall and others (1979:203–204) offer a detailed description of the structure and its engineering.[15] The tower kiva was badly burned. Marshall and others speculate that fire-hardening of the adobe mortar may have contributed to the structure's excellent state of preservation. Tree-ring dates from Kin Ya'a range from 1101 to 1106 and cluster at 1106 (Bannister, Robinson, and Warren 1970:25). The surrounding area is dotted with rubble mounds denoting small sites that composed the Kin Ya'a community, and a great kiva crowns a rise 200 m northwest of the great house. Some of these sites date from the 900s or earlier (Windes, personal communication, July 2002). Kin Ya'a may represent a great kiva–centered community brought into the Chacoan sphere of influence in the late Classic or Late Bonito period.

Despite the relatively low-lying terrain on which Kin Ya'a is positioned, the great house is visible from shrine 29SJ706 on South Mesa, 43 km to the northeast, through a small notch in the broad ridge north of Crownpoint. This intervisibility appears to be intentional—if either the shrine or Kin Ya'a had been located a few meters to the west or east, the two could not have seen each other. The Kin Ya'a tower kiva was built at the right spot and at the right height to be seen over the ridge from 29SJ706 on South Mesa. Hayes and Windes (1975:154–155) suggest that this "impressive bit of engineering" indicated that signaling and communication between the two areas was one of the functions of shrines and tower kivas.

Signaling alone does not seem the best explanation for construction of tower kivas. As Lekson (1986:52) explains, "a similar height could have been attained without the Tower Kiva." Furthermore, other nearby natural landforms offer better and less labor-intensive locations for signaling. An intervening mesa could have been circumvented by locating a signaling station on Lobo Mesa, a couple kilometers to the south. Kantner and Hobgood (2003) used GIS to demonstrate that tower kivas' extra height did not increase long-distance visibility. The Kin Klizhin great house would have been visible from West Mesa and South Mesa without the construction of a 9-m-high tower.

Tower kivas are highly symbolically charged structures. They dramatically represent balanced dualism between subterranean and vertical spaces. The kiva, a circular, subterranean, womb-like space, is juxtaposed with the tower, a rectangular, vertical, phallic-like space. Tower kivas may have symbolically balanced up and down, light and dark, sky and underworld, and possibly male and female. Both tower kivas and elevated kivas emphasize these kinds of oppositions, but tower kivas carry an added symbolic dimension. Tower kivas may represent not only balance but also movement, connections, or passages between upper and lower worlds or between past, present, and future. The structures may represent the vertically stacked worlds of Ancestral Pueblo origin stories (Marshall et al. 1979:204):

> It must be remembered that the ceremonial room or kiva, in modern mythology, represents the underworld out of which, according to legends, the early races of men emerged through an opening in the roof or hatchway.... [T]here may have been four kivas, one above another, to represent the underworlds in which the ancestors of the human race lived in succession before emerging into that in which we now dwell. [Fewkes 1917:14–15]

The tower kiva may have represented specific events from Pueblo mythology or, in a more general sense, may have symbolized several worlds or states of being. Kivas represent sites of connection or emergence between stacked worlds. The sipapu is a small hole in a kiva floor that, according to Pueblo tradition, represents the place of emergence from earlier worlds into this one, connecting the present world to past mythic events (Smith 1972). Perhaps the tower kiva is a sipapu writ large, linking not only vertical and subterranean dimensions but also past, present, and future.

Tower kivas may have represented all or none of these ideas—of course, it is impossible to know. When builders erected tower kivas in the early

1100s, they may have been experimenting with new ways to use space to represent core Chacoan ideas. As rivalries with Aztec intensified, construction of tower kivas in outlier communities southwest of Chaco may have helped strengthened canyon connections to the south. Or perhaps tower kivas represent rival factions' experiments with novel forms of ritual or public architecture.

Into the Post-Chacoan World

The flurry of Late Bonito–phase construction activity in Chaco Canyon lasted only a generation, perhaps less. In fact, builders may have left some great houses, such as Hillside Ruin, unfinished. Chacoans did not engage in any major great house construction after 1130, although they continued to use the structures for domestic purposes well into the 1200s. The decline of Chaco Canyon as a center place was almost certainly helped along by a second severe drought in the central San Juan Basin, between 1130 and 1180 (Vivian et al. 2006). During the ensuing two centuries, many Ancestral Puebloans moved north to the landscape of the northern San Juan and the Four Corners area. The population of the northern San Juan doubled between the late 1000s and the late 1200s, increasing from an estimated 6,000–7,000 to 12,000–14,000 people (Wilshusen 2002). By the mid-1200s, two-thirds of the population in the northern San Juan had aggregated into large pueblos (Varien 1999:148–149; Wilshusen 2002:117–118). Some Ancestral Puebloans continued to live in Chaco and some outlier communities in the San Juan Basin into the 1200s, but these gradually became domestic settlements with social life focused around the local community.

Perhaps for a time, Aztec succeeded at replacing Chaco as a ritual gathering place. One of the most intriguing clues to the nature of the Chaco–Aztec relationship is McElmo-style architecture. In the Totah area, Ancestral Puebloans erected at least ten McElmo-style great houses between 1115 and 1120, including Aztec East (McKenna and Toll 1992).[16] Aztec East consists of a balanced pair of compact, McElmo-style buildings surrounding a great kiva. Those who originally conceived Aztec planned for a great house on the east side, in the position of Chetro Ketl in Chaco, to complete the design. McElmo architecture may have come from farther to the north, to be utilized by builders at both Chaco and Aztec. Or Aztec builders may have adopted McElmo-style masonry in the 1110s as an attempt to co-opt and supercede this nouveau Chacoan style. Alternatively, the incorporation of McElmo buildings into the final construction phase at Aztec may represent the ultimate reintegration of Chaco and McElmo factions, resolving the tensions of the early 1100s. Although the Aztec East building site reflects a plan instituted by people who sought to replicate the Chacoan landscape, the ultimate execution of this plan reflects the ways in which labor, building styles, building functions, and social organization changed over more than a century. Builders did not complete construction at Aztec East until the 1240s.

If the leaders of Aztec succeeded at replacing Chaco Canyon as a gathering place, then its tenure as ritual center seems to have been short-lived. Although builders continued to work on Aztec West and Aztec East into the thirteenth century, they do not seem to have been actively expanding the original landscape design (Brown, Windes, and McKenna n.d.). Construction episodes were concentrated and far apart, unlike at Chaco during its heyday. Later Aztec great house additions tend to involve repairs, domestic room subdivisions, and the insertion of additional kivas.

The Pueblo III period (1150–1300) was a time of social upheaval, fluidity, and conflict, particularly in the northern San Juan (Billman, Lambert, and Leonard 2000; Kuckelman 2002; LeBlanc 1999:192–245; Varien 1999). At Aztec, Salmon, and other northern great houses, thirteenth-century inhabitants transformed the buildings into domestic structures. During the 1200s, inhabitants of Aztec West lived in rooms around the plaza and the great kiva. They used many of the rear rooms of the great house for refuse disposal and burial (Morris 1928). Similarly, at Salmon Ruin, people continued to live in the pueblo during the post-Chacoan period, between 1120 and 1280. Salmon residents gradually subdivided rooms, added new kivas, and made other modifications during this period (Reed 2006a). Ancestral Puebloans also aggregated in large pueblos to the south and west of the San Juan Basin, converting outlying Chacoan great houses such as Las Ventanas into residences.

Pueblo III builders erected new, large, domestic pueblos at sites such as Sand Canyon in the Four Corners area (Bradley 1992). They often situated these new sites around springs at the heads of canyons. Ancestral Puebloans also built large, new, domestic pueblos in the Cibola area and points southwest of Chaco, at sites such as Atse'e Nitsaa in Manuelito Canyon near Gallup (Fowler and Stein 1992:109–111). Unlike Chacoan great houses, these new pueblos were clearly intended as habitations. One characteristic of post-Chacoan pueblos is a change in the use of enclosed kivas. Large numbers of enclosed kivas characterize twelfth- and thirteenth-century pueblos in southwest Colorado, southeast Utah, northeast Arizona, and central New Mexico. Whereas Classic Bonito Chacoan great houses average one enclosed kiva for every 15 rooms, large pueblos average one kiva for every five or six rooms (Lipe 1989). This may represent a shift from kivas as sodality meeting rooms to kivas as household or domestic meeting facilities.

By the latter half of the thirteenth century, the last gatherings at Chaco were three to five generations in the past—they had long since passed from living memory. But powerful Chacoan tropes, including sacred geography, directionality, visibility, dualism, cyclical renewal, and social memory, continued to figure prominently in Pueblo worldviews. During the socially turbulent late thirteenth century in the northern San Juan, the Chacoan ideals of the past might have been invoked to help consolidate community identity. As clans and families aggregated into large pueblos, a real or an imagined shared Chacoan past would have been a point of social intersection or commonality. Bruce Bradley (1996) has recognized this, arguing that the D shape of Sand Canyon Pueblo might be a deliberate reference to Pueblo Bonito. Two prominent, late Pueblo III architectural features that allude to Chacoan ideas include McElmo towers and time bridges. Towers and time bridges reference key Chacoan themes, including visibility, verticality, balanced dualism, and social memory. The Ancestral Pueblo builders of these forms may have had several aims in mind: to restore some sense of Chacoan balance to the world, to help consolidate local community identity by connecting with a real or an imagined shared past, and finally, perhaps, to create a conduit into the next world.

McElmo Towers

The Pueblo III period towers of the Four Corners area lent their name to McElmo-style masonry (Vivian and Mathews 1965). The core-and-veneer, McElmo-style towers are two to three stories high and can be circular, square, or D-shaped (Fewkes 1916; Winter 1981:29). Ancestral Puebloans built McElmo towers on canyon rims, on mesa tops, and in canyon bottoms throughout the McElmo Canyon drainages and surrounding areas. Some towers, such as Painted Hand, in Canyons of the Ancients National Monument, are situated atop isolated boulders (plate 17). Others are incorporated into domestic pueblos. Towers likely had multiple, overlapping meanings and purposes. Some of the possibilities include defense (Lightfoot and Kuckelman 2001; Riley 1950; Schulman 1949), protection of agricultural resources (Johnson 2003; Winter 1981), line-of-sight communication (Wilcox and Haas 1994:217), ceremonialism (Fewkes 1916:219; Rohn 1971:86; Winter 1981:33), and astronomical observation (Williamson, Fisher, and O'Flynn 1977). But architecture always carries with it multiple layers of symbolism. In addition to whatever practical functions the towers served, they embodied an aesthetic reference to Chacoan ideological and spatial themes.

All towers, whether isolated atop boulders, constructed within pueblos, or standing sentinel in canyon bottoms, are attached to water, kivas, or other subterranean spaces. When Ancestral Pueblos built a tower within a pueblo roomblock, they commonly constructed a subterranean tunnel connecting the tower to a kiva (for example, Lancaster and Van Cleave 1954). Isolated towers, such as those at Painted Hand, are sometimes built atop hollowed-out boulders (Van Dyke, Ciborowski, and Throgmorton 2004). Towers at canyon heads, such as Horseshoe and Hackberry at Hovenweep National Monument, are frequently associated with springs (Winter 1981: 26). Towers in canyon bottoms, such as Lightning Tree, are also associated with water (Van Dyke and Throgmorton 2006). Kivas, subterranean spaces, and water sources are points of entry into, or emergence from, other worlds in many Pueblo oral traditions, including Hopi, Zuni, and Acoma (Parsons 1939:210–253; Stirling 1942:18–19). If similar symbolic connotations held true in the past, then most McElmo towers are situated atop an implied opening to the underworld.

This subterranean and celestial juxtaposition is a familiar one also symbolized by Chacoan tower kivas. McElmo towers may similarly represent a conduit across space and time, reaching back into the lower world of the past, through the world of the present, into a future world above. In Pueblo oral traditions, when times grew difficult during a succession of earlier worlds, human ancestors repeatedly escaped by climbing upwards into higher realms. In Hopi origin stories, the people in the third world were corrupt, engaging in violence and casting spells to cause sickness. When a flood threatened the world, the women built towers to reach the sky, but the towers fell down. The men planted reeds that grew through the sky, and the Hopi eventually emerged through the hole into this, the fourth world (Parsons 1939:237). King (2004) suggests that Ancestral Puebloans may have positioned towers atop openings to the lower world in an attempt to construct a pathway out of the social and environmental turmoil of the late thirteenth century.

Like the great houses and shrines of Chaco, McElmo towers also create line-of-sight connections to iconic landforms. Many towers along the McElmo drainages are situated to provide spectacular views of Sleeping Ute Mountain, a distinctive topographic reference point for the Four Corners region. Sleeping Ute Mountain, in turn, provides a vista south to Shiprock and the Chuska Mountains—the northwest edges of the old Chacoan world. Similarly, Hayes and Windes (1975:156) note that a number of towers on Mesa Verde provide line-of-sight connections to Huerfano Mountain—an iconic landform from the Chacoan era. One purpose of towers seems to have been to facilitate the continuation of an Ancestral Pueblo world linked by lines of sight between ancestral, symbolically charged, high places.

Table 8.3 Time Bridges in the Post-Chacoan World (as Identified by Fowler and Stein [1992])

Time Bridge	Time
Rocky Point → Navajo Springs	1150–1250 → 1050–1150
Post-Chacoan structures and kivas → Dittert Ruin	1150–1250 → 1050–1150
Ats'ee Nitsaa → Kin Hocho'i	1250–1325 → 1050–1150
Goodman Point → Casa Negra	1250–1325 → 1050–1150
Cliff Palace/Spruce Tree House → Far View House	1250–1325 → 1050–1150
Taylor Springs → Chambers	1250–1325 → 1050–1150

Roads to Ruins

References to the past continued and escalated in other parts of the Colorado Plateau during the post-Chacoan era. At the Pettit site, Saitta (1994) argues, a common memory of the Chacoan past was used to help integrate disparate groups and advance communalism instead of factionalism. At Hinkson Ranch, the continued use of the great kiva form may be a symbolic reference to Chaco (Kintigh 1994). In several locations on the Chacoan periphery, Ancestral Puebloans built "time bridges," like the one linking the Red Willow great house with the Los Rayos great kiva. These post-Chacoan roads through time connect thirteenth- or fourteenth-century sites with Chacoan great houses (table 8.3). For example, a road segment connects Atse'e Nitsaa with Kin Hocho'i, a twelfth-century Chacoan great house several miles away (Fowler and Stein 1992:116–117). Fowler and Stein coined the term *time bridge* to describe this phenomenon and argued that time bridges are "symbolic umbilicals that linked one age to another …tangible metaphor(s) for the unity of sacred space with ritual time" (Fowler and Stein 1992:117–118). The time bridge idea is similar to the role played by the Chaco Meridian in Lekson's (1999) Chaco-Aztec-Paquime scenario, although for Lekson, roads and connections point to where future sites will be positioned, as opposed to linking existing sites with the past. Post-Chacoan people may have been attempting to consolidate community identity or create their own brand of legitimacy through constructing references to a shared Chacoan past.

The memory of Chaco undoubtedly continued to influence Pueblo society for centuries and persists in Pueblo oral traditions today. Chaco is a place where ancestors paused on their migrations, where clans converged, and where people gained and exchanged ritual knowledge (Ferguson and Hart 1985:126; Kuwanwisiwma 2004). Hopi, Zuni, and several Eastern Pueblo traditions speak of a place called White House (Ellis 1967; Ortiz 1994), where ceremonial cycles originated. It is possible that White House is Chaco Canyon (Lekson and Cameron 1995).

Notes

1. *Totah*, or "Three Rivers," is a contemporary Navajo term for the area where these rivers come together near modern Farmington, New Mexico. I adopt it here as a convenient shorthand.

2. Following Marshall and others (1979:18) and a later discussion in this chapter, the central kiva at Salmon is an elevated kiva, not a true tower kiva. However, during the course of excavations in the 1970s, Irwin-Williams dubbed the feature "the tower kiva," and some archaeologists continue to use this term (Baker 2006:248; Reed 2006b).

3. One might argue that local emulators built Aztec North, because it resembled a great house on the outside but the builders did not employ the usual Chacoan construction techniques. I do not think that emulators built Aztec North. It is part of a large-scale, planned landscape that suggests sophisticated planning on the part of people very familiar with Chacoan design tenets.

4. Earl Morris (1919, 1921, 1924, 1928) excavated Aztec West in 1917–1918 under the auspices of the American Museum of Natural History.

5. The modular McElmo style appeared in the northern San Juan and Chaco Canyon during the early 1100s—it is discussed further below.

6. Published tree-ring dates include 1112rL, 1111rL, and 1113v (Robinson, Harrill, and Warren 1974:42).

7. Published tree-ring dates include 1063rL, 1058vv, and 1064r, but Lekson (1986:230) considers these dates to represent reused wood. The builders' strict adherence to the McElmo template and masonry strongly suggests that Chacoans erected Casa Chiquita in the early 1100s.

8. At Peñasco Blanco, a second-story kiva was added between 1120 and 1125 or later, using banded masonry (Lekson 1986:109). In addition, a McElmo unit was constructed of McElmo-style masonry atop a prepared terrace or platform to the northeast of the great house (Lekson 1986:109). Plaza enclosure by an arc of rooms or double walls usually dates to the very late 1000s or the early 1100s. At Pueblo Bonito in the early 1100s, the plaza was enclosed and then bisected by walls and rooms constructed on a north-south axis. The largest and last Classic Bonito–phase great kiva, Kiva A, was enclosed by this north-south group of rooms (Judd 1922:115, 1964:198–207; Lekson 1986:142; Vivian and Reiter 1960:66–70). At Chetro Ketl, the Great Kiva remained in use into the 1100s. Hawley (1934) considered the blocky sandstone masonry of the remodeled Court Kiva to date to 1100–1116. According to Lekson (1986:191–192), between 1095 and 1105, upper stories, including second-story rooms and an elevated kiva (Kiva N), were added over the north roomblock. After 1105, a row of rooms was added to the double-walled, plaza-enclosing arc, and other minor modifications were made. These include the "colonnade" wall along the plaza, which consists of some 13 square masonry columns spaced 1.3 m apart. The gaps between the columns were subsequently filled with masonry, and a row of irregular rooms added to the front. At Pueblo Alto, a number of late modifications were made, particularly along the west wing inside the plaza. The plaza was enclosed by a double-walled arc between 1100 and 1140. There is no evidence for occupation at Pueblo Alto after 1150 (Lekson 1986:209). The latest construction at Pueblo del Arroyo is also from the first decade of the 1100s (Vivian 1959:67–68).

9. A similar parallel wall with cells is found along the west exterior of the contemporaneous outlying Kin Bineola great house (Marshall et al. 1979:59).

10. Although the edges of Chaco Canyon block the view to great houses on the canyon floor, line-of-sight connections exist between Tsin Kletsin and all other canyon great houses via three shrines—29SJ1207 and 29SJ706 at the edge of South Mesa and 29SJ423 atop West Mesa. The link to Kin Ya'a is enabled only by the precise placement of 29SJ706 (Hayes and Windes 1975).

11. Marshall and others (1979:16) suggest that other true tower kivas may have existed at Haystack and Upper Kin Klizhin, but this interpretation remains conjectural in the absence of standing masonry or excavation.

12. It may be problematic to characterize any of these features as kivas in the traditional sense. Gwinn Vivian (personal communication, December 2006) points out that the elevated kivas at Chetro Ketl and Kin Kletso lack standard kiva floor features, although excavators did find kiva floor features in the elevated kiva at Salmon Ruin. We do not know what the floor features look like at Kin Klizhin and Kin Ya'a—neither has been excavated, and the upper floors have collapsed.

13. See Bannister 1965; Bannister, Robinson, and Warren 1970:24; Hewett 1905, 1936; Holsinger 1901; Judd 1954:57; Marshall and others 1979:69–72; Morrison 1876; Powers, Gillespie, and Lekson 1983; and Van Dyke and Powers 2002.

14. The three ledges extend around the inner circumference of the tower kiva, at 2.5 m, 3.25 m, and 5.15 m above the original ground surface. Marshall and others interpret the lowest ledge, which is 15–20 cm wide, as probably the roof of the lowest kiva and the floor of the middle kiva. Two 20-cm-diameter viga holes are present under this ledge. The highest ledge, which is 10 cm wide, is probably the roof of the middle kiva and the floor of the uppermost kiva. Marshall and others (1979:70) point out that it is located 2.7 m, or a full story, above the roof of the lowest kiva. The middle ledge, which is only 30 cm wide, does not seem to be high enough to constitute a separate story. Marshall and others interpreted it as a bench for the middle story of the three-story kiva. However, it might also represent remodeling.

15. The walls taper from a width of 1.5 m at the tower base to 40 cm at the fourth story. The tower kiva was constructed inside a rectangular room measuring 6.2 m north-south by 6.4 m east-west. The two lower stories of the kiva are relatively intact; the third and fourth stories are represented by a wall remnant in the northeast corner of the structure that reaches a standing height today of 10.25 m. On the north wall, vigas are located at 2.8 m, 5.7 m, and 8.6 m above the ground. Oddly, viga holes do not extend through to the interior of the kiva—Marshall and others suggest that either the holes were filled by stabilization or the exterior vigas supported scaffolding. Benches 10–20 cm wide are inset just above viga levels on the outside of the north wall; Marshall and others speculate that these helped taper the walls and also served as working platforms for the masons. On the interior of the kiva, breaks between the stories are represented by narrow benches 15–25 cm wide and 2.8 m apart, located directly above the exterior viga levels. Floor and roof beams were apparently set on these benches. A rectangular window is set into the north wall of the first and the second stories; this section of wall is absent for the third and fourth stories. The first-floor window is 40 by 35 cm and is located 2.2 m above the floor. The second-floor window is T-shaped, measures 39 by 10 cm on top and 27 by 15 cm on the bottom, and is located directly above the first-floor window.

16. These include Jackson Lake, Morris 39 Building 1, Morris 41 Building 16, LA 37601, Upper Barker, and the Holmes Group in the La Plata Valley, as well as Kello Blancett in the Animas Valley. Paul Reed and others are in the process of launching an initiative to further investigate Late Bonito great houses in this region and their relationships with one another, with Aztec, and with Chaco Canyon.

9 Lived Landscapes

On a recent commercial flight between Tucson and Colorado Springs, I had my face pressed against the glass as the plane passed directly over the San Juan Basin. Chacra Mesa, Fajada Butte, West Point, the Chaco River—all were etched on the Cretaceous seabed thousands of feet below us. As I strained to catch a glimpse of a great house or two, my seatmate on the aisle noticed my interest in the view and remarked, "Have you ever seen such an empty place?"

I was reminded of my first day in the field in the San Juan Basin, about fifteen years ago. At the end of a day digging test pits on Tohatchi Flats, everyone piled into the four-wheel-drive truck and waited for me to drive us back out to the highway. Confronted with an endless expanse of identical flat-topped buttes and mesas rising from scrub-covered sands, I tried to wind my way generally west. The bemused crew let me take a few wrong turns before steering me out through the labyrinth of two-tracks. When we reached the highway, I asked how they were able to navigate so easily on this empty, monotonous terrain. The crew members, all local residents, patiently explained to me that the mesas that surrounded us were each quite distinctive. Where I saw undifferentiated dunes dotted with four-wing saltbush, they saw the homes of relatives and the locations of past events. And they began to tell me stories. As a result of my experiences on that project, Tohatchi Flats is now a storied landscape for me as well. Today, as I drive through the project area on my way from Shiprock to Gallup, I pass the place where I excavated my first Basketmaker III site, the place where a crew member's truck broke an axle, the place where we adopted a stray dog, and, of course, the place where I got lost amidst the two-tracks on my first day in the field.

Places are made—meanings are inscribed onto landscapes—through ongoing, embodied, reflexive engagement. For my seatmate on the airplane and for me as a novice Basin archaeologist, the landscape appeared devoid of meaning, uncharted, and empty. We construct landscapes as we live them, building meaning out of our own experiences, as well as the stories, traditions, and past experiences of others. Landscapes are the lived, sensual milieus in which the social and material worlds intersect and mutually re-create each other. Human existence is apprehended through dwelling, through practice, through daily experiences in spaces charged with meanings, histories, and emotions. Landscapes both shape and reflect worldviews and ideologies. Meanings are constructed over time, through layers of experiences, knowledge, and stories. Pueblo culture is not static and unchanging, but threads of meaning stretch from the present far back into the Ancestral Pueblo past.

Landscapes may be thought of as multidimensional, encompassing the material spaces of the physical environment, the represented spaces of the imagination, and the perceived spaces of the senses (Lefebvre 1991). This tripartite organization carries over into the ways archaeologists have conceived of landscapes—as settlement patterns, as traditional cultural places, and as material windows into reflexively constructed pasts. My interpretations of Chacoan landscape are similarly woven from three interrelated kinds of evidence—archaeological data, ethnographic information, and phenomenological research. Archaeological data comprise architecture and features positioned on the topography. Ethnographic information details historic and contemporary Pueblo cosmographies and spatial meanings. Phenomenological research provides insights into sensual dimensions such as intervisibility, movement, and memory.

As a case study, Chaco illustrates intersections among landscape, spatial experience, sociopolitical complexity, and ideology. Chacoan leaders developed an ideology out of an Ancestral Pueblo worldview, elements of which can be traced back to the Basketmaker III period. The Ancestral Pueblo worldview had a strong spatial dimension. It encompassed key ideas about the social and cosmographic organization of the universe, including the concepts of sacred geography, visibility, balanced dualism, directionality, cyclical renewal, social memory, and center place. By the Classic Bonito phase, Chacoans had transformed elements of this worldview into a spatially formalized, shared ideology that mandated monumental construction and elaborate ceremonialism at the center place. The lived Chacoan landscape encouraged visitors to provide Chacoan leaders with legitimacy, emotional allegiance, and material support.

Six Centuries at Chaco

The roots of Chaco may be traced back at least as far as the Basketmaker III period, when incipient agriculturalists began to settle into village life. Seasonal rituals and a concern with cyclical renewal likely developed to help ensure fertility and rainfall and to keep the social world in balance. Large villages contained great pitstructures probably used for ritual and other community activities. During the Pueblo I period, northern Pueblo I sites such as McPhee Village presaged the development of Chacoan great houses. Ancestral Puebloans migrated south of the San Juan River at the end of the ninth century, founding new settlements along the Chuskan slopes, across the southern and western Basin, through Chaco Canyon, and into the Red Mesa Valley. Some communities were oriented around proto-great houses, some around great kivas, and a few around both. In Chaco Canyon, proto-great houses predominated.

During the Early Bonito phase, people living in dispersed proto-great house settlements began to gather seasonally at Chaco Canyon. Chaco was a logical place in which to carry out periodic agricultural rituals, because it resonated with elements of an Ancestral Pueblo worldview—sacred geography, visibility, balanced dualism, directionality, cyclical renewal, and social memory. Gatherings gradually increased in size as more communities began to participate.

In the Classic Bonito phase, there was a quantum shift in social organization at Chaco. Architecture and landscape were central to this transformation. Chacoans made monumental additions to Pueblo Bonito, Peñasco Blanco, and Una Vida. They built new great houses, great kivas, earthworks, and road segments, formalizing key elements of an Ancestral Pueblo worldview on the canyon landscape. Participants in ritual gatherings at Chaco came from communities throughout the San Juan Basin and perhaps beyond. Chacoans founded scores of new outliers, and both Chacoans and local outlier residents built formal, Bonito-style great houses and great kivas in existing communities. Periodic canyon rituals may have coincided with astronomical events such as solstices and lunar standstills. Inhabitants of outlier communities contributed their labor to Bonito-style architecture both at home and in Chaco Canyon. When people gathered in the canyon, their aesthetic experiences in that place confirmed and reinforced a Chacoan ideology, encouraging them to support the ritual and the social order, despite increasingly unequal access to social prestige and resources. By the final decades of the eleventh century, those who orchestrated and presided over ritual events in Chaco Canyon derived great status and prestige from their positions.

During the Late Bonito phase, new settlements grew in the northern San Juan. Aztec—a new outlier complex originally modeled after downtown Chaco—emerged as a rival center place. In response, canyon leaders attempted to redefine and reformalize Chaco as the ritual center of the Pueblo world. A new McElmo architectural style embodied familiar aspects of Chacoan ideology yet provided something new. Chacoans built six new great houses in the canyon and made additions to existing structures. Builders expanded core outlier great houses Kin Bineola and Pueblo Pintado into massive edifices and erected tower kivas at Kin Klizhin and Kin Ya'a. But by 1140, the center no longer held. The Chacoan ritual order disbanded, and the focus of Ancestral Pueblo settlement shifted once more to the peripheries of the San Juan Basin.

Ancestral Pueblo Worldview in the Chacoan Era

I have attempted to construct an interpretive argument that seeks not only to explain Chaco but also to shed light on the relationships between landscape and ideology. My interpretations are grounded in the assumptions that landscapes recursively structure and reflect worldviews and that shared elements of worldviews constitute archaeologically accessible dimensions of ideologies. Elements of a worldview shared by Chacoans and other Ancestral Puebloans are represented in archaeologically accessible material spaces, in the architecture and on the landscape. Both phenomenological perceptions and ethnographic representations provide lenses through which to construct one interpretation of that worldview. Phenomenology encourages us to think about visibility, movement, and layered emotional connections to places. Ethnography indicates the importance of sacred geography, balanced dualism, journeys, and cyclical renewal. Taking these together, I considered that an Ancestral Pueblo worldview during the Chacoan era would likely be concerned with one or more of the following themes:

1. *Sacred geography.* Unusual or highly visible natural places such as mountain peaks or springs might have been the sites of shrines or votive deposits.

2. *Visibility.* A concern with visibility might have been expressed through architectural prominence, site positions, and lines of sight connecting buildings with features and with topo-

graphic landmarks. Lines of sight and roads might have linked sacred places to Chaco.

3. *Movement.* Roads, ramps, and staircases in Chaco Canyon and nearby outlier great houses might have enhanced or restricted access and visibility and might have served as routes for ritual processions.

4. *Memory.* Buildings and features might have incorporated references to the recent past and to more distant ancestors.

5. *Cosmography.* Chacoan architecture and landscape might have represented cosmographic ideas such as cardinal directions, balanced dualism, and center place. These ideas might have been tied into the movements of the sun and moon.

As I examined canyon and outlier architecture and site positions and as I moved across the landscape, I investigated these interrelated themes, answering specific questions about the relationships between perceptions, representations, and material spaces.

Sacred Geography and Visibility

The open horizons of the San Juan Basin heighten the drama of elevated or oddly shaped, highly visible landforms such as Huerfano Mountain, Shiprock, Bennett Peak, Ford Butte, Fajada Butte, Hosta Butte, Mount Taylor, and Cabezon Peak. Mountain peaks topped with shrines mark the boundaries of the Tewa (Ortiz 1972) and Keresan (White 1960) worlds. Vivian (Vivian 1990:35), Hayes and Windes (1975), Lekson (2002a), and many others have noted the views of prominent peaks from Chaco Canyon. Hayes and Windes (1975) documented the existence of a canyon-wide shrine network and postulated that intervisibility was important across the San Juan Basin. My findings also support the importance of sacred geography and visibility at Chaco. Chacoan shrines, road segments, and strategically placed sites suggest that distinctive volcanic plugs, buttes, and mountain peaks held special significance across the Chacoan world, from the Basketmaker III through the Pueblo III periods.

Shabik'eshchee Village and Site 423, two large Basketmaker III villages in Chaco Canyon, are situated on high places. By the Early Bonito phase, Ancestral Puebloans were systematically siting proto-great houses and great kivas within sight of iconic landforms. Nearly all major Early Bonito settlements can see one or more isolated peaks. At Morris 33, Willow Canyon, Kin Bineola, and Peach Springs, Ancestral Puebloans positioned community architecture to create lines of sight to landmarks such as Shiprock, Bennett

Lived Landscapes   241

Peak, Hosta Butte, and Huerfano Mountain. Peñasco Blanco, arguably the most important Early Bonito proto-great house, sits on a high place with line-of-sight connections to Huerfano Mountain and to the Basketmaker III Site 423.

During the Classic Bonito phase, Chacoans transformed Peñasco Blanco into a highly visible great house. They positioned Pueblo Alto atop North Mesa with spectacular 360-degree visibility, and they sited Pueblo del Arroyo to align through South Gap with Hosta Butte. Road segments and other features underscore the importance of these site locations. Pueblo Alto and Pueblo del Arroyo were situated to maximize visual impact for travelers approaching the canyon from the north and south, respectively. A stone circle atop the north rim of Chaco Canyon aligns with Pueblo del Arroyo, South Gap, the South Road, and Hosta Butte. Roads not only emphasize the importance of certain highly visible great houses but also link Chaco Canyon with potentially significant topographic features. The North Road heads to Kutz Canyon; the South Road points to Hosta Butte. The Ah-Shi-Sle-Pah Road extends to Black Lake; the Chacra Face Road trends toward Cabezon Peak.

Classic- and Late Bonito–phase shrines demarcate points of visibility along Chacra Mesa, South Mesa, and West Mesa. They connect sites in the canyon, as well as in outlying areas of the Chacoan world. Site 1088 might have facilitated communication between Chaco and outliers in the southern and western San Juan Basin. Some shrines strategically created line-of-sight connections with significant landforms—for example, a shrine near Las Ventanas is positioned to create a visual link with Hosta Butte. And just as people at shrines or elevated great houses could see for vast distances, the sites could be seen from afar by outlier dwellers and by Chacoan visitors. Chaco Canyon itself is both a low and high place—although the canyon's interior is protected from view, Chacra Mesa is visible at great distances across the southern San Juan Basin, and West Point is visible from the flanks of the Chuska Mountains.

Canyon great houses in both high and low locations exhibit the solid mass, verticality, contrasting backgrounds, and clear forms characteristic of architecture built to be viewed, following Moore (1996). Outlier great houses also contain most of these characteristics, but there are interesting differences among them. Builders clearly meant for outlier great houses to be viewed. There is no such thing as a small, inconspicuous great house in a low place. However, there is no straightforward, inverse relationship between great house mass and verticality. Outlier great house builders often used more than one device to enhance visibility, including massive construction, vertical locations, and associations with dramatic landforms.

Outlier great house builders frequently exploited natural topography to heighten visual drama. Red Willow and Skunk Springs are massive great houses atop high mesas. Kin Bineola and Peach Springs are massive great houses that are not elevated but provide line-of-sight connections to iconic landforms. Chimney Rock, Escalon, Guadalupe, Bluff, Lowry, and Whirlwind are relatively small great houses in elevated locations—the former three are associated with distinctive, oddly shaped peaks. Andrews, Casamero, and Las Ventanas are associated with highly visible geologic formations. Builders positioned most outlier great houses with lines of sight to Chaco Canyon or to iconic Chacoan high places. In some cases, as at Las Ventanas and Kin Bineola, shrines facilitated these links.

The different methods builders employed to enhance the visibility of outlier great houses provide clues to different kinds of community interactions and relationships with Chaco. Andrews and Casamero, although neighbors, were visually isolated from each other, suggesting two independent communities. Although the Red Mesa Valley afforded less opportunity to create line-of-sight connections to significant peaks, a stone circle above the Andrews great house provides a view of Hosta Butte. Casamero contains no such line-of-sight connections—together with other aspects of Casamero's architecture, this suggests that Casamero might have been a colony once or twice removed from Chaco, with less close connections to the canyon or incomplete participation in a Chacoan sacred geographic schema. Most outlier great houses loom over their surrounding communities, but Whirlwind is visible only from afar, suggesting that visitors or neighbors were the intended audience, not local residents. The original settlers at Kin Bineola positioned the great house in alignment with distant Hosta Butte. Two hundred years later, Late Bonito builders bulked up Kin Bineola, perhaps competing with Chaco or attempting to confirm and solidify influence over the Kim-mi-ne-oli Valley. They not only built a huge structure with hundreds of rooms but also used double walls along the exterior to increase apparent mass. Nearly 200 km north of Chaco Canyon, the colonial Lowry great house provides a 360-degree view of surrounding landmarks, including Sleeping Ute Mountain and the La Plata Mountains—both with visual connections back to Chaco. Chimney Rock great house is positioned beneath Chimney Rock and Companion Rock to facilitate observation of the major lunar standstill—viewers at Chimney Rock can also see Huerfano Mountain far to the south. Although each of these great houses presents a unique situation, visibility is always a common denominator.

These observations reinforce the notion that sacred geography and visibility were key components of an Ancestral Pueblo worldview during Chacoan times. The observations also suggest ways in which we might explore the various intentions of great house builders and, by extension, the various kinds of outlier communities and relationships with Chaco.

Dualisms and Oppositions, Visibility and Movement

Balanced dualism is an organizing principle in many pueblos, particularly among the Tewa, Tiwa, and Rio Grande Keresans (Fox 1972; Ortiz 1969; White 1942). At Chaco, architectural symmetry may be traceable back as far as Shabik'eshchee Village, and it is strongly in evidence at McPhee Village. Dualistic symmetry is one of the guiding principles for the layout of Classic Bonito great houses and great kivas. It can also been seen in the paired opposition between great houses and great kivas. The vertical great house and its subterranean great kiva counterpart further represent a type of dualism that is pervasive on the Chacoan landscape—an opposition between the visible and the hidden. Great houses such as Pueblo Bonito were highly visible, yet many interior spaces, including kivas and the oldest part of the pueblo, were restricted from general view. An opposition between the visible and the hidden is represented at a meta-level by Chaco Canyon itself. Chacra Mesa is visible for many kilometers across the San Juan Basin, but the canyon interior is protected from view.

Chacoans used road segments to emphasize this vertical/visible and subterranean/hidden juxtaposition across several dimensions. The two major road segments extending from Chaco—the North Road and the South Road—balance each other in terms of direction and also in terms of the hidden (Kutz Canyon to the north) and the visible (Hosta Butte to the south). A similar hidden/visible dichotomy might be represented by the Ah-Shi-Sle-Pah Road (Black Lake) and the Chacra Face Road (Cabezon Peak), although these termini are less certain. Roads undoubtedly had cosmographic and symbolic purposes, but they also directed movement into and away from Chaco. It is easier to walk on road segments than on adjacent, unmodified terrain. In the canyon and at outliers, these roads were likely used for processions. As they led travelers to sites such as Pueblo Alto (in a high place, with excellent visibility) and Pueblo del Arroyo (in a low place, with more restricted visibility), road segments prescribed movement, creating spatial experiences that emphasized the visible and the hidden. Travelers moving across the dunes experienced an interesting "now you see it, now you don't" phenomenon when following prescribed approaches to Chaco along the roads. During the Late Bonito phase, builders seem to have taken this visible/hidden juxtaposition to yet another level, positioning great houses on the canyon landscape to exhibit high visibility (New Alto, Tsin Kletsin) or invisibility (Wijiji, Headquarters Site A).

The formal dualisms embodied by major Chacoan roads suggest that north, northwest, and south roads into Chaco Canyon may have been procession routes. These roads created specific kinds of visual experiences that culminated in the dramatic spectacle of particular great houses. Many outlier dwellers probably arrived in Chaco from the west, but travelers entering the canyon along the less formalized western route had different kinds of visual experiences. The Site 1088 cairn cluster can be seen from afar on a western approach to Chaco but is not visible to a traveler passing into the canyon directly under West Point. Although an impressive feature from some angles, Site 1088 does not seem designed to provide visual impact at the moment a visitor reaches Chaco (unlike Pueblo Alto, Pueblo del Arroyo, and Peñasco Blanco).

The visible/hidden opposition may be echoed in other arenas of the Chacoan material world. Kelley Hayes-Gilpin (personal communication, August 2006) believes this juxtaposition to be present in Chacoan rock art. Perhaps the pairing of the visible and the hidden echoed a contrast between public and secret ritual knowledge or activities—each the counterpart of the other, and both necessary for ceremonial undertakings.

Directionality and Celestial Events

Cardinal or intercardinal directions are important for all contemporary Pueblos, so it is not surprising that directionality has a deep history reaching back at least as far as Chaco. Archaeologists have long recognized a north/south organizing principle in Chaco Canyon (Fritz 1978; Lekson 1999; Marshall 1997). Chacoan directionality may have emerged out of concerns with sacred geography, visibility, and balanced dualism. The relationship among all these concepts is well illustrated by the North and the South roads. The celestial and subterranean directions correlate with visible and hidden architectural elements and are strongly represented at Chaco. Chacoans used cardinal or meridian orientations for some great kivas and great houses. East and west are less formally expressed on the Chacoan landscape, although they might be captured by the east-west-trending canyon itself.

Directionality is linked to the movements of celestial bodies. Cardinal alignments are also astronomical alignments, bisecting the movements of the sun and stars. Like farmers everywhere, Ancestral Puebloans were acutely aware of the sun's daily and seasonal peregrinations across the sky. Anna Sofaer and her colleagues (for example, Sofaer and Sinclair 1987) have demonstrated that Chacoans were concerned with solstices and equinoxes. More recently, Sofaer (1997) has argued that Chacoans marked lunar standstills as well. This latter interpretation is more controversial yet seems borne out by rock art, by certain great house alignments, and, perhaps most compellingly, by the position of the Chimney Rock outlier great house (Malville 2004). If Ancestral Puebloans were keeping track of the movements of the sun and moon on the horizon, then solstices, equinoxes, and standstills might have signaled occasions for people all over the Basin to gather in the canyon. There might also be another juxtaposition here between accessible/visible and restricted/hidden ritual knowledge. Solstices and equinoxes are easy to anticipate on an open horizon, but lunar standstills require tracking over 18.6 years. Chacoan lunar knowledge is more likely to have been the purview of specialists and, as Sofaer (1999) notes, served no useful agricultural purpose.

Cyclical Renewal and Social Memory

Rituals involve formal practices, liturgies, and performances of ceremonies that have been undertaken multiple times in the past (Moore and Myerhoff 1977). Pueblo ritual events are cyclical, repeating at prescribed intervals. In preparation for ritual events, Puebloans touch the past and make it new through such practices as replastering kivas and refurbishing masks. Periodic, repetitive ritual practices create the illusion of timelessness—as it is now, so it ever was. Thus, cyclical ritual is part of the larger process of social memory building. Architecture and landscape indicate that Chacoans referenced the past, through repeated cyclical events and through more general affirmations of continuity with distant ancestors.

Time and again, across the Basketmaker III–Pueblo III sequence, Puebloan peoples returned to landscapes occupied by ancestors, building new sites atop or next to old ones or constructing shrines on the locations where ancestors dwelled. Cyclical ritual may have its roots in Basketmaker III solar or agricultural observances. At Chaco, repeated additions and remodelings at great houses, great kivas, and other structures express cyclical renewal. Additions to great houses in Chaco Canyon over the course of three centuries maintained physical continuity with past events and ancestors. The founders of Peñasco Blanco, as well as the Classic Bonito builders of a J-shaped shrine atop Site 423, may have wanted to associate themselves with Basketmaker III ancestors. Memory lent symbolic power to the conversion of tenth-century domestic space into eleventh-century elite burial rooms at Pueblo Bonito. Mounds and berms may have been a form of constructed memory, standing in for large middens that would have signified long-term occupation. When Chacoans incorporated great kivas into the Bonito-style repertoire during the eleventh century, they may have been referencing Basketmaker III oversized pitstructures. During the late eleventh century and beyond, in Chaco Canyon and at outliers, Ancestral Puebloans built "time bridges" linking new buildings to those constructed by ancestors.

Some aspects of memory at Chaco, such as great house additions, great kivas, mounds, and roads, are highly visible, but others are deliberately hidden. Mills (n.d.) suggests that votive deposits sealed in great kiva niches or below roof pillars are a form of memory's counterpart—ritualized obliteration or forgetting. The elite burial rooms at Pueblo Bonito were screened from general view. As is evident in so many other aspects of Chacoan architecture and landscape, Chacoans juxtaposed both visible and hidden memory references.

Center Place

All these themes—sacred geography, visibility, balanced dualism, directionality, and social memory—come together to emphasize the most important idea in the Ancestral Pueblo worldview and the critical facet in a Chacoan ideology: the concept of Chaco Canyon as the center place. Center place figures prominently in most contemporary Pueblo migration stories, with Tewa, Keres, Hopi, and Zuni peoples each contending, for example, that they have now arrived in the center place where each was ordained to live (Dongoske et al. 1997; Ferguson and Hart 1985; Parsons 1939). The idea of the middle or center place has deep roots in Pueblo history. Although from a contemporary perspective, Puebloans do not consider Chaco Canyon to be the proper center place, Ancestral Puebloans might well have seen it that way a millennium ago.

For Ancestral Puebloans looking outwards from Chacoan high places, the canyon seemed ringed with high places—distant, storied peaks that likely held sacred significance. The canyon juxtaposed high and visible landforms with low and hidden spaces. Chaco Canyon was a hidden, protected space, but Chacra Mesa was a landform highly visible across the southern and western San Juan Basin. Perhaps Chaco seemed to be the point of balance between not only visible/hidden but also directional dualisms. Up and down, north and south, east and west—builders increasingly formalized these relationships on the surrounding landscape. Road segments balanced and connected opposing directions, high and low great houses, and visible and hidden natural spaces. The canyon was a fulcrum, a point of fixity halfway between these geographic opposites.

Perhaps time itself revolved around Chaco. Solar and lunar observations lent weight to the concept of Chaco Canyon as the center of the world; architecture and rock art marked the ways in which the sun and moon seemed to revolve around the canyon. The canyon was charged with the memory of Basketmaker ancestors and the tangible, centuries-old evidence of their presence. The repeated, cyclical celebration of rituals and traditions would have created a sense of continuity with the past and the future. Chaco Canyon seemed to be the place at which all these ideas intersected, the nexus to which all directions pointed. Perhaps Early Bonito ceremonial gatherings blossomed in Chaco, in part, because of the ways the canyon's natural topographic properties fit with elements of an Ancestral Pueblo worldview. By the Classic Bonito phase, Chacoan builders and participants thought of the canyon as the center place, the proper place in which to undertake ceremonies that served, in part, to keep the world in balance.

Ideology at Chaco

Chacoan architecture and landscape provide us with multiple, overlapping reflections of the major social and cosmographic beliefs shared by Ancestral Puebloans during the Bonito phases. Ancestral Pueblo worldview and Chacoan ideology intersect around the concept of center place. Ideology differs from worldview in that shared ideas, beliefs, and values assist in the promotion and legitimation of the interests of some groups and not others. Ideology works because some elements of both dominant and subordinate groups' ideologies are shared. Subjects are not dupes but consensually participate in unequal social and political situations because they resonate strongly with ideas shared by the dominant group.

If Chacoans and participating Ancestral Puebloans from across the greater San Juan Basin shared the belief that Chaco Canyon was the center place, then the canyon clearly would have been an important and appropriate location in which to conduct rituals necessary to Ancestral Puebloan life. The purpose of these rituals may have been to keep the world in balance, as well as to ensure rainfall and agricultural productivity. Great houses and great kivas were likely settings for these ceremonies, and the buildings housed ritual paraphernalia when not in use. Great house dwellers—descendants of the first settlers at canyon great houses—probably played key parts in the public elements of Chacoan rituals. They also may have maintained ceremonial secrets known only to a few but necessary for proper ritual performance. One of the major ways that ideologies are perpetuated is through the naturalization of beliefs so that they appear to be self-evident. By the Classic Bonito phase, it must have seemed natural and inevitable that great house leaders at the center place should be accorded higher status than other Puebloans.

Ritual is an effective vehicle for the creation, maintenance, and legitimation of power relationships, because ritual is ambiguous and multivocal, blending the political with the personal and the existential (Cohen 1979). Rituals involve formality—repetition, staging, acting, stylization, and order—which implies permanence and legitimacy, commanding the attention of audience and participants while simultaneously deflecting questions. "Ritual is a kind of tunnel into which one plunges, and where, since there is no possibility of turning either to right or left, the only thing to do is to follow" (Bloch 1983:42). At the same time, ritual enables individuals to claim legitimate authority within their roles as participants rather than on the basis of their individual identities (Kelly and Kaplan 1990:140). It is not the individual's will that seems to be expressed, but the requirements of the ritual. Ritual transforms the obligatory into the desirable (Turner 1967:30).

Aesthetic and emotionally charged practices such as ritual are powerful venues for the development and support of ideologies (Bell 1997; Bloch 1989; Kelly and Kaplan 1990). The Chacoan landscape carried emotional resonance for Ancestral Puebloans that dated back to Basketmaker III times. Emotional connections to place may have been part of the reason Early Bonito peoples settled in Chaco, amid sacred landmarks and ancestral villages. Ritual gatherings in the canyon would have heightened the aesthetic resonance of the place. Music, rhythm, poetry, dancing, color, costumes, acting—these elements of ritual would have helped create a heightened emotional state among participants (Cohen 1979:98). As social norms and categories are suffused with emotion, meaning is "condensed" (Turner 1967:29), and the distinctions between the poetic and the political are blurred (Geertz 1980). Following Walter Benjamin, Smith (2000) terms this process "rendering the political aesthetic."

Describing social change is easier than explaining how and why it happens. Archaeological explanations for Chaco often seem to founder on the moment that a subset of people at Chaco became elites, resorting to visions of aggrandizing or charismatic individuals. This transformation may be difficult for us to grasp because there was no one moment, no single individual or event. Rather, the emergence of Chacoan elites happened gradually over the Early Bonito phase, as a result of actions and beliefs shared by all members of Chacoan society. The concept of structuration helps explain how social change can be the cumulative result of large and small decisions made over centuries by people who could not have foreseen the consequences.

The notion of center place emerged from overlapping sets of ideas that had informed and reflected Ancestral Pueblo beliefs for centuries. By tracing the Ancestral Pueblo worldview back into the past, it becomes evident that sacred geography, visibility, cyclical rituals, and possibly dualism were important as far back as the Basketmaker III period. When Ancestral Puebloans left aggregated villages north of the San Juan River and scattered themselves across the San Juan Basin, they maintained shared elements of a worldview. Sacred geography, visibility, cyclical rituals, and dualism gained momentum during Pueblo I and Early Bonito times as Ancestral Puebloans positioned new settlements, laid out buildings, and established themselves within the shadows of Basketmaker ancestors. The concept of Chaco Canyon as center place took hold because it was grounded in elements of a shared, Ancestral Pueblo worldview. Once Ancestral Puebloans saw Chaco as the center place, ritual gatherings there seemed natural and inevitable, as did ritual leaders' growing authority.

By the Classic Bonito phase, some people at Chaco were being supported by the labor of others. Leaders were living in great houses, were buried in great houses, and were directing major building projects. They were better nourished and taller than their small house neighbors. Leaders may have overseen canyon agricultural production, but they probably did not go hungry in years of poor production. Other Ancestral Puebloans lived and farmed at small houses and at outliers. Outlier dwellers brought many things to Chaco—corn, turquoise, pottery, lithics, labor, and devotion. The canyon's natural topography encouraged visitors to think of Chaco as the center place.

As the people most closely associated with the great houses, Chacoan leaders likely directed monumental construction, including new great houses and additions, great kivas, earthworks, and roads. Skilled, experienced engineers and masons may have carried out the building designs, but the Chacoan leadership probably had a strong hand in their creation. On multiple, intersecting, overlapping levels, Classic Bonito architecture and landscape celebrate the Ancestral Pueblo worldview and emphasize Chaco Canyon as center place. These ideas were not merely symbolized by the buildings. Rather, approaches to Chaco, approaches to great houses, lines of sight, and the positioning of Bonito-style structures worked together to create a powerful spatial experience for human bodies moving through this landscape. Traveling to and through Chaco would have been an aesthetically and emotionally intense experience for Ancestral Puebloans. As canyon dwellers and visitors viewed and moved through Chacoan spaces, their perceptions reciprocally confirmed ideas about the nature of the world and their place in it, and they willingly transformed themselves into subjects. As leaders manipulated Chacoan spaces, they may have sought merely to celebrate, not to aggrandize. But the ultimate effect was to legitimate leaders' prestige and authority and to encourage Ancestral Puebloans to continue contributing labor and resources. In this way, at Chaco, the aesthetic became political.

Chacoan leaders were most likely descendants of the Early Bonito founders of major great houses, but these positions did not remain static over the course of 300 years. Given the limitations of archaeological data, it is easiest to think and talk about the desires of leaders, but this top-down perspective is only a small and skewed part of the picture. Future endeavors should focus on constructing more nuanced understandings of canyon society. Who were the people who founded new canyon great houses? Who moved out into the San Juan Basin during the Late Bonito phase to found major new outliers, including Aztec? Who were the people who supported, participated in, and challenged Chaco? The Chacoan landscape would have been perceived, accepted, and contested by a diverse array of Ancestral Puebloans. Men and women, young and old, outlier residents from near and far, members of diverse ethnic groups and sodalities, initiates and the uninitiated, all likely experienced Chaco differently. We need further investigation into outlier communities in terms of their internal organization and variable relationships with Chaco Canyon.

Beyond Chaco

As a case study, this interpretive work explores several points that may be useful to archaeologists and anthropologists interested in sociopolitical complexity, ideology, and landscape: Major social change can occur as the gradual, cumulative result of many individuals' decisions—we must be willing to look beyond prime movers and specific moments, placing change in larger historical context. Ideology is accessible to archaeologists through the medium of landscape. And phenomenology, if employed thoughtfully, can be a useful interpretive method.

Chaco presents an unusual instance of sociopolitical complexity in which ritual, not economics, serves as the basis for elites' power. Many anthropological models seeking to explain complexity see ritual as a veneer legitimating economic inequalities. Chaco encourages us to think about the obverse—economics may be a veneer legitimating ritual inequalities (Yoffee 2001). Many models for the emergence of social inequality are essentially "Great Man" theory—social change is driven by the behavior of greedy and ambitious groups or individuals. This has the effect of negating the actions of common people and of reducing all social change to a universal human will to power (Nietzche 1968). But we need not rely on prime movers or aggrandizers to explain the construction of monumental architecture and the rise of sociopolitical complexity. Complex sociopolitical regimes can arise as the cumulative result of many decisions, small and large, made over centuries by individuals who could not have foreseen the magnitude of resulting social and architectural changes. This "structurationist" perspective gets us out of the trap of "Great Man" history and places the power to effect change in the hands of human agents with differing and conflicting agendas and motivations.

It is important to consider time in our reconstructions, at multiple scales. Eleventh-century events at Chaco Canyon cannot be understood outside the context of some five centuries of earlier developments. And landscapes are palimpsests—humans constantly think about, reference, interact with, or reject the traces of pasts—both their own and others'. Classic Bonitians referenced Early Bonito ideas, Late Bonitians referenced the Classic phase, and so on, into the post-Chacoan era. Just as site location maps can conflate time by condensing hundreds of years of settlements into two dimensions, we tend to explain social change within short, manageable bursts. But this is not the only way to think about social transformations, including the emergence of inequalities. The same events may look very different when seen from the perspective of individual decisions made over days or even decades, as opposed to centuries.

Landscape and architecture can be important tools for archaeologists investigating less tangible aspects of the social past, including aesthetics and ideology. Because place making is integral to the reflexive construction of society, some aspects of ancient ideologies are materially and archaeologically accessible. Chaco's strong spatial orientation is not surprising, given the open horizons and dramatic landmarks of the Colorado Plateau (Tuan 1974). But landscapes embody worldviews and ideologies for many past peoples in diverse natural environments, including the Maya (Ashmore 1989) and ancient northern Europeans (Bradley 1998, 2000).

When we think about places and the meanings past peoples attached to them, top-down or static spatial representations such as maps and photographs cannot capture the richness of bodily experience. Phenomenological investigations can yield useful insights, particularly if employed judiciously and tempered with ethnographic information. In my reading of the Chacoan landscape, phenomenological experiments are just one line of evidence I draw upon to create a coherent interpretation that fits with empirical observations. A contemporary researcher's spatial experiences can provide only partial and distorted perspectives, but by moving through the landscape as past peoples did, it is possible to gain insights into past spatial perceptions and representations. I learned, for example, that Chacoans sited buildings in specific places and sought to create particular visible effects. Phenomenological investigators must not stop at describing particular views or sensations but should attempt to address the reasons ancient builders chose to construct and modify their spatial world in these particular ways.

At the same time, we archaeologists ought to strive to incorporate more sensuality into our methods, as well as our interpretations. Often, in our endeavors to objectify and legitimate archaeological knowledge, we too easily overlook or even negate the importance of the sensual. Emotion is one of the most compelling facets of ideology—where the heart is engaged, the body follows. The human experience encompasses emotional, aesthetic, and sensual dimensions, as well as rational decision-making behavior. Today, Native Americans, artists, scientists, archaeologists, and tourists engage with and are inspired by the Chacoan landscape. If this is true for modern visitors to the canyon, then how much more so for the ancient Chacoan, for whom and by whom the canyon architecture, with its multilayered uses and meanings, was constructed.

Coda

For a few brief centuries, Chaco Canyon was the center of the Ancestral Pueblo world. The white-plastered walls of Pueblo Bonito and Chetro Ketl gleamed brightly against a turquoise sky. Smoke steamed from kiva entrances, and the canyon was filled with the sounds of voices chanting, dogs barking, and the rasp of corn against rock. People came from diverse communities far and near to be part of feast days, to watch and participate in ceremony.

Today, in the remote stillness that is Chaco Canyon, thousand-year-old sandstone walls still shimmer in golden sunlight. Moons rise and set, hawks circle overhead, and the storied landscape lies breathing under the turquoise sky, holding the myriad meanings that peoples continue to inscribe upon this ancient center place.

> *In the seasons and among the people of the valley I was content. My spirit was quiet there. The silence was old, immediate, and pervasive, and there was great good in it. The wind of the canyons drew it out; the voices of the village carried and were lost in it. Much was made of the silence; much of the summer and winter was made of it.*
> *[Momaday 1976:154]*

References

Adams, E. Charles
1991   The Origin and Development of the Pueblo Katsina Cult. Tucson: University of Arizona Press.

Adler, Michael A.
1996   Fathoming the Scale of Anasazi Communities. In Interpreting Southwestern Diversity: Underlying Principles and Overarching Patterns. Paul R. Fish and J. Jefferson Reid, eds. Pp. 97–106. Anthropological Research Papers 48. Tempe: Arizona State University.

Adler, Michael A., and Richard H. Wilshusen
1990   Large-scale Integrative Facilities in Tribal Societies: Cross-cultural and Southwestern US Examples. World Archaeology 22(2):133–146.

Agnew, John A., and James S. Duncan, eds.
1989   The Power of Place: Bringing Together Geographical and Sociological Imaginations. London: Unwin-Hyman.

Akins, Nancy J.
1986   A Biocultural Approach to Human Burials from Chaco Canyon, New Mexico. Reports of the Chaco Center 9. Santa Fe, NM: National Park Service.
2003   The Burials of Pueblo Bonito. In Pueblo Bonito: Center of the Chacoan World. Jill E. Neitzel, ed. Pp. 94–106. Washington DC: Smithsonian Press.

Alcock, Susan E.
1993   Graecia Capta: The Landscapes of Roman Greece. Cambridge: Cambridge University Press.
2001   Reconfiguration of Memory in the Eastern Roman Empire. In Empires: Perspectives from Archaeology and History. Susan E. Alcock, Terence N. D'Altroy, Kathleen D. Morrison, and Carla M. Sinopoli, eds. Pp. 323–350. Cambridge: Cambridge University Press.
2002   Archaeologies of the Greek Past: Landscape, Monuments and Memories. Cambridge: Cambridge University Press.

Allen, Joseph W.
1972   The Mexican Wash Project: Archaeological Excavation along US Highway 666 near Buffalo Springs, New Mexico. Laboratory of Anthropology Notes 81. Santa Fe: Museum of New Mexico.

Althusser, Louis
1969   For Marx. Ben Brewster, trans. New York: Pantheon Books.
1971   Lenin and Philosophy. New York: Monthly Review Press.

Altman, Irwin, and Setha M. Low, eds.
1992   Place Attachment. New York: Plenum Press.

Altschul, Jeffrey H., and Edgar K. Huber
2000   Economics, Site Structure, and Social Organization during the Basketmaker III Period: A View from the Lukachukai Valley. *In* Foundations of Anasazi Culture: The Basketmaker–Pueblo Transition. Paul F. Reed, ed. Pp. 145–160. Salt Lake City: University of Utah Press.

Anschuetz, Kurt F., Richard H. Wilshusen, and Cherie L. Scheick
2001   An Archaeology of Landscapes: Perspectives and Directions. Journal of Archaeological Research 9(2):157–211.

Appadurai, Arjun
1988   Introduction: Place and Voice in Anthropological Theory. Cultural Anthropology 3(1):16–20.

Ashmore, Wendy
1989   Construction and Cosmology: Politics and Ideology in Lowland Maya Settlement Patterns. *In* Word and Image in Maya Culture: Explorations in Language, Writing, and Representation. William F. Hanks and Don S. Rice, eds. Pp. 272–286. Salt Lake City: University of Utah Press.
1991   Site Planning Principles and Concepts of Directionality among the Ancient Maya. Latin American Antiquity 2(3):199–226.
2002   Decisions and Dispositions: Socializing Spatial Archaeology. American Anthropologist 104(4):1172–1183.
2007   Building Social History at Pueblo Bonito: Footnotes to a Biography of Place. *In* The Architecture of Chaco Canyon, New Mexico. Stephen H. Lekson, ed. Pp. 179–198. Salt Lake City: University of Utah Press.

Ashmore, Wendy, and Bernard Knapp, eds.
1999   Archaeologies of Landscape: Contemporary Perspectives. Oxford: Blackwell Publishing.

Aveni, Anthony F.
1980   Skywatchers of Ancient Mexico. Austin: University of Texas Press.

Baker, Larry L.
1983   Stabilization of Guadalupe Ruin. Eastern New Mexico University Contributions in Anthropology 11. Portales: Eastern New Mexico University.

2006 Architecture of Salmon Pueblo. *In* Thirty-Five Years of Archaeological Research at Salmon Ruins, New Mexico. Paul F. Reed, ed. Pp. 245–276. Tucson, AZ: Center for Desert Archaeology; Bloomfield, NM: Salmon Ruins Museum.

n.d. Salmon Ruins: Architecture and Development of a Chacoan Satellite on the San Juan River. *In* Chaco's Northern Prodigies: Salmon, Aztec, and the Ascendancy of the Middle San Juan Region after AD 1100. Paul Reed, ed. Salt Lake City: University of Utah Press.

Baker, Larry L., and Stephen R. Durand, eds.
2003 Prehistory of the Middle Rio Puerco Valley, Sandoval County, New Mexico. Archaeological Society of New Mexico Special Publication 3. Portales: Archaeological Society of New Mexico.

Bannister, Bryant
1965 Tree-Ring Dating of the Archeological Sites in the Chaco Canyon Region, New Mexico. *In* Kin Kletso, A Pueblo III Community in Chaco Canyon, New Mexico, by Gordon R. Vivian and Tom Mathews. Southwestern Monuments Association Technical Series 6, Part 2. Pp. 116–202. Globe, AZ: Southwestern Monuments Association.

Bannister, Bryant, William J. Robinson, and Richard L. Warren
1970 Tree-Ring Dates from New Mexico A, G–H, Shiprock–Zuni–Mt. Taylor Area. Laboratory of Tree-Ring Research. Tucson: University of Arizona.

Barclay, Alistair, and Jan Harding, eds.
1999 Pathways and Ceremonies: The Cursus Monuments of Britain and Ireland. Neolithic Studies Group Seminar Papers 4. Oxford: Oxbow Books.

Barrett, John C.
1991 The Archaeology of Social Reproduction. *In* Landscape, Monuments, and Society: The Prehistory of Cranborne Chase. John Barrett, Richard Bradley, and M. Green, eds. Pp. 6–8. Cambridge: Cambridge University Press.
1994 Fragments from Antiquity: An Archaeology of Social Life in Britain, 2900–1200 BC. Oxford: Blackwell Publishing.

Basso, Keith H.
1996 Wisdom Sits in Places: Landscape and Language among the Western Apache. Albuquerque: University of New Mexico Press.

Begay, Richard M.
2004 Tsé Bíyah 'Anii'áhí: Chaco Canyon and Its Place in Navajo History. *In* In Search of Chaco: New Approaches to an Archaeological Enigma. David Grant Noble, ed. Pp. 54–60. School of American Research. Santa Fe, NM: SAR Press.

Bell, Catherine
1997 Ritual: Perspectives and Dimensions. New York and Oxford: Oxford University Press.

Bender, Barbara, ed.
1993 Landscape: Politics and Perspectives. Oxford, UK, and Providence, RI: Berg.

Benedict, Ruth
1931   Tales of the Cochiti Indians. Bureau of American Ethnology Bulletin 98. Washington DC: Smithsonian Press.

Benjamin, Walter
1968   The Work of Art in the Age of Mechanical Reproduction. *In* Illuminations, edited by Hannah Arendt. H. Zohn, trans. Pp. 217–251. New York: Schocken Books.

Bernardini, Wesley
1999   Reassessing the Scale of Social Action at Pueblo Bonito, Chaco Canyon, New Mexico. Kiva 64(4):447–470.

Bice, Richard A.
1983   The Sterling Site: An Initial Report. *In* Collected Papers in Honor of Charlie R. Steen, Jr. Nancy L. Fox, ed. Pp. 49–86. Papers of the Archaeological Society of New Mexico 8. Albuquerque: Archaeological Society of New Mexico.

Biella, Jan V.
1974   An Archaeological Assessment of the Exxon Uranium Mine Lease: Northwestern New Mexico. *In* Archaeological Reports: Cultural Resource Management Projects. Frank J. Broilo and David E. Stuart, eds. Albuquerque: Office of Contract Archeology, University of New Mexico.

Billman, Brian R., Patricia M. Lambert, and Banks L. Leonard
2000   Cannibalism, Warfare, and Drought in the Mesa Verde Region during the Twelfth Century AD. American Antiquity 65(1):145–178.

Blake, Emma
1998   Sardinia's Nuraghi: Four Millennia of Becoming. World Archaeology 30(1):59–71.

Blanton, Richard E., Gary M. Feinman, Stephen A. Kowaleski, and Peter N. Peregrine
1996   A Dual-Processual Theory for the Evolution of Mesoamerican Civilization. Current Anthropology 37(1):1–14.

Blinman, Eric
1989   Potluck in the Protokiva: Ceramics and Ceremonialism in Pueblo I Villages. *In* The Architecture of Social Integration in Prehistoric Pueblos. William D. Lipe and Michelle Hegmon, eds. Pp. 113–124. Crow Canyon Archaeological Center Occasional Paper 1. Cortez, CO: Crow Canyon Archaeological Center.

Bloch, Maurice
1983   From Blessing to Violence: History and Ideology in the Circumcision Ritual of the Merina of Madagascar. Cambridge: Cambridge University Press.
1989   Ritual, History, and Power: Selected Papers in Anthropology. London: Athlone.

Bowser, Brenda, ed.
2004   Toward an Archaeology of Place. Theme issue, Journal of Archaeological Method and Theory 11(1).

Bradfield, Wesley
1921   Economic Resources of Chaco Canyon. Art and Archaeology 11(1 & 2):36–38.

Bradford, James
1981   Historic Structure Report, Tsin Kletzin Ruin, Chaco Culture National Historical Park, New Mexico. Santa Fe, NM: Southwest Cultural Resources Center, National Park Service Southwest Regional Office.

Bradley, Bruce
1974   Preliminary Report of Excavations at the Wallace Ruin, 1969–1974. Southwestern Lore 40(3/4):63–71.
1992   Excavations at Sand Canyon Pueblo. In The Sand Canyon Archaeological Project: A Progress Report. William D. Lipe, ed. Pp. 79–98. Crow Canyon Archaeological Center Occasional Paper 2. Cortez, CO: Crow Canyon Archaeological Center.
1993   Wallace Ruin: Implications for Outlier Studies. In The Chimney Rock Archaeological Symposium. J. McKim Malville and Gary Matlock, eds. Pp. 72–75. US Department of Agriculture Forest Service General Technical Report RM-227. Fort Collins, CO: Rocky Mountain Forest Research and Experimental Station.
1996   Pitchers to Mugs: Chacoan Revival at Sand Canyon Pueblo. Kiva 61(3):241–255.

Bradley, Richard
1993   Altering the Earth: The Origins of Monuments in Britain and Continental Europe. Society of Antiquaries of Scotland Monograph Series 8. Edinburgh: Society of Antiquaries of Scotland.
1998   The Significance of Monuments: On the Shaping of Human Experience in Neolithic and Bronze Age Europe. London and New York: Routledge.
2000   An Archaeology of Natural Places. London and New York: Routledge.
2002   The Past in Prehistoric Societies. London and New York: Routledge.

Bradley, Richard, and Howard Williams, eds.
1998   The Past in the Past. Theme issue, World Archaeology 30(1).

Bradley, Ronna J., and Richard B. Sullivan
1994   A Study of Two Anasazi Communities in the San Juan Basin. Across the Colorado Plateau: Anthropological Studies for the Transwestern Pipeline Expansion Project, vol. IX. Albuquerque: University of New Mexico Office of Contract Archeology and Maxwell Museum of Anthropology.

Brady, James E., and Wendy Ashmore
1999   Mountains, Caves, Water: Ideational Landscapes of the Ancient Maya. In Archaeologies of Landscape: Contemporary Perspectives. Wendy Ashmore and A. Bernard Knapp, eds. Pp. 124–147. Oxford: Blackwell Publishing.

Brandi, James
1988   Lithic Analysis and Results. In The Casamero and Pierre's Outliers Survey: An Archaeological Class III Inventory of the BLM Lands Surrounding the Outliers, by Randy A. Harper, Marilyn K. Swift, Barbara Mills, James Brandi, and Joseph C. Winter. Pp. 99–114. Albuquerque: Office of Contract Archeology, University of New Mexico.

Brandt, Elizabeth
1977   The Role of Secrecy in a Puebloan Society. *In* Flowers in the Wind: Papers on Ritual, Myth, and Symbolism in California and the Southwest. T. C. Blackburn, ed. Pp. 11–28. Anthropological Papers 8. Socorro, NM: Ballena Press.
1980   On Secrecy and the Control of Knowledge: Taos Pueblo. *In* Secrecy: A Cross-cultural Perspective. S. K. Tefft, ed. Pp. 123–146. New York: Human Sciences Press.
1994   Egalitarianism, Hierarchy, and Centralization in the Pueblos. *In* The Ancient Southwestern Community: Models and Methods for the Study of Prehistoric Social Organization. Wirt H. Wills and Robert D. Leonard, eds. Pp. 9–23. Albuquerque: University of New Mexico Press.

Breternitz, Cory D., David E. Doyel, and Michael P. Marshall
1982   Bis sa'ani: A Late Bonito Phase Community on Escavada Wash, Northwest New Mexico. Navajo Nation Papers in Anthropology 14. Window Rock, AZ: Navajo Nation Cultural Resource Management Program.

Brew, John O.
1946   The Archaeology of Alkali Ridge, Southeastern Utah. Papers of the Peabody Museum 21. Cambridge, MA: Harvard University.

Brisbin, Joel M., Allen E. Kane, and James N. Morris
1988   Excavations at McPhee Pueblo (Site 5MT4475), A Pueblo I and Early Pueblo II Multicomponent Village. *In* Dolores Archaeological Program: Anasazi Communities at Dolores: McPhee Village. A. E. Kane and C. K. Robinson, comps. Pp. 63–403. Denver, CO: USDI Bureau of Reclamation.

Brown, Gary, Thomas C. Windes, and Peter McKenna
n.d.   Animas Anamnesis: Aztec Ruins, or Anasazi Capital? *In* Chaco's Northern Prodigies: Salmon, Aztec, and the Ascendancy of the Middle San Juan Region after AD 1100. Paul Reed, ed. Salt Lake City: University of Utah Press.

Brugge, David
1980   A History of the Chaco Navajos. Reports of the Chaco Center 4. Santa Fe, NM: Division of Chaco Research, National Park Service.

Bullard, William R., Jr.
1962   The Cerro Colorado Site and Pithouse Architecture in the Southwestern United States prior to AD 900. Papers of the Peabody Museum of American Archaeology and Ethnology 44(2). Cambridge, MA: Harvard University.

Bunzel, Ruth L.
1932   Introduction to Zuni Ceremonialism: Zuni Origin Myths, Zuni Ritual Poetry, Zuni Katcinas: An Analytical Study. *In* Forty-Seventh Annual Report of the Bureau of American Ethnology for the Years 1929–1930. Pp. 467–1086. Smithsonian Institution. Washington DC: Government Printing Office (GPO).

Bustard, Wendy
2003   Pueblo Bonito: When a House Is Not a Home. *In* Pueblo Bonito: Center of the Chacoan World. Jill E. Neitzel, ed. Pp. 80–93. Washington DC: Smithsonian Press.

In press Chaco Horrificus? *In* Multidisciplinary Approaches to Social Violence in the Prehispanic Southwest. D. Nichols and Patricia Crown, eds. Tucson: University of Arizona Press.

Buttimer, Anne
1993 Geography and the Human Spirit. Baltimore, MD: Johns Hopkins University Press.

Cameron, Catherine M.
1984 A Regional View of Chipped Stone Raw Material Use in Chaco Canyon. *In* Recent Research on Chaco Prehistory. W. James Judge and John D. Schelberg, eds. Pp. 137–152. Reports of the Chaco Center 8. Albuquerque, NM: Division of Cultural Research, National Park Service.
1995 Migration and the Movement of Southwestern Peoples. Journal of Anthropological Archaeology 14(2):104–124.
1997 The Chipped Stone of Chaco Canyon, New Mexico. *In* Ceramics, Lithics, and Ornaments of Chaco Canyon: Analysis of Artifacts from the Chaco Project, 1971–1978, vol. II: Lithics. Frances Joan Mathien, ed. Pp. 531–658. Santa Fe, NM: Publications in Archaeology 18G, National Park Service.
2001 Pink Chert, Projectile Points, and the Chacoan Regional System. American Antiquity 66(1):79–102.
2002 Sacred Earthen Architecture in the Northern Southwest: The Bluff Great House Berm. American Antiquity 67(4):677–695.

Cameron, Catherine M., and Stephen H. Lekson
2000 Preliminary Report on the 1998 Field Season at the Bluff Great House. Report submitted to the Bureau of Land Management (BLM), Bluff, UT. Boulder: Department of Anthropology, University of Colorado.

Cameron, Catherine M., and H. Wolcott Toll
2001 Deciphering the Organization of Production in Chaco Canyon. American Antiquity 66(1):5–13.

Carlson, John
1981 A Geomantic Model for the Interpretation of Mesoamerican Sites: An Essay in Cross-cultural Comparison. *In* Mesoamerican Sites and World-views: A Conference at Dumbarton Oaks, October 16 and 17, 1976. Elizabeth P. Benson, ed. Pp. 143–215. Washington DC: Dumbarton Oaks Research Library and Collections.

Carlson, Roy L.
1966 Twin Angels Pueblo. American Antiquity 31(5):676–682.

Carr, Christopher
1995 A Unified Middle-Range Theory of Artifact Design. *In* Style, Society, and Person: Archaeological and Ethnological Perspectives. Christopher Carr and Jill Neitzel, eds. Pp. 171–258. New York: Plenum Press.

Carroll, Alex, M. Nieves Zedeño, and Richard W. Stoffle
2004 Landscapes of the Ghost Dance: A Cartography of Numic Ritual. Journal of Archaeological Method and Theory 11(2):127–156.

Casey, Edward S.
1996 How to Get from Space to Place in a Fairly Short Stretch of Time: Phenomenological Prolegomena. In Senses of Place. Steven Feld and Keith H. Basso, eds. Pp. 13–52. School of American Research. Santa Fe, NM: SAR Press.
1997 The Fate of Place: A Philosophical History. Berkeley: University of California Press.

Cassells, E. Steve
1983 The Archaeology of Colorado. Boulder, CO: Johnson Books.

Chapman, Kenneth M.
1921 What the Potsherds Tell. Art and Archaeology 11(1 & 2):33–34.

Chenault, Mark L., and Thomas N. Motsinger
2000 Colonization, Warfare, and Regional Competition: Recent Research into the Basketmaker III Period in the Mesa Verde Region. In Foundations of Anasazi Culture: The Basketmaker–Pueblo Transition. Paul F. Reed, ed. Pp. 45–65. Salt Lake City: University of Utah Press.

Cohen, Abner
1979 Political Symbolism. Annual Review of Anthropology 8:87–113.

Connerton, Paul
1989 How Societies Remember. Cambridge: Cambridge University Press.

Conrad, Geoffrey W., and Arthur A. Demarest
1984 Religion and Empire: The Dynamics of Aztec and Inca Expansion. Cambridge: Cambridge University Press.

Cooper, Laurel M.
1995 Space Syntax Analysis of Chacoan Great Houses. Ph.D. dissertation, University of Arizona; University of Michigan Dissertation Services, Ann Arbor.

Cordell, Linda S.
1995 Tracing Migration Pathways from the Receiving End. Journal of Anthropological Archaeology 14(2):203–211.

Cordell, Linda S., W. James Judge, and June-el Piper, eds.
2001 Chaco Society and Polity: Papers from the 1999 Conference. New Mexico Archaeological Council Special Publication 4. Albuquerque: New Mexico Archaeological Council.

Cosgrove, Denis
1984 Social Formation and Symbolic Landscape. London: Croom Helm.
1993 The Palladian Landscape: Geographical Change and Its Cultural Representations in Sixteenth-Century Italy. University Park: Pennsylvania State University Press.

Craig, Douglas B., James P. Holmlund, and Jeffery J. Clark
1998 Labor Investment and Organization in Platform Mound Construction: A Case Study from the Tonto Basin of Central Arizona. Journal of Field Archaeology 25(3):245–259.

Creel, Darrell, and Charmion McKusick
1994 Prehistoric Macaws and Parrots in the Mimbres Area, New Mexico. American Antiquity 59(3):510–524.

Crown, Patricia, and W. H. Wills
2003 Modifying Pottery and Kivas at Chaco: Pentimento, Restoration, or Renewal? American Antiquity 68(3):511–532.

Cunnar, Geoffrey
1996 LA 80934: Excavations at Electric Raven Site. In Excavation of Gallup Station. Charles W. Wheeler, ed. Pp. 4-1 to 4-148. Pipeline Archaeology 1990–1993: The El Paso Natural Gas North System Expansion Project, New Mexico and Arizona, 4. Western Cultural Resource Management Report F074. Farmington, NM: Western Cultural Resource Management, Inc.

Cushing, Frank H.
1896 Outlines of Zuni Creation Myths. In Thirteenth Annual Report of the Bureau of American Ethnology for the Years 1891–1892. Pp. 321–447. Smithsonian Institution. Washington DC: GPO.
1966 Zuni Fetiches. In Second Annual Report of the Bureau of American Ethnology for
[1883] the Years 1880–1881. Smithsonian Institution. Washington DC: GPO. Reprint, Flagstaff, AZ: KC Publications, pp. 3–45.
1979 Zuni: Selected Writings of Frank Hamilton Cushing. Jesse Green, ed. Lincoln: University of Nebraska Press.

Damp, Jonathan E.
1999 Chuska Chronologies, Houses, and Hogans: Archaeological and Ethnographic Inquiry along N30-N31 between Mexican Springs and Navajo, McKinley County, New Mexico. Zuni Cultural Resource Enterprise Report 466, Research Series 10, Pueblo of Zuni.

Damp, Jonathan E., and Edward M. Kotyk
2000 Socioeconomic Organization of a Late Basketmaker III Community in the Mexican Springs Area, Southern Chuska Mountains, New Mexico. In Foundations of Anasazi Culture: The Basketmaker–Pueblo Transition. Paul F. Reed, ed. Pp. 95–113. Salt Lake City: University of Utah Press.

Davis, Mike
1992 City of Quartz: Excavating the Future in Los Angeles. New York: Vintage Books.

De Certeau, Michel
1984 The Practice of Everyday Life. Steven Rendall, trans. Berkeley and Los Angeles: University of California Press.

Dean, Jeffrey S.
1992   Environmental Factors in the Evolution of the Chacoan Sociopolitical System. *In* Anasazi Regional Organization and the Chaco System. David E. Doyel, ed. Pp. 35–44. Maxwell Museum of Anthropology Anthropological Papers 5. Albuquerque: University of New Mexico Press.

Dean, Jeffrey S., William H. Doelle, and Janet D. Orcutt
1994   Adaptive Stress, Environment, and Demography. *In* Themes in Southwest Prehistory. George J. Gumerman, ed. Pp. 53–86. School of American Research. Santa Fe, NM: SAR Press.

Dittert, Alfred E., Frank W. Eddy, and B. L. Dickey
1963   Evidence of Early Ceramic Phases in the Navajo Reservoir District. El Palacio 70(1-2):5–12.

Dobres, Marcia-Anne
2000   Technology and Social Agency: Outlining a Practice Framework for Archaeology. Oxford: Blackwell Publishing.

Dobres, Marcia-Anne, and John Robb
2000   Agency in Archaeology: Paradigm or Platitude? *In* Agency in Archaeology. Marcia-Anne Dobres and John Robb, eds. Pp. 3–17. London and New York: Routledge.

Dongoske, Kurt E., Michael Yeatts, Roger Anyon, and T. J. Ferguson
1997   Archaeological Cultures and Cultural Affiliation: Hopi and Zuni Perspectives in the American Southwest. American Antiquity 62(4):600–608.

Donley-Reid, Linda W.
1990   A Structuring Structure: The Swahili House. *In* Domestic Architecture and the Use of Space. Susan Kent, ed. Pp. 127–152. Cambridge: Cambridge University Press.

Doyel, David E., Cory D. Breternitz, and Michael P. Marshall
1984   Chacoan Community Structure: Bis sa'ani and the Chaco Halo. *In* Recent Research on Chaco Prehistory. W. James Judge and John D. Schelberg, eds. Pp. 37–54. Reports of the Chaco Center 8. Albuquerque, NM: Division of Cultural Research, National Park Service.

Dozier, Edward P.
1960   The Pueblos of the South-western United States. Journal of the Royal Anthropological Institute of Great Britain and Ireland 90(I-II):146–160.

Drager, Dwight L.
1976   Anasazi Population Estimates with the Aid of Data Derived from Photogrammetric Maps. *In* Remote Sensing Experiments in Cultural Resource Studies. Thomas R. Lyons, ed. Pp. 157–171. Reports of the Chaco Center 1. Albuquerque: National Park Service and University of New Mexico.

Duff, Andrew I.
1998   The Process of Migration in the Late Prehistoric Southwest. *In* Migration and Reorganization: The Pueblo IV Period in the American Southwest. Katherine A.

Spielmann, ed. Pp. 31–52. Anthropological Research Papers 51. Tempe: Department of Anthropology, Arizona State University.
2006 Participation, Place, and the Social Construction of Great House Communities. Paper presented at Materialities of Place: Current Investigations into Ancient Landscapes. Ruth M. Van Dyke, org. The 10th Biennial Southwest Symposium, Las Cruces, NM, January 13.

Duncan, James, and David Ley, eds.
1993 Place/Culture/Representation. London: Routledge.

Durand, Kathy Roler
2003 Function of Chaco-Era Great Houses. Kiva 69(2):141–169.

Durand, Stephen R., and Kathy Roler Durand
2000 Notes from the Edge: Settlement Pattern Changes at the Guadalupe Community. In Great House Communities across the Chacoan Landscape. John Kantner and Nancy Mahoney, eds. Pp. 101–108. Anthropological Papers 65. Tucson: University of Arizona Press.

Durand, Stephen R., Philip H. Shelley, R. C. Antweiler, and H. E. Taylor
1999 Trees, Chemistry, and Prehistory in the American Southwest. Journal of Archaeological Science 26(2):185–203.

Dutton, Bertha P.
1963 Sun Father's Way: The Kiva Murals of Kuaua. Albuquerque: University of New Mexico Press.

Dutton, Bertha P., and Miriam A. Marmon
1936 The Laguna Calendar. The University of New Mexico Bulletin 2. Anthropological Series, vol. 1, no. 2. Albuquerque: University of New Mexico.

Eagleton, Terry
1990 The Ideology of the Aesthetic. Oxford: Blackwell Publishing.
1991 Ideology: A Critical Reader. London: Verso.

Ebert, James I., and Robert K. Hitchcock
1980 Locational Modeling in the Analysis of the Prehistoric Roadway System at and around Chaco Canyon, New Mexico. In Cultural Resources Remote Sensing. Thomas R. Lyons and Frances Joan Mathien, eds. Pp. 169–207. Washington DC: National Park Service.

Eddy, Frank W.
1961 Excavation at Los Piños Phase Sites in the Navajo Reservoir District. Museum of New Mexico Papers in Anthropology 4. Santa Fe: Museum of New Mexico Press.
1977 Archaeological Investigations at Chimney Rock Mesa, 1970–72. Memoirs of the Colorado Archaeological Society 1. Boulder: Colorado Archaeological Society.

Edmonds, Mark
1999 Ancestral Geographies of the Neolithic: Landscapes, Monuments, and Memory. London and New York: Routledge.

Eggan, Fred
1950   Social Organization of the Western Pueblos. Chicago: University of Chicago Press.

Eliot, T. S.
1991   Burnt Norton. *In* T. S. Eliot, Collected Poems, 1909–1962. Pp. 175–181. New
[1935] York: Harcourt, Brace and Company.

Ellis, Florence Hawley
1966   The Immediate History of Zia Pueblo as Derived from Excavation in Refuse Deposits. American Antiquity 31(6):806–811.
1967   Where Did the Pueblo People Come From? El Palacio 74(3):35–43.

Ellis, Florence Hawley, and Lawrence Hammack
1968   The Inner Sanctum of Feather Cave. American Antiquity 33(1):25–44.

Emerson, Thomas E.
1997   Cahokian Elite Ideology and the Mississippian Cosmos. *In* Cahokia: Domination and Ideology in the Mississippian World. Timothy R. Pauketat, ed. Pp. 190–228. Lincoln: University of Nebraska Press.

English, Nathan B., Julio L. Betancourt, Jeffrey S. Dean, and Jay Quade
2001   Strontium Isotopes Reveal Distant Sources of Architectural Timber in Chaco Canyon, New Mexico. Proceedings of the National Academy of Sciences of the United States of America 98(21):11891–11896.

Farmer, James D.
2003   Astronomy and Ritual in Chaco Canyon. *In* Pueblo Bonito: Center of the Chacoan World. Jill E. Neitzel, ed. Pp. 61–71. Washington DC: Smithsonian Press.

Feinman, Gary M.
2000a Corporate/Network: A New Perspective on Leadership in the American Southwest. *In* Hierarchies in Action: Cui Bono? Michael W. Diehl, ed. Pp. 152–180. Center for Archaeological Investigations Occasional Paper 27. Carbondale: Southern Illinois University.
2000b Dual-Processual Theory and Social Formations in the Southwest. *In* Alternative Leadership Strategies in the Prehispanic Southwest. Barbara J. Mills, ed. Pp. 207–224. Tucson: University of Arizona Press.

Feinman, Gary M., Kent G. Lightfoot, and Steadman Upham
2000   Political Hierarchies and Organizational Strategies in the Puebloan Southwest. American Antiquity 65(3):449–470.

Feld, Steven
1996   Waterfalls of Song: An Acoustemology of Place Resounding in Bosavi, Papua New Guinea. *In* Senses of Place. Steven Feld and Keith Basso, eds. Pp. 91–135. School of American Research. Santa Fe, NM: SAR Press.

Feld, Steven, and Keith H. Basso, eds.
1996   Senses of Place. School of American Research. Santa Fe, NM: SAR Press.

Ferguson, T. J., and Roger Anyon
2001   Hopi and Zuni Cultural Landscapes: Implications of History and Scale for Cultural Resources Management. *In* Native Peoples of the Southwest: Negotiating Land, Water, and Ethnicities. Laurie Weinstein, ed. Pp. 99–122. Westport, CT: Bergin and Garvey.

Ferguson, T. J., and Chip Colwell-Chanthaphonh
2006   History Is in the Land: Multivocal Tribal Traditions in Arizona's San Pedro Valley. Tucson: University of Arizona Press.

Ferguson, T. J., Kurt E. Dongoske, Mike Yeatts, and Leigh J. Kuwanwisiwma
2000   Hopi Oral History and Archaeology. *In* Working Together: Native Americans and Archaeologists. Kurt E. Dongoske, Mark Aldenderfer, and K. Doehner, eds. Pp. 45–60. Washington DC: Society for American Archaeology.

Ferguson, T. J., and E. Richard Hart
1985   A Zuni Atlas. Norman: University of Oklahoma Press.

Fewkes, Jesse Walter
1916   Prehistoric Towers and Castles of the Southwest. Art and Archaeology 7(9):353–366.
1917   Archaeological Investigations in New Mexico, Colorado, and Utah. Smithsonian Miscellaneous Collections 68(1). Washington DC: Smithsonian Institution.

Fletcher, Thomas F., ed.
1994   Archaeological Data Recovery Excavations at the Sanders Great House and Six Other Sites along US Highway 191, South of Sanders, Apache County, Arizona. Report 471, Research Series 9. Pueblo of Zuni: Zuni Archaeological Program.

Force, Eric R., R. Gwinn Vivian, Thomas C. Windes, and Jeffrey S. Dean
2002   Relation of "Bonito" Paleo-channels and Base-Level Variations to Anasazi Occupation, Chaco Canyon, New Mexico. Arizona State Museum Archaeological Series 194. Tucson: University of Arizona Press.

Foucault, Michel
1977   Discipline and Punish: The Birth of the Prison. Alan Sheridan, trans. New York: Vintage Books, Random House.
1980   Power/Knowledge: Selected Interviews and Other Writings, 1972–1977. Colin Gordon, ed. New York: Pantheon.

Fowler, Andrew P., and John R. Stein
1992   The Anasazi Great House in Space, Time, and Paradigm. *In* Anasazi Regional Organization and the Chaco System. David E. Doyel, ed. Pp. 101–122. Maxwell Museum of Anthropology Anthropological Papers 5. Albuquerque: University of New Mexico Press.

Fowler, Andrew, John R. Stein, and Roger Anyon
1987   An Archaeological Reconnaissance of West-Central New Mexico: The Anasazi Monuments Project. Albuquerque, NM: Office of Cultural Affairs, Historic Preservation Division.

Fox, Robin
1972   Some Unsolved Problems of Pueblo Social Organization. *In* New Perspectives on the Pueblos. Alfonso Ortiz, ed. Pp. 71–85. School of American Research Advanced Seminar Series. Albuquerque: University of New Mexico Press.

Fritz, John M.
1978   Paleopsychology Today: Ideational Systems and Human Adaptation in Prehistory. *In* Social Archeology: Beyond Subsistence and Dating. Charles L. Redman, Mary Jane Berman, Edward V. Curtain, William T. Langhorn, Nina M. Versaggi, and Jeffrey C. Wanser, eds. Pp. 37–59. New York: Academic Press.

Geertz, Clifford A.
1980   Negara: The Theatre State in Nineteenth-Century Bali. Princeton, NJ: Princeton University Press.

Geuens, Jean-Pierre
1994   Visuality and Power: The Work of the Steadicam. Film Quarterly 47(2):8–16.

Geurts, Kathryn L.
2003   Culture and the Senses: Bodily Ways of Knowing in an African Community. Berkeley and Los Angeles: University of California Press.

Geuss, Raymond
1981   The Idea of a Critical Theory: Habermas and the Frankfurt School. Cambridge: Cambridge University Press.

Giddens, Anthony
1984   The Constitution of Society: Outline of the Theory of Structuration. Berkeley: University of California.

Gillespie, William B.
1986   Una Vida. *In* Great Pueblo Architecture of Chaco Canyon, New Mexico, by Stephen H. Lekson. Pp. 79–94. Albuquerque: University of New Mexico Press.

Gilpin, Dennis L.
2003   Chaco-Era Site Clustering and the Concept of Communities. Kiva 69(2):171–205.

Gilpin, Dennis, and Larry Benallie Jr.
2000   Juniper Cove and Early Anasazi Community Structure West of the Chuska Mountains. *In* Foundations of Anasazi Culture: The Basketmaker–Pueblo Transition. Paul F. Reed, ed. Pp. 161–174. Salt Lake City: University of Utah Press.

Gilpin, Dennis, Douglas D. Dykeman, and Paul F. Reed
1996   Anasazi Community Architecture in the Chuska Valley. Albuquerque: New Mexico Archaeological Council.

Gilpin, Dennis, and David E. Purcell
2000   Peach Springs Revisited: Surface Recording and Excavation on the South Chaco Slope, New Mexico. *In* Great House Communities across the Chacoan Landscape.

John Kantner and Nancy Mahoney, eds. Pp. 28–38. Anthropological Papers 65. Tucson: University of Arizona Press.

Gladwin, Harold S.
1945 The Chaco Branch: Excavations at White Mound and in the Red Mesa Valley. Medallion Papers 33. Globe, AZ: Gila Pueblo.

Gosden, Chris
1994 Social Being and Time. Oxford: Blackwell Publishing.

Gregory, Herbert E.
1916 The Navajo Country: A Geographic and Hydrographic Reconnaissance of Parts of Arizona, New Mexico, and Utah. United States Geologic Survey, Water Supply Paper 380, Washington DC.

Habermas, Jürgen
1976 Legitimation Crisis. London: Heinemann.

Halbwachs, Maurice
1975 Les Cadres Sociaux de la Mémoire. New York: Arno.
[1925]
1992 On Collective Memory, with an introduction by L. A. Coser, ed. and trans.
[1950] Chicago: University of Chicago Press.

Hamilakis, Yannis, Mark Pluciennik, and Sarah Tarlow, eds.
2002 Thinking through the Body: Archaeologies of Corporeality. New York: Kluwer/Plenum Publishers.

Hancock, Patricia M.
1990 Division of Conservation Archaeology Report no. 1871. Farmington, NM: San Juan County Museum Association.

Harper, Randy, Marilyn K. Swift, Barbara J. Mills, James Brandi, and Joseph C. Winter
1988 The Casamero and Pierre's Outliers Survey: An Archaeological Class III Inventory of the BLM Lands Surrounding the Outliers. Albuquerque: Office of Contract Archeology, University of New Mexico.

Harriman, Ray G., and Janet L. McVickar
1996 LA 80422: Aquila Caserio. In Investigations at an Early Anasazi Community in the Tohatchi Flats. Janet L. McVickar, ed. Pp. 3-1 to 3-221. Pipeline Archaeology 1990–1993: The El Paso Natural Gas North System Expansion Project, New Mexico and Arizona, 7. Western Cultural Resource Management Report F074. Farmington, NM: Western Cultural Resource Management, Inc.

Harrington, John
1916 The Ethnography of the Tewa Indians. In 29th Annual Report of the Bureau of American Ethnology for the Years 1907–1908. Pp. 29–636. Smithsonian Institution. Washington DC: GPO.

Harry, Karen G.
2005 Ceramic Specialization and Agricultural Marginality: Do Ethnographic Models Explain the Development of Specialized Pottery Production in the Prehistoric American Southwest? American Antiquity 70(2):295–319.

Hartung, Horst
1981 Monte Albán in the Valley of Oaxaca. In Mesoamerican Sites and World-views: A Conference at Dumbarton Oaks, October 16 and 17, 1976. Elizabeth P. Benson, ed. Pp. 41–70. Washington DC: Dumbarton Oaks Research Library and Collections.

Harvey, David
1989 The Condition of Postmodernity. Oxford: Blackwell Publishing.
1996 Justice, Nature, and the Geography of Difference. Oxford: Blackwell Publishing.

Hawley, Florence M.
1934 The Significance of the Dated Prehistory of Chetro Ketl, Chaco Canyon, New Mexico. Monographs of the School of American Research 2. Santa Fe, NM: SAR Press.
1938 The Family Tree of Chaco Canyon Masonry. American Antiquity 3(3):247–255.

Hayes, Alden C.
1964 The Archaeological Survey of Wetherill Mesa. Archaeological Research Series 7A. Washington DC: National Park Service, Department of the Interior.
1981 A Survey of Chaco Canyon Archaeology. In Archaeological Surveys of Chaco Canyon, New Mexico. Alden C. Hayes, David M. Brugge, and W. James Judge, eds. Pp. 1–68. Albuquerque: University of New Mexico Press.

Hayes, Alden C., David M. Brugge, and W. James Judge
1981 Archaeological Surveys of Chaco Canyon, New Mexico. Albuquerque: University of New Mexico Press.

Hayes, Alden C., and Thomas C. Windes
1975 An Anasazi Shrine in Chaco Canyon. In Papers in Honor of Florence Hawley Ellis. Theodore R. Frisbie, ed. Pp. 143–156. Papers of the Archaeological Society of New Mexico 2. Santa Fe: Archaeological Society of New Mexico.

Heidegger, Martin
1962 Being and Time. J. Macquarrie and E. Robinson, trans. Oxford: Blackwell Publishing.

Heitman, Carolyn, and Stephen Plog
2005 Kinship and the Dynamics of the House. In A Catalyst for Ideas: Anthropological Archaeology and the Legacy of Douglas Schwartz. Vernon L. Scarborough, ed. Pp. 69–100. School of American Research. Santa Fe, NM: SAR Press.

Herr, Sarah A.
1994 Great Kivas as Integrative Architecture in the Silver Creek Community, Arizona. M.A. thesis, University of Arizona.

2001   Beyond Chaco: Great Kiva Communities on the Mogollon Rim Frontier. Anthropological Papers 66. Tucson: University of Arizona Press.

Hewett, Edgar Lee
1905   Prehistoric Irrigation in the Navajo Desert. Records of the Past, vol. 4, pp. 325–329. Washington DC: Records of the Past Exploration Society.
1921   The Excavation of Chettro Kettle, Chaco Canyon, 1920. Art and Archaeology 11(1-2):45–58.
1922   The Chaco Canyon in 1921. Art and Archaeology 14(3):115–131.
1936   The Chaco Canyon and Its Monuments. School of American Research. Albuquerque: University of New Mexico Press; Santa Fe, NM: SAR Press.

Heyden, Doris
1981   Caves, Gods, and Myths: World-view and Planning in Teotihuacán. *In* Mesoamerican Sites and World-views: A Conference at Dumbarton Oaks, October 16 and 17, 1976. Elizabeth P. Benson, ed. Pp. 1–39. Washington DC: Dumbarton Oaks Research Library and Collections.

Hibben, Frank C.
1975   Kiva Art of the Anasazi at Pottery Mound. Las Vegas, NV: KC Publications.

Hieb, Louis A.
1979   Hopi World View. *In* Southwest. Alfonso Ortiz, ed. Pp. 577–580. Handbook of North American Indians, vol. 9, William C. Sturtevant, general ed. Washington DC: Smithsonian Press.

Hillier, Bill, and Julienne Hanson
1984   The Social Logic of Space. Cambridge: Cambridge University Press.

Himpele, Jeffrey
2003   The Gran Poder and the Social Movement of the Aymara Middle Class: A Video Essay. Visual Anthropology 14(2-3):207–244.

Hirsch, Eric, and Michael O'Hanlon, eds.
1995   The Anthropology of Landscape: Perspectives on Place and Space. Oxford: Clarendon Press.

Hodder, Ian, and Clive Orton
1976   Spatial Analysis in Archaeology. Cambridge: Cambridge University Press.

Holsinger, Stephan J.
1901   Report on Prehistoric Ruins of Chaco Canyon National Monument. Unpublished MS, General Land Office Letter "P," National Archives, Washington DC.

Houston, Stephen, and Karl Taube
2000   An Archaeology of the Senses: Perception and Cultural Experience in Ancient Mesoamerica. Cambridge Archaeological Journal 10(2):261–294.

Hurst, Winston B.
2000   Chaco Outlier or Backwoods Pretender? A Provincial Great House at Edge of the Cedars Ruin, Utah. *In* Great House Communities across the Chacoan Landscape. John Kantner and Nancy Mahoney, eds. Pp. 63–78. Anthropological Papers 65. Tucson: University of Arizona Press.

Ingold, Tim
1993   The Temporality of the Landscape. World Archaeology 25(2):152–174.

Irwin-Williams, Cynthia, Rex Adams, Paddy C. Johnson, M. Ann Bennett, E. Pierre Morenon, and Gordon Alan Davis
1975   Salmon Ruin Archaeological Investigations. Archaeological Completion Report 8. Washington DC: Division of Grants, Office of Archaeological and Historic Preservation, National Park Service, Department of the Interior.

Irwin-Williams, Cynthia, and Larry L. Baker, eds.
1991   Anasazi Puebloan Adaptation in Response to Climatic Stress, Prehistory of the Middle Rio Puerco Valley. Albuquerque, NM: Bureau of Land Management.

Irwin-Williams, Cynthia, and Phillip H. Shelley, eds.
1980   Investigations at the Salmon Site: The Structure of Chacoan Society in the Northern Southwest. Portales: Eastern New Mexico University Printing Services.

Jackson, J. B.
1984   Discovering the Vernacular Landscape. New Haven, CT: Yale University Press.

Jackson, William H.
1878   Report on the Ancient Ruins Examined in 1875 and 1877: Ruins of the Chaco Canyon, Examined in 1877. *In* United States Geological and Geographical Survey of the Territories, Embracing Colorado and Parts of Adjacent Territories. F. V. Hayden, ed. Pp. 411–450. Tenth Annual Report, 1876. Washington DC: GPO.

Jacobson, LouAnn
1984   Chipped Stone in the San Juan Basin: A Distributional Analysis. M.A. thesis, University of New Mexico.

Jalbert, Joseph P., and Catherine M. Cameron
2000   Chacoan and Local Influences in Three Great House Communities in the Northern San Juan Region. *In* Great House Communities across the Chacoan Landscape. John Kantner and Nancy Mahoney, eds. Pp. 79–90. Anthropological Papers 65. Tucson: University of Arizona Press.

Jeancon, Jean A.
1922   Archaeological Research in the Northeastern San Juan Basin during the Summer of 1921. The State Historical and Natural History Society of Colorado and the University of Denver.

Jeancon, Jean A., and Frank H. H. Roberts Jr.
1923   Further Archaeological Research in the Northeastern San Juan Basin of Colorado. The Colorado Magazine 1(1):3–10.

1924 Further Archaeological Research in the Northeastern San Juan Basin of Colorado during the Summer of 1922. The Colorado Magazine 1(2):65–70; 1(3):108–118; 1(4):163–173; 1(5):213–224; 1(6):260–276; 1(7):302–307.

Johnson, C. David
2003 Mesa Verde Region Towers: A View from Above. Kiva 68(4):323–340.

Johnson, Gregory A.
1982 Organizational Structure and Scalar Stress. In Theory and Explanation in Archaeology: The Southhampton Conference. Colin Renfrew, Michael Rowlands, and B. Segraves, eds. Pp. 389–421. New York: Academic Press.
1989 Dynamics of Southwest Prehistory—Far Outside, Looking In. In Dynamics of Southwest Prehistory. Linda S. Cordell and George J. Gumerman, eds. Pp. 371–389. Washington DC: Smithsonian Press.

Joyce, Rosemary
2003 Concrete Memories: Fragments of the Past in the Classic Maya Present. In Archaeologies of Memory. Ruth M. Van Dyke and Susan E. Alcock, eds. Pp. 104–125. Oxford: Blackwell Publishers.

Joyce, Rosemary, and Susan Gillespie, eds.
2000 Beyond Kinship: Social and Material Reproduction in House Societies. Philadelphia: University of Pennsylvania Press.

Judd, Neil M.
1922 Archaeological Investigations at Pueblo Bonito, New Mexico. Smithsonian Miscellaneous Collections 72(15):106–117. Washington DC: Smithsonian Institution.
1924 Two Chaco Canyon Pithouses. Annual Report of the Smithsonian Institution, 1922. Pp. 399–413. Washington DC: Smithsonian Institution.
1925 Everyday Life in Pueblo Bonito. National Geographic Magazine 58(3):227–262.
1927 The Architectural Evolution of Pueblo Bonito. Proceedings of the National Academy of Sciences 13(7):561–563.
1954 The Material Culture of Pueblo Bonito. Smithsonian Miscellaneous Collections 124. Washington DC: Smithsonian Institution.
1959 Pueblo del Arroyo, Chaco Canyon, New Mexico. Smithsonian Miscellaneous Collections 138(1). Washington DC: Smithsonian Institution.
1964 The Architecture of Pueblo Bonito. Smithsonian Miscellaneous Collections 147(1). Washington DC: Smithsonian Institution.

Judge, W. James
1979 The Development of a Complex Cultural Ecosystem in the Chaco Basin, New Mexico. In Proceedings of the First Conference on Scientific Research in the National Parks 3. Robert M. Linn, ed. Pp. 901–906. Washington DC: GPO.
1989 Chaco Canyon–San Juan Basin. In Dynamics of Southwest Prehistory. Linda S. Cordell and George J. Gumerman, eds. Pp. 209–261. Washington DC: Smithsonian Press.

1991 Chaco: Current Views of Prehistory and the Regional System. *In* Chaco and Hohokam: Prehistoric Regional Systems in the American Southwest. Patricia L. Crown and W. James Judge, eds. Pp. 11–30. School of American Research. Santa Fe, NM: SAR Press.

Judge, W. James, William B. Gillespie, Stephen H. Lekson, and H. Wolcott Toll
1981 Tenth-Century Developments in Chaco Canyon. *In* Collected Papers in Honor of Erik Kellerman Reed. Papers of the Archaeological Society of New Mexico 6. Albuquerque, NM: Archaeological Society of New Mexico Press.

Kane, Allen E.
1986 Prehistory of the Dolores River Valley. *In* Dolores Archaeological Program: Final Synthetic Report. David A. Breternitz, Christine K. Robinson, and G. Timothy Gross, comps. Pp. 353–435. Denver: Bureau of Reclamation, Department of the Interior.

Kantner, John
1996 Political Competition among the Chaco Anasazi of the American Southwest. Journal of Anthropological Archaeology 15(1):41–105.
1997 Ancient Roads, Modern Mapping. Expedition 39(3):49–51.
2003a Rethinking Chaco as a System. Kiva 69(2):207–227.

Kantner, John, ed.
2003b The Chaco World. Theme issue, Kiva 69(2).

Kantner, John, and Ronald Hobgood
2003 Digital Technologies and Prehistoric Landscapes in the American Southwest. *In* The Reconstruction of Archaeological Landscapes through Digital Technologies. Maurizio Forte, P. Ryan Williams, and James Wiseman, eds. Pp. 117–123. Oxford: Archaeopress.

Kantner, John, and Nancy Mahoney, eds.
2000 Great House Communities across the Chacoan Landscape. Anthropological Papers 65. Tucson: University of Arizona Press.

Kearns, Timothy M., ed.
1996 Investigations at Whirlwind Lake: An Anasazi Community in the Southern Chuska Valley. Pipeline Archaeology, 1990–1993: The El Paso Natural Gas North System Expansion Project, New Mexico and Arizona, vol. III (draft report). Farmington, NM: Western Cultural Resource Management, Inc.

Kearns, Timothy M., Janet L. McVickar, and Lori Stephens Reed
2000 The Early to Late Basketmaker III Transition in Tohatchi Flats, New Mexico. *In* Foundations of Anasazi Culture: The Basketmaker–Pueblo Transition. Paul F. Reed, ed. Pp. 115–142. Salt Lake City: University of Utah Press.

Kelley, Vincent C.
1950 Tectonics of the San Juan Basin. *In* Guidebook of the San Juan Basin, New Mexico and Colorado. Vincent C. Kelley, E. C. Beaumont, and Caswell Silver, eds. Pp. 124–131. Socorro: New Mexico Geological Society.

Kelly, John D., and Martha Kaplan
1990 History, Structure, and Ritual. Annual Review of Anthropology 19:119–150.

Kendrick, James W., and W. James Judge
2000 Household Economic Autonomy and Great House Development in the Lowry Area. *In* Great House Communities across the Chacoan Landscape. John Kantner and Nancy Mahoney, eds. Pp. 111–129. Anthropological Papers 65. Tucson: University of Arizona Press.

Kidder, Alfred V.
1962 An Introduction to the Study of Southwestern Archaeology with a Preliminary
[1924] Account of the Excavations at Pecos. Papers of the Southwest Expedition 1. Reprint, New Haven, CT: Yale University Press.

Kincaid, Chris, ed.
1983 Chaco Roads Project, Phase I: A Reappraisal of Prehistoric Roads in the San Juan Basin. Albuquerque, NM: Bureau of Land Management.

Kincaid, Chris, John R. Stein, and Daisy F. Levine
1983 Road Verification Summary. *In* Chaco Roads Project, Phase I: A Reappraisal of Prehistoric Roads in the San Juan Basin. Chris Kincaid, ed. Pp. 9/1–9/77. Albuquerque, NM: Bureau of Land Management.

King, Anthony
2004 Escaping Corruption: Conceptual Metaphor in Mesa Verde Towers. Undergraduate senior paper on file, Department of Anthropology, Colorado College, Colorado Springs.

King, Thomas F.
2003 Places That Count: Traditional Cultural Properties in Cultural Resource Management. Walnut Creek, CA: AltaMira Press.

King, Valerie C.
2003 The Organization of Production of Chuska Gray Ware Ceramics for Distribution and Consumption in Chaco Canyon, New Mexico. Ph.D. dissertation, University of New Mexico; University of Michigan Dissertation Services, Ann Arbor.

Kintigh, Keith W.
1994 Chaco, Communal Architecture, and Cibolan Aggregation. *In* The Ancient Southwestern Community: Models and Methods for the Study of Prehistoric Social Organization. Wirt H. Wills and Robert D. Leonard, eds. Pp. 131–140. Albuquerque: University of New Mexico Press.

Kluckhohn, Clyde
1939 Discussion. *In* Preliminary Report on the 1937 Excavations: Bc50-51, Chaco Canyon, New Mexico. Clyde Kluckhohn and Paul Reiter, eds. Pp. 151–162. University of New Mexico Bulletin 345. Anthropological Series, vol. 3, no. 2. Albuquerque: University of New Mexico Press.

Kluckhohn, Clyde, and Paul Reiter, eds.
1939   Preliminary Report on the 1937 Excavations: Bc50-51, Chaco Canyon, New Mexico. University of New Mexico Bulletin 345. Anthropological Series, vol. 3, no. 2. Albuquerque: University of New Mexico Press.

Kohler, Timothy A.
1992   Field Houses, Villages, and the Tragedy of the Commons in the Early Northern Anasazi Southwest. American Antiquity 57(4):617–635.

Küchler, Susanne
1993   Landscape as Memory: The Mapping of Process and Its Representation in a Melanesian Society. *In* Landscape: Politics and Perspectives. Barbara Bender, ed. Pp. 85–106. Oxford, UK, and Providence, RI: Berg Publishers

Kuckelman, Kristin
1988   Excavations at Masa Negra Pueblo (Site 5MT4477), A Pueblo I/Pueblo II Habitation. *In* Dolores Archaeological Program: Anasazi Communities at Dolores: McPhee Village. A. E. Kane and C. K. Robinson, comps. Pp. 405–555. Denver: Bureau of Reclamation, Department of the Interior.
2002   Thirteenth-Century Warfare in the Central Mesa Verde Region. *In* Seeking the Center Place: Archaeology and Ancient Communities in the Mesa Verde Region. Mark D. Varien and Richard H. Wilshusen, eds. Pp. 233–253. Salt Lake City: University of Utah Press.

Kus, Susan
1992   Toward an Archaeology of Body and Soul. *In* Representations in Archaeology. J.-C. Gardin and C. S. Peebles, eds. Pp. 168–177. Bloomington: Indiana University Press.

Kuwanwisiwma, Leigh
2004   Yupköyvi: The Hopi Story of Chaco Canyon. *In* In Search of Chaco: New Approaches to an Archaeological Enigma. David Grant Noble, ed. Pp. 41–47. School of American Research. Santa Fe, NM: SAR Press.

Kuwanwisiwma, Leigh, and T. J. Ferguson
2004   Ang Kuktota—Hopi Ancestral Sites and Cultural Landscapes. Expedition 46(2):2, 429.

Ladd, Edmund J.
1979   Zuni Social and Political Organization. *In* Handbook of North American Indians, vol. 9. William C. Sturtevant, general ed. Pp. 482–491. Washington DC: Smithsonian Press.
1983   Zuni Religion and Philosophy. Exploration:26–31.

Lancaster, James A., and Philip F. Van Cleave
1954   Excavations of the Sun Point Pueblo. *In* Archaeological Excavations in Mesa Verde National Park, Colorado, 1950, by James A. Lancaster, Jean M. Pinkley, Philip Van Cleave, and Don Watson. Pp. 88–111. National Park Service Archeological Research 2. Washington DC: National Park Service.

Lange, Charles H.
1959   Cochiti: A New Mexico Pueblo, Past and Present. Austin: University of Texas Press.

Lawrence, Denise L., and Setha M. Low
1990   The Built Environment and Spatial Form. Annual Review of Anthropology 19:453–505.

LeBlanc, Steven A.
1999   Prehistoric Warfare in the American Southwest. Salt Lake City: University of Utah Press.

Lechtman, Heather
1977   Style in Technology—Some Early Thoughts. *In* Material Culture, Styles, Organization, and Dynamics of Technology. Heather Lechtman and R. Merrill, eds. Pp. 3–20. New York: West Publishing.

Lefebvre, Henri
1991   The Production of Space. Donald Nicholson-Smith, trans. Oxford: Blackwell Publishing.

Leinau, Alice
1934   Sanctuaries in the Ancient Pueblo of Chetro Ketl. M.A. thesis, University of New Mexico. Unpublished MS, Chaco Center Archives, National Park Service and University of New Mexico, Albuquerque.

Lekson, Stephen H.
1986   Great Pueblo Architecture of Chaco Canyon, New Mexico. Albuquerque: University of New Mexico Press.
1988a   The Idea of the Kiva in Anasazi Archaeology. Kiva 53(3):213–234.
1988b   Sociopolitical Complexity at Chaco Canyon, New Mexico. Ph.D. dissertation, University of New Mexico.
1991   Settlement Patterns and the Chaco Region. *In* Chaco and Hohokam: Prehistoric Regional Systems in the American Southwest. Patricia L. Crown and W. James Judge, eds. Pp. 31–55. School of American Research. Santa Fe, NM: SAR Press.
1999   The Chaco Meridian: Centers of Political Power in the Ancient Southwest. Walnut Creek, CA: AltaMira Press.
2002a   Sky Determines. Paper presented at the 101st Annual Meeting of the American Anthropological Association, New Orleans, November 22.
2002b   War in the Southwest, War in the World. American Antiquity 67(4):607–624.

Lekson, Stephen H., ed.
1983   The Architecture and Dendrochronology of Chetro Ketl, Chaco Canyon, New Mexico. Reports of the Chaco Center 6. Albuquerque, NM: Division of Cultural Research, National Park Service.
2006   The Archaeology of Chaco Canyon: An Eleventh-Century Regional Center. School of American Research. Santa Fe, NM: SAR Press.
2007   The Architecture of Chaco Canyon, New Mexico. Salt Lake City: University of Utah Press.

Lekson, Stephen H., and Catherine M. Cameron
1995   The Abandonment of Chaco Canyon, the Mesa Verde Migrations, and the Reorganization of the Pueblo World. Journal of Anthropological Archaeology 14(2):184–202.

Lekson, Stephen H., Thomas C. Windes, and Peter J. McKenna
2006   Architecture. In The Archaeology of Chaco Canyon: An Eleventh-Century Regional Center. Stephen H. Lekson, ed. Pp. 67–116. School of American Research. Santa Fe, NM: SAR Press.

Lekson, Stephen H., Thomas C. Windes, John R. Stein, and W. James Judge
1988   The Chaco Canyon Community. Scientific American 256(7):100–109.

Lemonnier, Pierre
1986   The Study of Material Culture Today: Toward an Anthropology of Technical Systems. Journal of Anthropological Archaeology 5(2):147–186.

Leone, Mark P.
1988   The Georgian Order as the Order of Merchant Capitalism in Annapolis, Maryland. In The Recovery of Meaning. Mark P. Leone and Parker B. Potter, eds. Pp. 235–262. Washington DC: Smithsonian Press.

LeTourneau, Philippe D.
1997   Sources and Prehistoric Use of Black-Spotted Yellowish Brown Chert in West-Central New Mexico. Paper presented at the 62nd Annual Meeting of the Society for American Archaeology, Nashville, TN, April 5.

Levy, Jerrold E.
1992   Orayvi Revisited: Social Stratification in an "Egalitarian" Society. School of American Research. Santa Fe, NM: SAR Press.

Lightfoot, Ricky R.
1988   Roofing an Early Anasazi Great Kiva. Kiva 53(3):253–272.
1994   The Duckfoot Site, vol. 2: Archaeology of the House and Household. Crow Canyon Archaeological Center Occasional Paper 4. Cortez, CO: Crow Canyon Archaeological Center.

Lightfoot, Ricky R., and Kristin A. Kuckelman
2001   A Case of Warfare in the Mesa Verde Region. In Deadly Landscapes: Case Studies in Prehistoric Southwestern Warfare. Glen E. Rice and Steven A. LeBlanc, eds. Pp. 51–64. Salt Lake City: University of Utah Press.

Linford, Laurance D.
2000   Navajo Places: History, Legend, Landscape. Salt Lake City: University of Utah Press.

Lipe, William D.
1989   Social Scale of Mesa Verde Anasazi Kivas. In The Architecture of Social Integration in Prehistoric Pueblos. William D. Lipe and Michelle Hegmon, eds. Pp. 53–71.

Crow Canyon Archaeological Center Occasional Paper 1. Cortez, CO: Crow Canyon Archaeological Center.

Lipe, William D., Timothy A. Kohler, Mark D. Varien, J. Neal Morris, and Ricky Lightfoot
1988   Synthesis. *In* Dolores Archaeological Program: Anasazi Communities at Dolores: Grass Mesa Village. William D. Lipe, J. Neal Morris, and Timothy A. Kohler, eds. Pp. 1213–1276. Denver: US Department of the Interior, Bureau of Reclamation.

Lister, Robert H., and Florence C. Lister
1981   Chaco Canyon Archaeology and Archaeologists. Albuquerque: University of New Mexico Press.

Loebig, Douglas E.
2000   Red Willow Hamlet. *In* Excavations in the Northern Tohatchi Flats. Pipeline Archaeology, 1990–1993: The El Paso Natural Gas North System Expansion Project, New Mexico and Arizona, vol. V, book 2 of 3, chapter 5. Stephen W. Yost, ed. Western Cultural Resource Management Report F074. Farmington, NM: Western Cultural Resource Management, Inc.

Loebig, Douglas E., Stephen W. Yost, and Ruth M. Van Dyke
2000   Flowing Well Hamlet. *In* Excavations in the Northern Tohatchi Flats. Pipeline Archaeology, 1990–1993: The El Paso Natural Gas North System Expansion Project, New Mexico and Arizona, vol. V, book 2 of 3, chapter 4. Stephen W. Yost, ed. Western Cultural Resource Management Report F074. Farmington, NM: Western Cultural Resource Management, Inc.

Lomatewama, Ramson
1993   Drifting through Ancestor Dreams: New and Selected Poems. Flagstaff, AZ: Northland Publishing.

Low, Setha, and Denise Lawrence-Zúñiga, eds.
2003   The Anthropology of Space and Place: Locating Culture. Oxford: Blackwell Publishing.

Lowenthal, David
1985   The Past Is a Foreign Country. Cambridge: Cambridge University Press.

Luhrs, Dorothy
1935   The Excavation of Kin Nahazbas, Chaco Cañon, New Mexico. Unpublished MS, Chaco Center Archives, National Park Service and University of New Mexico, Albuquerque.

Lyons, Patrick D.
2003   Ancestral Hopi Migrations. University of Arizona Anthropology Series 68. Tucson: University of Arizona Press.

Lyons, Thomas R., and James I. Ebert, eds.
1978   Remote Sensing and Non-destructive Archaeology. Albuquerque, NM: National Park Service.

Lyons, Thomas R., and Robert K. Hitchcock
1977   Remote Sensing Interpretation of an Anasazi Land Route System. *In* Aerial Remote Sensing Techniques in Archaeology. Thomas R. Lyons and Robert K. Hitchcock, eds. Pp. 111–134. Reports of the Chaco Center 2. Albuquerque: National Park Service and University of New Mexico.

Mahoney, Nancy
2000   Redefining the Scale of Chacoan Communities. *In* Great House Communities across the Chacoan Landscape. John Kantner and Nancy Mahoney, eds. Pp. 17–27. Anthropological Papers 65. Tucson: University of Arizona Press.

Malville, J. McKim
1990   The Astronomy of Chimney Rock. Pagosa Springs, CO: Chimney Rock Interpretive Program, San Juan Mountains Association.

Malville, J. McKim, ed.
2004   Chimney Rock: The Ultimate Outlier. Lanham, MD: Lexington Books.

Malville, J. McKim, Frank W. Eddy, and Carol Ambruster
1991   Lunar Standstills at Chimney Rock. Archaeoastronomy (supplement to Journal for the History of Astronomy) 16:S43–S50.

Marshall, Michael P.
1982   Bis sa'ani Pueblo: An Example of Late Bonito Phase Great House Architecture. *In* Bis sa'ani: A Late Bonito Phase Community on Escavada Wash, Northwest New Mexico. Cory Dale Breternitz, David E. Doyel, and Michael P. Marshall, eds. Vol. 2, Part I, pp. 169–358. Navajo Nation Papers in Anthropology 14. Window Rock, AZ: Navajo Nation Cultural Resource Management Program.
1997   The Chacoan Roads: A Cosmological Interpretation. *In* Anasazi Architecture and American Design. B. H. Morrow and V. B. Price, eds. Pp. 62–74. Albuquerque: University of New Mexico Press.

Marshall, Michael P., and Anna Sofaer
1988   Solstice Project Investigations in the Chaco District, 1984 and 1985: The Technical Report. Unpublished MS, Laboratory of Anthropology, Santa Fe, NM.

Marshall, Michael P., John R. Stein, Richard W. Loose, and J. E. Novotny
1979   Anasazi Communities of the San Juan Basin. Albuquerque: Public Service Company of New Mexico.

Martin, Paul S.
1936   Lowry Ruin in Southwestern Colorado. Field Museum of Natural History Anthropological Series, vol. 23, no. 1. Chicago: Field Museum of Natural History.

Martin, Paul S., and John B. Rinaldo
1939   Modified Basket Maker Sites: Ackmen-Lowry Area, Southwestern Colorado (1938). Field Museum of Natural History Anthropological Series, vol. 23, no. 3. Chicago: Field Museum of Natural History.

Marx, Karl, and Friedrich Engels
1939   The German Ideology. New York: International Publishers.

Mathien, Frances Joan
1992   Women of Chaco: Then and Now. *In* Rediscovering Our Past: Essays on the History of American Archaeology. J. E. Reyman, ed. Pp. 103–130. Avebury, UK: Aldershot.
2003   Artifacts from Pueblo Bonito: One Hundred Years of Interpretation. *In* Pueblo Bonito: Center of the Chacoan World. Jill E. Neitzel, ed. Pp. 127–142. Washington DC: Smithsonian Press.

Mathien, Frances Joan, and Thomas C. Windes
1988   Historic Structure Report: Kin Nahasbas Ruin, Chaco Culture National Historical Park, New Mexico. Santa Fe, NM: Branch of Cultural Research, National Park Service.

Mathien, Frances Joan, and Thomas C. Windes, eds.
1987   Investigations at the Pueblo Alto Complex, Chaco Canyon, New Mexico, 1975–1979, vol III: Artifactual and Biological Analyses. Publications in Archeology 18F, Chaco Canyon Studies. Santa Fe, NM: National Park Service.

Mayer, Martin T.
1971   Tsin Kletzin–Pueblo Bonito Stabilization Report. Chaco Culture National Historical Park, New Mexico.

McCluskey, Stephen C.
1977   The Astronomy of the Hopi Indians. Journal for the History of Astronomy 8(3):174–195.

McGuire, Randall H.
1980   The Mesoamerican Connection in the Southwest. Kiva 46(1-2):3–38.
1992   A Marxist Archaeology. New York: Academic Press.

McGuire, Randall H., E. Charles Adams, Ben A. Nelson, and Katherine A. Spielman
1994   Drawing the Southwest to Scale, Perspectives on Macroregional Relations. *In* Themes in Southwest Prehistory. George J. Gumerman, ed. Pp. 239–265. Seattle: University of Washington Press.

McGuire, Randall H., and Dean J. Saitta
1996   Although They Have Petty Captains, They Obey Them Badly: The Dialectics of Prehispanic Western Pueblo Social Organization. American Antiquity 61(2):197–216.

McGuire, Randall H., and Ruth M. Van Dyke
In press Dismembering the Trope: Imagining Cannibalism in the Ancient Pueblo World. *In* Multidisciplinary Approaches to Social Violence in the Prehispanic Southwest. D. Nichols and Patricia Crown, eds. Tucson: University of Arizona Press.

McGuire, Randall H., and LouAnn Wurst
2003 O Where, O Where Has Ideology Gone? Paper presented at the Annual Meetings of the American Anthropological Association, Chicago, November 22.

McKenna, Peter J.
1984 Architecture and Material Culture of 29SJ1360, Chaco Canyon, New Mexico. Reports of the Chaco Center 7. Albuquerque, NM: Division of Cultural Research, National Park Service.

McKenna, Peter J., and H. Wolcott Toll
1992 Regional Patterns of Great House Development among the Totah Anasazi, New Mexico. *In* Anasazi Regional Organization and the Chaco System. David E. Doyel, ed. Maxwell Museum of Anthropology Anthropological Papers 5. Albuquerque: University of New Mexico Press.

McKenna, Peter J., and Marcia Truell
1986 Small Site Architecture of Chaco Canyon, New Mexico. Publications in Archaeology 18D. Santa Fe, NM: Division of Cultural Resources, National Park Service.

McLellan, George W.
1969 The Origin, Development, and Typology of Anasazi Kivas and Great Kivas. Ph.D. dissertation, University of Colorado; Ann Arbor: University of Michigan Publications.

McPherson, Robert S.
1992 Sacred Land, Sacred View: Navajo Perceptions of the Four Corners Region. Salt Lake City, UT: Charles Redd Center for Western Studies, Brigham Young University.

Meloy, Ellen
2002 The Anthropology of Turquoise. New York: Random House.

Merleau-Ponty, Maurice
1981 [1962] Phenomenology of Perception. C. Smith, trans. London: Routledge and Kegan Paul.

Miller, Daniel, and Christopher Tilley
1984 Ideology, Power, and Prehistory: An Introduction. *In* Ideology, Power, and Prehistory. Daniel Miller and Christopher Tilley, eds. Pp. 1–15. New Directions in Archaeology. Cambridge: Cambridge University Press.

Miller, James Marshall
1937 The Great Kivas of Chetro Ketl. M.A. thesis, University of Southern California. Unpublished MS, Chaco Center Archives, National Park Service and University of New Mexico, Albuquerque.

Mills, Barbara J.
1988 Chronological, Distributional and Functional Analyses of the Ceramic Assemblages from the Casamero and Pierre's Outliers. *In* The Casamero and

          Pierre's Outliers Survey: An Archaeological Class III Inventory of the BLM Lands Surrounding the Outliers. Randy A. Harper, Marilyn K. Swift, Barbara Mills, James Brandi, and Joseph C. Winter, eds. Pp. 59–98. Albuquerque: Office of Contract Archeology, University of New Mexico.
2002   Recent Research on Chaco: Changing Views on Economy, Ritual, and Power. Journal of Archaeological Research 10(1):65–117.
n.d.   Remembering While Forgetting: Depositional Practices and Social Memory at Chaco. In Memory Work: Archaeologies of Material Practices. Barbara J. Mills and William H. Walker, eds. School of American Research. Santa Fe, NM: SAR Press.

Mills, Barbara J., Andrea Carpenter, and William Grimm
1997   Sourcing Chuskan Ceramic Production: Petrographic and Experimental Approaches. Kiva 62(3):261–282.

Mindeleff, Victor
1989   A Study of Pueblo Architecture in Tusayan and Cibola. Washington DC:
[1891] Smithsonian Institution Press.

Momaday, N. Scott
1976   The Names. New York: Harper and Row.

Moore, Jerry D.
1996   Architecture and Power in the Ancient Andes: The Archaeology of Public Buildings. Cambridge: Cambridge University Press.

Moore, Sally F., and Barbara G. Myerhoff
1977   Introduction: Secular Ritual Forms and Meanings. In Secular Ritual. Sally F. Moore and Barbara G. Myerhoff, eds. Pp. 3–24. Amsterdam: Van Gorcum.

Morenon, Pierre E., and Ben Amick
1977   Summary of Energy Study Results in Chaco Canyon National Monument. Fort Burgwin Research Center, Southern Methodist University. Unpublished MS, Division of Cultural Research, National Park Service, Albuquerque, NM.

Morphy, Howard
1993   Colonialism, History, and the Construction of Place: The Politics of Landscape in Northern Australia. In Landscape: Politics and Perspectives. Barbara Bender, ed. Pp. 205–243. Oxford, UK, and Providence, RI: Berg.

Morris, Don, and David W. Kayser
1966   Ruins Stabilization of New Alto, Chaco Canyon National Monument, New Mexico. Globe, AZ: Ruins Stabilization Unit, National Park Service, Arizona Archaeological Center.

Morris, Earl H.
1915   The Excavation of a Ruin near Aztec, San Juan County, New Mexico. American Anthropologist 17(4):666–684.
1919   The Aztec Ruin. Anthropological Papers, vol. 26, Part I. New York: American Museum of Natural History.

1921	The House of the Great Kiva at the Aztec Ruin. Anthropological Papers, vol. 26, Part II. New York: American Museum of Natural History.
1924	Burials in the Aztec Ruin. Anthropological Papers, vol. 26, Parts III and IV. Pp. 139–225. New York: American Museum of Natural History.
1928	Notes on Excavations in the Aztec Ruin. Anthropological Papers, vol. 26, Part IV. New York: American Museum of Natural History.
1939	Archaeological Studies in the La Plata District: Southwestern Colorado and Northwestern New Mexico. Carnegie Institution of Washington Publication 519. Washington DC: Carnegie Institution.

Morris, Elizabeth Ann

1959	A Pueblo I Site near Bennett's Peak, Northwestern New Mexico. El Palacio 66(5):169–175.
1980	Basketmaker Caves in the Prayer Rock District, Northeastern Arizona. Anthropological Papers 35. Tucson: University of Arizona Press.

Morrison, C. C.

1876	Executive and Descriptive Report of Lieutenant C. C. Morrison, Sixth Cavalry, on the Operation of Party No. 2, Colorado Section, Field Session 1875, Appendix E. *In* Annual Report upon the Geographical Surveys West of the One-Hundredth Meridian, in California, Nevada, Utah, Colorado, Wyoming, New Mexico, Arizona and Montana, Being Appendix JJ of the Annual Report of the Chief of Engineers for 1876, by George M. Wheeler. Pp. 136–147. Washington DC: GPO.

Neitzel, Jill E.

1999	Examining Societal Organization in the Southwest: An Application of Multiscalar Analysis. *In* Great Towns and Regional Polities in the Prehistoric American Southwest and Southeast. Jill E. Neitzel, ed. Pp. 183–214. Albuquerque: University of New Mexico; Dragoon, AZ: Amerind Foundation.
2003a	Artifact Distributions at Pueblo Bonito. *In* Pueblo Bonito: Center of the Chacoan World. Jill E. Neitzel, ed. Pp. 107–126. Washington DC: Smithsonian Press.
2003b	The Organization, Function, and Population of Pueblo Bonito. *In* Pueblo Bonito: Center of the Chacoan World. Jill E. Neitzel, ed. Pp. 143–150. Washington DC: Smithsonian Press.

Nelson, Ben A.

1995	Complexity, Hierarchy and Scale: A Controlled Comparison between Chaco Canyon, New Mexico, and La Quemada, Zacatecas. American Antiquity 60(4):597–618.

Nelson, Ben A., Debra L. Martin, Alan C. Swedlund, Paul R. Fish, and George J. Armelagos

1994	Studies in Disruption: Demography and Health in the Prehistoric American Southwest. *In* Understanding Complexity in the Prehistoric Southwest. George Gumerman and Murray Gell-Mann, eds. Pp. 59–112. SFI Studies in the Sciences of Complexity 16. Reading, MA: Addison-Wesley.

Nials, Fred L.
1983   Physical Characteristics of Chacoan Roads. *In* Chaco Roads Project, Phase I. A Reappraisal of Prehistoric Roads in the San Juan Basin, 1983. Chris Kincaid, ed. Pp. 6-1 to 6-51. Albuquerque and Santa Fe, NM: Bureau of Land Management.

Nials, Fred, John Stein, and John Roney
1987   Chacoan Roads in the Southern Periphery: Results of Phase II of the BLM Chaco Roads Project. Albuquerque, NM: Bureau of Land Management.

Nietzche, Friedrich
1968   The Will to Power. Walter Kaufmann and R. J. Hollingdale, trans. New York: Random House.

Noble, David Grant, ed.
2004   In Search of Chaco: New Approaches to an Archaeological Enigma. School of American Research. Santa Fe, NM: SAR Press.

Obenauf, Margaret Senter
1980   The Chacoan Roadway System. M.A. thesis, University of New Mexico.
1983   Evaluation of Aerial Photography. *In* Chaco Roads Project, Phase I: A Reappraisal of Prehistoric Roads in the San Juan Basin. Chris Kincaid, ed. Pp. 4/1–4/21. Albuquerque, NM: Bureau of Land Management.
1991   Photointerpretation of Chacoan Roads. *In* Ancient Road Networks and Settlement Hierarchies in the New World. Charles D. Trombold, ed. Pp. 31–41. Cambridge: Cambridge University Press.

O'Bryan, Deric
1950   Excavations in Mesa Verde National Park, 1947–1948. Medallion Papers 39. Globe, AZ: Gila Pueblo.

O'Donovan, Maria
2002   New Perspectives on Site Function and Scale of Cerro de Trincheras, Sonora, Mexico: The 1991 Surface Survey. Arizona State Museum Archaeological Series 195. Tucson: University of Arizona Press.

Orcutt, Janet D., Eric Blinman, and Timothy A. Kohler
1990   Explanations of Population Aggregation in the Mesa Verde Region prior to AD 900. *In* Perspectives on Southwestern Prehistory. Paul E. Minnis and Charles L. Redman, eds. Pp. 196–212. Boulder, CO: Westview Press.

Ortiz, Alfonso
1965   Dual Organization as an Operational Concept in the Pueblo Southwest. Ethnology 4(4):389–396.
1969   The Tewa World: Space, Time, Being, and Becoming in a Pueblo Society. Chicago: University of Chicago Press.
1972   Ritual Drama and the Pueblo Worldview. *In* New Perspectives on the Pueblos. Alfonso Ortiz, ed. Pp. 135–161. Albuquerque: University of New Mexico Press.

Ortiz, Simon J.
1994   What We See: A Perspective on Chaco Canyon and Its Ancestry. *In* Chaco Canyon: A Center and Its World, by Mary Peck, Stephen H. Lekson, John R. Stein, and Simon J. Ortiz. Pp. 65–72. Santa Fe: Museum of New Mexico Press.
2002   Out There Somewhere. Tucson: University of Arizona Press.

Palkovich, Ann M.
1984   Disease and Mortality Patterns in the Burial Rooms of Pueblo Bonito: Preliminary Considerations. *In* Recent Research on Chaco Prehistory. W. James Judge and John D. Schelberg, eds. Pp. 103–113. Reports of the Chaco Center 8. Albuquerque, NM: National Park Service.

Palmer, Jay W.
1994   Copper Bells from Anasazi Sites. Blue Mountain Shadows 13:44–45.

Palmer, Jay W., M. G. Hollander, P. S. Z. Rogers, R. M. Benjamin, C. J. Duffy, J. B. Lambert, and J. A. Brown
1998   Pre-Columbian Metallurgy: Technology, Manufacture, and Microprobe Analyses of Copper Bells from the Greater Southwest. Archaeometry 40(2):361–382.

Papalexandrou, Amy
2003   Memory Tattered and Torn: Spolia in the Heartland of Byzantine Hellenism. *In* Archaeologies of Memory. Ruth M. Van Dyke and Susan E. Alcock, eds. Pp. 56–80. Oxford: Blackwell Publishing.

Parsons, Elsie Clews
1925   The Pueblo of Jemez. Papers of the Phillips Academy Southwestern Expedition 3. New Haven, CT: Yale University Press.
1939   Pueblo Indian Religion. Chicago: University of Chicago Press.

Pauketat, Timothy R.
2000   The Tragedy of the Commoners. *In* Agency in Archaeology. Marcia-Anne Dobres and John Robb, eds. Pp. 113–129. London: Routledge.

Peckham, Stewart L.
1958   Salvage Archaeology in New Mexico, 1957–1958: A Partial Report. El Palacio 65(5):161–164.
1969   An Archaeological Site Inventory of New Mexico, Part I. Unpublished MS, Laboratory of Anthropology, Museum of New Mexico, Santa Fe.

Pepper, George H.
1909   The Exploration of a Burial Room in Pueblo Bonito, New Mexico. *In* Anthropological Essays Presented to Frederick Ward Putnam in Honor of His Seventieth Birthday. Pp. 196–252. New York: G. E. Stechert and Company.
1920   Pueblo Bonito. Anthropological Papers, vol. 27. Washington DC: American Museum of Natural History.

Pierson, Lloyd M.
1949   The Prehistoric Population of Chaco Canyon, New Mexico: A Study in Methods

and Techniques of Prehistoric Population Estimation. M.A. thesis, University of New Mexico.

Pippin, Lonnie C.
1987   Prehistory and Paleoecology of Guadalupe Ruin, New Mexico. Anthropological Papers 107. Salt Lake City: University of Utah Press.

Plog, Fred, and Walter K. Wait, eds.
1982   The San Juan Tomorrow: Planning for the Conservation of Cultural Resources in the San Juan Basin. Santa Fe, NM: National Park Service, Southwest Region, in cooperation with the School of American Research.

Powers, Robert P.
1984   Regional Interaction in the San Juan Basin: The Chacoan Outlier System. In Recent Research on Chaco Prehistory. W. James Judge and John D. Schelberg, eds. Pp. 23–36. Reports of the Chaco Center 8. Albuquerque, NM: Division of Cultural Research, National Park Service.

Powers, Robert P., William B. Gillespie, and Stephen H. Lekson
1983   The Outlier Survey: A Regional View of Settlement in the San Juan Basin. Reports of the Chaco Center 3. Albuquerque, NM: National Park Service, Department of the Interior.

Proper, Michael J.
1997   Standing at the Foot of Guadalupe Ruin: Eleanor Site (ENM 883). M.A. thesis, Eastern New Mexico University, Portales.

Reed, Paul F.
2000   Fundamental Issues in Basketmaker Archaeology. In Foundations of Anasazi Culture: The Basketmaker–Pueblo Transition. Paul F. Reed, ed. Pp. 3–16. Salt Lake City: University of Utah Press.
2006a Salmon Pueblo: Chacoan Outlier and Thirteenth-Century Middle San Juan Community Center. In Thirty-Five Years of Archaeological Research at Salmon Ruins, New Mexico. Paul F. Reed, ed. Pp. 367–376. Tucson, AZ: Center for Desert Archaeology; Bloomfield, NM: Salmon Ruins Museum.

Reed, Paul F., ed.
2006b Thirty-Five Years of Archaeological Research at Salmon Ruins, New Mexico. Tucson, AZ: Center for Desert Archaeology; Bloomfield, NM: Salmon Ruins Museum.

Reed, Paul F., and Kathy N. Hensler, eds.
1999   Anasazi Community Development in Redrock Valley: Archaeological Excavations along the N33 Road in Apache County, Arizona. Navajo Nation Papers in Archaeology 33. Window Rock, AZ: Navajo Nation Archaeology Department.

Reed, Paul F., and Scott Wilcox
2000   Distinctive and Intensive: The Basketmaker III to Early Pueblo I Occupation of Cove-Redrock Valley, Northeastern Arizona. In Foundations of Anasazi Culture: The Basketmaker–Pueblo Transition. Paul F. Reed, ed. Pp. 69–93. Salt Lake City: University of Utah Press.

Reiter, Paul
1933   The Ancient Pueblo of Chetro Ketl. M.A. thesis, University of New Mexico.

Renfrew, Colin
2001   Production and Consumption in a Sacred Economy: The Material Correlates of High Devotional Expression at Chaco Canyon. American Antiquity 66(1):14–25.

Renfrew, Colin, and John F. Cherry, eds.
1986   Peer Polity Interaction and Socio-political Change. Cambridge: Cambridge University Press.

Reyman, Jonathan E.
1985   A Reevaluation of Bi-wall and Tri-wall Structures in the Anasazi Area. In Contributions to the Archaeology and Ethnohistory of Greater Mesoamerica. William J. Folan, ed. Pp. 293–333. Carbondale: Center for Archaeological Investigations, Southern Illinois University.

Riley, Carroll L.
1950   "Defensive" Structures in the Hovenweep Monument. El Palacio 57(11):339–344.

Roberts, Frank H. H., Jr.
1922   Report on the Work of the 1922 Season in the Piedra Parada Archaeological Field. University of Denver Bulletin 23(9).
1926–   Unpublished field notes, compiled and typed by Tom Windes in January 1978.
1927   Chaco Archives, University of New Mexico, Albuquerque.
1927   The Ceramic Sequence in the Chaco Canyon, New Mexico, and Its Relation to the Cultures of the San Juan Basin. Ph.D. dissertation, Harvard University.
1929   Shabik'eshchee Village: A Late Basket Maker Site in the Chaco Canyon, New Mexico. Bureau of American Ethnology Bulletin 92. Smithsonian Institution. Washington DC: GPO.
1932   The Village of the Great Kivas on the Zuni Reservation, New Mexico. Bureau of American Ethnology Bulletin 111. Smithsonian Institution. Washington DC: GPO.
1938   Chaco Canyon Masonry. American Antiquity 4(1):60–61.
1939   Archaeological Remains in the Whitewater District, Eastern Arizona, Part I: House Types. Bureau of American Ethnology Bulletin 121. Smithsonian Institution. Washington DC: GPO.

Robins, Michael R., and Kelley Hays-Gilpin
2000   The Bird in the Basket: Gender and Social Change in Basketmaker Iconography. In Foundations of Anasazi Culture: The Basketmaker–Pueblo Transition. Paul F. Reed, ed. Pp. 231–247. Salt Lake City: University of Utah Press.

Robinson, Tucker, Ruth M. Van Dyke, and Thomas C. Windes
2007   Shrines and Great House Intervisibility across the Chacoan Landscape. Poster presented at the 72nd Annual Meeting of the Society for American Archaeology, Austin, TX, April 27.

Robinson, William J., Bruce G. Harrill, and Richard L. Warren
1974   Tree-Ring Dates from New Mexico B: Chaco-Gobernador Area. Tucson: Laboratory of Tree-Ring Research, University of Arizona.

Rodman, Margaret C.
1992 Empowering Place: Multilocality and Multivocality. American Anthropologist 94(3):640–656.

Rohn, Arthur H.
1971 Mug House, Mesa Verde National Park, Colorado. Archeological Research Series 7-D, Wetherill Mesa Excavations. Washington DC: National Park Service.
1975 A Stockaded Basketmaker III Village at Yellow Jacket, Colorado. Kiva 40(3):113–119.

Roler, Kathy
1999 The Chaco Phenomenon: A Faunal Perspective from the Peripheries. Ph.D. dissertation, Arizona State University; University of Michigan Dissertation Services, Ann Arbor.

Roney, John R.
1992 Prehistoric Roads and Regional Integration in the Chacoan System. *In* Anasazi Regional Organization and the Chaco System. David E. Doyel, ed. Pp. 123–132. Maxwell Museum of Anthropology Anthropological Papers 5. Albuquerque: University of New Mexico Press.

Rowlands, Michael
1993 The Role of Memory in the Transmission of Culture. World Archaeology 25(2):141–151.

Roys, Lawrence
1936 Masonry of Lowry Ruin and of the Southwest. *In* Lowry Ruin in Southwestern Colorado, by Paul S. Martin. Pp. 115–142. Field Museum of Natural History. Anthropology 23(1). Chicago: Field Museum of Natural History.

Saitta, Dean
1994 The Political Economy and Ideology of Early Population Aggregation in Togeye Canyon, AD 1150–1250. *In* Exploring Social, Political, and Economic Organization in the Zuni Region. Todd L. Howell and Tammy Stone, eds. Pp. 47–60. Anthropological Research Papers 46. Tempe: Arizona State University.
1997 Power, Labor, and the Dynamics of Change in Chacoan Political Economy. American Antiquity 62(1):7–26.
1999 Prestige, Agency, and Change in Middle-Range Societies. *In* Material Symbols: Culture and Economy in Prehistory. John Robb, ed. Pp. 135–149. Center for Archaeological Investigations Occasional Paper 26. Carbondale: Southern Illinois University.

Schachner, Gregson
2001 Ritual Control and Transformation in Middle-Range Societies: An Example from the American Southwest. Journal of Anthropological Archaeology 20(2):168–194.

Schama, Simon
1996 Landscape and Memory. New York: Vintage Books.

Schelberg, John D.
1982 Economic and Social Development as an Adaptation to a Marginal Environment in Chaco Canyon, New Mexico. Ph.D. dissertation, Northwestern University.
1984 Analogy, Complexity, and Regionally Based Perspectives. *In* Recent Research on Chaco Prehistory. W. James Judge and John D. Schelberg, eds. Pp. 5–21. Reports of the Chaco Center 8. Albuquerque, NM: Division of Cultural Research, National Park Service.

Schulman, Albert
1949 Pre-Columbian Towers in the Southwest. American Antiquity 15(4):288–297.

Schwartz, Douglas W.
1984 Foreword. *In* New Light on Chaco Canyon. David Grant Noble, ed. Pp. ix–xi. School of American Research. Santa Fe, NM: SAR Press.

Sebastian, Lynne
1985 Archaeological Excavation along the Turquoise Trail: The Mitigation Program. Albuquerque: Office of Contract Archeology, University of New Mexico.
1992 The Chaco Anasazi: Sociopolitical Evolution in the Prehistoric Southwest. Cambridge: Cambridge University Press.

Sebastian, Lynne, and Jeffrey H. Altschul
2002 Settlement Pattern, Site Typology, and Demographic Analyses: The Anasazi, Archaic, and Unknown Sites. *In* An Archeological Survey of the Additions to Chaco Culture National Historic Park. Ruth M. Van Dyke and Robert Powers, eds. Unpublished MS, Chaco Center Publications in Archaeology, National Park Service, Santa Fe, NM, and Chaco Culture National Historic Park, Nageezi, NM.

Sever, Thomas L., and David W. Wagner
1991 Analysis of Prehistoric Roadways in Chaco Canyon Using Remotely Sensed Digital Data. *In* Ancient Road Networks and Settlement Hierarchies in the New World. Charles D. Trombold, ed. Pp. 42–53. Cambridge: Cambridge University Press.

Sharma, J. C.
1992 Temples of Champa in Vietnam. Nhà Xuất Bản Khoa Học Xã Hội, Hà Nội.

Shepard, Anna O.
1954 Rebuttal. *In* The Material Culture of Pueblo Bonito, by Neil M. Judd. Pp. 236–238. Smithsonian Miscellaneous Collections 124. Washington DC: Smithsonian Institution.

Shiner, Joel
1959 Stabilization of Wijiji, 1959. Globe, AZ: National Park Service Regional Stabilization Unit.

Sigleo, Anne C.
1981 Casamero: A Chacoan Site in the Red Mesa Valley, New Mexico. Unpublished MS, Chaco Center, National Park Service, Albuquerque, NM.

Sinclair, Rolf M., Anna Sofaer, and J. J. McCann Jr.
1987   Marking of Lunar Major Standstill at the Three-Slab Site on Fajada Butte. Bulletin of the American Astronomical Society 19:1043.

Smith, Adam T.
2000   Rendering the Political Aesthetic: Political Legitimacy in Urartian Representations of the Built Environment. Journal of Anthropological Archaeology 19(2):131–163.
2003   The Political Landscape: Constellations of Authority in Early Complex Polities. Berkeley and Los Angeles: University of California Press.

Smith, Watson
1952   Kiva Mural Decorations at Awatovi and Kawaika'a, with a Survey of Other Wall Paintings in the Pueblo Southwest. Papers of the Peabody Museum 38. Cambridge, MA: Harvard University.
1972   Prehistoric Kivas of Antelope Mesa, Northeastern Arizona. Papers of the Peabody Museum 39. P. 120. Cambridge, MA: Harvard University.
1990   When Is a Kiva? And Other Questions about Southwestern Archaeology. Tucson: University of Arizona Press.

Snead, James E., and Robert W. Preucel
1999   The Ideology of Settlement: Ancestral Keres Landscapes in the Northern Rio Grande. In Archaeologies of Landscape: Contemporary Perspectives. Wendy Ashmore and A. Bernard Knapp, eds. Pp. 169–197. Oxford: Blackwell Publishing.

Snygg, John, and Thomas C. Windes
1998   Long, Wide Roads and Great Kiva Roofs. Kiva 64(1):7–25.

Sofaer, Anna
1997   The Primary Architecture of the Chacoan Culture: A Cosmological Expression. In Anasazi Architecture and American Design. Baker H. Morrow and V. B. Price, eds. Pp. 88–132. Albuquerque: University of New Mexico Press.
1999   The Mystery of Chaco Canyon. Oley, PA: Bullfrog Films.

Sofaer, Anna, Michael P. Marshall, and Rolf M. Sinclair
1989   The Great North Road: A Cosmographic Expression of the Chaco Culture of New Mexico. In World Archaeoastronomy in the New World. Anthony F. Aveni, ed. Pp. 365–376. Cambridge: Cambridge University Press.

Sofaer, Anna, and Rolf Sinclair
1987   Astronomical Markings at Three Sites on Fajada Butte. In Astronomy and Ceremony in the Prehistoric Southwest. John B. Carlson and W. James Judge, eds. Pp. 43–70. Maxwell Museum of Anthropology Anthropological Papers 2. Albuquerque, NM: University of New Mexico Press.

Sofaer, Anna, Rolf Sinclair, and L. Doggett
1982   Lunar Markings on Fajada Butte, Chaco Canyon, New Mexico. In Archaeoastronomy in the New World. Anthony F. Aveni, ed. Pp. 169–181. Cambridge: Cambridge University Press.

Sofaer, Anna, V. Zinser, and Rolf Sinclair
1979   A Unique Solar Marking Construct. Science 206(4416):283–291.

Soja, Edward W.
1980   The Socio-spatial Dialectic. Annals of the Association of American Geographers 70:207–225.
1988   Postmodern Geographies: The Reassertion of Space in Critical Social Theory. New York: Verso.
1996   Thirdspace. Oxford: Blackwell Publishing.

Stein, John R.
1983   Road Corridor Descriptions. In Chaco Roads Project, Phase I: A Reappraisal of Prehistoric Roads in the San Juan Basin. Chris Kincaid, ed. Pp. 8/1–8/15. Albuquerque, NM: Bureau of Land Management.
1987   Architecture and Landscape. In An Archaeological Reconnaissance of West-Central New Mexico: The Anasazi Monuments Project. Andrew Fowler, John Stein, and Roger Anyon, eds. Pp. 71–103. Unpublished MS, New Mexico State Historic Preservation Division, Santa Fe.

Stein, John R., Dabney Ford, and Richard Friedman
2003   Reconstructing Pueblo Bonito. In Pueblo Bonito: Center of the Chacoan World. Jill E. Neitzel, ed. Pp. 33–60. Washington DC: Smithsonian Press.

Stein, John R., and Stephen H. Lekson
1992   Anasazi Ritual Landscapes. In Anasazi Regional Organization and the Chaco System. David Doyel, ed. Pp. 87–100. Maxwell Museum of Anthropology Anthropological Papers 5. Albuquerque: University of New Mexico Press.
1994   Anasazi Ritual Landscapes. In Chaco Canyon: A Center and Its World, by Mary Peck, Stephen H. Lekson, John R. Stein, and Simon J. Ortiz. Pp. 45–64. Santa Fe: Museum of New Mexico Press.

Stein, John R., and Peter J. McKenna
1988   An Archaeological Reconnaissance of a Late Bonito Phase Occupation near Aztec Ruins National Monument, New Mexico. Santa Fe, NM: National Park Service.

Stein, John R., and John Roney
1987   Appendix II: An Inventory of Sites Significant to the Study of Chacoan Roads in the Southern San Juan Basin. In Chacoan Roads in the Southern Periphery: Results of Phase II of the BLM Chaco Roads Project by Fred Nials, John Stein, and John Roney. Pp. 142–210. Cultural Resources 1. Albuquerque: New Mexico Bureau of Land Management.

Stein, John R., Judith E. Suiter, and Dabney Ford
1997   High Noon in Old Bonito: Sun, Shadow, and the Geometry of the Chaco Complex. In Anasazi Architecture and American Design. Baker H. Morrow and V. B. Price, eds. Pp. 133–148. Albuquerque: University of New Mexico Press.

Stevenson, Mathilda Coxe
1894   The Sia. Bureau of American Ethnology 11th Annual Report. Pp. 3–157.

Smithsonian Institution. Washington DC: GPO.
1904 The Zuni Indians. Bureau of American Ethnology 23rd Annual Report. Pp. 3–634. Smithsonian Institution. Washington DC: GPO.

Steward, Julian M.
1937 Ecological Aspects of Southwestern Society. Anthropos 32:87–104.
1955 Theory of Cultural Change. Urbana: University of Illinois Press.

Stirling, Matthew W.
1942 Origin Myth of Acoma and Other Records. Bureau of American Ethnology Bulletin 135. Smithsonian Institution. Washington DC: GPO.

Stodder, A. L. W.
1989 Bioarcheological Research in the Basin and Range Region. *In* Human Adaptations and Cultural Change in the Greater Southwest, by Alan H. Simmons, A. L. W. Stodder, Douglas D. Dykeman, and P. A. Hicke. Pp. 167–190. Arkansas Archeological Survey Research Series 32. Wrightsville, AR: Arkansas Archeological Survey.

Stuart, David E.
2000 Anasazi America: Seventeen Centuries on the Road from Center Place. Albuquerque: University of New Mexico Press.

Stuart, David E., and Rory P. Gauthier
1981 Prehistoric New Mexico: Background for Survey. Santa Fe, NM: Historic Preservation Bureau.

Swentzell, Rina
1992 Pueblo Space, Form, and Mythology. *In* Pueblo Style and Regional Architecture. Nicholas C. Markovich, Wolfgang F. E. Preiser, and Fred G. Sturm, eds. Pp. 23–30. New York: Van Nostrand Reinhold.

Taçon, Paul
1999 Identifying Ancient Sacred Landscapes in Australia: From Physical to Social. *In* Archaeologies of Landscape: Contemporary Perspectives. Wendy Ashmore and A. Bernard Knapp, eds. Pp. 33–57. Oxford: Blackwell Publishing.

Taussig, Michael
1993 Mimesis and Alterity. New York: Routledge.

Tedlock, Barbara
1983 Zuni Sacred Theater. American Indian Quarterly 7(3):93–110.

Thomas, Julian
1991 Rethinking the Neolithic. Cambridge: Cambridge University Press.
1993 The Politics of Vision and the Archaeologies of Landscape. *In* Landscape: Politics and Perspectives. Barbara Bender, ed. Pp. 19–48. Oxford, UK, and Providence, RI: Berg.
1996 Time, Culture, and Identity. London: Routledge.

Till, Jonathan
2001 Chacoan Roads and Road-Associated Sites in the Lower San Juan Region: Assessing the Role of Chacoan Influences in the Northwestern Periphery. M.A. thesis, University of Colorado.

Tilley, Christopher
1994 A Phenomenology of Landscape. Oxford, UK, and Providence, RI: Berg.
1999 Metaphor and Material Culture. Oxford: Blackwell Publishing.

Toll, H. Wolcott
1984 Trends in Ceramic Import and Distribution in Chaco Canyon. *In* Recent Research on Chaco Prehistory. W. James Judge and John D. Schelberg, eds. Pp. 115–135. Reports of the Chaco Center 8. Albuquerque, NM: National Park Service.
1985 Pottery, Production, and the Chacoan Anasazi System. Ph.D. dissertation, University of Colorado; University Microfilms, Ann Arbor, MI.
2001 Making and Breaking Pots in the Chaco World. American Antiquity 66(1):56–78.
2006 Organization of Production. *In* The Archaeology of Chaco Canyon: An Eleventh-Century Regional Center. Stephen H. Lekson, ed. Pp. 117–151. School of American Research. Santa Fe, NM: SAR Press.
n.d. The La Plata, the Totah, and the Chaco: Variations on a Theme. *In* Chaco's Northern Prodigies: Salmon, Aztec, and the Ascendancy of the Middle San Juan Region after AD 1100. Paul Reed, ed. Salt Lake City: University of Utah Press.

Toll, H. Wolcott, and C. Dean Wilson
2000 Locational, Architectural, and Ceramic Trends in the Basketmaker III Occupation of the La Plata Valley, New Mexico. *In* Foundations of Anasazi Culture: The Basketmaker–Pueblo Transition. Paul F. Reed, ed. Pp. 19–43. Salt Lake City: University of Utah Press.

Toll, H. Wolcott, Thomas C. Windes, and Peter J. McKenna
1980 Late Ceramic Patterns in Chaco Canyon: The Pragmatics of Modeling Ceramic Exchange. *In* Models and Methods in Regional Exchange. Robert E. Fry, ed. Pp. 95–118. Society for American Archaeology Papers 1. Washington DC: Society for American Archaeology.

Trigger, Bruce G.
1990 Monumental Architecture: A Thermodynamic Explanation of Symbolic Behavior. World Archaeology 22(2):119–132.

Truell, Marcia
1986 Part II: A Summary of Small Site Architecture in Chaco Canyon, New Mexico. *In* Small Site Architecture of Chaco Canyon, New Mexico, by Peter J. McKenna and Marcia Truell. Pp. 115–508. Publications in Archaeology 18D. Santa Fe, NM: Division of Cultural Resources, National Park Service.

Tuan, Yi-Fu
1974 Topophilia. Englewood Cliffs, NJ: Prentice-Hall.
1977 Space and Place: The Perspective of Experience. Minneapolis: University of Minnesota Press.

Turner, Christy G., II, and Jacqueline Turner
1999   Man Corn: Cannibalism and Violence in the Prehistoric American Southwest. Salt Lake City: University of Utah Press.

Turner, Victor W.
1967   The Forest of Symbols: Aspects of Ndembu Ritual. Ithaca, NY: Cornell University Press.

Tuwaletstiwa, Phillip
2000   Poovolli's Dream. Unpublished MS in possession of author, Kykotsmovi, AR.

Ucko, Peter, and Robert Layton, eds.
1998   The Archaeology and Anthropology of Landscape: Shaping Your Landscape. London: Routledge.

Van Dyke, Ruth M.
1996   Space and Power at Chacoan Outlier Communities. Paper presented at the 61st Annual Meeting of the Society for American Archaeology, New Orleans, April 13.
1997a   The Andrews Great House Community: A Ceramic Chronometric Perspective. Kiva 63(2):137–154.
1997b   Tracking the Trachyte Boundary: A Southern Perspective on Exchange and Interaction among Chacoan Communities. Paper presented in "Southwestern Archaeology: Chaco, Hohokam, and Beyond" at the 62nd Annual Meeting of the Society for American Archaeology, Nashville, TN, April 4.
1998   The Chaco Connection: Bonito-Style Architecture in Outlier Communities. Ph.D. dissertation, University of Arizona; University of Michigan Dissertation Services, Ann Arbor.
1999a   The Andrews Community: An Early Bonito Phase Chacoan Outlier in the Red Mesa Valley, New Mexico. Journal of Field Archaeology 26(1):55–67.
1999b   The Chaco Connection: Evaluating Bonito-Style Architecture in Outlier Communities. Journal of Anthropological Archaeology 18(4):471–506.
1999c   A Space Syntax Analysis of Guadalupe Ruin. American Antiquity 64(3):461–473.
2000   Chacoan Ritual Landscapes: The View from the Red Mesa Valley. In Great House Communities across the Chacoan Landscape. John Kantner and Nancy Mahoney, eds. Pp. 91–100. Anthropological Papers 65. Tucson: University of Arizona Press.
2001   Andrews Community Archaeological Research Project, 1999–2000. Report prepared for the BLM, Albuquerque, and the State of New Mexico, Santa Fe. Unpublished MS, NMCRIS Project 65869, Laboratory of Anthropology, Santa Fe, NM.
2002   The Chacoan Great Kiva in Outlier Communities: Investigating Integrative Spaces across the San Juan Basin. Kiva 67(3):231–248.
2003a   Bounding Chaco: Assessing Great House Architectural Variability across Time and Space. Kiva 9(2):117–139.
2003b   Memory and the Construction of Chacoan Society. In Archaeologies of Memory. Ruth M. Van Dyke and Susan E. Alcock, eds. Pp. 180–200. Oxford: Blackwell Publishing.
2004a   Chaco's Sacred Geography. In In Search of Chaco: New Approaches to an Archaeological Enigma. David Grant Noble, ed. Pp. 78–85. School of American Research. Santa Fe, NM: SAR Press.

2004b   Memory, Meaning, and Masonry: The Late Bonito Chacoan Landscape. American Antiquity 69(3):413–431.

2007   Great Kivas in Time, Space, and Society. *In* The Architecture of Chaco Canyon, New Mexico. Stephen H. Lekson, ed. Pp. 93–126. Salt Lake City: University of Utah Press.

n.d.   Sacred Landscapes: The Chaco–Totah Connection. *In* Chaco's Northern Prodigies: Salmon, Aztec, and the Ascendancy of the Middle San Juan Region after AD 1100. Paul Reed, ed. Salt Lake City: University of Utah Press.

Van Dyke, Ruth M., and Susan E. Alcock

2003   Archaeologies of Memory: An Introduction. *In* Archaeologies of Memory. Ruth M. Van Dyke and Susan E. Alcock, eds. Pp. 1–13. Oxford: Blackwell Publishing.

Van Dyke, Ruth M., Lauren Ciborowski, and Kellam Throgmorton

2004   Colorado College Survey of the Painted Hand Environs, Fall 2002: Canyons of the Ancients National Monument, Montezuma County, Colorado. Report prepared for the BLM, Denver, and Canyons of the Ancients National Monument, Dolores, CO. Unpublished MS, Anasazi Heritage Center, Dolores.

Van Dyke, Ruth M., and Robert Powers, eds.

2002   An Archaeological Survey of the Additions to Chaco Culture National Historic Park. Unpublished MS, Chaco Center Publications in Archaeology, National Park Service, Santa Fe, NM, and Chaco Culture National Historic Park, Nageezi, NM.

Van Dyke, Ruth M., and Kellam Throgmorton

2006   Colorado College Archaeological Survey of the Lightning Tree Tower Area, Canyons of the Ancients National Monument, Montezuma County, Colorado. Report prepared for the BLM, Denver, and Canyons of the Ancients National Monument, Dolores, CO. Unpublished MS, Anasazi Heritage Center, Dolores.

Varien, Mark D.

1999   Sedentism and Mobility in a Social Landscape. Tucson: University of Arizona Press.

Varien, Mark D., and Ricky Lightfoot

1989   Ritual and Nonritual Activities in Mesa Verde Region Pit Structures. *In* The Architecture of Social Integration in Prehistoric Pueblos. William D. Lipe and Michelle Hegmon, eds. Pp. 73–88. Crow Canyon Archaeological Center Occasional Paper 1. Cortez, CO: Crow Canyon Archaeological Center.

Vivian, R. Gordon

1940   New Rooms and Kiva Found in Pueblo Bonito. Southwestern Monuments Report suppl. (February):127–130.

1947   Ruins Stabilization, Chaco Canyon National Monument, Pueblo Alto (New Alto), 1947. Globe, AZ: National Park Service Mobile Unit, Southwestern National Monuments.

1959   The Hubbard Site and Other Tri-Wall Structures in New Mexico and Colorado. Archaeological Research Series 5. Washington DC: National Park Service, Department of the Interior.

Vivian, R. Gordon, and Tom W. Mathews
1965   Kin Kletso: A Pueblo III Community in Chaco Canyon, New Mexico. Southwest Monuments Association Technical Series 6, Part 1. Globe, AZ: Southwest Monuments Association.

Vivian, R. Gordon, and Paul Reiter
1960   The Great Kivas of Chaco Canyon and Their Relationships. Monographs of the School of American Research and the Museum of New Mexico 22. Santa Fe: SAR Press.

Vivian, R. Gwinn
1972   Prehistoric Water Conservation in Chaco Canyon. Final technical report to the National Science Foundation, grant no. GS-3100, Washington DC.
1983   Identifying and Interpreting Chacoan Roads: An Historical Perspective. In Chaco Roads Project, Phase I: A Reappraisal of Prehistoric Roads in the San Juan Basin. Chris Kincaid, ed. Pp. 3/1–3/18. Albuquerque, NM: Bureau of Land Management.
1989   Kluckhohn Reappraised: The Chacoan System as Egalitarian Enterprise. Journal of Anthropological Research 45(1):101–113.
1990   The Chacoan Prehistory of the San Juan Basin. New York: Academic Press.
1997a Chacoan Roads: Function. Kiva 63(1):35–67.
1997b Chacoan Roads: Morphology. Kiva 63(1):7–34.
2000   Basketmaker Archaeology at the Millennium: New Answers to Old Questions. In Foundations of Anasazi Culture: The Basketmaker–Pueblo Transition. Paul F. Reed, ed. Pp. 251–257. Salt Lake City: University of Utah Press.

Vivian, R. Gwinn, Dulce N. Dodgen, and Gayle Harrison Hartmann
1978   Wooden Ritual Artifacts from Chaco Canyon, New Mexico: The Chetro Ketl Collection. Anthropological Papers 32. Tucson: University of Arizona Press.

Vivian, R. Gwinn, Carla R. Van West, Jeffrey S. Dean, Nancy Akins, Mollie Toll, and Thomas C. Windes
2006   Chaco Ecology and Economy. In The Archaeology of Chaco Canyon: An Eleventh-Century Regional Center. Stephen H. Lekson, ed. Pp. 45–66. School of American Research. Santa Fe, NM: SAR Press.

Voll, Charles B., and Martin T. Mayer
1964   1964 Stabilization of Casa Chiquita Ruin, Chaco Canyon National Monument, New Mexico. Unpublished MS, National Park Service Western Archaeological and Conservation Center, Tucson, AZ.

Wagstaff, J. M.
1987   The New Archaeology and Geography. In Landscape and Culture: Geographical and Archaeological Perspectives. J. M. Wagstaff, ed. Pp. 26–36. Oxford: Blackwell Publishing.

Walker, William H.
2002   Stratigraphy and Practical Reason. American Anthropologist 104(1):159–177.

Ward, Christine
2004   Exploring Meanings of Chacoan Community Great Houses through Chipped Stone: A Biographical Approach. Ph.D. dissertation, University of Colorado; University of Michigan Dissertation Services, Ann Arbor.

Ware, John A.
2001   Chaco Social Organization: A Peripheral View. *In* Chaco Society and Polity: Papers from the 1999 Conference. Linda S. Cordell, W. James Judge, and June-el Piper, eds. Pp. 79–93. New Mexico Archaeological Council Special Publication 4. Albuquerque: New Mexico Archaeological Council.
2002   What Is a Kiva? The Social Organization of Early Pueblo Communities. *In* Culture and Environment in the American Southwest: Essays in Honor of Robert C. Euler. David A. Phillips Jr. and John A. Ware, eds. Pp. 79–88. Anthropological Research Papers 8. Phoenix: SWCA.

Ware, John A., and George J. Gumerman
1977   Remote Sensing Methodology and the Chaco Canyon Prehistoric Road System. *In* Aerial Remote Sensing Techniques in Archaeology. Thomas R. Lyons and Robert K. Hitchcock, eds. Pp. 135–167. Reports of the Chaco Center 2. Albuquerque: National Park Service and University of New Mexico.

Warren, A. Helene
1967   Petrographic Analyses of Pottery and Lithics. *In* An Archaeological Survey of the Chuska Valley and the Chaco Plateau, New Mexico, by Arthur H. Harris, James Schoenwetter, and A. Helene Warren. Pp. 104–134. Museum of New Mexico Research Records 4. Albuquerque: Museum of New Mexico.
1977   Geology and Mineral Resources of the White Rock Canyon and the Cochiti Area, Sandoval County, New Mexico. *In* Archeological Investigations in Cochiti Reservoir, New Mexico, vol. 1. Jan V. Biella and R. C. Chapman, eds. Pp. 15–30. Albuquerque: Office of Contract Archeology, University of New Mexico.

Washburn, Dorothy
1974   Nearest Neighbor Analysis of Pueblo I–II Settlement Patterns along the Rio Puerco of the East, New Mexico. American Antiquity 39(2):315–335.

Weber, Max
1947   The Theory of Economic and Social Organization. New York: Free Press.

Weigand, Phil C.
1994   Observations on Ancient Mining within the Northwestern Regions of the Mesoamerican Civilization, with Emphasis on Turquoise. *In* In Quest of Mineral Wealth: Aboriginal and Colonial Mining and Metallurgy in Spanish America. A. K. Craig and R. C. West, eds. Pp. 21–35. Geoscience and Man 33. Baton Rouge: Department of Geography and Anthropology, Louisiana State University.

Weigand, Phil C., and Garman Harbottle
1993   The Role of Turquoise in the Ancient Mesoamerican Trade Structure. *In* The American Southwest and Mesoamerica: Systems of Prehistoric Exchange. Jonathan E. Ericson and Timothy G. Baugh, eds. Pp. 159–177. New York: Plenum Press.

Wendorf, Fred, Nancy Fox, and Orian L. Lewis
1956   Pipeline Archaeology. Santa Fe, NM: Laboratory of Anthropology; Flagstaff: Museum of Northern Arizona.

Weslowski, L. V.
1981   Native American Land Use along Redondo Creek. *In* High-Altitude Adaptation along Redondo Creek. Craig Baker and Joseph C. Winter, eds. Albuquerque: Office of Contract Archeology, University of New Mexico.

Wheelbarger, Linda
n.d.   Puebloan Communities on the South Side of the Middle San Juan River. *In* Chaco's Northern Prodigies: Salmon, Aztec, and the Ascendancy of the Middle San Juan Region after AD 1100. Paul Reed, ed. Salt Lake City: University of Utah Press.

White, Leslie A.
1942   The Pueblo of Santa Ana, New Mexico. Memoirs of the American Anthropological Association 60. Menasha, WI: American Anthropological Association.
1960   The World of the Keresan Pueblo Indians. *In* Culture in History: Essays in Honor of Paul Radin. Stanley Diamond, ed. Pp. 53–64. New York: Columbia University Press.
1962   The Pueblo of Sia, New Mexico. Bureau of American Ethnology Bulletin 184. Smithsonian Institution. Washington DC: GPO.
1973   The Acoma Indians. Glorieta, NM: Rio Grande Press.
[1932]

Whitehouse, Harvey
1992   Memorable Religions: Transmission, Codification and Change in Divergent Melanesian Contexts. Man 27(4):777–797.

Whiteley, Peter M.
1985   Unpacking Hopi "Clans": Another Vintage Model Out of Africa? Journal of Anthropological Research 41(4):359–374.
1986   Unpacking Hopi "Clans," II: Further Questions about Hopi Descent Groups. Journal of Anthropological Research 42(1):69–79.

Whitten, Penelope
1982   Excavations at the Crawford Site: A Basketmaker III–Pueblo I Site near Crownpoint, New Mexico. Contributions to Anthropology 307. Bloomfield, NM: Division of Conservation Archaeology, San Juan County Archaeological Research Center and Library.

Wilcox, David R.
1993   The Evolution of the Chacoan Polity. *In* The Chimney Rock Archaeological Symposium. J. McKim Malville and Gary Matlock, eds. Pp. 76–90. USDA Forest Service General Technical Report RM-227.

Wilcox, David R., and Jonathan Haas
1994   The Scream of the Butterfly: Competition and Conflict in the Prehistoric Southwest. *In* Themes in Southwest Prehistory. George J. Gumerman, ed. Pp. 211–238. School of American Research. Santa Fe, NM: SAR Press.

Willey, Gordon
1953   Prehistoric Settlement Patterns in the Viru Valley, Peru. Bureau of American Ethnology Bulletin 155. Smithsonian Institution. Washington DC: GPO.

Williamson, Ray, H. J. Fisher, and D. O'Flynn
1977   Anasazi Solar Observatories. *In* Native American Astronomy. Anthony F. Aveni, ed. Pp. 203–218. Austin: University of Texas Press.

Wills, Wirt H.
2000   Political Leadership and the Construction of Chacoan Great Houses, AD 1020–1140. *In* Alternative Leadership Strategies in the Prehispanic Southwest. Barbara J. Mills, ed. Tucson: University of Arizona Press.
2001   Ritual and Mound Formation during the Bonito Phase in Chaco Canyon. American Antiquity 66(3):433–451.

Wills, Wirt H., and Thomas C. Windes
1989   Evidence for Population Aggregation and Dispersal during the Basketmaker III Period in Chaco Canyon, New Mexico. American Antiquity 54(2):347–369.

Wilshusen, Richard H.
1986   The Relationship between Abandonment Mode and Ritual Use in Pueblo I Anasazi Protokivas. Journal of Field Archaeology 13(2):245–254.
1988   Sipapus, Ceremonial Vaults, and Foot Drums (Or, A Resounding Argument for Protokivas). *In* Dolores Archaeological Program: Supporting Studies: Additive and Reductive Technologies. Eric Blinman, Carl J. Phagan, and Richard H. Wilshusen, comps. Pp. 649–671. Denver: Bureau of Reclamation, Department of the Interior.
1989   Unstuffing the Estufa: Ritual Floor Features in Anasazi Pit Structures and Pueblo Kivas. *In* The Architecture of Social Integration in Prehistoric Pueblos. William D. Lipe and Michelle Hegmon, eds. Pp. 89–111. Crow Canyon Archaeological Center Occasional Paper 1. Cortez, CO: Crow Canyon Archaeological Center.
2002   Estimating Population in the Central Mesa Verde Region. *In* Seeking the Center Place: Archaeology and Ancient Communities in the Mesa Verde Region. Mark D. Varien and Richard H. Wilshusen, eds. Pp. 101–120. Salt Lake City: University of Utah Press.

Wilshusen, Richard H., and Eric Blinman
1992   Pueblo I Village Formation: A Reevaluation of Sites Recorded by Earl Morris on Ute Mountain Ute Tribal Lands. Kiva 57(3):251–269.

Wilshusen, Richard H., and Scott G. Ortman
1999   Rethinking the Pueblo I Period in the San Juan Drainage: Aggregation, Migration, and Cultural Diversity. Kiva 64(3):369–399.

Wilshusen, Richard H., and Ruth M. Van Dyke
2006   Chaco's Beginnings. *In* The Archaeology of Chaco Canyon: An Eleventh-Century Regional Center. Stephen H. Lekson, ed. Pp. 211–259. School of American Research. Santa Fe, NM: SAR Press.

Wilshusen, Richard H., and Mark D. Varien
1996   Estimating Prehistoric Population for the Mesa Verde Region: Using New Methods to Interpret Old Data. Report submitted to the Colorado Historical Society, Denver.

Wilshusen, Richard H., and C. Dean Wilson
1995   Reformatting the Social Landscape in the Late Pueblo I–Early Pueblo II Period: The Cedar Hill Data in Regional Context. In The Cedar Hill Special Treatment Project: Late Pueblo I, Early Navajo, and Historic Occupations in Northwestern New Mexico. Richard H. Wilshusen, comp. Pp. 43–80. Research Paper 1. Dolores, CO: La Plata Archaeological Consultants.

Windes, Thomas C.
1977   Typology and Technology of Anasazi Ceramics. In Settlement and Subsistence along the Lower Chaco River: The CGP Survey. Charles A. Reher, ed. Pp. 279–370. Albuquerque: University of New Mexico Press.
1978   Stone Circles of Chaco Canyon, Northwestern New Mexico. Reports of the Chaco Center 5. Albuquerque, NM: National Park Service, Department of the Interior.
1984   A View of Cibola Whiteware from Chaco Canyon. In Regional Analysis of Prehistoric Ceramic Variation: Contemporary Studies of the Cibola Whitewares. Alan P. Sullivan and Jeffrey L. Hantman, eds. Pp. 94–119. Anthropological Research Papers 31. Tempe: Arizona State University.
1986   Pueblo Alto. In Great Pueblo Architecture of Chaco Canyon, New Mexico, by Stephen H. Lekson. Pp. 192–209. Albuquerque: University of New Mexico Press.
1987   Investigations at the Pueblo Alto Complex, Chaco Canyon, New Mexico, 1975–1979, vols. I and II, parts 1 and 2. Chaco Canyon Studies, Publications in Archeology 18F. Santa Fe, NM: National Park Service.
1991   The Prehistoric Road Network at Pueblo Alto, Chaco Canyon, New Mexico. In Ancient Road Networks and Settlement Hierarchies in the New World. Charles D. Trombold, ed. Pp. 111–131. Cambridge: Cambridge University Press.
1993   The Spadefoot Toad Site: Investigations at 29SJ 629 in Marcia's Rincon and the Fajada Gap Pueblo II Community, Chaco Canyon, New Mexico. Reports of the Chaco Center 12. Santa Fe, NM: Branch of Cultural Research, Division of Anthropology, National Park Service.
2003   This Old House: Construction and Abandonment at Pueblo Bonito. In Pueblo Bonito: Center of the Chacoan World. Jill E. Neitzel, ed. Pp. 14–32. Washington DC: Smithsonian Press.
n.d.a   Early Puebloan Occupations in the Chaco Region: Excavations and Survey of Basketmaker III and Pueblo I Sites, Chaco Canyon, New Mexico. Reports of the Chaco Center 13. Santa Fe, NM: National Park Service, Department of the Interior.
n.d.b   Sighting along the Grain: Differential Wood Use at Salmon Ruin. In Salmon Ruins: Chacoan Outlier and Thirteenth-Century Pueblo in the Middle San Juan Region. Paul F. Reed, ed. Salt Lake City: University of Utah Press.

Windes, Thomas C., Rachel M. Anderson, Brian K. Johnson, and Cheryl A. Ford
2000   Sunrise, Sunset: Sedentism and Mobility in the Chaco East Community. *In* Great House Communities across the Chacoan Landscape. John Kantner and Nancy Mahoney, eds. Pp. 39–59. Anthropological Papers 65. Tucson: University of Arizona Press.

Windes, Thomas C., and Dabney Ford
1992   The Nature of the Early Bonito Phase. *In* Anasazi Regional Organization and the Chaco System. David E. Doyel, ed. Pp. 75–86. Maxwell Museum of Anthropology Anthropological Papers 5. Albuquerque: University of New Mexico Press.
1996   The Chaco Wood Project: The Chronometric Reappraisal of Pueblo Bonito. American Antiquity 61(2):295–310.

Windes, Thomas C., and Peter J. McKenna
2001   Going against the Grain: Wood Production in Chacoan Society. American Antiquity 66(1):119–140.

Winter, Joseph C.
1981   Anasazi Agriculture at Hovenweep II: The Development and Use of Towers. Contract Abstracts and CRM Archeology 2(2):28–36. Albuquerque: University of New Mexico Press.

Woods, Janet McC.
1934   Excavation of the Court Kiva, Chetro Ketl. Unpublished MS, Chaco Center Archives, National Park Service and University of New Mexico, Albuquerque.

Woodson, Kyle M.
1999   Migrations in Late Anasazi Prehistory: The Evidence from the Goat Hill Site. Kiva 65(1):63–84.

Yoffee, Norman
1994   Memorandum to Murray Gell-Mann Concerning: The Complications of Complexity in the Prehistoric Southwest. *In* Understanding Complexity in the Prehistoric Southwest. George J. Gumerman and Murray Gell-Mann, eds. Pp. 341–358. SFI Studies in the Sciences of Complexity, XIV. Reading, MA: Addison-Wesley.
2001   The Chaco "Rituality" Revisited. *In* Chaco Society and Polity: Papers from the 1999 Conference. Linda S. Cordell, W. James Judge, and June-el Piper, eds. Pp. 63–78. New Mexico Archaeological Council Special Publication 4. Albuquerque: New Mexico Archaeological Council.

Yost, Stephen W., and Ruth M. Van Dyke
1996   Excavations at LA 82627/2509 (The Blackbird Site). *In* Investigations at Nine Sites in the Southern Tohatchi Flats and Adjacent Uplands. Pipeline Archaeology, 1990–1993: The El Paso Natural Gas North System Expansion Project, New Mexico and Arizona, vol. VIII, book 2, chapter 14. Farmington, NM: Western Cultural Resource Management, Inc.

Young, M. Jane
1988 Signs from the Ancestors: Zuni Cultural Symbolism and Perceptions of Rock Art. Albuquerque: University of New Mexico Press.

Zedeño, M. Nieves
1997 Landscapes, Land Use, and the History of Territory Formation: An Example from the Puebloan Southwest. Journal of Archaeological Method and Theory 4(1):67–103.

Zeilik, Michael
1986 The Ethnoastronomy of the Historic Pueblo: Moon Watching. Archaeoastronomy (supplement to Journal for the History of Astronomy) 17:S1–S22.

Zukin, Sharon
1991 Landscapes of Power: From Detroit to Disney World. Berkeley: University of California Press.

Index

Numbers followed by *f* indicate figures and numbers followed by *t* indicate tables.

Aboriginal Australians, 40
Acoma, 15, 47, 57, 132–33, 149
Adler, Michael A., 125
aesthetic dimensions, of ideology, 32–33
aggregation, in Pueblo I period, 70–71, 73
agriculture: and climate of Chaco Canyon, 17; and northern expansion of Chaco in Late Bonito phase, 206–207
Ah-Shi-Sle-Pah Road, 44, 145, 151, 155–57, 165, 166, 199n12
Alkali Ridge, 72–73
Allentown/Whitewater, 81*t*
Amick, Ben, 156
Andes, and monumental architecture, 118
Andrews: Bonito-style architecture and Chacoan influence on, 176, 181t, 196; earthworks and middens at, 192; and great kiva settlements of Early Bonito phase, 81*t*, 88–89, 104n11; plan of, 172*f*, 177*f*; ramp and approach to, 191; and visibility, 181*t*, 186–87, 243
Animas River, 209
Anyon, Roger, 134n11
ArcGIS, 8
archaeology: current interpretations of Chaco, 3; and history of occupation at Chaco, 17–25; history of research at Chaco, 2–3; landscapes and studies of place and social reality, 4–7, 9; and perspectives on Chacoan social and political organization, 25–35; phenomenology and interpretation of landscapes, 8, 39, 238
Archaic sites, in Chaco Canyon, 18
architecture: Chacoan ideology and Bonito-style at Chaco, 115–28, 132–33; Chacoan ideology and Bonito-style at outliers, 171, 173, 183–98; outliers and boundaries of Chacoan world, 178–83; visible landscape and monumental, 40–41. *See also* great houses; great kivas; kivas; pitstructures; plazas; shrines; stone circles; towers
art: and balanced dualism in Chacoan rock art, 245; commemorative functions of, 46; and emotional dimensions of ideology, 32–33
astronomical alignments: and cardinal directions in landscape of Chaco, 245–46; and cardinal directions in Pueblo cosmography, 53; and ceremonies at Chaco during Classic Bonito phase, 55, 108, 132. *See also* lunar movements; solstice ceremonies
Atse'e Nitsaa, 56, 234
Awatovi, 55
Aztec, 25, 149, 204*f*, 206, 208*t*, 209–13, 230–31, 235n3

balanced dualism: and Bonito-style architecture at Chaco, 115, 116, 117, 120–21, 126, 131; and Bonito-style architecture at outliers, 183, 196–97; continued importance of in post-Chacoan world, 232; and Kin Bineola in Late Bonito phase, 225; and landscape of Chaco in Late Bonito phase, 220, 223, 224; and phenomenological interpretation of Chaco landscape, 244–45; and roads, 150; and sacred geography of Chaco, 140; and Salmon Ruin in Late Bonito phase, 207; as theme in contemporary Pueblo cosmography, 53–54; and villages of Pueblo I period, 74–75
Basketmaker III period: and Early Bonito phase settlements, 92; and history of occupation of Chaco Canyon, 18; and orientation of

305

pitstructures, 116; and roots of Chaco, 63–70, 102n2; and site superposition by Pueblo II components, 192; and social memory at Classic Bonito-phase Chaco, 128; and social mobility in San Juan Basin, 62; subdivision of sites into cultural variants, 102n1
Basso, Keith, 4, 11
Bc 51 (small house), 119*t*
Bennett Peak, 15, 93, 94
Big House, 134n11
Bis sa'ani, 210
Blackbird site, 182
Black Lake, 151, 156, 157
Bloch, Maurice, 249
Bluff great house, 167n2, 172*f*, 181*t*, 191, 193
Bradley, Bruce, 122, 232
Breternitz, Cory D., 171
Brugge, David M., 103n6
Bureau of Land Management, 36n8, 145, 150, 160
burials: and elites at Pueblo Bonito, 29–30, 36n9, 107, 122; and environmental problems at end of Classic Bonito phase at Chaco, 207
Bustard, Wendy, 103n8

Cabezon Peak, 15, 96, 142, 185, 187
Candelaria. *See* Las Ventanas
cardinal directions: continued importance of in post-Chacoan world, 232; and landscape of Chaco in Late Bonito phase, 220, 223, 224; and orientation of Chacoan great houses, 116–17, 132; and phenomenological interpretation of Chacoan landscape, 245–46; as theme in contemporary Pueblo cosmography, 49–54
Casa Abajo, 79*t*
Casa Chiquita, 214*t*, 216*f*, 217, 219, 220, 223
Casa del Rio site, 80*t*
Casamero site, 172*f*, 179, 181*t*, 187, 188, 189*f*, 243
Casa Patricio, 199n13
Casa Rinconada, 123*t*, 124, 125, 126, 127*f*
Casey, Edward S., 39
Cedar Hill, 79*t*, 84
center place: and Bonito-style architecture at Chaco, 115–28, 132–33; and Bonito-style architecture at outliers, 183; decline of Chaco as in Pueblo III period, 230; Early Bonito phase and emergence of Chaco as, 98–102; and outlier communities, 144; and phenomenological interpretation of landscape at Chaco, 247–48; and ritual gatherings at Chaco during Classic Bonito phase, 106–15; and roads, 150; as theme in contemporary Pueblo cosmography, 53, 54, 57
ceramics: and Chuska-Chaco relationship, 24, 157–58, 168n6; Early Bonito phase assemblages at Chaco, 78, 82, 85–86; and Pueblo I period in San Juan Basin, 76–77; redecoration of at Chaco, 55, 56; and roads, 150
ceremonial center, emergence of Chaco as in Early Bonito phase, 99–100. *See also* center place; ritual
Chaco Canyon: Basketmaker III roots of, 63–70; Bonito-style architecture and ideology, 115–28, 183–98; and boundaries of Chacoan world, 178–83; current archaeological interpretations of, 3; description of physical landscape, 12–17; Early Bonito phase and development of proto-great houses, 78–97; Early Bonito phase and emergence of as center place, 98–102; earthworks and ideology of during Classic Bonito phase, 129–31; ethnography and interpretation of landscape, 47–60; history of archaeological research at, 2–3; landscape of during Late Bonito phase, 213–24; northern expansion in Late Bonito period, 202–13; overview of history of occupation, 17–25; perspectives on sociopolitical organization, 25–35; phenomenology and experience of landscape at, 7–9, 38–47, 237–53; Pueblo I period and origins of, 70–78; Pueblo III period and post-Chacoan world, 230–35; and ritual gatherings during Classic Bonito phase, 106–15; and roads during Classic Bonito phase, 144–64; and sacred geography during Classic Bonito phase, 140–44; topography of, 11–12; and worldview of ancestral and colonial outliers, 173–78. *See also* architecture; great houses; ideology; outlier communities; ritual; roads; social organization
Chaco Center, 26–27, 145
Chaco Digital Initiative, 10n1
Chaco Meridian, 234
Chaco Phenomenon, 22
Chaco Plateau, 12, 13–14
Chaco Project, 10n1, 63
Chaco River, as route for travel, 157–59, 166
"Chaco River Corridor," 86
Chaco Slope, 12–13

Chaco Wash, 14, 17, 35n1
Chacra Face Road, 44, 157, 163
Chacra Mesa, 14, 140, 157
Chan Chan (Chimu), 42
Cherry, John F., 42
Chetro Ketl: approach to, 154; ceremonies and exotic materials at, 108; and great kivas, 123t, 124, 125, 126, 235n8; lunar standstill and orientation of, 117, 134n9; plan of, 112f; remodeling of in Late Bonito phase, 218, 235n8; sequence of construction, 113; size of, 119t
Chimney Rock (geographic feature), 15, 110f, 176, 243
Chimney Rock site, 109–11, 172f, 176, 178, 181t, 190, 243, 246
Chimu (Peru), 42
Chuskan Mountains: ceramics and relationship with Chaco, 24, 157–58, 168n6; and Early Bonito phase ceramics in Chaco, 85–86, 99; and outlier communities, 167n3; slopes of as source of raw materials for Chaco, 24, 157–58
Classic Bonito phase, and overview of Chaco, 19–21, 339–40. *See also* architecture; great houses; ideology; outlier communities
climate, of San Juan Basin, 16–17. *See also* drought
Clys Canyon, 153
colonialism. *See* outlier communities
Companion Rock, 15, 110, 176
Coolidge, 81t
copper. *See* exotic materials
core-and-veneer masonry, and great houses, 19, 118, 179–80, 198n6, 216
corporate strategies, 30
cosmography: definition of, 241; influence of Chacoan ideology on modern Pueblo, 48; and phenomenological interpretation of Chaco landscape, 9; and roads, 148–51; themes in contemporary Pueblo, 49–59. *See also* ideology; worldview
Coyote Canyon Road, 145
Crown, Patricia, 55, 68–69, 121
Cushing, Frank H., 52
cyclical renewal: and Basketmaker III period, 69–70; and Bonito-style architecture at outliers, 191–95; continued importance of in post-Chacoan world, 232; and phenomenological interpretation of Chaco landscape, 246–47; as theme in contemporary Pueblo cosmography, 54–56. *See also* remodeling

dance, and contemporary Pueblo cosmography, 58
dating: of construction sequence at Guadalupe site, 104n10; of great kivas in Chaco, 123t; of roads, 145. *See also* dendrochronology
De Certeau, Michel, 39, 43
dendrochronology: and history of occupation of Chaco Canyon, 17–18; and lunar events at Salmon Ruin, 208; and remodeling of outliers, 192; and reuse of wood in McElmo style, 235n7
direct historical approach, 47
directionality. *See* cardinal directions
disuse, of Pueblo I pitstructures, 103n4
Dolores Archaeological Project, 35n4, 71
Doyel, David E., 171
drought, and northern expansion of Chaco in Late Bonito phase, 206. *See also* climate
dualism. *See* balanced dualism
dual processual theory, 30
Dye Brush/Dzil Nda Kai, 81t

Eagleton, Terry, 31, 32
Early Bonito phase: and emergence of Chaco as center place, 98–102; overview of Chaco during, 339–40; and rise of proto-great houses, 78–97
earthworks: and Chacoan ideology during Classic Bonito phase, 129–31, 132, 135n15; and Kin Bineola mound, 226; and outlier great houses, 191, 193, 197
East Chaco Canyon, and roads, 163–64
Eastern Pueblos, 47, 53
East Road, 44, 151, 163–64
Edge of the Cedars site, 202–203
egalitarian interpretation, of sociopolitical organization at Chaco, 26, 27
Eleanor site, 198n7
Eliot, T. S., 201
elites: and burials at Pueblo Bonito, 29–30, 36n9, 107, 122; and interpretations of sociopolitical organization at Chaco, 28–30, 250–51; and ritual gatherings at Chaco during Classic Bonito phase, 106–15. *See also* hierarchical organization; power; social organization
El Llano, 79t, 198–99n10
Ellis, Florence Hawley, 58, 227, 235n8
El Rito, 81t
emotional dimensions, of ideology, 32–33, 253
Escalon, 172f, 181t, 190–91, 199n10
Escavada Wash, 14, 15, 17

Index   307

ethnography, and phenomenological interpretation of Chacoan landscape, 47–60, 238. *See also* origin myths; Pueblo(s)
existentialism, 38
exotic materials: and burials at Pueblo Bonito, 29–30, 36n9, 107; and ceremonial paraphernalia at Chaco, 108; and Classic Bonito phase at Chaco, 25; and interpretations of sociopolitical organization of Chaco, 28, 29

Fajada Butte, 14, 142, 162, 163, 164
Fajada Gap, and roads, 162–63
faunal studies, and Chuska-Chaco relationship, 24
Feinman, Gary M., 30
Feld, Steven, 39
Ferguson, T. J., 105
Fewkes, Jesse Walter, 229
Force, Eric R., 17, 35n1, 100
Ford, Dabney, 90, 103n8, 126–27, 133n4
Ford Butte, 15, 93, 94*f*
Foucault, Michel, 27
Fowler, Andrew, 134n11, 234
Friedman, Rich, 103n8, 133n4, 134n8, 160
Fritz, John M., 116, 222

game theory, 29
geography, and archaeological studies of landscapes, 5, 6, 10n3. *See also* sacred geography; topography
geology, and physical landscape of Chaco Canyon, 12–15
Giddens, Anthony, 34
Gladwin, Harold S., 103n5
Grass Mesa Village, 74–75, 76
Great Bend, 79*t*
great houses: Chacoan ideology and Bonito-style, 116–22, 131, 141; formal approaches to, 44–45; and great kivas during Classic Bonito phase, 125–26; and Late Bonito phase in Chaco Canyon, 213–24; location of in Chaco Canyon, 23*f*; outliers and Classic Bonito architecture, 172*f*, 183–84, 197; and overview of occupation history of Chaco, 19–21; and plazas, 60n1; as public spaces during Classic Bonito phase at Chaco, 111–15; and roads, 165, 166; shrines and line-of-sight connections with, 142–43; visibility and visual impact of, 41–43, 242–43. *See also* outlier communities; Peñasco Blanco; proto-great houses; Pueblo Alto; Pueblo Bonito; Pueblo del Arroyo

great kivas: and Bonito-style architecture at outliers, 184, 198n3; and Chaco as center place in Classic Bonito phase, 122–28, 131; and Early Bonito phase in Chaco Canyon, 84, 89–91, 104n12; and outlier communities, 36n7; and overview of occupation history of Chaco, 21; and Pueblo I period, 75–76. *See also* kivas
great pitstructures, and Basketmaker III period, 35n3, 63, 67–69, 128
Guadalupe: access to, 190; avifauna and ritual practices at, 190; dating of construction sequence at, 104n10; plan of, 172*f*; and proto-great houses in Early Bonito phase, 80*t*, 88; visibility and line-of-sight networks of, 96, 181*t*, 185, 187

Halfway House, 152, 186
Hammack, Lawrence, 58
Hart, E. Richard, 105
Hawley, Florence. *See* Ellis, Florence Hawley
Hayes, Alden C., 103n6, 141–42, 221, 228–29, 233, 241
Hayes-Gilpin, Kelley, 56, 245
Haystack D, 81*t*
Headquarters Site A, 214*t*, 216*f*, 218, 223, 224
Heidegger, Martin, 38, 39
herraduras, and Chacoan roads, 147
Hewett, Edgar Lee, 9n1, 134n5
hierarchical interpretation, of sociopolitical organization of Chaco, 27. *See also* elites
Hillside Ruin, 218
Hinkson Ranch, 234
Hobgood, Ronald, 229
Hogback, 79*t*, 84
Hopi, 47–48, 53, 55, 57, 109, 149, 233, 234
Hosta Butte: and balanced dualism of roads, 150, 155, 159–60; and line-of-site connections of Classic Bonito outliers, 186–87; and line-of-sight connections of Early Bonito sites, 94, 95–96, 97; and orientation of Late-Bonito Kin Bineola, 225; and topography of San Juan Basin, 15, 140
Huerfano Mountain, 15, 97, 233
Hungo Pavi, 112*f*, 113, 117, 119*t*, 123*t*, 224
Husserl, Edmund, 38
Hyde Expedition (1896–1900), 9n1

ideology: and archaeological studies of landscapes, 5–6; and Bonito-style architecture at Chaco, 115–28, 132–33; and Bonito-style architecture at outlier communities, 183–98; Early Bonito phase and emergence of shared Chacoan, 101–102; emotional dimensions of, 32–33, 253; and perspectives on sociopolitical organization of Chaco, 31–33; and phenomenological interpretation of Chaco landscape, 9, 248–51; and roads during Classic Bonito phase, 144–64. *See also* balanced dualism; center place; cosmography; memory; movement; sacred geography; symbolism; visibility; worldview

Irwin-Williams, Cynthia, 104n10, 235n2

Jackson Staircase, 43, 154
Jaquez, 206
Jemez, 40, 57, 58
Johnson, Gregory A., 26
Judd, Neil M., 10n1, 19, 29, 36n9, 104n9, 134n7
Judge, W. James, 10n1, 26–27, 28, 103n6

Kant, Immanuel, 38
Kantner, John, 28, 29, 188, 198n8, 229
katsina masks, 55
Kawaika'a, 55
Keres linguistic group, 50–52, 53, 54, 57, 58, 149
Kidder, A. V., 16, 78
Kim-mi-ne-oli Wash, 225, 226
Kin Bineola, 79t, 80t, 95–96, 134n9, 204f, 208t, 225–26, 236n9, 243
King, Anthony, 233
Kin Hocho'i, 56, 234
Kin Kletso, 214t, 216f, 217, 219, 220, 223
Kin Klizhin, 77, 160, 199n13, 204f, 208t, 227–30
Kin Nahasbas, 80t, 88, 90, 97, 123t, 124, 133n3, 163
Kin Nizhoni, 199n13
Kin Ya'a, 160, 204f, 208t, 227–30, 236n10
kivas: and outlier great houses, 180; and post-Chacoan pueblos, 231; ratio to rooms in Classic Bonito-phase great houses at Chaco, 121; remodeling of Chacoan, 55. *See also* great kivas; orbiter kivas; tower kivas
Kluckhohn, Clyde, 26, 90
Kutz Canyon, 150

labor: and Chaco as center place during Classic Bonito phase, 106–15; and construction of Kin Bineola in Late Bonito phase, 226; and remodeling of great houses in Late Bonito phase, 218–19; and social organization of Chaco, 250

Laguna, 47
Lake Valley, 79t
landscape: and archaeological studies of place and social reality, 4–7, 9; Bonito-style architecture and Chacoan ideology, 115–28; description of physical at Chaco, 12–25; earthworks and Chacoan ideology, 129–31; ethnography and interpretation of Chacoan, 47–60; and Late Bonito phase in Chaco Canyon, 213–24; memory, visibility, and sacred geography in Early Bonito phase, 91–97; and northern expansion of Chaco during Late Bonito phase, 202–13; of outlier communities, 182–83; phenomenology and interpretation of Chacoan, 7–9, 38–47, 237–53; and ritual gatherings at Chaco during Classic Bonito phase, 106–15; roads and Chacoan ideology, 144–64; and sacred geography of Chaco, 140–44
Las Ventanas site, 172f, 181t, 187
Late Bonito phase: in central San Juan Basin, 225–30; and history of occupation of Chaco, 21; and landscape of Chaco Canyon, 213–24; and northern expansion of Chaco, 202–13; and outlier communities, 25; overview of Chaco during, 240
Lefebvre, Henri, 6
Lekson, Stephen H., 10n1, 33, 48, 53, 103n8, 104n9, 111–12, 114, 130, 133n4, 134n5, 134n7, 149, 150, 183, 191, 209, 219, 220, 229, 234, 235n7–8, 241
line-of-sight networks: between outliers and Chaco Canyon, 186–87, 197; and boundaries of Chacoan world, 180, 182; and Early Bonito phase sites, 94–95, 97; and Late Bonito phase great houses, 221; and location of shrines, 141–44; and McElmo towers in Pueblo III period, 233; and visibility of Chacoan great houses, 42, 141. *See also* visibility
Lister, Robert, 10n1
lithics, and Chuskan materials at Chaco, 24
Lizard House, 218
Loma Alta, 89, 90
Lomatewama, Ramson, 61
Los Aguajes, 156
Los Rayos great kiva, 81t, 193, 195
Lowry Ruin, 202–206, 208t, 243
lunar movements: and construction of Salmon Ruin in Late Bonito phase, 208; and directionality in Chaco landscape, 245–46; and positioning of outliers, 134n9; and rituals

Index   309

at Chaco, 109–11. *See also* astronomical alignments

macaws. *See* exotic materials
maps, and interpretation of Chaco landscape, 8
MapTech Terrain Navigator, 8
Marshall, Michael P., 149, 150, 167–68n5, 171, 227, 228, 235n2, 236n11, 236n14–15
Mathews, Tom W., 17, 19, 216, 220
Maya, 41, 109
McElmo style: and towers in Pueblo III period, 232–33; and veneer styles of Chacoan great houses, 19, 21, 216–17, 219, 230
McGuire, Randall H., 27
McKenna, Peter, 35n5, 143, 209, 212
McPhee Village, 74–75, 76
Meddler Mound, 134n11
Meloy, Ellen, 137
memory: and Bonito-style architecture at outliers, 183, 191–95, 196–97; continued importance of to Pueblo society in post-Chacoan world, 232, 234–35; and Early Bonito phase proto-great houses, 83, 91–97; and great kivas at Chaco during Classic Bonito phase, 128; and landscape of Chaco in Late Bonito phase, 220, 222, 224 ; and phenomenological interpretation of Chaco landscape, 8–9, 45–47, 246–47; and remodeling during Classic Bonito phase at Chaco, 121; as theme in contemporary Pueblo cosmography, 54, 55, 56, 59
Merleau-Ponty, Maurice, 38
middens: and Chacoan ideology during Classic Bonito phase, 130; of Early Bonito phase proto-great houses, 84, 192
migrations: away from San Juan Basin in Pueblo III period, 25; and increases in population of Early Bonito settlements, 89
military, and power in sociopolitical organization of Chaco, 28
Miller, Daniel, 27
Mills, Barbara J., 247
Momaday, N. Scott, 1, 12, 58
Moore, Jerry, 40–41, 45, 118, 166, 242
Morenon, Pierre E., 156
Morris, Earl, 93, 119, 235n4
Morris 33, 79*t*, 84, 93
Morris 41, 206
Mount Taylor, 15, 97, 142–43, 188*f*
movement: definition of, 241; and phenomenological interpretation of Chaco landscape, 8–9, 43–45, 244–45; and themes in contemporary Pueblo cosmography, 56–59. *See also* processions; ramps; roads; staircases
Museum of New Mexico, 134n5
My Son (Vietnam), 40
Mystery of Chaco Canyon, The (film 1999), 117

Narbona Pass chert, 24
National Geographic Society, 10n1
Navajo, 15, 48
Neo-Darwinian evolution, 29
network strategies, 30
New Alto, 153, 160–61, 214*t*, 216*f*, 217
Newcomb, 79*t*, 84
North Road, 43–44, 145, 148–50, 152–55, 165, 166
North Ruin, 205, 206

oral tradition. *See* ethnography; origin myths; Navajo; Pueblo(s)
orbiter kivas, 208
origin myths: roads and Chacoan ideology, 149–50; and sipapu in Puebloan cosmography, 56–57; and tower kivas of Late Bonito phase, 229; and towers of Pueblo III period, 233
Ortiz, Alfonso, 54, 90
Ortiz, Simon, 132–33, 137, 145
Ortman, Scott G., 74, 90
outlier communities: ancestral and colonial types and worldview of, 171, 173–78, 196; and Bonito-style architecture, 171, 173, 174–83; and boundaries of Chacoan world, 178–83; and Chaco as center place, 144; and Chuskan ceramics, 168n6; and northern expansion of Chaco in Late Bonito phase, 202–13; and overview of occupation history of Chaco, 22, 25; and roads, 167; variability in size and layout of, 35–36n7; visibility and visual impact of, 243

Padilla Well, 80*t*, 86, 158, 199n13
Paleoindian sites, in Chaco Canyon, 18
Palmer, Doug, 167n1
Peach Springs: as ancestral outlier of Classic Bonito phase, 174–75, 181*t*; plan of, 172*f*; and proto-great houses in Early Bonito phase, 81*t*, 93, 97; and social memory, 192; and visibility, 185–86, 243
Pecos Classification, 18, 78
Peñasco Blanco: approaches to, 156, 157, 159; as Early Bonito phase settlement, 80*t*, 96, 94–95, 97; expansion of in Classic Bonito phase, 112; and great kivas, 123*t*; orienta-

tion of, 116, 117; plan of, 129f; remodeling in Pueblo III period, 235n8; and roads, 165; and visibility, 119t, 224, 242
Pepper, George H., 29, 36n9
Pettit site, 56, 234
phenomenology, and experiential interpretation of landscape at Chaco, 7–9, 38–47, 152, 237–53
photography, and interpretation of Chaco landscape, 8
Pierre's outlier, 152, 167n1
Pigg site, 205–206
"pilgrimage fair" model, 28
pitstructures: and Basketmaker II period, 63, 64f, 103n4; and Pueblo I period, 75–76; and site superposition in Pueblo II period, 192–93. *See also* great pitstructures
place: and human understanding of existence, 38–39; reflexive engagement and meaning of, 238; use of term, 4
plazas, and great houses, 60n1
Plog, Steve, 10n1
political organization, and perspectives on Chacoan social structure, 25–35. *See also* elites; power; social organization
population: estimates for during Classic Bonito phase at Chaco, 21; increases at Early Bonito phase settlements, 88–89. *See also* migrations
power: and archaeological studies of landscape, 6; and perspectives on sociopolitical organization of Chaco, 27–31; visibility and invisibility in construction of, 40
Powers, Robert P., 26–27
processions: and Ah-Shi-Sle-Pah Road, 166; and formal routes for movement, 45; possible route between Pueblo Bonito and Casa Rinconada, 127f; and roads in contemporary Pueblo cosmography, 57
proto-great houses: and Pueblo I period, 19; and Early Bonito phase, 78–97; and outlier communities, 174, 192; use of term, 103n7
Pueblo(s): Chacoan influences on post-Chacoan world, 25, 232; cyclical renewal and ritual events, 246; ethnography and interpretation of Chacoan landscape, 47–60; high places in oral traditions of, 15; and McElmo towers of Pueblo III period, 233; memory, movement, and cosmography in physical and imagined landscapes of modern, 9; and middens as sacred space, 130. *See also* Acoma; Eastern Pueblos; Hopi; Keres linguistic group; Laguna; Tewa linguistic group; Western Pueblos; Zuni
Pueblo Alto: earthworks and evidence for feasting, 130, 135n15, 150; orientation of and cardinal directions, 117, 223; plan of, 112f; remodeling of in Late Bonito phase, 235n8; roads and approaches to, 153–54, 160–61, 165, 166, 242; sequence of construction at, 113; and social memory, 222, 223; visibility of and Chacoan ideology, 118, 119t, 153, 161, 242
Pueblo Bonito: and Chaco as center place, 118, 121; and Early Bonito phase, 87, 90, 97, 101, 103n8; and earthworks, 130–31; and exotic materials in burials, 29–30, 36n9, 107, 122; and exotic materials as evidence of rituals, 108; orientation of, 116–17; and great kivas, 123t, 124, 126–27; plan of, 112f, 119t, 129f; and processional route, 127f; and proto-great houses, 80t; and remodeling in Classic Bonito phase, 113, 114; and remodeling in Late Bonito phase, 218; and remodeling in Pueblo III period, 235n8; and visibility of Late Bonito phase great houses, 224
Pueblo del Arroyo: plan of, 112f; roads and approaches to, 150, 155, 160, 161–62, 165; remodeling of in Late Bonito phase, 218, 235n8; sequence of construction at, 113; visibility of and Chacoan ideology, 118, 119t, 161–62, 166, 242
Pueblo Pintado, 80t, 88, 97, 134n9, 163–64, 226
Pueblo I period: and roots of Chaco, 70–78, 99, 103n4–6; and site superposition by Pueblo II components, 192–93; and social mobility in San Juan Basin, 62, 92
Pueblo II period: and architectural style of great houses, 180; and site superposition of Basketmaker II and Pueblo I pitstructures, 192–93
Pueblo III period: and continued Chacoan influence in post-Chacoan world, 230–35; and core-and-veneer masonry, 180; and great kivas, 56; and migration away from central San Juan Basin, 25

ramps, 43, 191, 197, 199n12. *See also* staircases
redistribution: Early Bonito phase and emergence of Chaco as center place, 98; and interpretations of sociopolitical organization at Chaco, 27, 28
Red Mesa Valley, 24, 89, 90, 97

Index 311

Red Willow-Los Rayos road, 193, 195
Red Willow site, 172f, 181t, 193–95, 197, 243
Reed, Paul, 209, 236n16
Reiter, Paul, 126
remodeling: of Basketmaker III structures, 70; of great houses in Late Bonito phase, 218–19; of great houses in Pueblo III period, 235n8; of kivas at Chaco during Classic Bonito phase, 121, 126; of outlier great houses, 192. *See also* cyclical renewal
Renfrew, Colin, 27, 42
ritual: and Aztec site in post-Chacoan world, 230–31; and Chaco as center place in Classic Bonito phase, 106–15, 132–33; and concept of ritual landscape, 183; and cyclical renewal in Pueblo cosmography, 246; Early Bonito phase and emergence of Chaco as ceremonial center, 98–102; and great pitstructures of Basketmaker III period, 68–69; ideology and phenomenological interpretation of Chaco landscape, 248–49; and interpretations of sociopolitical organization of Chaco, 30–31. *See also* astronomical alignments; ceremonial centers; processions; shrines; solstice ceremonies
roads: and Chacoan ideology in Classic Bonito phase, 144–67, 199n13; identification of in San Juan Basin, 36n8; and landscape of outliers, 193, 195; locations of in Chaco Canyon, 23f, 138–39f; and northern expansion of Chaco during Late Bonito phase, 206, 209; and overview of occupation history of Chaco, 22; and phenomenological interpretation of Chacoan landscape, 43–45, 242, 244–45; and themes in contemporary Pueblo cosmography, 57; and time bridges in post-Chacoan world, 234. *See also* movement
Roberts, Frank H. H., Jr., 63, 65
Roberts' Small Pueblo, 218
Robins, Michael R., 56
Roney, John R., 22, 145, 148

sacred geography: as aspect of spatial experience in Pueblo ethnography, 59; continued importance of in post-Chacoan world, 232; definition of, 240; and Early Bonito phase landscape of Chaco, 91–97; and landscape of Chaco during Classic Bonito phase, 140–44; and phenomenological interpretation of Chaco landscape, 241–44
Saitta, Dean, 27, 30, 31, 56, 234

Salmon Ruin, 149, 186, 204f, 207–209, 231, 235n2
Sand Canyon Pueblo, 56, 232
San Juan Basin: climate of, 16–17; Early Bonito phase communities in, 82f; and landscape of Early Bonito phase, 91–97; Late Bonito phase in central region of, 225–30; migration away from in Pueblo III period, 25; physiographic subregions of, 12–14; and settlement patterns in Pueblo I period, 72–78; social mobility during Basketmaker III and Pueblo I periods, 62; and topography of Chaco Canyon, 11–12, 14–16
San Mateo, 81t
Schelberg, John D., 26–27
School of American Research, 9n1, 134n5
Schwartz, Douglas W., 14
Sebastian, Lynne, 28, 29, 100
settlement patterns: and archaeological study of landscape, 5; and Pueblo I period in San Juan Basin, 72–78
Shabik'eshchee Village, 18, 63, 64–65, 67, 69, 101, 128, 241
shell. *See* exotic materials
Shiprock, 15, 92, 93, 94
shrines: and boundaries of Chacoan world, 180, 182; and Late Bonito phase great houses, 221–22; and line-of-sight connections in Pueblo III period, 236n10; location of in Chaco Canyon, 138–39f; and pilgrimage routes in modern Pueblo cosmography, 58; roads and siting of, 147, 150, 152, 157, 158–59; and visibility, 141–44, 187, 242
signaling, and tower kivas, 229
Sinclair, Rolf M., 149, 167–68n5
sipapu, and origin myths, 56–57, 149, 229
Site 423: and Basketmaker III communities of sites, 66; and Chacoan shrines, 142; and Chaco as center place, 101; and Classic Bonito great kivas, 128; defensive location of, 67; Early Bonito sites and line-of-sight connections to, 94, 241; and ritual burning of pitstructures, 69; roads and approaches to, 156, 157. *See also* 295J423 site
Site 1088, 143, 158, 166, 182, 186, 245
Skunk Springs: and Chuskan ceramics, 158; and Classic Bonito outliers, 169–71, 172f, 181t; and Early Bonito settlements in San Juan Basin, 84–86; line-of-sight connections and visibility of, 94, 198n9, 243
Sleeping Ute Mountain, 233

Smith, Adam T., 6, 32–33, 249
social memory. *See* memory
social organization: and Bonito-style architecture at outliers, 196; and community organization in Early Bonito phase, 89–91; and perspectives on Chacoan political structure, 25–35; and phenomenological interpretation of Chaco landscape, 249–51; and understanding of Classic Bonito architectural and political developments at Chaco, 21–22. *See also* elites; labor; political organization; power; settlement patterns
sodalities, and hierarchical social relationships at Chaco, 107
Sofaer, Anna, 109, 117, 134n9, 149, 150, 167–68n5, 222
solstice ceremonies, 55, 108
South Fork, 77, 80t
South Gap, 155, 159–62
South Mesa, 14, 160
South Road, 44, 145, 150, 155, 159–62, 165, 166
Southwest: and use of term *landscape*, 5
spatial perceptions and spatial representations, definition of, 6, 7. *See also* cardinal directions; landscape; place
Squaw Springs, 79t, 84
staircases, 43, 191, 197. *See also* ramps
Standing Rock, 81t, 97
Stein, John R., 33, 103n8, 126–27, 130, 133n4, 134n8, 134n11, 156, 160, 169, 183, 184, 185, 191, 234
Sterling, 206
stone circles, 138–39f, 155, 187
structuration, and interpretations of sociopolitical organization of Chaco, 33–35, 249
Suiter, Judith E., 126–27
symbolism: and concept of symbolic entrainment, 42; and McElmo great houses of Late Bonito phase, 219; and McElmo towers in Pueblo III period, 233. *See also* cosmography; ideology

Taçon, Paul, 91
Taussig, Michael, 179
Taylor, Mount. *See* Mount Taylor
Tewa linguistic group, 49–50, 53, 54, 57, 90, 149, 220
Thomas, Julian, 8
Tikal ceremonial complex (Maya), 41
Tilley, Christopher, 8, 27
time bridges, 234, 247
Toh-La-Kai, 182

Toll, H. Wolcott, 26–27, 56, 167n3, 192
Toltecs, 28
topography: of Chaco Canyon, 11–12, 23f; and visibility of outlier great houses, 184–90. *See also* geography
Totah region, and Chacoan periphery, 206, 235n1
tower(s), McElmo-style in Late Bonito phase, 232–33
tower kivas, in Late Bonito phase, 207, 227–30, 236n14–15
transportation, and roads, 147
Trigger, Bruce G., 3
Truell, Marcia, 35n5
Tse Bee Kintsoh, 81t
Tsin Kletsin, 214t, 216f, 217, 221–23, 236n10
Tuan, Yi-Fu, 6, 39
Turner, Christy G., II & Jacqueline, 28, 249
turquoise. *See* exotic materials
Tuwaletstiwa, Phillip, 37
29SJ423 site, 18, 23f, 63–64, 215f
29SJ1253 site, 80t, 90, 97, 123t, 139f, 215f
Twin Angels site, 149

Una Vida, 80t, 88, 97, 112, 116, 119t, 123t
University of New Mexico, 10n1
Upper Twin Angels mound, 149, 168n5
Urartian state, 32–33

Van Dyke, Ruth M., 41, 103n7, 143, 160, 198n8
veneer styles: and great houses of Classic Bonito phase, 19, 20f, 119–20, 134–35n12, 179, 198n5; and great houses of Late Bonito phase, 216. *See also* core-and-veneer masonry
violence: burials at Chaco and evidence for, 207; evidence for in Basketmaker III period, 102n3; and interpretations of power in sociopolitical organization at Chaco, 28
visibility: as aspect of spatial experience in Pueblo ethnography, 59; and Basketmaker III settlements, 67; and Bonito-style architecture at outliers, 184–90, 196–97; and boundaries of Chacoan world, 180; of Classic Bonito great houses at Chaco, 118, 141; continued importance of in post-Chacoan world, 232; definition of, 240–41; and Early Bonito phase proto-great houses, 83, 91–97; of Late Bonito phase great houses, 221–24, 228–29; and phenomenological interpretation of Chaco

landscape, 8–9, 241–45; and Pueblo I period communities, 77. *See also* line-of-sight networks
visible landscapes, and phenomenological interpretation of Chaco, 39–43
Vivian, R. Gordon, 10n1, 17, 19, 108, 126, 134n7, 216, 220
Vivian, R. Gwinn, 26, 35n1, 36n8, 90, 116, 140, 143, 167n1, 214, 219, 236n12, 241
Vivian's Staircase, 151, 157

Walker, William H., 102–103n3
Ware, John A., 133n1
Weber, Max, 27
West Chaco River, 157–59, 166
Western Pueblos, 47
West Mesa, 14, 160
West Point, 86, 143–44, 159
West Road, 151, 157
Whirlwind, 172*f*, 181*t*, 187, 189–90, 197, 243
White House, in Pueblo oral tradition, 234–35
White Mound Village, 89, 90, 103n5
Wijiji, 214*t*, 216*f*, 217, 223, 224
Wilcox, David R., 28
Willow Canyon, 79*t*, 93

Wills, Wirt H., 28, 30–31, 55, 68–69, 121, 135n15–16
Wilshusen, Richard H., 35n4, 74, 90, 103n3–4, 103n7, 125
Wilson, C. Dean, 56, 192
Windes, Thomas C., 18, 21, 65, 77, 88, 90, 97, 103n6, 103n8, 133n4, 141–42, 143, 145, 155, 164, 209, 212, 221, 228–29, 233, 241
worldview: of ancestral and colonial outliers, 173–78; Chacoan era and ancestral Pueblo, 240–48; Early Bonito phase and shared Chacoan ideology, 101–102; influence of Chacoan ideology on modern Pueblo, 48, 232; and definitions of ideology, 31–32. *See also* cosmography; ideology

Yoffee, Norman, 30–31
Young, M. Jane, 52

Zuni: and classification of contemporary Pueblo groups, 47; and cosmography, 52, 53, 54, 55, 57, 58, 108; and kivas, 126, 135n14; and memory of Chaco, 234–35; and plastering of walls, 134n10